COMPANIES AND CLIMATE CHANGE

Companies lie at the heart of the climate crisis and are both culpable for, and vulnerable to, its impacts. Rising social and investor concern about the escalating risks of climate change are changing public and investor expectations of businesses and, as a result, corporate approaches to climate change. Dominant corporate norms that put shareholders (and their wealth maximization) at the heart of company law are viewed by many as outdated and in need of reform. *Companies and Climate Change* analyzes these developments by assessing the regulation and pressures that impact energy companies in the UK, with lessons that apply worldwide. In this work, Lisa Benjamin shows how the Paris Agreement, climate and energy law in the EU and the UK, and transnational human rights and climate litigation, are regulatory and normative developments that illustrate how company law can and should act as a bridge to progressive corporate climate action.

Lisa Benjamin is Assistant Professor at Lewis & Clark Law School. Professor Benjamin was a corporate and commercial lawyer in London for seven years before teaching international environmental and company law at the University of The Bahamas. She became an advisor to the Government of The Bahamas on climate change, including representing the country at the UNFCCC negotiations and as part of the Paris Agreement negotiations. She is currently a member of the UNFCCC Compliance Committee (Facilitative Branch) which assesses country reports under the Kyoto Protocol.

CAMBRIDGE STUDIES ON ENVIRONMENT, ENERGY AND NATURAL RESOURCES GOVERNANCE

Cambridge Studies on Environment, Energy and Natural Resources Governance publishes foundational monographs of general interest to scholars and practitioners within the broadly defined fields of sustainable development policy, including studies on law, economics, politics, history, and policy. These fields currently attract unprecedented interest due both to the urgency of developing policies to address climate change, the energy transition, food security and water availability and, more generally, to the progressive realization of the impact of humans as a geological driver of the state of the Earth, now called the "Anthropocene."

The general editor of the series is Professor Jorge E. Viñuales, the Harold Samuel Chair of Law and Environmental Policy at the University of Cambridge and the Founder and First Director of the Cambridge Centre for Environment, Energy and Natural Resource Governance (C-EENRG).

Companies and Climate Change

THEORY AND LAW IN THE UNITED KINGDOM

LISA BENJAMIN

Lewis & Clark College

CAMBRIDGE
UNIVERSITY PRESS

University Printing House, Cambridge CB2 8BS, United Kingdom

One Liberty Plaza, 20th Floor, New York, NY 10006, USA

477 Williamstown Road, Port Melbourne, VIC 3207, Australia

314–321, 3rd Floor, Plot 3, Splendor Forum, Jasola District Centre, New Delhi – 110025, India

79 Anson Road, #06-04/06, Singapore 079906

Cambridge University Press is part of the University of Cambridge.

It furthers the University's mission by disseminating knowledge in the pursuit of education, learning, and research at the highest international levels of excellence.

www.cambridge.org
Information on this title: www.cambridge.org/9781108484671
DOI: 10.1017/9781108689243

© Lisa Benjamin 2021

This publication is in copyright. Subject to statutory exception and to the provisions of relevant collective licensing agreements, no reproduction of any part may take place without the written permission of Cambridge University Press.

First published 2021

A catalogue record for this publication is available from the British Library.

ISBN 978-1-108-48467-1 Hardback

Cambridge University Press has no responsibility for the persistence or accuracy of URLs for external or third-party internet websites referred to in this publication and does not guarantee that any content on such websites is, or will remain, accurate or appropriate.

To my parents and Philip. Thank you.

Contents

Acknowledgements *page* xiii

1 **Introduction** 1
  1.1 The Climate Crisis 2
  1.2 Climate Action 4
  1.3 The Causal Relationship between Companies and Climate Change 5
  1.4 Company Law and Climate Change 6
  1.5 Varying Corporate Forms 9
  1.6 Systemic Barriers and Opportunities: Short-Termism, CSR and Societal Expectations 13
  1.7 Climate Risks and Corporate Transitions: The United Kingdom as a Model 16
  1.8 Structure of the Book 18

2 **Theorising the Company in the Context of Climate Change** 20
  2.1 Corporate Theories and Norms in the Context of Climate Change 21
  2.2 Impact of Corporate Theories and Norms on the Environment and the Climate 31
  2.3 Alternative Climate-Friendly Corporate Theories 37
  2.4 Conclusion 44

3 **English Company Law and Climate Change** 46
  3.1 Corporate Governance Reviews in the United Kingdom and the Takeover Code 47
  3.2 The Common Law Position Prior to 2006 52
  3.3 Company Law Review Steering Group Reports 61

	3.4	The Companies Act 2006 and Climate Concerns	63
	3.5	Post-2006 Case Law	71
	3.6	Conclusion	74
4	**International and Transnational Climate Change Law and Policies**		78
	4.1	International Treaties on Climate Change	80
	4.2	Corporate Social Responsibility and Private Environmental Governance	90
	4.3	International Codes of Conduct and Private Transnational Initiatives	102
	4.4	Conclusion	110
5	**Domestic Climate and Energy Regulation**		113
	5.1	Regulating Companies	114
	5.2	Climate and Energy Regulation in the European Union	118
	5.3	Climate and Energy Regulation in the United Kingdom	119
	5.4	Energy Market Reform in the United Kingdom	122
	5.5	Market Mechanisms	131
	5.6	Companies' Approaches to Trading Mechanisms	138
	5.7	Conclusion	139
6	**Companies, Human Rights and Climate Litigation**		141
	6.1	Companies and Human Rights	143
	6.2	Human Rights as an Environmental Concern to Companies: The Development of the UN Norms	144
	6.3	The United Nations Guiding Principles	146
	6.4	The OECD Guidelines and National Contact Points	147
	6.5	Broader Effect of the United Nations Guiding Principles on Companies	147
	6.6	Climate Change and Human Rights	149
	6.7	Climate Change Litigation	151
	6.8	The Convergence of Human Rights-Based Climate Litigation against Companies	164
	6.9	The Oslo Global Principles and Enterprise Principles	167
	6.10	Some Stumbling Blocks to Climate Litigation Efforts against Companies	169
	6.11	Conclusion	171
7	**Fiscal Barriers and Incentives to Corporate Climate Action**		173
	7.1	Fossil-Fuel Subsidies	174
	7.2	Carbon Taxes	181

	7.3 Institutional Investors and Climate Change	187
	7.4 Sustainable Investment and Environment, Social and Governance Factors	200
	7.5 The Divestment Movement	205
	7.6 Shareholder Climate Action via Resolutions	207
	7.7 Impact of Initiatives on Companies	209
	7.8 Conclusion	211
8	**Conclusion**	214
	8.1 Key Findings	215
	8.2 What the Future Holds for Companies in the Context of Climate Change	223
	8.3 Final Thoughts	227
Index		231

Acknowledgements

There are so many people who contributed to this work. This monograph represents a culmination of ideas that I have been working on and presenting for several years. I would like to thank Matt Gallaway and everyone at Cambridge University Press who supported me and helped me to refine the scope of the work. I would also like to thank the anonymous reviewers of the initial book proposal, and the editor of the Cambridge University Press monograph series, Jorge Viñuales.

I would like to thank the following individuals in particular (in alphabetical order) for their comments and reviews of various iterations of this project over the years: Stelios Andreadakis, Daniel Attenborough, Janet Dine, Marc Moore, Meinhard Doelle, Thomas Hale, Veerle Heyvaert, Emily Jones, Hari Osofsky, Jacqueline Peel, Melissa Powers, Lavanya Rajamani, Sara Seck, Joana Setzer, Harro van Asselt and Horace Yeung.

Parts of this monograph were presented at several different events, and I would like to thank the participants at these events who provided valuable feedback and comments: American Society of International Law, Institute of the Environment, University of Minnesota's The Road to Paris: Multidimensional Action to Address Climate Change (2015), University of Oxford Faculty of Law, International Environmental Law Interest Group, ASIL and the University of Minnesota Energy Transition Lab's Regulating the Energy Transition Conference (2016), the University of Oslo's Time and Sustainability Conference (2018), Aarhus University's Climate Litigation Conference (2018), Vermont Law School's Corporations and Climate Change Conference (2018) and the Association for Law, Property and Society, Corporate Energy Transitions Panel (2019). Last (but not least), I would like to thank Akriti Bhargava for her invaluable research assistance.

1

Introduction

The world is facing a climate emergency, and companies lie at the heart of this crisis. Companies contribute a staggering amount of greenhouse gas (GHG) emissions to the atmosphere, and so are central to the problem of climate change. Companies can (and some already have) also harness technology, know-how and capital to contribute to climate solutions. In addition to this dual role, companies themselves are vulnerable to climate risks. Climate risks are therefore bidirectional for companies; these entities create climate risks through their activities but are also subject to these risks. Some industries such as energy, utilities, agriculture and forestry are more culpable (and more vulnerable) than others. In the climate context, companies therefore have a public role and arguably a public responsibility, as their emissions negatively affect society at large. Yet companies are governed primarily by private law. In fact, corporate theories such as shareholder primacy and shareholder wealth maximisation have long influenced corporate activity and company law, particularly in the Anglo-American context, and have fuelled the corporate approach to climate change. This book argues that these private theories and norms are outdated in the Anthropocene, and new approaches to climate change should be adopted by companies and by company law.

Companies are artificial legal creations which have facilitated enormous economic growth and wealth over the past few centuries. From a legal perspective, Anglo-American corporate directors' duties are fairly flexible, with few specific duties required of directors within corporate statutes. It is perhaps due to this tremendous discretion afforded to directors that companies have become such powerful vehicles of wealth creation. This extraordinary accumulation of wealth and power has been accompanied by significant wealth inequality and negative environmental impacts, the climate crisis being one of these. Greenhouse gases are perhaps the greatest or 'mother of all' negative externalities[1] produced by corporate activity, and their production and the consequential changes to the climate they fuel, are posing extraordinary risks to society, financial systems and the companies themselves, amounting to an existential threat to human existence.

The theory and law of companies in the context of climate change have been understudied, but are extremely important. It is the malleability that corporate law directors' duties afford that provides the most hope that companies will provide more and better solutions to the climate crisis. The backdrop of capitalism and the commodification of the environment are never far from the premise of this book, and these interrelated issues have had a suppressive effect on corporate climate action. As Janet Dine notes, to consider competing models of corporate governance is to consider competing models of capitalism.[2] Globalisation facilitated the high mobility of capital, and supported the explosive growth of transnational corporations (or TNCs). TNCs are the main focus of this book due to their tremendous contribution to GHG emissions. However, companies are not alone in their facilitation of and benefit from the neoliberal capitalist system. Other financial actors such as banks, international financial institutions, hedge funds, institutional investors, management consultants and accounting firms exercise pressure on companies to externalise environmental and social costs.[3] Many of these actors are also incorporated as companies, and so the theories and laws covered in this book may also apply to them. Any changes to company law and theory must be accompanied by changing approaches of capital to climate change and climate risks. This book focuses on the theory and law of companies in the context of climate change, with an emphasis on the United Kingdom.

1.1 THE CLIMATE CRISIS

The current period of human existence has been named the age of the Anthropocene, or the human epoch. This refers to a geological age in which anthropogenic activities are the primary driver of changes to Earth's climate, geology and ecology.[4] Anthropogenic GHG emissions are a significant driver of observed planetary changes. The 1992 United Nations Framework Convention on Climate Change (UNFCCC) defines climate change as anthropogenic, being 'a change of climate which is attributed directly or indirectly to human activity that alters the composition of the global atmosphere and which is in addition to natural climate variability

---

[1] Richard Tol, 'The Economic Effects of Climate Change' (2009) 23(2) *Journal of Economic Perspectives* 29, 29.
[2] Janet Dine, 'Corporate Regulation, Climate Change and Corporate Law: Challenges and Balance in an International and Global World' (2015) 26 Eur. Bus. L. Rev. 173, 174.
[3] Doris Fuchs, *Business Power in Global Governance* (Lynne Rienner 2007), 111.
[4] The Anthropocene is an unofficial unit of geologic time; see www.nationalgeographic.org/encyclopedia/anthropocene (accessed 20 July 2020).

observed over comparable time periods'.[5] Climate change has been attributed to the natural and anthropogenic emissions of GHGs. Human activity leads to emissions of four main GHGs: carbon dioxide, nitrous oxide, methane and halocarbons.

The Intergovernmental Panel on Climate Change (IPCC) is the main international scientific body on climate change and issues periodic assessment reports. The IPCC concluded with very high confidence (a nine out of ten likelihood) that the global average net effect of human activity since 1750 has been one of warming.[6] GHG emissions, and the resulting impacts from climate change, account for a large and growing share of global environmental damage, estimated to constitute between 69 and 73 per cent of all externalities from 2008 to 2050.[7] The most recent IPCC Assessment Report stated that the concentrations of atmospheric carbon dioxide, methane and nitrous oxide are unprecedented in comparison with the past 800,000 years.[8]

The increase in GHG emissions from pre-industrial times is attributed primarily to fossil-fuel emissions and, secondly, to net land use changes such as deforestation.[9] Fossil-fuel combustion and industrial processes now account for approximately 78 per cent GHG emission increases from 1970 to 2010.[10] Fossil-fuel combustion on its own accounts for approximately 90 per cent of total global carbon dioxide emissions (excluding emissions from forest fires and wood burning).[11]

Emission rates are generally increasing, despite global mitigation policies. The IPCC estimates that GHG emissions increased between 1970 and 2010, with larger absolute increases occurring more recently, between 2000 and 2010.[12] Emissions continued to rise annually through 2018.[13] Further increases will lead to further warming, which in turn will lead to long-lasting and potentially irreversible changes to the climate system.[14] These changes will lead to impacts on ecosystems and

---

[5] United Nations Framework Convention on Climate Change (adopted 9 May 1992, entered into force on 21 March 1994) (UNFCCC), art. 1.2.
[6] Intergovernmental Panel on Climate Change, 'Climate Change 2007: Synthesis Report' (2008), 37, www.ipcc.ch/pdf/assessment-report/ar4/syr/ar4_syr.pdf (accessed 4 May 2020).
[7] UNEP Finance Initiative and Principles for Responsible Investment, 'Universal Ownership: Why Environmental Externalities Matter to Institutional Investors' (2010), 5, www.unepfi.org/fileadmin/documents/universal_ownership_full.pdf (accessed 31 July 2020).
[8] Intergovernmental Panel on Climate Change, 'Climate Change 2014: Synthesis Report' (2014), 4, www.ipcc.ch/pdf/assessment-report/ar5/syr/AR5_SYR_FINAL_SPM.pdf (accessed 4 May 2020).
[9] IPCC (n 6), 37.
[10] IPCC (n 8), 4.
[11] Jos G. J. Olivier, Greet Janssens-Maenhout and Jeroen A. H. W. Peters, 'Trends in Global CO$_2$ Emissions' (PBL Netherlands Environmental Assessment Agency 2012), 20.
[12] IPCC (n 7), 4.
[13] United Nations Environment Programme, 'The Emissions Gap Report 2019: A UNEP Synthesis Report' (UNEP, Nairobi, November 2019), iv.
[14] IPCC (n 8), 8.

people which are 'severe, pervasive and irreversible'.[15] At certain ecological or climate tipping points, impacts become irreversible. Near-term choices on emissions can lead to what the IPCC refers to as 'lock-ins or irreversibilities' in the climate system.[16] These events could lead to runaway climate change.

The impacts of climate change are likely to be catastrophic in many countries. Climate impacts are also systemic and non-linear. Due to the complexity of climate science, many of these impacts are as yet unknown and uncertain. This means that there is no certainty that human systems and societies will be able to adapt to all of the changes. At the end of 2019, the United Nations Secretary-General, António Guterres, stated that the point of no return on climate change is in sight, and hurtling towards us.[17]

1.2 CLIMATE ACTION

The main international agreement on climate change is the Paris Agreement, concluded in 2015. Under this agreement, countries submitted nationally determined contributions to emission reductions. Parties also agreed global temperature goals – to keep global mean temperature increases to 'well below 2°C', with an aspirational goal of 1.5°C, compared to pre-industrial averages.[18] Currently, the world is not on track to meet either of these goals, and current estimates, taking into account the Paris pledges, anticipate a 3.2–3.4°C rise.[19] In order to meet the global temperature goal of well below 2°C, net global emissions will have to approach zero by the second half of this century.[20] This will require steep declines in the carbon intensity of all sectors, including the energy sector.[21] While it is still possible to reach the 2°C global goal, the window is 'closing fast'[22] in order to do so. We have approximately ten years to get a handle on the climate crisis and bend the curve of emissions towards net zero by 2050.

The International Energy Agency estimates that global emissions should peak in 2020, which means ending coal and oil use within the next few years.[23] A transition to low- or zero-carbon sources in the energy sector is a critical piece of the global

---

[15] Ibid.
[16] Ibid., 87.
[17] Associated Press, 'U.N. Chief Warns of "Point of No Return" on Climate Change' 2 December 2019, www.nbcnews.com/news/world/u-n-chief-warns-point-no-return-climate-change-n1093956 (accessed 10 July 2020).
[18] Article 4, UNFCCC, The Paris Agreement, FCCC/CP/2015/L.9.
[19] UNEP (n 13), ix.
[20] IDDRI and SDSN, 'Pathways to Deep Decarbonization' Interim 2014 iii, www.iddri.org/Publications/Pathways-to-deep-decarbonization-Interim-2014-Report (accessed 10 August 2015).
[21] Ibid., iii.
[22] Ibid., ix.
[23] OECD and IEA, 'World Energy Outlook Special Report, Energy and Climate Change' (2015), 13, www.iea.org/publications/freepublications/publication/WEO2015SpecialReport onEnergyandClimateChange.pdf (accessed 10 August 2019).

response to climate change,[24] as two-thirds of all anthropogenic GHG emissions result from the energy sector.[25] Power must be produced almost exclusively from zero- or low-carbon sources in all countries in order to reach this goal.[26] Business-as-usual responses or incremental changes will not be sufficient.[27] Amid the coronavirus pandemic, 2020 is anticipated to be the warmest year on record, with an estimated 1.2°C rise, illustrating that we have much work to do, and quickly, if we are to avoid climate catastrophe. Companies have a large and critical role to play in this transition.

1.3 THE CAUSAL RELATIONSHIP BETWEEN COMPANIES AND CLIMATE CHANGE

Companies are major contributors to the climate crisis through the emission of GHGs. Richard Heede's quantitative analysis of historic fossil fuel and cement production records of ninety leading investor-owned, state-owned and nation-state producers of oil, natural gas, coal and cement concluded that 63 per cent of cumulative worldwide emissions of carbon dioxide and methane from 1854 to 2010 were attributed to these 'carbon major'[28] entities. Investor-owned entities contributed the majority of these emissions, 315 gigatonnes, followed closely by nation states, and state-owned fossil fuel and cement-producing entities.[29] Of the eighty-five existing entities examined, fifty-four were headquartered in developed countries, and seven Anglo-American companies appear in the top twenty of emitters.[30] Two English companies, BP and Anglo American, appear in the top twenty carbon-major emitters, emitting 2.74 per cent (or 35,837 Mt CO_{2e}) and 0.50 per cent (or 7,242 Mt CO_{2e}), respectively of global totals.[31] Five US companies – Chevron, ExxonMobil, ConocoPhillips, Peabody Energy and CONSOL Energy – appear in the top twenty, emitting 3.52 per cent (or 51,096 Mt CO_{2e}), 3.22 per cent (or 46,672 Mt CO_{2e}), 1.16 per cent (or 16,866 Mt CO_{2e}), 0.86 per cent (or 12,432 Mt CO_{2e}) and 0.63 per cent (or 9.096 Mt CO_{2e}), respectively.[32] Anglo-American corporate approaches to climate change are therefore critical.

The majority of these emissions originate from activities such as fossil-fuel combustion, flaring, venting, fugitive or vented methane, fuel use by those entities and

---

[24] IDDRI and SDSN (n 20), x; OECD/IEA (n 23), 3.
[25] OECD/IEA (n 23), 20.
[26] IDDRI and SDSN (n 20), 35.
[27] Ibid., x.
[28] Richard Heede, 'Tracing Anthropogenic Carbon Dioxide and Methane Emissions to Fossil Fuel and Cement Producers, 1854–2010' (2014) 122(1) *Climatic Change* 229, 229.
[29] Ibid., 234.
[30] Ibid., 236.
[31] Ibid., 237.
[32] Ibid.

cement production.³³ The twenty largest investor- and state-owned energy companies are responsible for 29.5 per cent of all global industrial emissions, and the ten largest investor-owned companies alone are responsible for 15.8 per cent of global emissions through 2010.³⁴

Half of the total carbon and methane emissions have been produced since 1984,³⁵ indicating that emission levels are not abating. In a sample of 153 large companies, Caring for Climate (C4C) estimated that these companies were responsible for the release of approximately 2,107 million metric tonnes of carbon dioxide in 2010 alone.³⁶ The CDP (previously the Carbon Disclosure Project) found that the emissions from the largest fifty emitters actually increased by 1.65 per cent since 2009.³⁷ These fifty global companies emitted 73 per cent of total Global 500 emissions in 2013.³⁸

The role of companies as major contributors to climate change is therefore enormous. Contributions by companies to GHG emissions are so great that Heede concludes that the vast productive capacity and reserves of 'carbon major' entities, combined with their profit-seeking motives, mean that these companies and nation states arguably control 'the future of the planetary climate system'.³⁹ It is likely then, as the climate change crisis becomes more severe, corporate GHG emissions will be subjected to further scrutiny and regulation. This is already occurring in some jurisdictions, particularly in the United Kingdom. This leads to the question of what regulations are companies currently subject to, and what would be the best mechanism(s) to mediate corporate contributions to climate change in the future. Corporate theory and law have largely been overlooked as a tool to incentivise and facilitate corporate climate action, and this book hopefully goes some way towards filling that gap.

1.4 COMPANY LAW AND CLIMATE CHANGE

The modern company evolved during the nineteenth century's Industrial Revolution, and was primarily used as a vehicle to pool assets to enable large-scale investments.

---

[33] Ibid., 234.
[34] Ibid.
[35] Ibid.
[36] Caring for Climate, 'Caring for Climate Progress Report 2012' (May 2012), 7, www.unglobalcompact .org/library/1121 (accessed 4 May 2020).
[37] CDP, 'Sector Insights: What Is Driving Climate Change Action in the World's Largest Companies?' Global 500 Climate Change Report (2013), 8, www.pwc.com/mu/en/pressroom/ assets/g500_2013_report_embargoed__500bst_12_september_2013.pdf (accessed 1 July 2020). Scope 1 emissions are those emitted directly from sources the company owns or controls. Scope 2 emissions are indirect emissions that arise from the consumption of products/services of a company. The Global 500 are the largest companies by market capitalisation included in the FTSE Global Equity Index Series.
[38] Ibid.
[39] Heede (n 28), 237–8.

1.4 Company Law and Climate Change

The United Kingdom was the site of some of the earliest company law statutes of this time, including the Joint Stock Companies Act of 1844 which expanded access to the incorporation of companies, and the Limited Liability Act of 1855 which established that shareholders were not liable for any debts of the company they invested in, provided they had fully paid for their shares. These legal innovations allowed for the pooling of large amounts of capital, with fairly low risks for investors, within the corporate form. These companies then built railroads, bridges, factories and other infrastructure and industry which drove the Industrial Revolution forward.[40]

While these companies maintained a level of public and social character, due in part to their government-based charter,[41] automatic chartering and the lifting of restrictions on the size and scope of corporate activities led to the morphing of companies away from public-facing entities into purely for-profit entities.[42] This movement took off in the latter half of the next century, partly due to a theoretical understanding of companies existing to serve only shareholder interests. In particular the period from the 1970s to the 1990s saw the emergence of several neoliberal ideologies which remain prevalent today. From the 1970s onwards, trends of deregulation by politicians, combined with theories such as shareholder wealth maximisation, formed the foundation for Anglo-American approaches to company law and corporate regulation.[43] These powerful neoliberal paradigms did not recognise negative corporate externalities as problematic, and emphasised deregulation in a global context.[44] The 1980s, in particular, was a critical time, witnessing corporate takeovers in the United States and United Kingdom, and the rise of capital markets as drivers of productivity.[45] Due to these socio-economic developments, TNCs now command financial and human resources of a magnitude previously unseen.[46] These developments led to the principles of shareholder primacy and wealth maximisation becoming the dominant driving forces behind Anglo-American corporate activities.

Many shareholder primacists take an economic approach to the role and function of a company. In their view, the overall objective of a company is to serve the interests of the whole of society but primarily through increasing profits for

---

[40] British trading companies and the English chartering system were the roots of the American corporation, Barnali Choudhury and Martin Petrin, *Corporate Duties to the Public* (Cambridge University Press 2019), 11.
[41] Ibid., 10.
[42] Ibid., 13.
[43] Ibid., 17.
[44] Dine (n 2), 174.
[45] William M. Bratton and Michael L. Wachter, 'The Case against Shareholder Empowerment' (2010) 158 U. Pa. L. Rev. 653, 669.
[46] Fuchs (n 3), 2.

shareholders – the pursuit of social efficiency in economic terms.[47] As a result, the main, and sometimes only, objective of a company is to increase the wealth of its shareholders. The shareholder wealth maximisation norm is considered by shareholder primacists as the best means of achieving overall social efficiency, although they do acknowledge there are differing opinions over whether this is empirically correct.[48]

One of the key themes of the shareholder primacy norm is that it privileges the role and value of shareholders within a company, thereby diminishing the role of other, non-shareholder constituents, such as the environment. In addition, shareholder primacists do not value the contributions made to companies by the environment, nor attempt to decrease negative externalities, such as GHG emissions, as this may detract from the profitability of the company.

According to shareholder primacists, any attempt at environmental protection is mainly viewed as an agency cost to be avoided.[49] The global atmosphere thereby becomes a free polluting ground for companies to exploit. Dealing with climate change reduces shareholder wealth as it diverts assets from other investments that may be more profitable for shareholders.[50] Shareholder primacy, in its strong form, also reduces the role of state intervention in a company. This approach to the company is inadequate when the climate is viewed as an important stakeholder in the company. Companies rely on a stable climate in order to operate. However, under the shareholder primacy norm, non-shareholders can be excluded from consideration by company law, and must rely instead on regulation external to the company for protection. The shareholder primacy and wealth maximisation norms may also have influenced recent amendments to English company law through Section 172 of the United Kingdom's Companies Act 2006, and have had a pervasive and systemic impact on Anglo-American company law, and company law around the world.

Despite their pervasive character, these corporate norms do not always dominate interpretations of directors' duties. Company law has often balanced shareholder power with directorial discretion, with directors often being privileged in that balance.[51] Directors are consistently provided with a certain amount of discretion

---

[47] John Armour, Henry Hansmann and Reinier Kraakman, 'What Is Corporate Law?' in Reinier Kraakman et al. (eds.), *The Anatomy of Corporate Law: A Comparative and Functional Approach* (2nd ed., Oxford University Press 2009), 28–9.
[48] Ibid., 29.
[49] Paddy Ireland, 'Company Law and the Myth of Shareholder Ownership' (1999) 62 *MLR* 32, 33; Marc T. Moore and Antoine Reberioux, 'Revitalizing the Institutional Roots of Anglo-American Corporate Governance' (2011) 40(1) *Economy and Society* 84, 85; Diane Denis, 'Corporate Governance and the Goal of the Firm: In Defence of Shareholder Wealth Maximization' (2016) 51 *The Financial Review* 467, 479.
[50] Audrey Wen-hsin Hsu and Tawei Wang, 'Does the Market Value Corporate Responses to Climate Change?' (2013) 41(2) *The International Journal of Management Science* 195, 195.
[51] Bratton and Wachter (n 45), 659.

or leeway by courts in how and for whom they exercise their discretion, provided it is linked to some benefit to the company. This book challenges traditional corporate norms as being outdated and inappropriate in the context of climate change, and illustrates how even a shareholder-centric jurisdiction such as the United Kingdom can move towards a more climate-friendly approach to company law and climate regulation.

1.5 VARYING CORPORATE FORMS

There are several different types of corporate forms that are often available to shareholders. By far the most popular of these forms, particularly in the developed world, has been the for-profit company. For-profit companies can be either small, private (or close) companies with only a few shareholders, or large companies with thousands of shareholders. In the Anglo-American for-profit company, there is often a unitary board of directors which establishes and monitors corporate policies. The board can delegate management to other officials, and shares are owned by shareholders who are afforded varying degrees of power and control in certain circumstances. While directors can also be shareholders, they occupy two different roles – the directors manage the company and shareholders own shares.

The power of the corporate form was advanced considerably by the seminal English House of Lords case of *Salomon* v. *Salomon*.[52] This case held that even within a small private for-profit company, where there were only seven shareholders, those shareholders were not responsible for the debts of the company as it was a separate legal entity. The intertwined principles of limited liability and separate legal personality established the for-profit company as a low-risk vehicle for investors to pool capital. It also allowed groups of companies to flourish, with the parent company in the role of a shareholder not being liable for the debts of its subsidiaries.[53]

Companies can be private in that they do not offer their shares for sale to the public, with pre-emption rights often included in their founding documents to restrict sales to third parties. They can also be public, and/or listed on a public stock exchange such as the London Stock Exchange or New York Stock Exchange. Non-profit companies also exist, such as companies limited by guarantee, which do not distribute profits back to their shareholders. Charitable incorporated organizations or community interest companies in the U.K., and Benefit Companies in the U.S., are newer forms of social enterprise corporate models.

---

[52] [1897] AC 22.
[53] *Re Southard and Company Ltd.* [1979] 1 WLR 1198.

Community interest companies (CICs) were developed in the U.K. in 2005 as part of a larger social enterprise policy.[54] CICs are primarily limited companies that operate not for the benefit of their shareholders, but instead for the benefit of an identified community.[55] Profits are to be dedicated to these community interests. While these entities are allowed to pay dividends to shareholders, these are capped, and an asset lock ensures that assets must be preserved and not sold for the profit of shareholders.[56] CICs have a statutory obligation to ensure the company meets the needs of the community interest, and must file an annual report demonstrating how they have done so. These types of companies have struck a balance by accepting higher level of constraints upon profitability, in exchange for providing a clear signal regarding their community purposes.[57] CICs can be used as a legal vehicle to attract private capital and distribute benefits to local communities,[58] although they may be more appropriate for the non-profit sector rather than for the private sector.[59]

Benefit companies were introduced in the U.S. in 2010, and are designed to be 'for profit' companies.[60] Originally developed in Delaware, benefit companies have spread throughout several states in the U.S.. B Lab is a private, non-profit company that certifies its own type of B-corporations, and has been a major lobbying force behind the passing of benefit company legislation in various states.[61] Legislation on benefit companies varies from state to state, but essentially it is designed to allow these companies to work in the best interests of those stakeholders who are materially affected by benefit companies. These obligations are identified in the certificate of incorporation of the benefit company.[62]

---

[54] Alex Nicholls, 'Institutionalizing Social Entrepreneurship in Regulatory Space: Reporting and Disclosure by Community Interest Companies' (2010) 35 *Accounting, Organization and Society*, 394, 396.
[55] Department of Business Innovation and Skills, 'Office of the Regulator of Community Interest Companies: Information and Guidance Notes' Chapter 1 (November 2012), 3, www.gov.uk/government/organisations/office-of-the-regulator-of-community-interest-companies (accessed 8 May 2019).
[56] Ibid, 10–11.
[57] Timothy Edmonds, 'Briefing Paper No. 03426, Community Interest Companies' (30 April 2014), 6, http://researchbriefings.files.parliament.uk/documents/SN03426/SN03426.pdf (accessed 8 May 2019).
[58] Carol Liao, 'Limits to Corporate Reform and Alternative Legal Structures' in Beate Sjåfjell and Benjamin J. Richardson (eds.), *Company Law and Sustainability: Legal Barriers and Opportunities* (Cambridge University Press 2015), 292Adam Brown, David Cox and Roy Pinnock, 'United Kingdom: Community Benefits Incorporated: Shale and Other Contentious Infrastructure' (2013) *International Energy Law Review*, 2–3.
[59] Liao (n 58) 295.
[60] Karsten Engsig Sorensen and Mette Neville, 'Social Enterprises: How Should Company Law Balance Flexibility and Credibility?' (2014) 15(2) *European Business Organization Law Review* 5, 6.
[61] J Haskell Murray, 'Social Enterprise Innovation: Delaware's Public Benefit Corporation Law' (2014) 4 *Harvard Business Law Review* 345, 348.
[62] Sean W Brownridge, 'Canning Plum Organics: The Avant-Garde Campbell Soup Company Acquisition and Delaware Public Benefit Corporations' (2014) 39 Del. J. Corp. L. 703, 710.

Benefit companies are explicitly designed to have a corporate purpose that creates positive social impacts.[63] There are also mandatory requirements to report on the company's social and environmental performance using independent third-party accreditation.[64] These companies were developed against the backdrop of shareholder primacy,[65] and therefore put forward alternative models of the company, but they are still for-profit companies and there may be inherent tensions between shareholder wealth maximization and public beneficiaries.[66] The model law on benefit companies does not provide directors with clarity on how they are to weigh and balance competing interests.[67] In addition, model laws on benefit companies are permissive and not mandatory, and so they merely allow directors to consider non-shareholder interests.[68]

The low-profit company was first introduced in 2008 in Vermont.[69] It is often conceived of as a 'hybrid' between the non-profit company and the for-profit company. It is designed to allow both investments geared towards profit-making, and also towards donations.[70] It must be incorporated with an explicit charitable mission, and profit-making is designed as a secondary consideration to its social mission.[71]

The increasing number of social enterprise oriented corporate forms demonstrates a renewed desire to pursue socially-sensitive corporate approaches. To varying degrees, they lessen the pressure on directors to work solely to enhance the wealth of shareholders. However, most social enterprise entities are still closely-held companies which might not rise to the level which attract regulatory scrutiny as public and transnational companies do,[72] particularly on emissions.

In addition to social enterprise companies, hybrid forms which mix the benefits of partnerships and companies have also been created, such as Limited Liability Partnerships (or LLPs), as well as Limited Liability Corporations (or LLCs) found in the United States. In addition to these hybrid forms, older forms of a traditional

---

[63] 'The Need and Rationale for the Benefit Corporation: Why It Is the Legal Form That Best Addresses the Needs of Social Entrepreneurs, Investors and Ultimately, the Public' (White Paper, 18 January 2013), 1, http://benefitcorp.net/policymakers/benefit-corporation-white-paper (accessed 8 May 2019).
[64] Ibid.
[65] Ibid, 838.
[66] Brownridge (n 62) 710.
[67] Murray (n 61) 365; Alicia E. Perloples, 'Delaware Public Benefit Corporations 90 Days Out: Who's Opting In?' (2014) 14 U.C. Davis Bus. L. J., 247, 252.
[68] Liao (n 58) 304.
[69] Daniel S Kleinberger, 'A Myth Deconstructed: "The Emperor's New Clothes" on the Low-Profit Limited Liability Company' (2010) 35 Delaware J. Corporate Law 879, 879.
[70] Florida Senate Issue Brief, 'An Overview of Low-Profit Limited Liability Companies (L3Cs)' (October 2010), 1, www.flsenate.gov/UserContent/Session/2011/Publications/InterimReports/pdf/2011-210cm.pdf (accessed 8 May 2019).
[71] Ibid; Liao (n 56) 299.
[72] Alina S. Ball, 'Social Enterprise Governance' (2016) 18 U. Pa. J. Bus. L. 919, 933.

for-profit company, but which has a very different type of shareholder, are state-owned companies. The majority (or all) of their shares are usually owned by a government. In these companies, there is a mix of both public duty and private obligation.[73] These companies are often used to further their government's economic and development aims,[74] but the states which own and often operate them may also owe duties under other laws, including international environmental law.

Heede's carbon major study highlights that a significant proportion of carbon majors are state-owned companies. Of the top 90 carbon-majors, 50 are investor-owned and 31 are state-owned companies.[75] A large number of the top twenty emitting state-owned enterprises are located in developing countries such as Iran, China and Saudi Arabia, all of which are parties to the Paris Agreement.[76] Many of these state-owned companies are also investing aggressively in other developing countries, as well as in Europe, the U.S. and Japan. While generalizations about the role of business in global governance often refers to large, market-integrated entities based in industrialised countries,[77] and it is these entities which are the main focus of this book, this approach is slowing changing, and so some examples of corporate relationships to climate change from developing countries are also provided.

Except for companies limited by guarantee, all of these types of companies focus to a greater or lesser degree on profit making. Traditional for-profit companies put a heavier emphasis on this approach to corporate operations, whereas state-owned companies may, for example, follow government directives more strictly, depending on their government's policies in a particular industry. Directors of public companies may be subject to more pressure to produce short-term profits than directors in private companies and so are the main focus of this book, but pressures around profitability persist in private companies as well.[78] Social enterprise companies may weigh competing social and environmental demands more heavily than profit making, but are also subject to corporate norms around profitability, although to a lesser degree than traditional for-profit companies.

This book focuses on the traditional for-profit company as it is the most popular corporate form, and most subject to corporate norms of shareholder primacy and wealth maximization. Many recent regulatory developments are also focused on

---

[73] Larry Catá Backer, 'The Human Rights Obligations of State-Owned Enterprises: Emerging Conceptual Structures, Principles and National and International Law and Policy' (2017) 50 Vand. J. Transt'l L. 827, 832.
[74] Ibid., 835.
[75] Heede (n 28), 231.
[76] Although Iran has yet to ratify the Paris Agreement.
[77] Fuchs (n 3), 6; David Vogel, *The Market for Virtue: The Potential and Limits of Corporate Social Responsibilities* (Brookings 2006), 111.
[78] Vogel (n 77), 72.

public companies, as well as on TNCs.[79] These norms also influence, to a lesser extent, social enterprise companies as well as state-owned companies. In all of these companies, directors are afforded some degree of discretion in how they manage the business, and are subject to varying degrees of climate barriers as well as opportunities.

1.6 SYSTEMIC BARRIERS AND OPPORTUNITIES: SHORT-TERMISM, CSR AND SOCIETAL EXPECTATIONS

The pressure to maximize shareholder wealth is not a legal requirement, but instead a corporate norm that has been interpreted by capital markets in particular to focus on short-term wealth creation. While traditional interpretations of shareholder primacy did not mandate a short-term approach, the subsequent focus on the reduction of agency costs has ushered in a large element of short-termism, often quarterly, into shareholder primacy.[80] The liberalisation of capital markets and the introduction of electronic trading in the 1980s compounded this short-term approach.[81] The simultaneous rise of institutional investors during that same period meant that portfolio managers became overly concerned with the quarterly earnings of companies, as their own performance was assessed quarterly.[82] This in turn put pressure on directors to manage companies in order to maximize short-term returns for shareholders, particularly in for-profit companies.

An emphasis on short-term profitability diverts attention away from focusing on issues such as climate change, which directors often (mistakenly) interpret to only have long-term impacts. This short-termism is fuelled by a larger capitalist system which emphasizes and prioritizes economic growth and exploitation of natural resources, leading to what Wright and Nyberg have deemed a 'creative self-destruction' where economic growth and climate change are the ultimate manifestation of both progress and devastation.[83] The threat of climate change is deeply and

---

[79] This book uses both the terms transnational corporations as well as multinational companies. TNCs it is the main term used by the United Nations in a number of agreements, but the OECD favours the term multinational corporations (or MNCs) and this is used particularly where OECD guidelines are covered. This book also uses the term company law as this is the traditional name used in the English jurisdiction as opposed to corporate law used predominantly in the U.S., but the descriptor 'corporate' is also used.

[80] Brian R Cheffins, 'Corporate Law and Ownership Structure: A Darwinian Link?' (2002) 25 UNSWLF 346, 361; John Grinyer, Alex Russell and David Collison, 'Evidence of Managerial Short-termism in the UK' (1998) 9 British Journal of Management 13, 19; David Millon, 'Shareholder Social Responsibility' (2012–2013) 36 Seattle U. L. Rev. 911, 913.

[81] Eduard Gracia, 'Short-Term Thinking and the Winner-Takes-All Market', Deloitte Consulting 6, https://papers.ssrn.com/sol3/papers.cfm?abstract_id=445260 (accessed 31 March 2020).

[82] Jill E. Fisch, 'Securities Intermediaries and the Separation of Ownership from Control' (2010) 33 Seattle U. L. Rev. 877, 883.

[83] Christopher Wright and Daniel Nyberg, Climate Change, Capitalism and Corporations: Processes of Creative Self-Destruction (Cambridge University Press 2015), 1.

fundamentally connected to global capitalism.[84] Any action on climate change, even by companies, must also be supported by different approaches to growth and the natural environment in the global economic system.

While this book focuses on climate change, it is not the only environmental crisis the world is facing. Levels of biological diversity are approaching or passing irreversible tipping points, and pose significant risks to human society.[85] Sustainable approaches must be adopted, and be respectful of planetary boundaries.[86] The Sustainable Development Goals, agreed in 2015, are an important part of the 2030 global development agenda. SDG Goal 13 focuses on climate change, and states that climate change measures must be integrated into national policies, strategies and planning, efforts on climate finance must be scaled up, as must resilience and adaptive capacities in all countries to climate hazards.[87] The law, including company law, has an important role to play in both fuelling and addressing environmental sustainability generally.[88] The SDG Goal 13 refers back to the UNFCCC and the international climate regime, which is one of the main drivers of corporate climate action covered in this book.

The traditional corporate approach to environmental issues has been through the use of corporate social responsibility (CSR) movements and initiatives. CSR has varying definitions, but is itself a product of neoliberal political economies and so is business-driven and often focuses on win-win scenarios,[89] where the environment is protected but profits are also made. Unfortunately environmentally friendly investments are not always profitable in the short term. So while there is a market for virtue, as social enterprise companies illustrate, Vogel notes it is often a niche one.[90] CSR can encourage firms to go 'beyond compliance', but CSR initiatives do not check the operations of the most irresponsible businesses.[91]

The deficiencies of CSR do not mean that companies are entirely immune from social pressure. Companies are often referred to as 'corporate citizens', reflecting both their status as legal persons but also reflecting the role they play in society.[92]

---

[84] Ibid, 6.
[85] IPBES, 'Global Assessment Report on Biodiversity and Ecosystem Services' (2019), https://ipbes.net/global-assessment (accessed 20 July 2020).
[86] Johan Rockstrom et al., 'A Safe Operating Space for Humanity' (2009) 461 Nature, 472.
[87] UNDP, Sustainable Development Goal 13, www.undp.org/content/undp/en/home/sustainable-development-goals/goal-13-climate-action.html#targets (accessed 22 July 2020).
[88] See generally, Beate Sjåfjell and Benjamin J. Richardson (eds.) *Company Law and Sustainability: Legal Barriers and Opportunities* (Cambridge University Press 2015).
[89] Peter Newell, 'CSR and the Limits of Capital' (2008) 39(6) *Development and Change* 1063, 1069.
[90] David Vogel, 'The Low Value of Virtue' (June 2005) *Harvard Business Review*, 26; Vogel (n 77), xvi.
[91] Peter Newell, 'Citizenship, Accountability, and Community: The Limits of the CSR Agenda' (2005) 31(3) *International Affairs* 541, 542.
[92] Wright and Nyberg (n 83), 23. Fuchs notes the concept of 'corporate citizenship' was developed in the U.S. as a way to enshrine corporate individualism and corporate rights (n 3), 49.

Companies rely on a social licence to operate, meaning they must be concerned with, and engage with, societal demands and pressures for a number of reasons. While some of these reasons may be purely philanthropic, or are efforts to protect their reputation, companies can often feel a 'compliance pull'[93] to conform to even voluntary or soft law mandates both nationally and internationally. Companies use these social mandates to both avoid critics and regulation, but also to attract benefits to themselves. Companies are very interested in the skills (as employees), tastes (as consumers) and capital (as investors) of the public, and millennials in particular, who in turn are often concerned about climate change. Companies also benefit from public goods such as the atmosphere, and as beneficiaries they are expected by society to take on public duties.[94]

Companies have direct or instrumental power to make decisions that will affect the lives of many, as well as structural power.[95] Structural power is exercised by the high mobility of capital, and the ability of TNCs in particular to punish or reward governments for policy choices.[96] Their structural power enables them to set the regulatory agenda, both nationally and internationally.[97] TNCs have tremendous power and influence, rivalling that of states, and can also lobby governments for special regulatory treatment.[98] Due to their power, companies can act as rule makers.[99] Business engages in global governance through self-regulation such as CSR and private-public governance initiatives.[100] In the process of creating the rules, companies themselves also create a large quantity of norms, participate in governance, and so may themselves have a 'quasi-regulatory function.'[101] As private entities, companies can create autonomous governance systems.[102] They can create or participate in transnational regime complexes, including in the climate arena, alongside of states.[103] The approaches that companies take to climate change are, therefore, extremely important.

---

[93] Veerle Heyvaert, 'Transnationalization of Law: Rethinking Law Through Transnational Environmental Regulation' (2017) 6 *Transnational Environmental Law* 205, 216.
[94] Choudhury and Petrin (n 40) 4.
[95] Fuchs (n 3), 64; Choudhury and Petrin (n 40), 28.
[96] Fuchs (n 3), 64.
[97] Ibid.
[98] Joseph E. Stiglitz, 'Multinational Corporations: Balancing Rights and Responsibilities' (2007) 101 Am. Soc'y Int'l L. Proc., 16.
[99] Choudhury and Petrin (n 40), 29.
[100] Ibid.
[101] Moore and Reberioux (n 49) 85.
[102] Larry Catá Backer, 'Private Actors and Public Governance Beyond the State: The Multinational Corporation, the Financial Stability Board, and the Global Governance Order' (2011) 18(2) *Indiana Journal of Global Legal Studies* 751, 756.
[103] Kenneth W. Abbott, 'Strengthening the Transnational Regime Complex for Climate Change' (2014) 3(1) *Transnational Environmental Law* 57, 65. Although some authors challenge the power of companies to regulate; Jan Tullberg, 'Illusions of Corporate Power: Revisiting the Relative Powers of Corporations and Governments' (2004) 52 *Journal of Business Ethics* 325, 328.

1.7 CLIMATE RISKS AND CORPORATE TRANSITIONS: THE UNITED KINGDOM AS A MODEL

Climate change poses tremendous risks to companies, and to the entire global financial system. The risks of climate change are estimated to negatively impact a significant portion of global assets, with up to 30% of global manageable assets at risk.[104] Between now and the end of the century, this could lead to between four to forty-three trillion dollars' worth of assets at risk.[105] A 3°C rate of warming by the end of the century has the potential to reduce the level of global GDP by 21%.[106] Failure of climate change mitigation and adaptation ranked as the number one risk, by impact, in the 2020 Global Risks Report, and number two by likelihood over the next ten years.[107]

Failure of climate policy in the 2020s could lead to increased transition risks, with firms and markets having to adjust more rapidly. This will in turn lead to higher costs, greater economic disruptions and potentially draconian interventions by panicked policy-makers.[108] Greater understanding of climate risks could make long-term borrowing unavailable, impact insurance costs and availability, reduce the terminal value of assets, and trigger capital reallocation and asset re-pricing.[109] Highly exposed industries, therefore, may be disincentivized from highlighting climate risks where this would have a negative financial impact on them. Over 200 of the world's largest companies anticipate that climate change could cost them up to US$1 trillion, with much of the economic pain felt in the next five years.[110] Despite this, very few firms are adequately assessing climate risks. In 2019, the Bank of England warned that climate change will require a massive reallocation of capital, and if companies and industries fail to adjust, they will fail to exist.[111] Acting on climate change makes sense for companies, particularly those in highly exposed sectors, even if it means short term losses, longer term adjustments, or even business transitions.

---

[104] Global manageable assets are the total stock of assets held by non-bank financial institutions. The Economist Intelligence Unit, The Cost of Inaction: Recognising Recognizing the value at risk from climate change 8 (2015), https://eiuperspectives.economist.com/sites/default/files/The%20cost%20of%20inaction_0.pdf (accessed 1 July 2020).
[105] Ibid., 2; Allie Goldstein et al., 'The Private Sector's Climate Change Risk and Adaptation Blind Spots' (2018) 9 *Nature Climate Change* 18, 18.
[106] Oxford Economics, 'Global Modelling the Economic Cost of Global Warming' 6 July 2020, 1.
[107] World Economic Forum, 'The Global Risks Report 2020' (15th ed.), 7.
[108] Ibid, 33.
[109] McKinsey Global Institute, 'Climate Risk and Responses Physical Hazards and Socioeconomic Impacts' (January 2020), viii.
[110] Mark Green, 'World's Biggest Firms Foresee $1 Trillion Climate Cost Hit' 3 June 2019, www.reuters.com/article/us-climate-change-companies-disclosure/worlds-biggest-firms-foresee-1-trillion-climate-cost-hit-idUSKCN1T50CF.
[111] www.bankofengland.co.uk/news/2019/april/open-letter-on-climate-related-financial-risks.

The G20 countries constitute 78% of global emissions.[112] Only four of those G20 countries have committed to net-zero emissions by 2050.[113] The U.K. is one of those four countries. Despite the political upheaval of Brexit, the U.K. adopted a net-zero emissions target in 2019. It was the first country to adopt climate legislation in 2008, which incorporated national emissions targets through the Climate Change Act. It also updated its Companies Act in 2006 to adopt an enlightened shareholder value approach to directors' duties.

The English jurisdiction is an important part of the Anglo-American tradition of company law, has substantial jurisprudence on the objective of companies and the obligations of directors, and has a record of innovation and export of its company law model.[114] Many countries around the world adopted a form of corporate theory and/or company law which originated from the English legal model, and there are connections between English corporate governance reforms and corporate governance regulation at the international level as well, particularly the OECD Principles of Corporate Governance.[115] While the new enlightened shareholder value model is critiqued for retaining and even entrenching a shareholder primacy model, the U.K. approach to climate change includes a clear regulatory overlap between company law and climate change laws. While this overlap only relates to reporting of climate risks at the moment, it will likely stretch beyond that narrow thematic window to encompass larger responsibilities of companies and corporate directors on climate change and climate risk in the future.

These regulatory developments in the U.K. indicate a direction of travel for corporate and climate law in the future in the U.K., and around the world, and so the U.K. is the major jurisdictional focus of this book. Examples of regulations and legal developments from other jurisdictions are also included, from the U.S., the EU, Australia and Canada, as well as some developing countries such as India, Pakistan, the Philippines and South Africa. The U.K. approach could be a potential model for future regulatory and fiscal developments. Despite being a stronghold for the shareholder primacy theory, it recently adopted a net-zero national emissions target, and is adopting more progressive energy and financial strategies to achieve that target, which include corporate obligations and regulations. This book will assess the various aspects of these as well as international regulatory developments to assess the evolving role of companies in the context of climate change.

---

[112] UNEP (n 12), vi.
[113] Ibid., vii.
[114] Shawn Donnelly, 'Corporate Governance and the Company Law Review in Britain' in Byong-Man Ahn, John Halligan and Stephen Wilks (eds.), *Reforming Public and Corporate Governance* (Edward Elgar 2002), 256.
[115] Alan Dignam, 'Exporting Corporate Governance: U.K. Regulatory Systems in a Global Economy' (2000) Company Lawyer 70.

1.8 STRUCTURE OF THE BOOK

The central thesis of this book is that climate change is forcing a reinterpretation of corporate norms and laws, and that company law should act as a bridge, and not a barrier, to corporate climate action. This book will look at company law and corporate theory, as well as other regulatory efforts and developments which affect companies, through the lens of climate change. The risks of climate change are so great they now challenge how we think about companies and the traditional role they have played in society. This book interrogates the theory and law affecting companies in the context of climate change, and finds that many of the norms and laws that regulate this space are outdated, and in fact are subject to dramatic changes as society, policy makers, financial regulators, investors and companies themselves better understand the risks and opportunities that climate change poses.

The obvious place to start this inquiry is with longstanding corporate norms, and the Anglo-American theory of corporate law in particular, which animates so much of the judicial interpretation of corporate statutes. These theories have dominated corporate responses to climate change for many decades, but these responses have been largely inadequate as a tool to manage the climate crisis, and this relationship is explored in Chapter 2. Because of their influence, Chapter 2 focuses mainly on U.S. and U.K. corporate theories. Chapter 3 looks at how these norms have influenced company law, looking primarily at U.K. common law, and the flexibility it traditionally provided to directors. This discretion has arguably been restricted by the amendments to directors' duties in the U.K. Companies Act 2006.

In addition to corporate law and theory, companies are also affected by international environmental law. The Paris Agreement in particular has had a significant influence on U.K. national climate regulation, including the decision to move to net-zero emissions by 2050. Despite the resurgence of shareholder primacy in the Companies Act 2006, international environmental law, CSR and public-private initiatives have significantly influenced corporate responses to climate change. These initiatives and evolving corporate approaches to climate change are assessed in Chapter 4.

Domestic emission measures as well as national legislative efforts to transition energy markets away from fossil fuels and towards renewable energy also significantly affect companies. Emissions reporting mandates, energy market reform regulation, as well as emissions trading schemes all have an impact and have been influenced by the international initiatives covered in Chapter 4. These national measures are explored in Chapter 5, including carbon trading mandates in the EU ETS, and the influence of Brexit on the U.K.'s approach to carbon trading.

In addition to these directed, and state-controlled regulatory measures, companies are also affected by climate litigation and human rights law, which have both evolved in the past few years by directly targeting companies as a site of legal attention, if not direct liability. Chapter 6 looks at human rights regulation and

1.8 Structure of the Book

climate litigation from the perspective of multinational companies, which are often the focus of attention of these initiatives. Climate litigation is appearing in a number of countries, predominantly the U.S. and the EU. But it is not confined to the developed world, and litigation efforts in developing countries such as Peru, The Philippines, and Pakistan are also investigated in Chapter 6.

Finally, companies require capital. Fiscal measures and increased awareness regarding climate change by financiers who provide capital to companies is changing the face and attention of these actors and therefore of capital markets. If capital is directed away from fossil fuels and towards renewable energy, companies may be motivated to transition their energy sources and business models accordingly.[116] The impact of carbon taxes, trade measures at the WTO, as well as concerns from institutional investors are covered in Chapter 7.

There are, of course, a number of areas of the law which also directly and indirectly impact companies in the realm of climate change, but due to space limitations this book focuses specifically on areas of the law which are of primary relevance to for-profit companies, with a particular emphasis on TNCs. The Conclusion ties these regulatory efforts in various jurisdictions together, and explores where theories and laws are evolving, and may continue to evolve, towards a more climate-friendly corporate approach.

---

[116] On the role of capital in climate action, see generally, Megan Bowman, 'Development and Global Sustainability: The Case for 'Corporate Climate Finance' (2014) Harvard College Review of Environment and Society, www.hcs.harvard.edu/~res/2014/05/development-and-global-sustainability-the-case-for-corporate-climate-finance/ (accessed 1 August 2020).

2

Theorising the Company in the Context of Climate Change

In August 2019, members of the Business Roundtable gathered to redefine corporate responsibility, by adopting a modern standard that meets the long-term needs of all stakeholders, as opposed to just the short-term needs of shareholders.[1] The Business Roundtable consists of 181 chief executives of some of the largest US companies, and acts as a supra-corporate lobby and a forum for the development of common corporate political stances.[2] The organisation has been issuing Principles of Corporate Governance since 1978. To be clear, the Business Roundtable is not a traditionally progressive actor.[3] Its 2019 statement was couched as a 'redefinition' of the purpose of the corporation in order to promote an economy that serves all Americans. This statement represents a significant departure from all of the organisation's previous statements since 1997, which focused attention exclusively on shareholders. The 2019 statement specifically stated that it signifies a move away from shareholder primacy. Directors of the Business Roundtable's members – such as Accenture, Amazon, Apple, BP, Chevron, The Coca-Cola Company, 3M, Gap Inc., GE, General Motors, IBM and Goldman Sachs – also committed to incorporating sustainable practices in order to protect the environment.[4] How aggressively these companies will act to implement the 2019 statement remains to be seen. However, this statement is historic as it moves away from traditional corporate norms such as

---

[1] Business Roundtable, 'Business Roundtable Redefines the Purpose of a Corporation to Promote "An Economy That Serves All Americans"' (19 August 2019), www.businessroundtable.org/business-roundtable-redefines-the-purpose-of-a-corporation-to-promote-an-economy-that-serves-all-americans (accessed 24 May 2020).
[2] Doris Fuchs, *Business Power in Global Governance* (Lynne Rienner 2007), 76.
[3] Ibid., who notes the Business Roundtable was responsible for the defeat of proposals for the creation of a consumer protection agency, stricter antitrust regulation, revision and elimination of deadlines in the Clean Air Act Amendments in the 1970s and the defeat of the Clinton administration's healthcare plan in the 1990s.
[4] Business Roundtable (n 1).

shareholder primacy and shareholder wealth maximisation which, as illustrated in this chapter, have been the dominant theoretical approaches to the company.

2.1 CORPORATE THEORIES AND NORMS IN THE CONTEXT OF CLIMATE CHANGE

The theories and norms that underpin company law are highly influential. Norms are guidelines or non-binding values which regulate behaviour. The most dominant of these norms in the corporate context include agency theory, law and economics theories, shareholder primacy norm and shareholder wealth maximisation norm. Shareholder primacy and shareholder wealth maximisation norms developed out of both agency theories and law and economics theories. Although rarely legally binding in any jurisdiction, corporate theories, and the norms they have spawned, guide directors when they apply and interpret company law. As a result, these dominant theories and norms are directly relevant to corporate decision-making around climate change. They are examined here through the lens of climate change to establish how they impact environmental decision-making by directors, and climate change in particular.

The shareholder primacy norm reifies and privileges shareholders and their interests, elevating them to a central position of concern for the company and its directors. At the same time, the norm marginalises and makes subservient the interests of non-shareholders, including society overall, the environment and the atmosphere. Law and economics theorists have given the shareholder primacy norm an economic interpretation, with an almost exclusive focus on the economic interests of shareholders and maximisation of their wealth. Application of these norms has led to a focus on short-term, often quarterly, profitability. While traditional shareholder primacy and wealth maximisation norms did not mandate a short-term approach, the subsequent focus on the reduction of agency costs combined with larger structural market conditions has ushered in a large element of short-termism into the norms' interpretation and application.[5]

The focus on shareholder wealth maximisation combined with short-termism is often incompatible with the long-term time frames of climate change, and the long-term perspectives directors need to adopt in order to assess and manage the impacts and risks of climate change in the short, medium and long term. Shareholder primacy and short-term wealth maximisation encourage the company and its man-

---

[5] Brian R. Cheffins, 'Corporate Law and Ownership Structure: A Darwinian Link?' (2002) 25 UNSW L. J. 346, 361; John Grinyer, Alex Russell and David Collison, 'Evidence of Managerial Short-Termism in the UK' (1998) 9 *British Journal of Management* 13, 19; David Millon, 'Shareholder Social Responsibility' (2012) 36 Seattle U. L. Rev. 911, 913.

agers to externalise costs, which include environmental damage and negative externalities such as GHG emissions. Therefore, shareholder primacy and wealth maximisation norms pose considerable barriers to corporate action in the context of climate change.

Corporate norms and actions are interconnected and can influence and shape one another. Companies themselves create many norms and values, and so corporate activity on its own has a 'quasi-regulatory function'.[6] The concerns and imperatives of shareholder primacy and wealth maximisation norms shaped academic and practitioner approaches to, and narratives of, company law. The rise of the shareholder primacy and wealth maximisation norms tells us a story about how these powerful paradigms can shape cultural practices.[7] These norms have legitimised corporate action that sidelines climate concerns in favour of short-term shareholder concerns. If climate change is not considered by corporate theorists as important enough to be a central concern for companies, the issue will be left to other regulatory or market approaches to manage. Company law focuses primarily on the protection and advancement of the interests of shareholders, therefore relegating issues such as climate change to law, specifically environmental or energy law, considered external to company law. These external laws and regulations are inadequate to counter the powerful imperatives of short-term profit-making. This dynamic also creates situations of conflict, whereby companies and their managers and directors may be tempted to violate non-corporate regulations or voluntary corporate initiatives in order to adhere to internal, short-term norms.

The emphasis on shareholder primacy and short-term wealth maximisation has implications for the role and function of company law in the context of climate change. Scholarly analysis has failed to identify company law and directors' duties as a potential regulatory response to climate change.[8] Shareholder primacy and short-term wealth maximisation norms, as currently interpreted, therefore lead to negative impacts on the climate. These norms and theories were developed over time and built upon one another. Their historical interpretations provide insights into their limitations and future potential for assessing and managing large-scale and systemic risks such as climate change. Norms and theories, as well as the directors' duties they inform, are not static concepts. They have and will evolve over time. Competing theories have also developed over time, and these may provide a more cogent picture of the company in the context of climate change.

---

[6] Marc T. Moore and Antoine Reberioux, 'Revitalizing the Institutional Roots of Anglo-American Corporate Governance' (2011) 40(1) *Economy and Society* 84, 85.

[7] Lyman Johnson, 'Reclaiming an Ethic of Corporate Responsibility' (2002) 70 Geo. Wash. L. Rev. 957, 965.

[8] Sarah Barker, 'Directors' Personal Liability for Corporate Inaction on Climate Change' (2015) 67(1) *Governance Directions* 21; Janet Dine, 'Corporate Regulation, Climate Change and Corporate Law: Challenges and Balance in an International and Global World' (2015) 26 Eur. Bus. L. Rev. 173.

2.1.1 The Beginnings of Agency Theory and Shareholder Primacy

Corporate theory has failed to adequately and consistently explain (absent certain circumstances such as takeovers) what or whose objective a company serves, and therefore to whom directors owe duties to. This may be due to many factors, including the wide varieties and types of company and a historical misunderstanding of the shareholders as the 'owners' of the company. Perhaps due to this rationalising void, certain theories and norms have sprung up which focus only on the relationship between directors and shareholders.

At the beginning of the twentieth century, the focus on the relationship between directors and shareholders intensified as the ownership of shares began to diverge from the control of the company. During this time, American and English companies experienced a revolutionary shift from the majority of companies being shareholder-controlled to being director-controlled entities.[9] Ownership of companies became widely dispersed amongst hundreds and then thousands of shareholders. Small, private and closely held corporations gave way to large, publicly traded companies.

As a result of these developments, ownership of shares in a company became separated from the control of that company. The control shifted into the hands of directors as a result. This shift coincided with a transition in the nature of companies. Companies transitioned from largely public service–type entities, undertaking quasi-public projects in the Industrial Revolution era, to private entities, undertaking a wide variety of business activities.[10] These two simultaneous shifts laid the foundation for the development, and eventual dominance, of agency theories and the shareholder primacy norm.

Adolf Berle and Gardiner Means captured the shift in control from shareholders to directors in their seminal work, *The Modern Corporation and Private Property*.[11] The authors were concerned that these great transitions in the nature of corporate activities and the characteristics of control would lead to the company becoming a dominant but largely uncontrolled institution.[12] In response, they developed two related and influential doctrines which still characterise the modern corporation: (1) that it had become so dominant that it exercised a tremendous amount of control and influence over society, and (2) that the separation of ownership from control had broken the traditional property relationship between the shareholder and the company.[13] The rupture of this relationship between the shareholder and the company

---

[9] Brian R. Cheffins, 'Are Good Managers Required for a Separation of Ownership and Control?' (2004) 13(4) *Industrial and Corporate Change* 591, 597.
[10] Walter Werner, 'Corporate Law in Search of Its Future' (1981) 81(8) Colum. L. Rev. 1611, 1641.
[11] Adolf A. Berle and Gardiner C. Means, *The Modern Corporation and Private Property* (first published 1932, Transaction 1991).
[12] Ibid., 46.
[13] Ibid., 4.

in theory rendered shareholders vulnerable to the power and excesses of management.[14] Given such wide powers of control, managers could focus on the needs of the business and perhaps even their own needs, instead of the interests and needs of the shareholders. Shareholders would have to incur costs, generally known as agency costs, in order to refocus the minds of directors in their direction. Berle and Means' concern about agency costs spawned generations of agency theorists, and has had wide and persistent implications for company law and theory. Their theory also led to the elevation of shareholder interests, and marginalisation of all other interests within the company.

Initially, Berle and Means considered that neither regulation nor shareholders would be adequate monitors of corporate activity.[15] However, in a subsequent debate with Merrick Dodd, Berle changed his mind, concluding that shareholders were the only practical and appropriate monitor of the company. He argued that any power held by directors is held on trust for, and for the benefit of, the shareholders.[16] Directors, therefore, become agents of the shareholders. This statement, made in his famous 1931 essay published in the *Harvard Law Review*, was the genesis of the shareholder primacy approach.[17] While Berle was primarily concerned with constraining the power of corporations and their managers by using shareholders as monitors, his approach elevated and cemented the role of shareholders as central and fundamental within corporate theory.

While Berle's approach (that directors are agents of the shareholders) has become the dominant theoretical model of the company, it remains contested today, just as it was at the time of its introduction. During the 1930s, Berle engaged in an extended academic debate with Dodd. Their debate focused not just on whose interests directors serve but also on the broader topics of what the nature and objectives of a company are and should be. Dodd challenged Berle's assumptions that the sole function of a company is to make profits for its shareholders.[18] Instead, Dodd focused on the company as an entity which could take into account and value the views of all of its constituents, not just its shareholders.

In Dodd's analysis, if the company is a separate entity, there is no reason why shareholders should be privileged within it. Dodd's theory makes room for other non-shareholder constituents to have their views and interests considered by the company. He felt that companies should be accountable to the public as a whole due to their tremendous influence on public life.[19] Dodd's focus was on the

---

[14] Ibid.
[15] It is important to note that Berle and Means were equally concerned that regulation would not be adequate to constrain the power of companies, and therefore the company should not protect shareholder interests to the exclusion of all other constituents. Ibid., 313.
[16] Adolf A. Berle Jr, 'Corporate Powers as Powers in Trust' (1931) 44(7) Harv. L. Rev., 1049.
[17] William W. Bratton and Michael L. Wachter, 'Shareholder Primacy's Corporatist Origins: Adolf Berle and The Modern Corporation' (2008) 34 J. Corp. L. 99, 148.
[18] E. Merrick Dodd, 'For Whom Are Corporate Managers Trustees?' (1932) 45 Harv. L. Rev. 1145.
[19] Ibid., 1149.

company's impacts on society, and so his understanding of the company more easily accommodates the tremendous impacts that companies have on the climate in the modern day.

Dodd's theory marked the beginning of stakeholder theories, which provide alternative and competing theories to the corporate form. The debate between Berle and Dodd reflects early tension between the shareholder primacy and stakeholder theories, and laid the groundwork for the later development of these norms and theories. It also illustrates that from an early date, shareholder primacy was a contested theory. Berle eventually changed his mind, conceding that Dodd was correct, illustrating that he was always a reluctant shareholder primacy theorist.[20] Despite his reversal, Berle's theory of directors as agents, and shareholder primacy, developed over time to become the dominant corporate theory.

2.1.2 *Agency Costs and Shareholder Primacy*

The majority of scholarly analyses of Berle and Means' work focused on agency costs and how to minimise them. The issue of agency costs remains the central focus of company law and corporate theory. Agency theorists' central concern is that the separation of ownership from control would lead untrustworthy managers to pursue their own self-interest, and not the interests of shareholders. Agency theories assume that when a principal delegates decision-making authority to an agent, the principal cannot assume the agent will act in the interests of the principal at all times and at zero cost. Agency costs will have to be incurred by shareholders to discipline directors and help focus their attention back to shareholder concerns. Directors can be incentivised to do this and disciplined by several mechanisms, such as increasing shareholder rights, raising executive compensation, hostile takeovers and market forces.

This focus on agency costs was, and is, underpinned by a theoretical assumption that shareholders are the principal constituents of the company, and therefore their interests should be the primary, and exclusive, consideration of directors. Agency theorists elevate the role of shareholders and their interests, contributing to the dominance of the shareholder primacy norm. The agency approach reduces a complex set of relationships within the company to focus entirely on the relationship between the directors and the shareholders. This approach relegates any non-shareholder stakeholder to 'bystanders' within the company.[21] It minimises the role and interests of non-shareholders, including the environment. This myopic focus on

---

[20] Adolf A. Berle Jr, '"Control" in Corporate Law' (1985) 19 U. San Fran. L. Rev. 229, 235. Dodd also moderated his views, E. Merrick Dodd Jr, 'Book Review, *Bureaucracy and Trusteeship in Large Corporations* by Marshall E. Dimock and Harold K. Hyde' (1941) 9 U. Chi. L. Rev. 538, 546–7.
[21] Lucian Arye Bebchuk, 'The Case for Increasing Shareholder Power' (2005) 118(3) Harv. L. Rev. 833, 913.

shareholders thus led to the diminishing, and almost complete disregard of the interests and concerns of non-shareholder constituents, such as the environment, in company law scholarship. Non-shareholder constituents barely figure in the agency theorist literature. The agency approach facilitates, and in fact encourages, negative impacts on the environment if the corporate activities which generate these impacts are profit-maximising and therefore in the assumed interest of shareholders.

Although Berle and Means were equally concerned with the company's dominance and negative influence in society, the majority of company law scholarship discarded this concern after adopting the shareholder primacy theory. The issue of the separation of ownership from control, and its attendant agency problem, instead became the major focus of these theorists, particularly agency theorists, who have come to dominate company law theory.[22] The rise of shareholder primacy theorists coincided with the emergence of the law and economics theories that proposed free-market solutions to problems of ownership and control in an effort to minimise agency costs.[23]

2.1.3 *Law and Economics, and Shareholder Wealth Maximisation*

The law and economics movement served as the catalyst that catapulted shareholder primacy to the dominant position it now enjoys in the corporate law academy. The movement began in the 1950s with theorists such as Richard Posner, Gary Becker, Ronald Coase and Harold Demsetz. The movement came to the forefront between 1960 and 1980, and still prevails today in corporate scholarship. It uses neoclassical economic analysis to explain legal outcomes and relationships within the company.[24] Law and economics theorists put forward two rationales for shareholder primacy: first, it is contractually what the parties have agreed to, and second, it leads to economic efficiency.[25] Law and economics theorists reconceptualised the company from the perspective of neoclassical economics. From this perspective, the company and its managers should focus almost exclusively on making profits for shareholders.

The fundamental assumption underlying law and economics theory is that the company is involved in a continuous struggle in the marketplace, where only the rational (i.e. profit-maximising) will survive.[26] These theorists built on agency

---

[22] Mark S. Mizruchi, 'Berle and Means Revisited: The Governance and Power of Large US Corporations' (2004) 33(5) *Theory and Society* 579, 596.
[23] Henry G. Manne, 'The "Higher Criticism" of the Modern Corporation' (1962) 62(3) Colum. L. Rev. 399.
[24] Daniel H. Cole and Peter Z. Grossman, *Principles of Law and Economics* (Prentice Hall 2004), 56.
[25] Jill E. Fisch, 'Measuring Efficiency in Corporate Law: The Role of Shareholder Primacy' (2005) 31 J. Corp. L. 637, 650.
[26] Herbert A. Simon, 'Theories of Decision-Making in Economics and Behavioural Science' (1959) 49(3) *The American Economic Review* 253, 254.

theories by assuming that both principal and agent in the company were rational, wealth-seeking and utility maximisers.[27] They relied on neoclassical economic concepts such as self-interest and economic rationality, and applied them to corporate actors. They assumed, therefore, that shareholders, being economically rational actors, would only relinquish control to managers if those managers served their economic interests.[28] As a result, the theory characterises all shareholders and directors as profit-seeking actors. The theory has been critiqued for focusing exclusively on economic behaviour, motivated purely by self-interest. Lynn Stout caricatures the law and economics shareholder as a mythical *Homo economicus*, exclusively rational with stable preferences, self-interested and exclusively concerned with profit maximisation.[29] The theory places exclusive emphasis on the profit-making ability of the company, for the benefit of shareholders, and subsequently gave rise to the shareholder wealth maximisation norm.

2.1.4 Shareholder Wealth Maximisation and Contractarians

Law and economics theorists believe that shareholders only invest in order to make a profit, and shareholders' economic interests should be the primary concern of directors. Shareholder wealth maximisation becomes the sole function of the company, and any other concerns, such as environmental, become costs that reduce the profitability of the company.

Law and economics theories adopted two models of the company: the company as owned by its shareholders, and shareholders as the residual claimants of a web of contracts which make up the company. In both of these models, the environment and the mounting impacts of climate change do not figure as a concern to be catered for by the company.

The model of shareholders as owners has diminished in relevance today and has been severely criticised. In the 1970s, the model was most famously promoted by Milton Friedman, who argued that the sole social responsibility of company executives was to make as much money as possible for shareholders, while conforming to basic rules of society.[30] His approach highlighted the focus on shareholder wealth

---

[27] Mahmoud Ezzamel and Robert Watson, 'Organizational Firm, Ownership Structure and Corporate Performance: A Contextual Empirical Analysis of UK Corporations' (1993) 4 *British Journal of Management* 161, 164.

[28] Harold Demsetz, 'The Structure of Ownership and the Theory of the Firm' (1983) 26 J. L. & Econ. 375, 385–7.

[29] Lynn A. Stout, 'The Mechanisms of Market Inefficiency: An Introduction to the New Finance' (2002) 28 J. Corp. L. 635, 660.

[30] Milton Friedman, 'A Friedman Doctrine – The Social Responsibility of Business Is to Increase Its Profits', *The New York Times* (New York, 13 September 1970), www.nytimes.com/1970/09/13/archives/a-friedman-doctrine-the-social-responsibility-of-business-is-to.html (accessed 1 March 2020). Shareholder primacists argued that shareholders were owners as they bore the risk of any losses to the company and the benefit of any profits. Even if they no longer held any direct control over the corporation, they held indirect control through the right to elect and remove

maximisation to the detriment of all other social responsibilities. It also illustrated the anti-regulation position of shareholder primacy theorists, which has persisted over the decades in varying degrees. His approach saw the sole role of law to remove impediments to corporate profitability. An impediment would include environmental and GHG emission regulation, which would decrease the profitability of shareholders by imposing the costs of those emissions on the company instead of society.

The shareholder-as-owner model of the corporation as epitomised by Friedman has given way to a contractarian analysis of the company – that the company is a web or nexus of contracts. This approach reconceptualised the company as a series of privately ordered, consensual contracts agreed amongst the participants of the company. But this approach also privileges shareholders and their wealth maximisation. The parties to this series of contracts are assumed to be driven by self-interest to find optimal contracting solutions that maximise profits.[31]

The nexus of contracts approach rejected the shareholder as owner model, because if shareholders were owners, the company could not be reduced simply to a network of consensual contracts.[32] This left the role of shareholder as the primary constituent of the company in an uncertain position. In theory, under a pure nexus of contracts approach, there should be no contractual party who deserves to have their rights and interests prioritised. Instead, every party should be able to negotiate their way to primary position. Arguably then, the high cost of GHG emissions imposed on society, and the risks climate change poses to companies, would afford the atmosphere and the environment a place at the negotiating table, and environmental rights should be prioritised within the company. However, contractarians use the incompleteness of contract and agency cost theories to fill this gap and maintain the primacy of shareholders and their profits within the company.

Contractarians do this through the hypothetical bargain analysis. In a hypothetical bargain, they assume that all parties would choose shareholder wealth maximization and structure their contractual relationships accordingly. The reason shareholder wealth maximization is the default choice is based on the understanding that this norm serves all interests of the constituents of the company, including society.[33] Contractarians assume that the best way to achieve aggregate social welfare

---

directors, see Melvin A. Eisenberg, 'The Conception That the Corporation Is a Nexus of Contract, and the Dual Nature of the Firm' (1998) 24 J. Corp. L. 819, 825. Dine assesses the World Bank Reports on the Observance of Standards and Codes Initiative and determines even this global institution mistakenly considers shareholders as owners of the company, (n 8), 182–3.

[31] Frank H. Easterbrook and Daniel R. Fischel, 'The Corporate Contract' (1989) 89(1) Colum. L. Rev. 1416, 1421.

[32] Eisenberg (n 30), 825.

[33] Michael Bradley, Cindy A Schipani, Anant K Sundaram and James P Welsh, 'The Purposes and Accountability of the Corporation in Contemporary Problems' (1999) 62(3) L. and Contemporary Problems 9, 38.

is to make managers directly accountable to shareholders.[34] In their view, this is the most welfare enhancing and economically efficient approach. While they concede that non-shareholder interests are legitimate and deserve protection, they argue that these interests are better catered for by mechanisms outside of company law, for example by employment or environmental law.[35]

Although not all shareholder primacists are contractarians, contractarians still regard shareholder interests as the primary focus of company law. This is because shareholders are considered to be the residual claimants who bear the entire risk of the corporate enterprise, and are entitled to any residual profits.[36] Shareholders are considered to be vulnerable participants in the company because other constituents, such as employees or creditors, have contractual, prioritised rights to fixed payments.[37] However, shareholders are not the only constituents who make firm-specific investments or are vulnerable to the negative impacts of corporate activities. Other constituents of the company, such as employees and local communities, can also be classed as residual risk-bearers, and may also want to participate in the life of the company.[38] Contractarians counter this argument by stating that non-shareholders could protect their interests by contracting for greater rights and interests in the company. The reason they do not is because they are unwilling to pay for this privilege, and so shareholders value exclusive rights to directors' duties more.[39]

Contractarians do not ignore social concerns, but they do sideline them. They argue that social concerns are most efficiently catered for by producing profits for shareholders.[40] This analysis of the company breaks down in the case of negative externalities such as GHG emissions which are pushed outside of the company and paid for by non-shareholders. While this is profitable for the company in the short term, it is certainly not welfare-enhancing or cost effective for society as a whole. The rising costs of climate change for companies and society at large should afford

---

[34] Henry Hansmann and Reinier Kraakman, 'The End of History for Corporate Law' (2000) 89 Geo. L. J. 439, 441.
[35] Ibid, 441–2.
[36] Stephen M. Bainbridge, 'The Case for Limited Shareholder Voting Rights' (2005) 53 UCLA L. Rev. 601, 604; Stelios Andreadakis, 'Enlightened Shareholder Value: Is It the New Modus Operandi for Modern Companies?' in S Boubaker et al. (eds.), *Corporate Governance: Recent Developments and New Trends* (Springer-Verlag 2012), 416.
[37] John Armour, Henry Hansmann and Reinier Kraakman, 'What Is Corporate Law?' in Reinier Kraakman et al. (eds.), *The Anatomy of Corporate Law: A Comparative and Functional Approach* (2nd ed., Oxford University Press, 2009), 14.
[38] Lynn A. Stout, 'Bad and Not-so-bad Arguments for Shareholder Primacy' (2001) 75 S. Cal. L. Rev. 1189, 1194.
[39] Jonathan R Macey and Geoffrey P Miller, 'Corporate Stakeholders: A Contractual Perspective' (1993) 43(2) U. Toronto L. J. 401, 402.
[40] Diane Denis, 'Corporate Governance and the Goal of the Firm: In Defence of Shareholder Wealth Maximization' (2016) 51(4) *The Financial Review* 467, 479.

the issue significant attention by directors, but this does not occur under these corporate theories.

2.1.5 Negative Externalities and Law and Economics

An externality is a cost or benefit resulting from an economic activity. Externalities or spillover effects are defined by Cole and Grossman as "some of the costs or benefits associated with the transactions [are] not borne by those participating in the transaction but are externalized to others."[41] Externalities, therefore, can be both positive and negative. A negative externality is a cost which affects a party that did not choose to incur a cost. The most common example of a negative externality is pollution. GHG emissions have been described as "the mother of all externalities"[42] and "the greatest negative meta-externality ever imposed by economic systems on the natural world."[43] The cost of environmental damage caused by the world's 3,000 largest publicly listed companies was estimated at US$2.15 trillion, constituting one third of all global environmental damage.[44] Climate change could cause even more economic costs, as it is expected to negatively impact between US$4.2–43 trillion of the world's manageable assets (worth approximately US$143 trillion) by the end of the century.[45] In the United States alone it is estimated that climate change will lead to hundreds of billions of dollars' worth of losses for economic sectors by the end of the century.[46]

Even though it has such tremendous negative impacts on society, human health, welfare and safety, traditional law and economics based corporate theory does not adequately consider the harmful effects pollution, such as GHG emissions, have on society. The law and economics movement adopted neoclassical economics precepts and applied them to corporate actors. This approach assesses all company constituents from the perspective of their ability to produce profits for the company and its shareholders. In the case of the environment, this can lead to the economic commodification of environmental goods and services, and the encouragement of negative externalities. If it is more profitable to externalise environmental costs, then externalities are encouraged and the costs of GHG emission are pushed outside of the company and onto society.

---

[41] Cole and Grossman (n 24), 13.
[42] Richard Tol, 'The Economic Effects of Climate Change' (2009) 23(2) *Journal of Economic Perspectives* 29, 29.
[43] Rosetta Lombardo and Giovanni D'Orio, 'Corporate and State Social Responsibility: A Long-Term Perspective' (2012) 3 *Modern Economy* 91, 92.
[44] UNEP Finance Initiative and Principles for Responsible Investment, 'Universal Ownership: Why Environmental Externalities Matter to Institutional Investors' (2011) 3.
[45] The Economist Intelligence Unit, 'The Cost of Inaction: Recognising the Value at Risk from Climate Change' (2015) 2.
[46] US Global Change Research Program, 'Fourth National Climate Assessment: Volume II, Impacts, Risks, and Adaptation in the United States' (2018) 25.

Environmental or climate concerns do not figure prominently in agency, shareholder primacy or contractarian approaches to the company. They focus solely on shareholders and short-term profit making, and subsequently encourage negative externalities such as GHG emissions.

2.2 IMPACT OF CORPORATE THEORIES AND NORMS ON THE ENVIRONMENT AND THE CLIMATE

Law and economics theories view the firm as a privately ordered, nexus of contracts. They also see minimal or no role for state intervention or regulation in the firm. These theorists also often see transactional cost reduction, and consequentially increased profits, as the primary goal of the company. One of the major normative goals of the law and economics movement is to increase social welfare through the maximisation of profits.[47] It is unclear, however, whether this means increasing profits or the value of the firm. Shareholder primacists often conflate the two, sometimes using shareholder value as the determinant factor. It is also unclear whether the focus of shareholder primacists is on long-term or short-term profitability. Although there is some conflicting evidence, many theorists consider that shareholder wealth maximization should be considered in the long-term. However in practice, the shareholder primacy and the shareholder wealth maximization norms have been interpreted as requiring a focus on short-term profits, to the detriment of the long-term value of the firm. They also marginalize any focus on long-term and systemic issues that may affect society and the company, such as climate change.

The contractarian approach to the firm as an exclusively private entity has a number of implications for the climate. Companies are major producers of negative externalities, and emitters of greenhouse gases. However, the contractarian approach privileges shareholders as the primary constituent of the company to the detriment of the interests and values of other stakeholders, and has a strong influence on Anglo-American company law.[48] It focuses on shareholder wealth maximization as the most important function of the company, and therefore can lead to a myopic focus on short-term profitability, and an economic commodification of the environment and encouragement of negative externalities such as greenhouse gas emissions. The approach diminishes the role of public regulation and the judiciary, hence reframing company law as almost an entirely default, voluntary arrangement. It diminishes the concept of a firm as an entity capable of serving a variety of interests, and reduces it to a largely contractual sphere. There are three major effects

---

[47] Armour, Hansmann and Kraakman (n 37) 28.
[48] The Company Law Review Steering Group, *Modern Company Law for a Competitive Economy* (Great Britain Department of Trade and Industry 1999) 15. See also Sarah Worthington, 'Reforming Directors Duties' (2001) 64(3) *MLR* 439, 443 and 447 and Dine (n 8), 181.

of the shareholder primacy theory and shareholder wealth maximization on the relationship between companies and climate change.

2.2.1 An Exclusive Focus on Shareholders by Company Law

The shareholder primacy norm privileges shareholders, and their interests, as central to the company and minimises the role and interests of non-shareholder constituents such as the environment. As a result of the dominance of the shareholder primacy norm, the interests and roles of other non-shareholder constituents have been marginalised and made subservient to the interests of shareholders. The hypothetical bargain analysis applied by the nexus of contract theory privileges and reifies shareholders as the only rational investors in a firm.[49] This is often not the case.[50] The environment is not an entity that can specifically contract with the company, either at the time of formation of the company, or through the company's lifetime, and therefore is unable to exercise its rights or interests through contract. It is also not clear that shareholders are actually any more vulnerable than other participants in the company. Shareholders have a number of rights accorded to them under company law such as the right to formulate the company's constitution, attend annual general meetings, vote on specific intra-company issues, appoint and remove directors and ultimately to exit the company if they are unhappy. It is much easier to sell shares with a view to reinvesting elsewhere than to leave permanent employment.

Other constituents do not have as many rights as shareholders within a company, and may in fact be more vulnerable to directorial opportunism and self-interest.[51] The evidence of environmental damage and greenhouse gas emissions produced by companies is clear evidence of the vulnerability of the environment and the climate to company activities. Non-shareholder constituents can be more vulnerable to ex-post opportunism by directors, but the shareholder-centric view of company law has sidelined their interests.[52] As a result, this private, contractual model of the company breaks down in the case of environmental damage and negative externalities such as GHG emissions.

---

[49] Thomas A. Smith, 'The Efficient Norm for Corporate Law: A Neotraditional Interpretation of Fiduciary Duty' (1999) 98(1) Michigan L. Rev. 214, 236; Hao Zhang and Andrew Keay, 'An Analysis of Enlightened Shareholder Value in Light of Ex Post Opportunism and Incomplete Law' (2011) 8(4) Eur. Company and Financial L. Rev. 445, 456.

[50] Shareholders are a fluid, and not a homogenous group and therefore their interests and incentives may vary (See Fisch (n 25) 649 and they may not always invest rationally (see Stout (n 29), 660). In addition, shareholders can be described as only one of many residual claimants who make investments in the firm and expect benefits over and above their contractual entitlements (see Stout (n 38) 1194; and Margaret M. Blair and Lynn A. Stout, 'A Team Production Theory of Corporate Law' (1999) 85(2) Virginia L. Rev. 247).

[51] Zhang and Keay (n 49) 456; Dine (n 8) 173.

[52] Ibid.

2.2 Impact of Corporate Theories & Norms

The contractarian analysis of the company provides a limited to almost non-existent ability for directors to consider either long-term risks to the company such as climate change, or non-shareholder interests. In addition, shareholder primacy ignores distributive consequences of directors' decisions when they focus exclusively on shareholder profits.[53] This leads to negative externalities, such as greenhouse gas emissions, being an acceptable part of doing business in the shareholder-primacy world. It also leads to wealth reallocation by directors towards shareholders, leaving others, mainly the public, to pick up the costs of these externalities. These others are often the climate vulnerable, who are the least able to withstand the impacts of climate change. According to contractarians, environmental interests should be dealt with not by company law, but by regulation external to company law. As a result, the shareholder primacy approach to the company, as traditionally interpreted, does not provide an adequate mechanism for companies to mediate and remedy their contributions to climate change.

2.2.2 Focus on Short-Term Profitability

Contractarians argue that overall societal wealth can be achieved by providing profitable returns for shareholders.[54] A heavy reliance on the shareholder wealth maximization norm has led to a myopic focus by directors on short-term profits and a shift towards predominant short-term thinking generally.[55] This focus on short-term profitability is not necessarily a part of shareholder wealth maximization, but is due in large part to the norm's adoption and interpretation by directors and the pressures of financial markets. In fact, the norm is primarily about focusing on long-term profitability of the company, not short-termism. According to many contractarians, the role of shareholder wealth maximization is to seek long-term shareholder value or gain. Jensen states that the value maximization norm means that corporate managers should make all decisions so as to increase the total long-run market value of the firm.[56] Hansmann and Kraakman describe the primary aim of company law as striving to increase long-term shareholder value.[57] While descriptions of shareholder

---

[53] Wai Shun Wilson Leung, 'The Inadequacy of Shareholder Primacy: A Proposed Corporate Regime that Recognizes Non-Shareholder Interests' (1996–1997) 30 *Columbia Journal of Law and Social Problemss* 587, 606.

[54] Steven M. H. Wallman, 'The Proper Interpretation of Corporate Constituency Statutes and Formation of Director Duties' (1991–1992) 21 Stetson L. Rev. 163, 168.

[55] Grinyer, Russell and Collison (n 5) 19; Cheffins (n 5) 361; Eduard Gracia, 'Corporate Short-Term Thinking and the Winner-Takes-All Market' (2003) 6, https://papers.ssrn.com/sol3/papers.cfm?abstract_id=445260, (accessed 24 May 2020); Jill E. Fisch, 'Securities Intermediaries and the Separation of Ownership from Control' (2010) 33 Seattle U. L. Rev. 877, 883; Millon (n 5) 914.

[56] Michael C. Jensen, 'Value Maximization, Stakeholder Theory, and the Corporate Objective Function' (2001) 12(2) *Business Ethics Quarterly* 235, 236 (defining the value of the firm as the sum of all financial claims on firms including equity, debt, warrants and preferred stock).

[57] Hansmann and Kraakman, (n 34) 440.

wealth maximization often incorporate a long-term view, its application does not always (or even typically) clearly distinguish between time horizons,[58] shareholder value, firm value and individualized share price, or provide specific guidance to directors on which values they should prioritize. In contrast, market forces have interpreted shareholder wealth maximization as prioritizing short-term profits, and reconstructed the norm as creating a significant barrier to corporate action on climate change.[59]

The rise of institutional investors has meant that portfolio managers are overly concerned with the quarterly earnings of companies, as their own performance is assessed quarterly.[60] As a result, they often focus on the current market price of the company and not on the long-term value of the firm, leading to a short-term bias.[61] Investors' profit horizons vary. For example, hedge funds and mutual funds are often short-term investors, whereas some institutional investors, such as pension funds, may have longer-term investment horizons.[62] By and large, however, investors focus on short-term profit making.

The liberalisation of capital markets and the introduction of electronic trading in the 1980s compounded this short-term approach.[63] Managers absorbed this short-term thinking, and started to manage the company for short-term gain, forgoing investments in longer-term projects such as research and development.[64] In a study of directors of U.K. companies, a large proportion of finance managers stated that their company was likely to behave in a way that conformed to considerations of short-term accounting profit.[65] This managerial behaviour was primarily attributed to their beliefs about the preference of capital markets for short-term earnings.[66] Managerial behaviour biased towards short-term goals can lead to inappropriate decisions that impair the long-term value of the company and the interests of other stakeholders.[67]

---

[58] Lisa Benjamin and Stelios Andreadakis, 'Corporate Governance and Climate Change: Smoothing Temporal Dissonance to a Phased Approach' (2019) 40(4) *Business Law Review* 146.

[59] Lisa Benjamin, 'The Road to Paris Runs Through Delaware: Climate Litigation and Directors' Duties' (2020) 2 Utah L. R. 313; Janet Dine, 'Corporate Regulation, Climate Change and Corporate Law: Challenges and Balance in an International and Global World' (2015) 26(1) *Eur. Bus. L. Rev.* 173.

[60] Jill Fisch, 'Securities Intermediaries and the Separation of Ownership from Control' (2010) 23 Seattle U. L. Rev. 877, 883.

[61] Lipton and Rosenblum, 'A New System of Corporate Governance: The Quinquennial Election of Directors' (1991) 58(1) U. Chicago L. Rev. 187, 206.

[62] Lisa Fairfax, 'Making the Corporation Safe for Shareholder Democracy' (2008) 69 Ohio St. L. J. 53, 83.

[63] Gracia (n 55) 6.

[64] Grinyer, Russell and Collison (n 5) 19.

[65] Ibid., 21.

[66] Ibid., 21.

[67] Fisch (n 25) 638.

It is not clear whether contractarians advocate short-term profitability or long-term profitability as the driving force behind the shareholder wealth maximization norm.[68] Allen notes that company law had effectively papered over this conflict between long-term and short-term profit maximisation.[69] Many theorists in fact advocate for long-term wealth maximization. However, share value is so focused on shareholders that it will often exclude value provided by and to non-shareholders.[70] Market forces also lead directors to focus on short-term profits.

There is no clear delineation in the dominant theories between profits and shareholder wealth. Profits are not always a good indicator of shareholder wealth, as corporate profits can be used by directors for other firm activities, and not just issued as dividends to shareholders.[71] Weak product markets, and the existence of monopolies, may mean that social wealth could in fact be weakened by shareholder wealth maximization.[72] Some contractarians have acknowledged that the efficient capital market hypothesis failed in the financial crisis of 2008 as a result of the misplaced faith in the proposition that market price is always efficient.[73] During the more recent COVID-19 health crisis, market-based approaches failed to provide sufficient resilience within supply chains.

There is clear evidence that although traditional theoretical approaches advocate for shareholder wealth maximization in the long-term, its interpretation by directors, under market pressures, can lead to a short-term bias in managerial preferences, and a focus on short-term profitability. This approach leads to interests and risks which are considered long-term, such as climate change, being diminished or even ignored by managers. Contractarians view the firm as a privately ordered organization, and this perspective may leave little room for regulatory intervention to balance competing interests within the company and to ensure a long-term perspective, and so disincentivizes corporate support for internalizing the costs of GHG emissions.

2.2.3 Encouragement of Negative Externalities and Greenhouse Gases

Standard neoclassical economic theory provides that a "properly functioning market should always maximize productive and allocative efficiency."[74] Its beginning

---

[68] Andrew Keay, 'Getting to Grips with the Shareholder Value Theory in Corporate Law' (2010) 39 Comm. L. World Rev. 358, 371.
[69] William T. Allen, 'Our Schizophrenic Conception of the Business Corporation' (1992–1993) 14 Cardozo L. Rev. 261, 271.
[70] Fisch (n 25) 644.
[71] Andrew Keay and Radoula Adamopoulou, 'Shareholder Value and UK Companies: A Positivist Inquiry' (2012) 13(1) Eur. Business Org. L. Rev. 1, 21.
[72] Mark Roe, 'The Shareholder Wealth Maximization Norm and Industrial Organization' (2001) 149(6) U Pennsylvania L Rev 2063, 2065–2066.
[73] Ronald J Gilson and Reinier Kraakman, 'Market Efficiency after the Fall: Where Do We Stand Following the Financial Crisis?' in Claire A. Hill and Brett H. McDonnell (eds.), *Research Handbook on the Economics of Corporate Law* (Edward Elgar 2012), 473.
[74] Cole and Grossman (n 24) 13.

premise is a perfectly functioning and competitive market that assumes several things, such as complete information held by buyers and sellers, that participants can enter the market without cost, that market participants always react rationally to changes in market conditions, and that all cost and benefits fall within the market, creating no externalities.[75] Externalities are an example of market failure as they provide a subsidy to the producer that does not absorb the cost of the externality. The product, therefore, is cheaper than it should be to produce, so it then, in a perfect market, should be inefficient to produce.[76]

As an artificial entity, the company is incentivised to externalise costs onto those whose interests are not catered for by the firm.[77] This may be increasingly the case where managers focus almost exclusively on the pursuit of short-term profitability for shareholders. This short-term bias will curtail corporate social responsibility or other expenditures in companies which often require long-term investment horizons as this would reduce current earnings.[78] Long-term expenditures could include climate-friendly corporate decisions like incorporating a more sustainable approach to supply chain management, operations, production and in the case of energy companies, transitioning their business models towards cleaner energy. Contractarians focus on a very narrow range of interests of internal constituents,[79] and assume that contractual strategies can correct externalities.[80] The shareholder primacy theory as interpreted by contractarians absolves company law from dealing with externalities.

Heede's quantitative analysis of historic fossil fuel and cement production records of 90 leading investor-owned, state-owned and nation-state producers of oil, natural gas, coal and cement concluded that 63% of cumulative worldwide emissions of carbon dioxide and methane from the year 1854 to 2010 were attributed to these carbon-major entities.[81] It is clear that companies are responsible for a large amount of greenhouse gas emissions that they currently treat as externalities. This represents not only market inefficiency, but also a reallocation of wealth to shareholders, as non-shareholder constituents are asked to absorb the costs and negative effects of climate change. The environment may be a more vulnerable constituent of the company than shareholders, and yet is not appropriately catered for by the

---

[75] Ibid.
[76] Ibid. Coase, in the law and economics vein, took a novel approach to externalities when he proposed that stopping a negative externality imposed costs on the polluter, and, therefore, the problem of negative externalities was reciprocal, Ronald Coase, 'The Problem of Social Cost' (1960) 3 J. L. and Economics 1, 2.
[77] Kent Greenfield and D. Gordon Smith, 'Debate: Saving the World with Corporate Law?' (2007) 57 Emory L. J. 947, 959; Dine (n 8), 174.
[78] Millon (n 5) 911–2.
[79] David Millon, 'New Directions in Corporate Law Communitarians, Contractarians, and the Crisis in Corporate Law' (1993) 50 Wash & Lee L. Rev. 1373, 1378.
[80] Ibid., 1379.
[81] Richard Heede, 'Tracing Anthropogenic Carbon Dioxide and Methane Emissions to Fossil Fuel and Cement Producers, 1854–2010' (2014) 122(1) *Climatic Change* 229, 229.

shareholder primacy or shareholder wealth maximization norms. As a result of these three major impacts, traditional corporate norms such as shareholder primacy and shareholder wealth maximization are outdated and inappropriate for the task of governing companies in the context of climate change.

2.3 ALTERNATIVE CLIMATE-FRIENDLY CORPORATE THEORIES

While shareholder primacy and shareholder wealth maximization norms dominate corporate scholarship, these theories and norms are not without their critics. As the Berle and Dodd debate illustrates, shareholder primacy has always been critiqued for not providing a comprehensive understanding of relationships within the company. A number of theorists find the focus on profits to be unclear, reference to share price unreliable,[82] and the exclusive focus on shareholders and profits to be injurious to other constituents of the company. The 2008 financial crisis led some theorists to question the appropriateness of the shareholder primacy approach, and even the efficient capital markets hypothesis. Despite the continued dominance of the shareholder primacy and contractarian approaches, alternative theories have always provided competing understandings of the corporate form and whose interests it should serve. These theories provide a more comprehensive and climate-friendly version of the company.

2.3.1 *The 'Stakeholder Approach'*

The major alternative theory to shareholder primacy is the stakeholder approach. Richard Freeman popularized it in the 1980s, providing a definition of stakeholders as "any group or individual who can affect, or is affected by, the achievement of a company's purpose."[83] The definition traditionally includes shareholders, but also employees, customers, suppliers, and environmentalists.[84] It would not necessarily include the environment or atmosphere as it focuses on individuals or groups of individuals. Other stakeholder theories divided stakeholders into two main groups: primary stakeholders, whose ongoing contributions the company needs to survive (such as customers, shareholders, suppliers, employees and public groups such as governments and communities), and secondary stakeholders who influence or affect the company, such as the media.[85] Stakeholder theory's foundational assumption is that values are necessary within the company, and that the focus on profits is too

---

[82] Lynn Stout, 'Share Price as a Poor Criterion for Good Corporate Law' (Jan 2005) U California L & Economics Research Paper Series, 5.
[83] R. Edward Freeman, *Strategic Management: A Stakeholder Approach* (Cambridge University Press 2010), iv.
[84] Ibid.
[85] Max B. E. Clarkson, 'A Stakeholder Framework for Analyzing and Evaluating Corporate Social Performance' (1995) 20(1) *The Academy of Management Review* 92, 106–107.

narrow a justification for the purpose of the company.[86] As applied to climate change, under stakeholder theories, companies could and should consider the environment a primary stakeholder and therefore provide a more climate-friendly approach to companies and corporate law.[87]

There are a number of different stakeholder theories, including communitarianism and progressive corporate law theories, as well as Dodd's approach to the company from the 1930s. Dodd viewed the company as a social rather than purely private entity. The communitarian movement is associated with management theorist and business ethics scholar, Amitai Etzioni. The communitarian approach to the company views all of the participants of the company as part of one community with shared goals and bonds.[88] Like Dodd, communitarians are more concerned with the social effects of companies, and are more willing to use regulation to discipline corporate excesses.[89] The progressive company law approach derived from both communitarianism and stakeholder theory, and proposes that companies have more social obligations than just shareholder wealth maximization.[90] It recasts companies as public institutions with public obligations, and focuses on how to reform companies from within, by using company law instead of external regulation.[91] These theories highlight the social impacts and role of the company, and the potential role of company law in regulating corporate impacts on society such as climate change.

Stakeholderism suffers from a number of potential defects, including that the definition of a stakeholder is nebulous, and the balancing of various interests is difficult.[92] In addition, directors may not always know what each stakeholder considers to be a benefit.[93] As a result, directors may be accountable to no one as they are left without a clear decisional rule.[94] Stakeholder theories have similarities to Dodd's approach to the company. He focused on the company as an entity, an approach taken up by a number of other alternative theories such as the team production theory and entity theories.

---

[86] R. Edward Freeman, Andrew C. Wicks and Bidhan Parmar, 'Stakeholder Theory and "The Corporate Objective Revisited"' (2004) 15(3) *Organizational Science* 364, 364.

[87] Nardia Haigh and Andrew Griffiths, 'The Natural Event as a Primary Stakeholder: The Case of Climate Change' (2009) 18 *Business Strategy and the Environment* 347, 351.

[88] Amitai Etzioni, 'A Communitarian Note on Stakeholder Theory' (1998) 8(4) *Business Ethics Quarterly* 679, 679.

[89] Millon (n 80) 1379.

[90] Cynthia A. Williams, 'Corporate Social Responsibility in an Era of Economic Globalization' (2001–2002) 35 U. C. Davis L. Rev. 705, 716.

[91] Lawrence E. Mitchell (ed.), *Progressive Corporate Law* (Westview Press 1995), xiv.

[92] Andrew Keay, 'Stakeholder Theory in Corporate Law: Has It Got What It Takes?' (2010) 9 J. Global L. & Bus. 249, 259, 278; Andreadakis (n 36) 419.

[93] Andrew Keay, 'Ascertaining the Corporate Objective: An Entity Maximization and Sustainability Model' (2008) 71(5) Modern L. Rev. 663, 676.

[94] Roberto Romano, 'A Guide to Takeovers: Theory, Evidence and Regulation' (1992) 9 Yale L. J. on Reg., 119, 172.

2.3.2 *Team Production and Entity Theories*

Margaret Blair and Lynn Stout developed the team production theory as an alternative theory to explain the public company. In their view, shareholder primacy is not adequately reflected in company law,[95] and so their team production model provides an alternative explanation of the public company. While the team production model pays closer attention to the contributions and deserved benefits of constituents other than shareholders, it does not identify specifically with stakeholderism, but instead builds on the nexus of contracts theory.[96] According to the team-production model, the gap-filling role in the contractual model should be filled not by residual claimants such as shareholders, but by a board of directors.[97]

The team production model relies heavily on the concept of the company as an entity. A few English theorists developed this concept into a new entity maximisation and sustainability model, and an entity maximisation and viability principle.[98] A number of theorists argue that company law has failed to clearly articulate the actual objective of companies,[99] and both the shareholder primacy and stakeholder theories failed to completely explain the company. An entity approach to the company better explains its objectives and relationships with other constituents.

Keay developed a new entity maximisation and sustainability model (EMS) of the company. Entity maximisation focuses on the common interest of all constituents who have invested in the firm, not by prioritizing one group over the other, but by focusing on the long-term reputation of the organization as an entity.[100] Entity sustainability calls for the company to focus on issues that affect its survival, such as environmental considerations.[101] According to Keay, unlike team production, which provides a theory of the firm, EMS provides a normative objective of the company.[102]

Attenborough further develops the entity concept into the entity maximisation and viability principle (EMV).[103] The EMV concept consists of two elements, the first of which is the duty to respect, protect and fulfill the interests of those involved

---

[95] Blair and Stout (n 50) 291.
[96] Ibid., 320.
[97] Ibid., 320.
[98] The entity theory of corporate law is not new. At the end of the 19th and beginning of the 20th century, three approaches to corporate law were debated, the 'fiction' or 'artificial entity' theory, the 'contract/association' theory and the 'real entity' theory. See Cheffins (n 7) 478–9.
[99] Daniel Attenborough, 'How Directors Should Act When Owing Duties to the Companies' Shareholders: Why We Need to Stop Applying *Greenhalgh*' (2009) 20(10) Intl. Co. and Commercial L. Rev. 1, 1. See also L. S. Sealy, '"Bona Fides" and "Proper Purposes" in Corporate Decisions' (1989) 15 Monash U. L. Rev. 265, 269; Keay (n 92) 663; Alistair Alcock, 'An Accidental Change to Directors' Duties?' (2009) 30 Company Lawyer 1, 5.
[100] Kaey (n 95) 685.
[101] Ibid., 691–2.
[102] Ibid., 696–7.
[103] Daniel Attenborough, 'Giving Purpose to the Corporate Purpose Debate: An Equitable Maximization and Viability Principle' (2011) 32(1) Legal Studies 4.

in or affected by the activities of the company.[104] This duty would mitigate actual and potential damage caused by the company,[105] such as environmental pollution. The second element involves facilitating the viability of the entity itself, separate and apart from the interests of the shareholders.[106] Rather than attempting to prioritise and balance the interests of a number of stakeholders of the company, EMV instead focuses on the viability of the entity defined by its ability to survive without violating the duty to respect, protect and fulfill. The viability of the entity is important only if social and public interests (protected through the duty to respect, protect and fulfill) are not harmed along the way.[107]

These entity theorists provide an alternative, and arguably more balanced approach, to the company than the shareholder primacy theory. These theories, as well as the team production theory, are more appropriate to govern companies in the Anthropocene. These theories specifically allow for the company to operate while catering for social and public interests, which would include climate change. Other theorists argue that companies in fact have always had public duties, and the traditional approach to shareholder wealth maximization is no longer viable in today's society, and a recalibrated corporate purpose which balances broader stakeholder interests as part of the corporate mission.[108]

It is clear that the traditional shareholder primacy and shareholder wealth maximization norms are detrimental to and disincentivize corporate climate action. They should be altered and updated in order to be better able to cater for systemic and catastrophic risks such as climate change. Shareholder concerns should be balanced against other concerns such as climate change. Where the risks of climate change to society and to these corporate entities are significant, they should be balanced against the profit imperative by directors. Where climate action will provide a benefit to the company, even in the long-term, climate action should be taken by directors. The EMS and EMV entity theories would facilitate this balancing exercise by directors. The level and scale of the climate action should vary in proportion to the contributions that company made (and is making) to climate change, as well as its technological and human capacity. Firms which are part of systemically important financial or supply systems, such as banks, insurers, and manufacturers of essential goods and services, and fossil fuel intensive industries, should have elevated requirements to consider, mitigate and manage climate risks, and take climate action. Firms that are too big to fail should essentially be too big not to consider climate risks, and should act appropriately to minimize these risks to not only their organizations, but also to society at large. The team production and

---

[104] Ibid., 15.
[105] Ibid., 15.
[106] Ibid., 16.
[107] Ibid., 33.
[108] Barnali Choudhury and Martin Petrin, *Corporate Duties to the Public* (Cambridge University Press 2019), 56–7.

particularly the EMV and EMS entity theories provide a more appropriate and climate-friendly understanding of the company.

Despite the proliferation of alternative theories of the company, none have risen to the dominant position occupied by traditional shareholder primacy and shareholder wealth maximization approaches to the company. However, English company law has not adopted a stakeholder or entity approach to the company, instead adopted the enlightened shareholder value approach.

2.3.3 *The United Kingdom Enlightened Shareholder Value Approach*

English law moved to the enlightened shareholder value approach to the company with the turn of the twenty-first century. The Labour Government, through the Department of Trade and Industry, established the Company Law Review Steering Group (CLRSG) in 1998 to consider reforms to the existing 1995 Companies Act. A comprehensive review of company law of this kind had not taken place for over forty years. As part of its review, the CLRSG produced four major strategy documents,[109] and provided what it considered to be the role and objective of companies. The CLRSG borrowed heavily from the contractarian approach to companies.[110]

The CLRSG considered two approaches to describe what the objective of companies should be: the enlightened shareholder value approach (ESV), and the pluralist approach. The pluralist approach was described as directors paying equal attention to all constituents and stakeholders. The ESV approach was described as the approach currently enshrined in English law; that the role of companies was to generate maximum value for shareholders, as this approach was often the best means of providing for overall prosperity and wealth.[111] The CLRSG considered that the pluralist approach would distract directors by forcing them to manage competing considerations at the expense of economic growth and international competitiveness.[112] The pluralist approach to company law reform was therefore discarded.

The CLRSG adopted the ESV approach to the reform of the Act, as it was considered to be consistent with the ultimate objective of companies. The aim of company law was "to provide a framework to promote the long-term health of companies, taking into account both the interests of shareholders and broader corporate social and environmental responsibilities."[113] The principle of ESV, therefore, was to include a balance between both shareholder interests and broader non-shareholder interests. The CLRSG describes ESV as follows:

---

[109] The Company Law Review Steering Group (n 48).
[110] Ibid., 'The Strategic Framework' 10, 15; Worthington (n 48) 443.
[111] 'The Strategic Framework' (n 48) 37.
[112] Ibid., 44.
[113] Trade and Industry Committee, 'The White Paper on Modernizing Company Law: Sixth Report of Session 2002–2003' (HC 439 2003) 10.

...it sets as its basic goal for directors the success of the company in the collective best interests of shareholders. But it also requires them to recognise, as the circumstances require, the company's need to foster relationships with its employees, customers and suppliers, its need to maintain its business reputation and its need to consider the company's impact on the community and the working environment.[114]

The ESV approach recognizes that a company's long-term success is dependent not only upon satisfying shareholder interests, but valuing relationships with non-shareholder constituents as well. In this regard, it differs from shareholder primacy by recognizing and potentially valuing the contributions of non-shareholder constituents to the success of the firm. The ESV principle would ensure that directors at least consider non-shareholder constituents,[115] and consider the impact of corporate activities on these stakeholders.[116] However, even though it considers the impacts of the company on stakeholders including the environment, it still prioritises the primacy of shareholders in this balancing equation. The ESV principle was adopted through s172 of the Companies Act 2006, and as a result, English legal doctrine has incorporated, and been influenced by, the shareholder primacy norm.[117] Different jurisdictions adopt a stronger or weaker form of shareholder primacy. As the birthplace of the law and economics movement, the U.S. has relied more heavily on shareholder primacy and shareholder wealth maximization.

2.3.4 U.S. Approaches to Corporate Law

Corporate laws in the United States were similarly built on principles of shareholder primacy which have been dominant for the last several decades. In the United States, fiduciary duties are made up of two primary duties: those of care and loyalty, with the duty of good faith being a subsidiary duty of loyalty.[118] Delaware corporate law is particularly shareholder-focused and profit-centric. This was most recently illustrated by the 2010 case of *eBay Domestic Holdings* v. *Newmark*,[119] where the Delaware Supreme Court stated, 'Having chosen a for-profit corporate form, the craigslist directors are bound by the fiduciary duties and standards that accompany that form. Those standards include acting to promote the value of the corporation for the benefit of its stockholders.'[120] The duty of loyalty, as interpreted by Delaware Supreme Court in *Stone* v. *Ritter*,[121] provides that directors have a responsibility to

---

[114] The Company Law Review Steering Group, Final Report (n 48) 1.
[115] The Company Law Review Steering Group, Strategic Framework (n 48) 41–2.
[116] Trade and Industry Committee (n 113) 7.
[117] Dine (n 8) 184–5.
[118] *Stone v. Ritter*, 911 A.2d 362, 367 (Del. 2006).
[119] 16 A.3d1 (Del. Ch. 2010).
[120] Ibid., 105.
[121] *Stone* (n 118) at 371.

ensure that appropriate information and reporting systems are established by management to ensure compliance with key regulatory regimes.[122] The duty of loyalty can be violated if directors demonstrate a conscious disregard for their responsibilities.[123] The case of *Re Caremark International Inc. Derivative Litigation*,[124] established a high threshold to meet for violation of the duty of loyalty for lack of oversight. These are now often referred to as 'Caremark duties'. These duties establish that only in limited circumstances, high profile oversight failures could be regarded as not just gross negligence by directors but instead as acts of disloyalty for sustainable or systemic failure to assure a reasonable information and reporting system exists for regulated activities.

Similarly, according to the Delaware Supreme Court in *In Re Walt Disney Company Derivative Litigation* (the *Disney* case),[125] acts of bad faith include where a director intentionally acts with a purpose other than that of advancing the best interests of the corporation, where she acts with the intention to violate applicable law or intentionally fails to act in the face of a known duty to act, demonstrating a conscious disregard for her duties.[126] The later case of *Re Citigroup Inc Shareholder Derivative Litigation*[127] in the context of the 2008 financial crisis, made it even more difficult for directors to be found in breach of their duties for systemic risk oversight failures.[128]

The U.S. business judgment rule provides a large dose of discretion to business decisions made by directors.[129] This rule is a process-based one, where courts are not concerned with the content of the decision made by a director, but instead with the process by which the decision was made.[130] Absent illegality, fraud or self-dealing, courts under the business judgment rule presume that directors have employed their own appropriate business judgment to the issue at hand.[131] While originally an abstention rule, Fershee notes that the increasing turn in Delaware towards profitability may convert the business judgment rule away from an abstention rule to a more intrusive standard assumed by courts, marking a significant departure from its historical interpretations.[132]

---

[122] Ibid., 8–71.
[123] Ibid., 370.
[124] 698 A.2d 959 (Del. Ch. 1996).
[125] *In re Walt Disney Co. Derivative Litig.*, 906 A.2d 27 (Del. 2006).
[126] Ibid., 67.
[127] 964 A 2d 106 (Del. Ch. 2009).
[128] Marc T. Moore, 'Redressing Risk Oversight Failure in UK and US Listed Companies: Lessons from the RBS and Citigroup Litigation' (2017) 18 *Eur. Bus. Org. Law Rev.* 733, 743–6.
[129] See Stephen M. Bainbridge, *Corporate Law* 125 (2d ed. 2009).
[130] *Stone* (n 118) at 367.
[131] See *Brehm v. Eisner*, 746 A.2d at 255.
[132] Joshua P. Fershee, 'The End of Responsible Growth and Governance?: The Risks Posed by Social Enterprise Enabling Statutes and the Demise of Director Primacy' (2018) 19 *Tenn. J. Bus. L.* 361, 363.

However, the 2019 Business Roundtable statement may signal a changing direction in the context of directors' duties. This statement illustrates that despite the shareholder-centric nature of the U.S. jurisdiction, directors in the U.S. are themselves reconsidering their duties and approaches, and whose interests they serve. Whether and how this 2019 statement is implemented by directors remains to be seen. The COVID-19 health crisis combined with demands for racial justice in the United States highlight rising social concerns and shifting public norms, which may in turn influence corporate norms.

Light highlights the close relationship between corporate law and environmental law in the U.S., by illustrating that the law of corporations, including securities law, antitrust law, and bankruptcy law, all play a crucial role in a corporation's decision making and actions that impact the environment.[133] Securities law applicable to corporations in the U.S. can affect the environmental decisions made by corporations through disclosure obligations,[134] for example, by incentivizing publically-listed corporations to alter their behaviour to disclose favourable data, even if not mandated to.[135] Similarly, antitrust law can influence a corporation's environmental behaviour through various mechanisms including private environmental governance of common pool resources such as forests, fisheries and the atmosphere.[136] Company law is therefore closely bound to environmental outcomes and the climate crisis, and has an important role to play in mitigating and managing climate change.

2.4 CONCLUSION

Although there are a number of competing company law theories, none of them have risen to such prominence as the shareholder primacy and wealth maximization norms, which remain the dominant theories in company law today, particularly in the U.S. and the U.K.. While these theories are more dominant in the U.S., they have also been sticky in the U.K. as well, although to a lesser degree. The agency analysis of the company has become so prevalent and pervasive that many theorists believe that only shareholder primacy and wealth maximization can discipline directors to work exclusively for shareholders. Under this model, other constituents' interests are sidelined and relegated to contractual mechanisms or external regulation in order to gain any protection. The shareholder primacy approach reconceptualises the firm as an organization almost completely ordered through private, market-based, consensual arrangements.[137]

---

[133] Sarah E. Light, 'The Law of the Corporation as Environmental Law' (January 2019) 71 Stan. L. Rev. 137, 160.
[134] Ibid., 165.
[135] Ibid., 167.
[136] Ibid., 178.
[137] Alan Wolfe, 'The Modern Corporation: Private Agent or Public Actor?' (1993) 50 Wash & Lee L. Rev. 1673, 1673.

2.4 Conclusion

This approach to the firm as an exclusively private entity has a number of implications for the climate. Under the shareholder primacy model, stakeholder constituents such as the environment are excluded from protection by company law, and expected to seek protection from contractual arrangements or regulatory mechanisms outside of company law, such as environmental law or market mechanisms. Shareholder primacy under the contractarian analysis also diminishes the concept of a firm as an entity capable of serving a variety of interests, and reduces it to a largely contractual sphere. Under the contractual model of shareholder primacy, there remains very little to no opportunity for the environment as a non-shareholder constituent to contract with the company.

The contractual model of the company does not prioritise or protect the interests of the environment and wider society from the negative impacts of greenhouse gas emissions by companies. The shareholder primacy norm privileges shareholders as the primary constituent of the company and of company law, to the detriment of the interests and values of other stakeholders. It focuses solely on efficiency and shareholder wealth maximization as the sole purpose of the firm. This approach can lead to a myopic concentration on short-term profits, an economic commodification of the environment, and the encouragement of negative externalities. As a result, the shareholder primacy norm combined with the prevalence of short-term management approaches is inadequate to constrain companies' contributions to climate change. These norms are increasingly outdated, and should be reconsidered. In particular, climate change and other systemic environmental risks should be balanced against shareholder interests where these risks are significant and corporate action can mitigate and manage them. Viewing the company as an entity with a long-term existence is a more appropriate theoretical approach and is more amenable to balancing a variety of interests, including, but not only, those of shareholders. Corporate norms and theories are not static concepts, and climate change itself, combined with shifting social norms, is challenging these traditional theoretical approaches to the company, and therefore motivating changes to company law itself within certain jurisdictions.

The subsequent chapter will focus on English company law, and how and to what extent the shareholder primacy approach has exerted its influence in the drafting and interpretation of the law, if in slightly more 'enlightened' terms.

3

English Company Law and Climate Change

This chapter explores the contours of English company law in the context of climate change, starting with corporate governance reviews from 1992 to present day, the period of English case law before 2006, and finally the enlightened shareholder value position under the Companies Act 2006. English common law, as well as the Companies Act, and the obligations of directors' duties under Section 172 in particular, apply to all types of companies, although other parts of the Act apply to different sizes and types of companies. The corporate governance reports for the most part strongly reflect a shareholder primacy and agency approach to company law outlined in the previous chapter. These reports apply specifically to public companies listed on a stock exchange.[1]

English common law prior to the Companies Act 2006 reserved a large amount of discretion for directors, with the predominant legal test being that directors owed duties to the company as an entity (or the company 'as a whole'). Only a slim line of case law dictated that directors owed duties to shareholders. This is surprising as several theorists, many of whom were examined in the previous chapter, determined that by the company, the common law meant current and future shareholders, and therefore that the shareholder primacy theory was always a part of Anglo-American company law duties. But this view is not well reflected in the case law itself, and this Chapter concludes that English case law, at least prior to the Companies Act 2006, did not reflect the shareholder primacy approach. This means that directors could take environmental concerns such as climate change into account, even above the interests of shareholders, if that approach benefited the company as an entity.

Despite the deference provided to directors in the common law, only one environmental case prior to 2006 is closely connected with directors' duties. This

---

[1] Although externally managed investment companies which have a differently constituted board and company structure can use the Association of Investment Companies' Corporate Governance Code.

may reflect the common understanding, or misunderstanding, that environmental rights and duties were not the concern of company law itself, but were best handled by regulation external to the company. This approach was and is strongly reflected in corporate governance codes. Unlike the common law, many corporate governance reviews and codes placed the shareholder at the heart of the company. From the Cadbury Review in 1992, to the 2018 UK Corporate Governance Code, shareholders feature prominently in these reports and regulatory codes. It is not until the CLRSG reports in the early 2000s that the stakeholder approach was seriously considered as a part of company law, although even then the CLRSG took a largely economic and contractarian view of the company.[2] The CLRSG reports laid the groundwork for the Companies Act 2006, and section 172 of the Act provides the most up-to-date approach to directors' duties under English company law. This chapter will conclude with an analysis of the impact, if any, Section 172 has or will have on directors' approaches to climate change, and its interaction with previous common law approaches.

3.1 CORPORATE GOVERNANCE REVIEWS IN THE UNITED KINGDOM AND THE TAKEOVER CODE

Many corporate governance reviews since 1992 have assumed and explicitly referred to either shareholders as owners of the company, and/or placed their interests at the heart of the company. This approach stands in stark contrast to English common law interpretations of directors' duties prior to 2006. It is not until the CLRSG review that stakeholders appear in the corporate governance reviews at all. Until that time, it had merely been assumed, arguably incorrectly, that English company law prioritised shareholder interests above all others, including those of the environment. This approach may reflect a misunderstanding by the business community of the role that company law itself had ascribed to shareholders. Alternatively, this may also reflect a co-option by the business community of the law and economics approach to the company, and entrenchment of the shareholder primacy approach.

3.1.1 The Cadbury Report

The first corporate governance report in the United Kingdom was published in 1992 by the Committee on the Financial Aspects of Corporate Governance. Named after the Chairman of the Committee, Adrian Cadbury, the Cadbury Review was a watershed report for its time. It provided a simple yet enduring definition of

---

[2] See Section 3.4 of this chapter.

corporate governance, being 'the system by which companies are directed and controlled',[3] and its main recommendation was the establishment of a voluntary Code of Best Practice for all listed companies. The Cadbury Report did not advocate for statutory intervention into corporate governance, because '[s]tatutory measures would impose a minimum standard and there would be a greater risk of boards complying with the letter, rather than with the spirit, of their requirements'.[4] Instead, the Cadbury Report developed the 'comply or explain' procedure, whereby listed companies would either comply with the voluntary Code of Best Practice, or have to explain any departures from it. The Cadbury approach of 'voluntarism' to corporate regulation has become an enduring legacy of corporate governance both in England and abroad. The Cadbury Report became the springboard for other international corporate governance initiatives such as the 1999 OECD Principles of Corporate Governance.[5]

The Committee that drafted the report was a private-sector initiative, established by non-governmental agencies such as the Financial Reporting Council (FRC), the London Stock Exchange and the accountancy profession. The Committee was established in order to address the growing mistrust of corporate reporting and governance due to a number of corporate scandals. These included the disappearance of pension fund manager Robert Maxwell and the collapse of Polly Peck and the Bank of Credit and Commerce International groups of companies.[6] The Cadbury Report was an effort to stave off government intervention in corporate affairs in the wake of these scandals.[7] The 'comply or explain' approach established a non-binding code of conduct, which constitutes the 'most liberal version of regulation after complete deregulation'.[8] The most recent Combined Code of Corporate Governance in 2018 firmly entrenches the 'comply or explain' approach first advocated by the Cadbury Report, and so the voluntary approach to corporate governance remains the primary approach.

---

[3] Sir Adrian Cadbury, *Report of the Committee on the Financial Aspects of Corporate Governance* (Financial Reporting Council and the London Stock Exchange 1992) para 2.5. ("Cadbury Report")

[4] Ibid., para 1.10.

[5] Cally Jordan, 'Cadbury Twenty Years on' (2013) 58(1) Villanova L. Rev. 1, 6; Ian Jones and Michael Pollitt, 'Understanding How Issues in Corporate Governance Develop: Cadbury Report to Higgs Review' (2004) 12(2) *Corporate Governance*, 164; Dine notes how the OECD framework heavily depends on shareholder primacy, Jane Dine, 'Corporate Regulation, Climate Change and Corporate Law: Challenges and Balance in an International and Global World' (2015) 26 Eur. Bus. L. Rev. 173, 183.

[6] Colin Boyd, 'Ethics and Corporate Governance: The Issues Raised by the Cadbury Report in the United Kingdom' (1996) 15(2) *Journal of Business Ethics* 167, 168.

[7] Jones and Pollitt (n 5) 169.

[8] Stelios Andreadakis, 'Research Notes: Regulatory or Non-Regulatory Corporate Governance: A Dilemma Between Statutes and Codes of Best Practice' (2008) 4(3) *Journal of Contemporary European Research* 253, 254.

The Cadbury Report clearly placed shareholders at the heart of corporate governance, referring to shareholders as the owners of the company,[9] responsible for making directors act in their interests.[10] It is not until 2008 that language describing shareholders as owners of the company was dropped from the Code. Despite this change in language, corporate governance reports have firmly adopted the agency view of companies, stating that 'the issue for corporate governance is how to strengthen the accountability of boards of directors to shareholders'.[11] Other stakeholders are not mentioned in the reports at all, except for only the most recent versions. The main principle of the Code is that directors are responsible for the success of 'the company', and to meet the interests of shareholders 'and others' – although who 'the others' are is not explained.[12] In the 2010 version of the Code, the language of the long-term success of the company was adopted,[13] perhaps in response to the CLRSG reports and Companies Act 2006. In the 2018 version of the Code, the impact of the financial crisis on stakeholders, in particular, was emphasised, along with the sustainable, long-term success of the company.[14]

3.1.2 *Subsequent Corporate Governance Reports*

A number of corporate governance reviews followed the Cadbury Review. The Greenbury Review in 1995 looked at the remuneration of directors, and again focused on the interests of shareholders.[15] The 1998 Hampel Review was prepared in order to review the efficacy of both the Cadbury and Greenbury Reviews. The Hampel Review focused on both corporate accountability and business prosperity.[16] Although the Hampel Review mentions that stakeholders who have a relevant interest in the company should be taken into account,[17] the focus of directors' duties, according to this report, is again on the shareholders, both present and future, and on long-term shareholder value.[18] As in Cadbury, the Hampel Review focused on the need to

---

[9] Cadbury Report (n 3) para 6.1. As a result of the financial crisis in 2008, the Prime Minister requested a review of corporate governance of UK banks and financial institutions, which led to the Walker Report in 2009. Although this review only applied to these types of entities, it also refers to shareholders as owners of the company. Sir David Walker, *A Review of Corporate Governance in UK Banks and Other Financial Industry Entities* (Association of Chartered Certified Accountants 2009) 12. ("Walker Report")
[10] Cadbury Report (n 3) para 6.6.
[11] Ibid., para 6.1.
[12] Ibid., Principle A1.
[13] Financial Reporting Council, *The UK Corporate Governance Code* (June 2010) para 1.
[14] Financial Reporting Council, *The UK Corporate Governance Code* (July 2018).
[15] Sir Richard Greenbury, *Directors Remuneration* (Study Group Chaired by Sir Richard Greenbury 1995), paras 4.2 and 6.16 ("Greenbury Review").
[16] Sir Ronnie Hampel, *Final Report* (Committee on Corporate Governance 1998), para 1.1 ("Hampel Report").
[17] Ibid., para 1.3.
[18] Ibid., para 1.18.

restrict regulatory interference with companies.[19] This focus on shareholders, shareholder value and restricting regulation of companies is firmly in line with the shareholder value and law and economics approach to the company.

In 1999 the Institute of Chartered Accountants published the Turnbull Guidance for Directors on certain aspects of the Combined Code of Corporate Governance. The Turnbull Report highlighted the need to safeguard both shareholders' investments and the assets of the company, reflecting the shareholder wealth maximisation approach.[20] Until 1999, these private-industry motivated reports, codes and guidance all placed shareholders at the heart of corporate governance as the primary, and in most cases, the only constituent, whose interests directors should protect. They all firmly reflected the shareholder primacy view of the company.

In 2002, the Government commissioned businessman Derek Higgs to review the role and effectiveness of non-executive directors in the wake of chronic corporate underperformance. The Higgs Report does not mention shareholders as owners of the company, but refers instead to the obligation of directors to act in the interests of 'the company' and to promote its success.[21] Despite this more subtle approach, John Armour, Simon Deakin and Suzanne Konzelmann note that the Higgs Review still adopts a shareholder primacy philosophy.[22]

The 2016 edition of the UK Corporate Governance Code released by the FRC describes the goal of the company as the sustainable success of the entity over the longer term.[23] The Code describes directors as being primarily accountable to shareholders, who are also described as the main focus of the Code.[24] However, the Code does recognise that other non-shareholder constituents do make contributions to the company, and that directors are encouraged to recognise their contributions and listen to their views, provided they are relevant to the overall approach to governance.[25] The Code calls for directors to work for the best interests of the company, but is still largely shareholder-centric, with some acknowledgement paid

---

[19] Helen Short, 'Corporate Governance: Cadbury, Greenbury and Hampel – A Review' (1999) 7 (1) *Journal of Financial Regulations and Compliance* 57, 58.

[20] Sir Nigel Turnbull, *Internal Control: Guidance for Directors on the Combined Code* (The Institute of Chartered Accountants in England & Wales 1999), para 2 ("Turnbull Report"); Dominic Elliot, Steve Letza, Martina McGuinness and Clive Smallman, 'Governance, Control and Operational Risk: The Turnbull Effect' (2000) 2(3) *Risk Management* 47, 50.

[21] Sir Derek Higgs, *Review of the Role and Effectiveness of Non-executive Directors* (Secretary of State for Trade and Industry 2003), 5 and 6, Principles A1 and A.3.3 ("Higgs Report").

[22] John Armour, Simon Deakin and Suzanne J. Konzelmann, 'Shareholder Primacy and the Trajectory of UK Corporate Governance' (2003) 41(3) *British Journal of Industrial Relations* 531, 532.

[23] Financial Reporting Council, *The UK Corporate Governance Code* (April 2016) para 4, see also the 2018 version of the Code (n 14) para 1

[24] FRC 2016 (n 23), para 9.

[25] Ibid.

to other constituents. This version of the Code reflects the enlightened shareholder value approach to the company.

3.1.3 *The Takeover Code*

The Takeover Code (or the City Code on Takeovers and Mergers) was first published as a non-binding code of conduct regulating takeovers in 1968, and is administered by an independent body, The Panel on Takeovers and Mergers. It has developed into a binding instrument regulated by Part 28 of the Companies Act 2006. The Takeover Code consists of a set of general principles and rules to ensure fairness and coherence in takeover situations. General Principle 3 and Rule 21 of the Code prevent unilateral or defensive action by a company's board when subject to an actual or imminent takeover bid.[26] Often known as the 'non-frustration' principle, directors are prohibited from frustrating a takeover without the approval of the shareholders. The non-frustration principle has considerable support in the United Kingdom, and is consistent with a strong shareholder rights approach.[27] Compared to the United States, where powers to prevent a takeover are often granted to directors, Bernard Black and John Coffee have noted that the limited defensive powers granted to directors in the United Kingdom may reflect weaker directorial powers in the British system.[28]

The strong shareholder emphasis in the Takeover Code, as well as in Corporate Governance Reports and Guidance, demonstrate that private industry certainly advocated for, and believed the law reflected – the shareholder primacy norm. In the case of the Takeover Code, strong powers are granted to shareholders in takeover situations. This may result from the mistaken assumption by the business community that the law required directors to pay attention to shareholders' interests. It may also reflect a co-option by the business community of the shareholder wealth maximisation norm, and the contractarian analysis of companies, which then found their way into these industry-motivated reports, codes and guidance. These reports certainly reflect the agency view of company law that focuses only on shareholders and ex post director opportunism,[29] and do not give much attention or scope to non-shareholder constituents. But this approach arguably does not reflect the position of English company law prior to 2006, which provided directors with significant

---

[26] Panel on Takeovers and Mergers, *The Takeover Code: The City Code on Takovers and Mergers* (2016) ("Takeover Code"), www.thetakeoverpanel.org.uk/the-code/download-code (accessed 22 July 2020).
[27] David Kershaw, 'The Illusion of Importance: Reconsidering the UK's Takeover Defence Prohibition' (2007) 56 I.C.L.Q. 267, 268.
[28] Bernard S. Black and John C. Coffee, 'Hail Britannia? Institutional Investor Behaviour under Limited Regulation' (1994) 92(7) Michigan L. Rev. 1997, 2026.
[29] Hao Zhang and Andrew Keay, 'An Analysis of Enlightened Shareholder Value in light of Ex Post Opportunism and Incomplete Law' (2011) 8(4) Eur. Company and Financial L. Rev. 445, 456.

deference and thereby scope to consider and account for environmental issues such as climate change.

3.2 THE COMMON LAW POSITION PRIOR TO 2006

The English company law developed out of partnership law, and early Companies Acts drew from the partnership concept that partners were an integral element of the partnership itself.[30] For example, the Joint Stock Companies Act 1856 stated that seven or more persons formed *themselves* into a company.[31] In these early Acts, the company was equivalent to its creators, or its shareholders.[32] These early deed of settlement companies were fundamentally different from their modern-day counterparts, with a focus on shareholders as an integral part of the company.[33] Under this older approach, directors acted as trustees who managed the business on behalf of the beneficiaries, or shareholders, who held unlimited liability and also had an interest in the assets of the company.[34] The common law reflected this understanding of directors as trustees for shareholders, and shareholders as a sort of 'cestui que' trust, whose interests were of paramount importance in the company's affairs.[35] This approach of company law very clearly reflects Berle's theory of directors acting in the exclusive interests of the shareholders. However, company law and corporate statutes moved away from this centralisation of shareholders.

The Companies Act 1862 changed this approach considerably. Shareholders were no longer *the* company, but instead the company was made 'by but not of shareholders'.[36] The emergence of limited liability for shareholders, limited to the unpaid portion of their shares, also accompanied this concept of separate legal personhood for a company. Therefore, by the second half of the nineteenth century, incorporation of a company was seen to be the establishment of a completely separate legal entity, which was 'emptied' or 'cleansed' of shareholders.[37] The company as a legal entity separate and apart from its shareholders reflects the modern understanding of company law and the corporate entity. The development of the company as a

---

[30] Paddy Ireland, 'Company Law and the Myth of Shareholder Ownership' (1999) 62(1) M.L.R. 32, 38.
[31] Andrew Keay, 'Ascertaining the Corporate Objective: An Entity Maximization and Sustainability Model' (2008) 71(5) Modern L. Rev. 663, 681; Paddy Ireland, 'Corporate Governance, Stakeholding, and the Company: Towards a Less Degenerate Capitalism?' (1996) 23(3) J. L. Society 287, 301; Paddy Ireland, Ian Grigg-Spall and Dave Kelly, 'The Conceptual Foundations of Modern Company Law' (1987) 14(1) J. L. Society 149, 150.
[32] Ireland, Grigg-Spall and Kelly (n 31) 150.
[33] Lorraine Talbot, *Critical Company Law* (Routledge Cavendish 2008) 153.
[34] Ibid.
[35] David Kershaw, 'The Path of Corporate Fiduciary Law' (2012) 8 N.Y.U. J. L. Business 395, 430–3, who cites the case of *Aberdeen Railway* v. *Blaikie Brothers* [1854] UKHL 1 to demonstrate that shareholders, as *cestui que trust*, could ratify directorial self-dealing.
[36] Ireland, Grigg-Spall and Kelly (n 31) 150.
[37] Ireland (n 30) 301.

separate legal entity in law changed the nature of fiduciary duties of directors accordingly, with directors owing duties to the company, and not to the shareholders.[38]

The concept of the company as a separate legal entity has not been an easy one for the law to digest and explain. The judicial concept of separate legal personality has changed and shifted over the years.[39] Initially, the company was viewed as its assets, then as a function of its assets, with the emphasis on profit-making for shareholders, and, finally, from the 1980s onward, as a competitive contractual entity as illustrated in Chapter 2.[40] A number of academics argue that the shifting judicial understanding of the nature of the corporate entity has had a corresponding effect on the judicial approach to directors' duties.[41] The result is divergent decisions in the common law as to whether directors owe duties to 'the company' as an entity, or to shareholders themselves. However, the majority of the pre-Companies Act 2006 decisions appear to follow the entity approach to the company – that directors owe duties to the company as a separate legal entity.

The historical approach from the early nineteenth century, when shareholders were deemed to be the company itself, led some academics to point to an ambiguity within company law when it dealt with directors' duties. This ambiguity, at times, conflated the interests of the company entity with the interests of shareholders. As Alan Dignam notes, this ambiguity could be a direct hangover from the historical concept that shareholders *were* the company. He writes,

> A strict adherence to the idea of shareholders 'being' the company created tension between the core principle that the company is separate from the shareholders and the principle of judicial consideration of the extent to which directors have an independent power conferred upon them in the articles. How can shareholders be both separate from the company and the substance of the company at the same time?[42]

Judicial understandings of the company took some time to shed this historical misunderstanding, but slowly evolved away from considering the shareholders as the sole and primary concern of directors, replacing them with the company as an entity.

An alternative, and more appealing, argument is that any judicial ambivalence found in the case law may not be due to a historical misunderstanding, but in fact

---

[38] Talbot (n 33) 159; Separate legal personality became a fundamental tenant of English Company Law through 1897 House of Lords case of *Salomon v. A. Salomon and Co. Ltd.* [1897] AC 22, affirmed by several cases, such as *Macaura v. Northern Assurance Co. Ltd.* [1925] AC 619; *Lee v. Lee's Air Farming Ltd.* [1961] AC 12; *Prest v. Petrodel* [2013] UKSC 34.
[39] Talbot (n 33) 154–5.
[40] Ibid.
[41] Ibid.; Keay (n 31); Ireland (n 30); Ireland, Grigg-Spall and Kelly (n 31).
[42] Alan Dignam, 'The Future of Shareholder Democracy in the Shadow of the Financial Crisis' (2012–2013) 36 Seattle U. L. Rev. 639, 664.

may be purposeful, with the judiciary exercising deference to the commercial expertise of directors through use of what may be deemed to be the 'business judgment rule'.[43] English common law displays more deference than ambivalence, leaving the directors a large amount of discretion as to whose interests they prefer when making directorial decisions, provided their decisions benefit the company as an entity.

A majority of cases prior to 2006 support this view, as the judiciary has consistently referred to the company as an entity when discussing fiduciary duties. The most often cited example of this test is found in the early and leading judgment of *Percival v. Wright*.[44] In this case, a shareholder who sold his share to the company objected when the directors did not disclose that they were negotiating a buy-out of the company. It was held that directors are not the trustees for individual shareholders, and Justice Eady rejected arguments by the plaintiff's counsel that, as shareholders are beneficiaries, the assets of the company belong to the shareholders in equity.[45] As a result, the interests of shareholders are made subservient to the greater interests of the company as an entity. This case marks a significant shift in understanding from shareholders as 'partners', to the view of the company as representing the assets of the company.[46]

In the case of *Hutton v. West Cork Railway Company*,[47] the directors were not allowed to disperse the remaining assets of an insolvent company to the company's employees and directors as this was deemed to be a charitable act that would not advance the interests of the company. Interestingly, a number of comments were made regarding whether this type of 'charitable' behaviour would be acceptable by directors if the company was a going concern, and not in or approaching insolvency. Bowen LJ noted that a railway company could send its porters for tea at the company's expense if such an act would ultimately be for the company's benefit. Any act that does not benefit the shareholders directly can be allowed if it ultimately benefits the company, and leads to its success.[48] As a result, if directors were to prefer climate interests to shareholder interests, and this led to the future success of the company, this act would not be contrary to English company law.

---

[43] The business judgment rule has a definition under US law: 'a presumption that in making a business decision the directors of a corporation acted on an informed basis, in good faith and in the honest belief that the action taken was in the best interest of the company'. *Aronson v. Lewis* 473 A.2d 805, 812 (Del. 1984). English law does not have an official business judgment rule test within the common law, but relies instead on statutory duties of honesty and good faith, although Andre Tunc notes that English law has an unarticulated business judgment rule encapsulated in judicial reluctance to interfere with directors' decisions, see Andre Tunc, 'The Judge and the Businessman' (1986) 102 L.Q.R. 549. The term is used here to highlight the deference often showed by the judiciary to the commercial expertise of directors.

[44] [1902] 2 Ch 421.

[45] Ibid., 423–4, 426.

[46] Talbot (n 33) 161.

[47] [1883] Ch D 654.

[48] Ibid.

The seminal case of *Re Smith and Fawcett Limited*[49] established the traditional English law test that the directors act in the interests of the company, interpreted as the 'general interests of the company as a whole'.[50] This phrase has had enduring value in company law, and the case clearly established that directors have the power to decide what is in the best interests of the company.[51] Eve J, in the case of *Re Lee Behrens and Company*[52], sets out three questions that would establish whether directors have complied with their fiduciary duties. These were, 1) is the transaction reasonably incidental to carrying on the company's business, 2) is it a bona fide transaction and 3) is it done for the benefit of and to promote the prosperity of the company?[53] This tripartite test clearly focused on the company and not on the shareholders. If directorial attention to climate concerns passed this three-tier test, these concerns may then surpass attention to shareholder interests, even if this involved some sacrificing of shareholder profits. The test of the company as a whole allows directors sufficient flexibility to pay attention to climate concerns and would even make room for profit-sacrificing climate-friendly behaviour, if the ultimate objective benefits the company as an entity.

As a result of this main line of authority, it is clear that English case law prior to 2006 did not reflect or even mandate the shareholder primacy norm, and therefore environmental and climate concerns could dictate directorial decisions if they led to the betterment of the company as a whole. Under this approach, the potential effects of climate change could warrant attention of directors and justify some profit-sacrificing measures to reduce GHG emissions by companies, if this ultimately led to the company's success.

Some shareholder primacy theorists, however, have pointed to a slimline of English authority that advocates for shareholder primacy. The case of *Greenhalgh v. Arderne Cinemas*[54] developed a definition that focused exclusively on shareholders. In this case, Lord Evershed stated that 'bona fide for the benefit of the company' did not mean the company as a commercial entity distinct from the corporators, but meant the corporators as a general body.[55] He stated that directors must look at the hypothetical member and ask whether the proposed action is to this person's benefit. This view reduces directors' duties solely to considering shareholder interests, and has been criticised by academics. Daniel Attenborough states that *Greenhalgh* is simply bad law, and subsequent cases have repeated Evershed's dicta without the

---

[49] [1942] 1 Ch 304.
[50] Ibid 308.
[51] D. J. Bakibinga, 'Directors' Duty to Act Bona Fides in the Interest of the Company' (1990) 39(2) I.C.L.Q. 451, 451.
[52] [1932] 2 Ch 46.
[53] Ibid., 51. See also *Fulham Football Club v. Cabra* [1992] WL 895734 CA.
[54] [1951] 1 Ch 286.
[55] Ibid., 291.

requisite analysis.[56] Ross Grantham notes that there was no evidence that Evershed meant to establish a general principle.[57] Len Sealy states that although the company as a whole has a 'notoriously elusive meaning',[58] the better view is to focus not on corporators as *Greenhalgh* does, but instead to focus on the corporate body as that is what matters most.[59]

In fact, Evershed in *Greenhalgh* sought to rely on the cases of *Shuttleworth v. Cox Bros and Company*[60] and *Sidebottom v. Kershaw, Leese and Company Ltd*.[61] In the latter case, counsel for the respondents argued that the company as a whole meant every individual shareholder. However, a close reading of Lord Sterndale's judgment shows that he stated that the respondents' counsel's argument was 'very difficult to follow'[62] and that the matter had already been settled by the *Allen v. Gold Reefs of West Africa*[63] case, which referred to the company as a whole. *Shuttleworth v. Cox* simply affirmed the *Sidebottom v. Kershaw* decision, and so it is unclear which cases, if any, Evershed relied on for his statements.[64]

Only one pre-2006 company law case specifically deals with environmental issues. In *re Waste Recycling Group Plc*,[65] the company applied to the court to approve a scheme of arrangement for a capital restructuring under Section 425 of the Companies Act 1985. The scheme included a reduction of capital in order to carry out a takeover of the company by a private entity. The majority (99.7 per cent) of the shareholders approved the scheme, but one minority shareholder, Mr Davis, objected. Mr Davis was concerned that an environmental company should be subject to public oversight and not be operated by a private entity. Justice Lloyd summarised his concerns as follows:

> He says – and this seems to be a fair comment from observations – that particular companies with operations which have an environmental impact – whether positive or negative – often attract the attention of shareholders who buy shares more with a

---

[56] Daniel Attenborough, 'How Directors Should Act When Owing Duties to the Companies' Shareholders: Why We Need to Stop Applying *Greenhalgh*' (2009) 20(10) Intl. Co. and Commercial L. Rev. 1, 1.
[57] Ross Grantham, 'The Doctrinal Basis of the Rights of Company Shareholders' (1998) 57(3) C.C.L.J. 554, 567.
[58] L. S. Sealy, '"Bona Fides" and "Proper Purposes" in Corporate Decisions' (1989) 15 Monash U. L. Rev. 265, 269.
[59] Ibid., 270.
[60] [1927] 1 Ch 154.
[61] [1920] Ch Div 154.
[62] Ibid., 164–5.
[63] [1900] 1 Ch 656.
[64] *Gaiman and Others v. National Association for Mental Health* [1969] 1 Ch 317, supports the *Greenhalgh* judgment, although this case dealt with a company limited by guarantee, as well as *Multinational Gas and Petrochemical Co v. Multinational Gas and Petrochemical Services* [1983] 1 Ch 258, which states that shareholders are the company when it is solvent.
[65] [2003] EWHC 2065 (Ch).

3.2 The Common Law Position Prior to 2006

desire to try to hold directors to account in respect of environmental interests than just on dividend or other financial return.[66]

Although Justice Lloyd appeared to have some sympathy with Mr Davis' assertions, he decided that the court had no ability to distinguish between the subjective reasons for holding shares, either for environmental oversight or purely financial gain.

The relative lack of environmental cases under English company law may mean that English directors did not appreciate the largely entity approach of English common law, and assumed that environmental and climate issues were better dealt with by complying with environmental regulations. Climate issues (largely through climate litigation) also have only recently gained legal traction, and the Climate Change Act 2008 was passed after the 2006 Companies Act. One of the few English company law decisions that specifically deals with non-shareholder constituents[67] is the *Parke* v. *Daily News*[68] case, which prohibited directors from making ex gratia payments to employees on the sale of the assets of the newspaper. Plowman J determined that the sale of the newspaper was in the interests of the shareholders, but the payment to employees was not in the interests of the company.[69]

The dearth of English cases that deal specifically with non-shareholder constituents such as the environment, and particularly employees, is curious as Section 309 (the precursor of Section 172) of the Companies Act 1985 stated that, 'the matters to which the directors of a company are to have regard in the performance of their functions include the interests of the company's employees in general, as well as the interests of its members'. Chronologically, the Section 309 placed the interests of employees before those of the shareholders; however, employees could not enforce this provision through a derivative action, and it was therefore deemed to be a 'lame duck' provision.[70] This may foreshadow the effectiveness of Section 172 for the environment, as there are similarly no mechanisms for non-shareholder constituents to enforce the provisions of Section 172. The lack of environmental company law cases in the United Kingdom also points to the general assumption by directors that company law was not an appropriate forum for environmental issues, reflecting shareholder primacy normative approaches to the company.

While US company law was based on pre-2006 English common law, American jurisprudence more firmly reflects the shareholder wealth maximisation norm,

---

[66] Ibid., para 10.
[67] There are a number of cases that deal specifically with creditors, particularly on the insolvency of the company.
[68] [1962] 1 Ch 927. Note that Lord Cullen in the Scottish case of *Dawson International* v. *Coats Paton* [1989] 5 BCC 405, 409 casts doubt on the *Parke* v. *Daily News* approach.
[69] *Parke* (n 68) 963.
[70] Andrew Keay, 'Tackling the Corporate Objective: An Analysis of the United Kingdom's "Enlightened Shareholder Value Approach"' (2007) 29 Sydney L. Rev. 577, 593.

particularly in Delaware. The statement in *Dodge* v. *Ford Motor Co* [71] that 'A business corporation is organised and carried on primarily for the profit of the stockholders' is often touted as establishing shareholder wealth maximisation as intrinsic in US law. However, academics have questioned whether this case establishes such a sound principle.[72] The 1968 case of *Shlensky* v. *Wrigley*[73] established that the Wrigley company did not have to install lights to enable night baseball games, even though it would be more profitable. In this case, the President of the Board stated he was concerned not to negatively affect the quality of life of the surrounding neighbourhood as the reasons why night lights were not installed.

The circumstances in a takeover situation are very different. For example, *Revlon Inc.* v. *MacAndrews & Forbes Holdings Inc.*[74] is often cited as establishing that directors must pay attention to shareholders' profitability, but this has since been narrowed to the circumstances of a takeover by the case of *Paramount Communications Inc.* v. *Time Inc.*[75] As highlighted in Chapter 2, in the recent case of *eBay Domestic Holdings Inc.* v. *Newmark*,[76] a Delaware court noted, 'Having chosen a for-profit corporate form, the craigslist directors are bound by the fiduciary duties and standards that accompany that form. Those standards include acting to promote the value of the corporation for the benefit of its stockholders'. This re-entrenched shareholder primacy and wealth maximisation principle, particularly in Delaware, although this decision has also been criticised.[77] Outside of Delaware, many other US states also have constituency statutes which require directors to pay attention to non-shareholder interests.[78]

Australia has a less-entrenched shareholder primacy approach. In particular, the unique enforcement role of the Australian Securities and Investments Commission under the Corporations Act 2001 provides that entity with wide investigatory and prosecutorial powers for breaches of directors' duties. Sarah Barker notes that the Australian business judgment rule also, unlike the US approach, is usually ineffective to cure a breach of the Act.[79] Therefore, the Australian jurisdiction may be less

---

[71] 170 N.W. 668, 684 (Mich. 1919).
[72] Lynn A Stout 'Why We Should Stop Teaching *Dodge* v. *Ford*' (2008) Cornell L Faculty Publications Paper 724; and D. Gordon Smith 'The Shareholder Primacy Norm' (1998) 23 J. Corp. L. 277, 315.
[73] 237 N.E.2d 776 (Ill. App. Ct. 1968).
[74] 506 A.2d 173 (Del. 1986)
[75] 571 A.2d 1140 (Del. 1989) and *Re Trados Inc.* 73 A.3d 17 (Del. 2013).
[76] 16 A.3d 1 (Del. Ch 2010).
[77] David A. Wishnick, 'Corporate Purposes in a Free Enterprise System: A Comment on *eBay* v. *Newmark*' (2012) 121 Yale L. J. 2405.
[78] These were passed in the late 1980s and early 1990s as a result of the uptick in takeovers and are found in about thirty states, but are largely permissive and have rarely been used to challenge directors' decision making. See for example Oregon ORS. §60.357(5), or Georgia Ga. CodeAnn.§ 14-2-202(b)(5)(1989).
[79] Sarah Barker, 'An Introduction to Directors' Duties in Relation to Stranded Assets Risks' in Ben Caldecott (ed.) *Stranded Assets and the Environment Risk, Resilience and Opportunity* (Routledge 2018), 217.

shareholder-centric and directors in this jurisdiction be more open to liability for breach of duty where they are willfully blind to the risks of stranded assets in particular.[80] A legal opinion by two prestigious legal academics in Australia noted that litigation for breach of Section 180(1) of the Australian *Corporations Act 2001* in the context of climate change was in fact likely.[81] The lawyers noted that as a matter of Australian law, company directors *can*, and in some cases *should* be considering the impact on their business of climate change risks, to the extent they intersect with the interests of the firm.[82] These risks implicated directors and imposed obligations on them to inform themselves, disclose the risks as part of financial reporting frameworks, and take such steps as they may see fit to take.

While various jurisdictions within the Anglo-American corporate law evidence varying levels of shareholder primacy, the UK judiciary has, for the most part, gifted a wide amount of discretion (absent self-dealing and dishonesty) to directors to manage the company as they deem fit in the interests of the company as a whole. There is a slimline of authority that does advocate for shareholder primacy as a common-law duty, but Evershed's judgment in the *Greenhalgh* case is questionable. This inconsistency within the judgments may simply evidence an unfolding of a historical misunderstanding of the proper role of shareholders within the company. But the main authorities display a purposeful approach by the judiciary to provide directors with sufficient commercial (and therefore legal) space to manage companies as they deem fit, according to the business judgment rule. Prior to 2006, the statutory provisions of the Companies Acts, as interpreted by case law, provided directors with a large amount of discretion to determine what the best interests of the company meant.[83] They did this by adopting the phrase 'the company as a whole', although the phrase has been interpreted as having a 'notoriously elusive meaning'.[84]

A number of academics have seized on the judicial reticence within the common law to tell directors what to do, with the conclusion that English common law mandates that directors must act in the interests of the shareholders. For example, Lorraine Talbot argues that directors owe duties to capital, and to shareholders alone.[85] Brenda Hannigan notes that although the common law has stated that directors owe duties to promote the success of the company for the benefit of the

---

[80] Ibid., 210.
[81] For a comprehensive assessment of Australian directors' duties, see Barker (n 79).
[82] Noel Hutley S.C. and Sebastian Hartford-Davis, 'Climate Change and Directors' Duties' (Supplementary Memorandum of Opinion, 26 March 2019), 2.
[83] Although, note that courts will intervene in exceptional circumstances where directors have acted bona fides and within their powers, *Ultraframe Ltd* v. *Fielding* [2005] EWHC 1638 (Ch).
[84] Sealy (n 58) 269; This ambiguity led Dignam to question, 'Why is there no definitive case that ultimately determines a director's obligations when faced with a difference between his or her honest view as to the future strategic direction of the company and the shareholders' differing views?' Dignam (n 42) 666
[85] Talbot (n 33) 131.

members as a whole, and for most purposes this means the entity, this calls for a balancing of the short- and long-term interests of the shareholders.[86] Richard Nolan points out that the purpose of the company has not changed in 150 years; it is primarily a vehicle to raise capital and to make and distribute profits.[87] Davy Wu has stated that the common law has always reflected the shareholder primacy approach, stating, 'To hold that members' interests represent the company's interests is just a recognition of the shareholder primacy principle that has long been deeply embedded in company law'.[88]

As stated above, except for a very slimline of cases, the majority of English law authority does not support these contentions. Pre-2006, the judiciary in England persistently refused to decide that directors must only pay attention to shareholder interests, and instead pointed directors towards taking care of the company as an entity. Alistair Alcock states that pre-existing common law often, but not always, aligned the benefit of the company with the interests of its current shareholders, and provided directors with a large amount of discretion.[89] He states, 'That discretion allowed an enlightened shareholder value approach, perhaps entity maximisation and even some profit sacrificing social responsibility. It did not enforce rigid shareholder 'supremacy'.[90] Attenborough notes that the common law was often 'surprisingly ambivalent'[91] when it came to defining management's primary duties, and Stephen Copp notes that there were some cases that advocated for shareholder primacy, and some that did not.[92]

There is clearly ambiguity within the common law as to what the interests of the company actually mean, but most pre-2006 cases in the United Kingdom demonstrated that directors did not always have to act in the interests of the shareholders alone.[93] As a result, the shareholder primacy approach has not always been firmly entrenched as part of English company law.[94] The judiciary instead adopted an entity approach to the corporation, largely reflecting Dodd's and not Berle's approach to the company. Even though the common law fell short of

---

[86] Brenda Hannigan, *Company Law* (4th edn, OUP 2016) 216.
[87] R. C. Nolan, 'The Continuing Evolution of Shareholder Governance' (2006) 65(1) C.L.J. 92, 97.
[88] Davy Ka Chee Wu, 'Managerial Behavior, Company Law, and the Problem of Enlightened Shareholder Value' (2010) 31 *Company Lawyer*, 53.
[89] Alistair Alcock, 'An Accidental Change to Directors' Duties?' (2009) 30 *Company Lawyer* 362, 366.
[90] Ibid.
[91] Daniel Attenborough, 'Book Review Andrew Keay The Enlightened Shareholder Value Principle and Corporate Governance' (2013) 76(5) M.L.R. 940, 940.
[92] Stephen F. Copp, 's172 of the Companies Act 2006 Fails People and Planet?' (2010) 31 *Company Lawyer*, 406, 407–8.
[93] Charlotte Villiers, 'Directors' Duties and the Company's Internal Structures under the UK Companies Act 2006: Obstacles for Sustainable Development' (2010) U Oslo Faculty of Law Legal Studies Research Paper Series No. 2010-03, 105, 106–8.
[94] Andrew Keay, 'Moving Towards Stakeholderism? Constituency Statutes, Enlightened Shareholder Value, and More: Much Ado about Little?' (2011) 22(1) E. Business L.R. 1, 22.

advocating for a stakeholder approach, it provided directors with sufficient flexibility to manage the company in a way they deemed the most appropriate in the circumstances. This common law approach afforded directors the flexibility to consider, and even prioritise, environmental and climate concerns over shareholder profits, if that ultimately benefitted the company. This approach changed dramatically with the CLRSG reports, which adopted a contractarian analysis of the company through the enlightened shareholder value approach.

3.3 COMPANY LAW REVIEW STEERING GROUP REPORTS

Historically, English Companies Acts have provided minimal legislative guidance to directors on how they should perform their duties. As analysed above, this approach was designed to provide directors with a significant amount of flexibility and deference. Section 172 of the Companies Act 2006 took a directional shift, providing a much fuller list of objectives that directors are now required to take into account. This approach was encapsulated in what the CLRSG determined was the enlightened shareholder value approach.

Academics are split as to whether this new legislative approach provides for a new stakeholder approach to managing companies, or whether Section 172 further entrenches the shareholder value approach adopted by previous corporate governance reports. Section 172 explicitly mentions the environment as a stakeholder for the first time in English company law, and required the reporting of some environmental information under Section 417,[95] but it is debatable whether this statutory change will have any real impact on climate concerns, as upon closer analysis it subordinates environmental concerns to shareholder interests.

The Labour Government, through the Department of Trade and Industry, established the CLRSG in 1998 to consider reforms to the existing Companies Act. A comprehensive review of company law of this kind had not taken place for over forty years. The CLRSG stated that the role of companies was to facilitate the operation of market forces through contractual and other relationships, although in cases of market failure, the CLRSG acknowledged that other interventions would be justified.[96] Accordingly, the objective of the reform of the Companies Act 1985 was to achieve competitiveness and the efficient creation of wealth from the corporate enterprise.[97] The primary objective of the review, and consequently any changes to company law, would be designed to extract as much value from the company as possible in order to increase national competitiveness, thereby reflecting a

---

[95] This business review obligation in Section 417 was replaced by The Companies Act 2006 (Strategic Report and Directors' Report) Regulations 2013 with new strategic review obligations in Section 414.
[96] The Company Law Review Steering Group, *Modern Company Law for a Competitive Economy* (Great Britain Department of Trade and Industry 1999) 15.
[97] Ibid., 36; Dine (n 5), 184.

shareholder wealth maximisation approach. The, arguably secondary, aim of the reform would also be 'to minimize the negative impacts of corporate activity on participants and to maximize welfare more widely'.[98] The latter objective points to a welfarist objective of companies, but was qualified as the CLRSG stated it only applied to the extent it was appropriate to use the mechanics of company law to achieve these aims.[99] The CLRSG approach to the company and its objectives therefore largely adopted a law and economics perspective.

The CLRSG considered two approaches to describe what the objective of companies should be: the enlightened shareholder value approach (or ESV), and the pluralist approach. The ESV approach was described as the approach which reflected current English law: that the role of companies was to generate maximum value for shareholders, as this approach was often the best means of providing for overall prosperity and wealth.[100] This was arguably not the case, as the prior analysis of pre-2006 common law has shown.

The CLRSG considered that the pluralist approach would distract directors by forcing them to manage competing considerations at the expense of economic growth and international competitiveness.[101] The CLRSG adopted the ESV approach to reform the Act, as this was considered to be consistent with the ultimate objective of companies. The reports clearly stated that existing English law reflects shareholder wealth maximisation,[102] and that the company is to be run for the benefit of its shareholders.[103] The reports describe the company in contractual terms, reflecting the contractarian approach, stating that companies 'can be viewed largely as contractual entities, created and controlled under agreements entered into by members and directors'.[104] This perspective clearly reflects a wealth maximisation, utility-maximising, law and economics, and contractarian approach to company law. However, unlike the strong form of contractarianism, the review noted that there may be room for regulation in order to secure wider social interests.[105]

Despite this theoretical approach, the CLRSG was still concerned about short-termism. The report stated that the position of English law on directors' duties was misunderstood, determining that directors understood the law as requiring them to adopt a short-term focus on profits in order to satisfy their shareholders, which was not in fact correct.[106] This failure by directors to adopt a long-term approach to a

---

[98] Ibid.
[99] Ibid.
[100] Ibid., 37.
[101] Ibid., 44.
[102] Ibid., 37, 38.
[103] The Company Law Review Steering Group, *Modern Company Law for a Competitive Economy: Developing the Framework* (A Consultation Document from the CLSG March 2000) 9.
[104] Ibid., 10.
[105] Ibid., 10.
[106] CLRSG, *Developing the Framework* (n 103) 40.

company's success suggested to the CLRSG that there was a strong case for making the current law more explicit in the new Section 172,[107] by providing for a long-term vision that would necessitate the taking into account of wider interests.[108] The reports stated that the vast majority of responses they received favoured keeping the basic rule that directors act for the benefit of shareholders, that is shareholder primacy, but also supported a more 'inclusive' way of accomplishing this goal.[109]

The CLRSG failed to consider that this legal approach was in fact incorrect, and the law prior to 2006 did not actually mandate shareholder primacy. In short, according to the CLRSG, although the overall objective of the company should be pluralist in ensuring maximum welfare for all, the means of achieving this should recognise the realities of running a corporate enterprise, that is shareholder primacy.[110] While these statements appear to be contradictory, the overall consensus of the CLRSG was that companies are to be run for the primary benefit of the shareholders. The restatement of directors' duties advocated by the CLRSG was taken to depend on two pillars:

1) An 'inclusive' statement of directors' duties that restates their legal position that the company should be operated in the ultimate interests of its members, but that also takes into account wider relationships; and
2) A new mandatory operating and financial review (OFR) for all public and large private companies that would include social and environmental impacts.[111]

The CLRSG's reports led to several changes in company law, ultimately codified in the Companies Act 2006. In relation to the corporate objective, Section 172 of the Companies Act 2006 sets out the enlightened shareholder value approach.

3.4 THE COMPANIES ACT 2006 AND CLIMATE CONCERNS

The 2006 Companies Act codifies seven directors' duties, six of which are fiduciary duties. Of the fiduciary duties, the duty to promote the success of the company is the principal duty.[112] This duty is found in Section 172(1) which states that directors have the duty to promote the success of the company for the benefit of its members. This is followed by a non-exhaustive, more inclusive list of non-shareholder constituents and considerations in Sections 172(1)(a)–(f). Under Section 172(d), when exercising

---
[107] Ibid., 40.
[108] Ibid., 49.
[109] Ibid., 10.
[110] Ibid., 14.
[111] The Company Law Review Steering Group, *Modern Company Law for a Competitive Economy: Completing the Structure* (A Consultation Document from the CLRSG, 2000) 33.
[112] Alexia Staker and Alice Garton, 'Directors' Liability and Climate Risk: United Kingdom – A *Country Paper*' (Commonwealth Climate Law Initiative 2018), 10.

the duty under Section 172(1), directors must have regard to the impact of the company's operations on the community and the environment. This is the first time environmental concerns have appeared in statutory form under English company law. Despite its mention, the structure of Section 172 means that success of companies is to be achieved primarily for the benefit of shareholders, in priority to the interests of non-shareholders such as the environment. An outstanding issue debated by academics was whether the interests of non-shareholders would be considered as independent priorities (more in line with the pluralist approach), or whether non-shareholder interests could only be considered where they are consistent with the success of the company and the members' interests. The analysis is relevant for climate change to determine what, if any, impact does the new Section 172 have on the environment and the climate. In particular, are climate concerns post-2006 allowed to balance out or even trump the concerns of shareholders?

The CLRSG reports provide an actual hierarchy that directors are to consider, as follows:

1) Obeying the corporate constitution;
2) Promoting what directors calculate (in good faith) would promote the success of the company for the members' benefit;
3) As part of the process in 2), directors should take account of factors they believe (in good faith) are relevant for the purpose in 2).[113]

According to this hierarchy, it is clear that shareholder interests are meant to predominate over any other concerns, including climate concerns. A number of writers note that Section 172 only requires directors to consider non-shareholder interests when the pursuit of those interests would promote the success of the company.[114] For the first time, a company statute lists shareholder benefits as part of the definition of the success of the company. Under the pre-2006 common law, shareholder interests were not necessarily automatically equated with the interests of the company as a whole. However, Section 172 has removed the old statutory language, and replaced it with the obligation to promote the success of the company, with an explicit reference to shareholders.

Arguably the new Companies Act now focuses on shareholder supremacy, and, should directors pay too much attention to the other constituencies listed, to the detriment of the company, they may be in breach of their duties.[115] The new Section 172 actually shifts the focus from the company as an entity to the shareholders.[116] As a result, directors can take into account non-shareholder interests only when they serve the economic interests of the company and its shareholders. When this is not

---

[113] Ibid., 40.
[114] John Lowry, 'The Duty of Loyalty of Company Directors: Bridging the Accountability Gap Through Efficient Disclosure' (2009) 68(3) C.L.J. 607, 616; Keay (n 94) 29; Dine (n 5), 184.
[115] Alcock, (n 89) 367.
[116] Keay (n 94) 22.

3.4 The Companies Act 2006 and Climate Concerns

the case, directors may be free to disregard non-shareholder interests, and instead pursue matters that promote the success of the company.[117] Climate concerns may not be prioritised over shareholder concerns if they do not promote the success of the company *and* the shareholders. This differs from the position under pre-2006 common law where climate concerns could trump shareholder concerns if their pursuit would benefit the company. Under Section 172, shareholder concerns are elevated to be equal to the interests of the company.

If success of the company is equated with shareholder interests and profits, is there a difference between ESV and shareholder wealth maximisation at all? The CLRSG certainly advocated for a shareholder value approach to company law, but did want to add nuance to the definition of shareholder value by making it 'enlightened'.[118] The enlightened element of shareholder value, according to Hao Zhang and Andrew Keay, was what they deem the 'principle of due consideration for the interests of non-shareholder stakeholders'.[119] Under this principle, directors should have due consideration for non-shareholder interests while working towards shareholder wealth maximisation.[120]

Shareholder wealth maximisation and non-shareholder interests are not always compatible. Margaret Hodge, in the Parliament debate on Section 172, couched the two sets of interests as complementary,[121] but Carrie Bradshaw notes it is dangerous to assume a ready compatibility between shareholder and non-shareholder interests.[122] Where environmental concerns reap profits for companies and shareholders, then an easy compatibility between Section 172(1) and (1)(d) can be achieved. In the case of climate change, reducing the emission of GHGs is often incompatible with increasing profits, at least in the short term, as these emissions are currently not restricted or taxed significantly. In fact, the example of climate change was specifically mentioned in the Hansard debates regarding the impact of Section 172.

In the Hansard debates regarding the Bill, the compatibility between environmental and shareholder concerns was stressed by the then Attorney General Lord Goldsmith. According to Lord Goldsmith, the government's view was that the best way to promote environmentally and socially responsible conduct by companies was to demonstrate how this behaviour can lead to business success.[123] There may, of course, be times when environmental interests and shareholder interests coincide. But this is not always the case, and is less likely if GHG emissions are treated as

---

[117] Success was deemed to be the core objective of Section 172, although the CLRSG left the definition of success up to directors. See CLRSG, *Completing the Structure* (n 111) 39.
[118] Zhang and Keay (n 29) 451.
[119] Ibid., 446.
[120] Ibid., 451; Andreadakis, (n 8) 420.
[121] Margaret Hodge, 'Companies Act 2006, Duties of Company Directors, Ministerial Statements, Department of Trade and Industry' (June 2007), 2.
[122] Carrie Bradshaw, 'The Environmental Business Case and Unenlightened Shareholder Value' (2013) 33(1) L.S. 141, 148.
[123] HL Deb 6 February 2006, vol 678, col GC273.

negative externalities. Lord Avebury, in the Hansard debates, pointed out this very issue, using the example of carbon emissions. He stated:

> In many, if not most, cases, the success of the company is dependent on its ability to continue damaging the environment, and within a fairly distant time horizon, making large parts of the globe uninhabitable. The airlines, for example, are spewing enormous amounts of CO_2 and low molecular weight hydrocarbons into the upper atmosphere, contributing to a rise in temperature which is likely to result in the melting of polar icecaps and the raising of sea levels by 18 metres. How do British Airways, for instance, 'have regard to' this undesirable side-effect of their normal business?[124]

Lord Avebury advocated for Section 172 of the Bill to include minimum environmental standards, as opposed to leaving companies' conduct subject to only voluntary codes of conduct.[125] Lord Goldsmith's response to this suggestion was to confirm that including minimum environmental standards in Section 172 would reflect the pluralist approach to company law, which was rejected by the CLRSG. According to Lord Goldsmith, environmentally responsible conduct would have to be subordinate to, or simply a means of achieving, shareholder value.[126] One of the three reasons for the subordination of environmental concerns to shareholder interests was that company law was not considered by the government as the appropriate forum to pursue corporate social responsibility.[127]

As a result, where climate and shareholder interests collide, and there is no economic case for inclusive ESV, Section 172 requires that shareholder interests predominate.[128] As a result, ESV only appears to be 'enlightened' when the interests of the climate coincide with the profit motive of shareholders. In other words, ESV is enlightened when environmental, including climate interests, conveniently fall in line with shareholder wealth maximisation. When these interests do not align, ESV appears to reflect the shareholder primacy and shareholder wealth maximisation norms, and climate concerns become subordinate to shareholder interests.

Through Section 172, environmental interests are reduced to purely economic denominators.[129] Bradshaw notes that ESV does not sanction profit-sacrificing behaviour on behalf of the environment, and therefore it does not provide a sufficiently direct means to mediate negative environmental externalities.[130] According to Arad Reisberg, because Section 172 has no enforcement mechanisms for non-shareholders, its benefits for the environment are elusive, and environmental groups would have to

---

[124] Ibid., col GC266.
[125] Ibid., col GC267.
[126] Ibid., col GC273.
[127] Ibid.
[128] Luca Cerioni, 'The Success of the Company in s172(1) of the UK Companies Act 2006: Towards an "Enlightened Director Primacy?"' (2008) 4 Original L. Rev. 8, 16.
[129] Bradshaw (n 122) 142.
[130] Ibid., 156–7.

either buy shares in the company in order to bring a derivative action, or rely on existing shareholders to bring a derivative action for breach of directors' duties.[131] The lack of enforcement options for stakeholders within Section 172 is a deficiency in the Act, making their already subservient position to shareholders even weaker.[132]

Many obstacles may bar suits against the company, including that the directors are the wrongdoers and still in control, as well as costs, leading to very few derivative actions being initiated.[133] This enforcement problem with Section 172 contributes to the provision being ineffective, and 'largely educational'.[134] In fact, Section 172 may make all stakeholders, including shareholders, worse off as shareholders now have to compete with other constituents' views.[135]

The provisions of the Companies Act 2006 only contemplate a pluralist balancing of interests subject to the overarching requirement to promote the success of the company, for the benefit of the members or shareholders, as the final determining issue.[136] Rosemary Langford argues that any other approach would be unworkable, and would require a deeper revision of company law to effect such stakeholder promotion and protection.[137] As a result, Section 172 is shareholder-centric, and provides a subservient place in the law for environmental and climate interests. Even in this subservient role, stakeholder interests are unenforceable through derivative actions.

Some academics have been more positive about the change to the statutory provisions on directors' duties. According to this more positive view of Section 172, the statute does modify the obligation of good faith in that it will now include the failure to consider the factors listed in section 172(1).[138] Deryn Fisher argues that, although section 172 will not force directors to consider the interests of third parties, it must be seen as a largely normative measure that, when combined with stakeholder pressure, the prevailing commercial climate, and a few enlightened shareholders, will encourage a more inclusive and longer-term view of what constitutes the success of the company.[139] ESV is considered as a 'hybrid' between shareholder

---

[131] Arad Reisberg, 'Derivative Claims Under the Companies Act 2006: Much Ado About Nothing?' (2008) UCL Legal Studies Research Paper No. 09-02, 14.

[132] Collins C. Ajibo, 'A Critique of ESV: Revisiting the Shareholder Primacy Theory' (2014) 2(1) Birkbeck L. Rev. 37, 50; Rosemary Teele Langford, 'Best Interests: Multifaceted but not Unbounded' (2016) 75(3) C.L.J. 505, 510; Dine (n 5), 187.

[133] Andrew Keay and Michelle Welsh, 'Enforcing Breaches of Directors' Duties by a Public Body and Antipodean Experiences' (2015) 15(2) J. Corporate L. Studies 255, 256.

[134] Andrew Keay, 'The Duty to Promote the Success of the Company: Is it Fit for Purpose?' (2010) U Leeds School of Law, Centre for Business Law and Practice Working Paper 1, 30.

[135] Villiers (n 93) 8.

[136] Langford (n 132) 526.

[137] Ibid.

[138] Ibid., 622.

[139] Deryn Fisher, 'The Enlightened Shareholder – Leaving Stakeholders in the Dark: Will Section 172(1) of the Companies Act 2006 Make Directors Consider the Impact of their Decisions on Third Parties?' (2009) 20(1) Intl Co Commercial L Rev 10, 15–16.

wealth maximisation and stakeholderism,[140] or as a 'third-way' compromise between shareholder value and the stakeholder model.[141]

Section 172 is innovative because for the first time directors have a statutory obligation to have regard to the impact of the company's operations on both the community and the environment. 'Have regard to' is not intended to constitute merely a tick-box exercise on behalf of directors. In fact, the Companies (Miscellaneous Reporting) Regulations 2018, section 414 CZA now requires directors to publish a statement of how the directors have had regard to the elements of Section 172 (called a Section 172 statement). The provisions of Section 172(1)(d) mean that directors must now consider or think about the impact the company's operations may have on the community and the environment. If those impacts are sufficiently serious, and if those impacts lead directors to the conclusion that the proper course is to do something positive for the environment,[142] then directors will have a new duty to act on behalf of the environment. But 'have regard to' does not mean 'give primacy to', leading to a conclusion that some degree of legal or reputational damage may be acceptable if the long-term value of the company will increase as a result.[143] This could include not acting to mitigate GHGs, particularly if no legal requirement or financial penalty exists to decrease them. Acting on behalf of the environment is only justifiable under Section 172(1)(d) if it increases the long-term profitability of the company.[144] Therefore, when environmental interests and long-term shareholders' interests collide, Section 172(1)(d) would not support profit-sacrificing climate-friendly behaviour.

There are further issues with the effectiveness of Section 172(1)(d) for climate change. In particular, the term environment is vague and almost incapable of a single definition.[145] The provision links both the environment together with the community,[146] and therefore it is not clear whether environmental considerations stand alone in directorial decisions, or whether impacts have to be on both the environment and the community in order to be considered. In addition, Section 417 of the Act required directors to disclose certain information, including environmental information under

---

[140] Ibid., 10.
[141] Sarah Kiarie, 'At Crossroads: Shareholder Value, Stakeholder Value and Enlightened Shareholder Value: Which Road Should the United Kingdom Take?' (2006) 17 Intl. Co. Commercial L. Rev. 329, 339. See also Cynthia A. Williams and John M. Conley, 'An Emerging Third Way? The Erosion of the Anglo-American Shareholder Value Construct' (2005) 38 Cornell Int'l. L. J. 493, 496.
[142] Arad Reisberg and Ian Havercroft, 'Directors' Duties Under Companies Act 2006 and the Impact of the Company's Operations on the Environment' UCL Centre for Commercial Law (December 2010), footnote 30.
[143] Clifford Chance LLP, 'Corporate Law Tools Project Jurisdiction: UK' Mandate of the Special Representative of the Secretary-General on the Issue of Human Rights and International Corporations and other Business Enterprises (2009), para 10.1.
[144] Villiers (n 93) 8.
[145] Reisberg and Havercroft (n 142) 20.
[146] Ibid., 29.

Section 417(5)(b)(i), to shareholders.[147] The provision was designed to work together with Section 172 in order to ensure the enlightened part of ESV. But inconsistencies existed between Section 172 and Section 417(5)(b)(i) which reduced their combined effectiveness. While Section 172(1)(d) links the environment together with the community, Section 417(b) only mentioned environmental matters on its own.[148] In addition, while Section 172(1)(d) refers to the impact of the company's operation on the environment, Section 417(d) referred instead to environmental matters (including the impact of the company's business on the environment), which is arguably a wider consideration.

Concerns regarding the effectiveness of Section 172 on its own were so serious, that on 11 January 2006, advocacy group Friends of the Earth launched a judicial review of the then government's decision to remove the OFR's requirements under Section 417 and replace it with the business review provisions.[149] The judicial review was subsequently withdrawn, but the removal of the OFR drew criticism from many stakeholders, including environmental NGOs.[150] Friends of the Earth was particularly critical about the replacement of the OFR with the Business Review in Section 417. They pointed to a number of deficiencies when the two were compared. These included the fact that the Business Review had a lower level of audit than the OFR, had no mandatory reporting standards, focused only on the impact of environmental issues on the company and lacked a forward-looking approach.[151]

The lack of forward-looking disclosure requirements is particularly detrimental in the case of climate change, because climate impacts are anticipated to be largely in the future. If a company has no anticipated future emissions levels or reductions of GHGs, it will be difficult to anticipate its contributions to, and therefore the full effects of, climate change. Prior to the Companies Act 2006, there were a number of issues with corporate non-financial reporting. At the time, and even today, companies struggle with non-financial performance reporting, and often connect non-financial reporting automatically to profits.[152] The deficiencies of Section 417 in terms of environmental reporting are significant, as the section does not provide clear guidelines on reporting or uniform standards for companies. There is no guidance on the meaning of impact on the environment under the statute, and so Section 417 failed to make environmental reporting by companies more effective.[153]

---

[147] Section 417 has been largely replaced by s 414.
[148] Reisberg and Havercroft (n 142) 29.
[149] Friends of the Earth, 'Judicial Review Win: How We Stopped the Government Pricing People Out of Taking It to Court' (27 September 2017), https://friendsoftheearth.uk/legal-and-planning/judicial-review-win-how-we-stopped-government-pricing-people-out-taking-it-court (accessed 6 July 2020).
[150] Ibid.
[151] Friends of the Earth Judicial Review (n 149) para 50.
[152] Villiers (n 93) 24.
[153] Reisberg and Havercroft (n 142) 39.

The Corporate Responsibility Coalition (or CORE) in the United Kingdom is made up of a number of environmental and social NGOs, including Amnesty International, ActionAid, Friends of the Earth, Traidcraft, War on Want and the World Wildlife Fund, and was one of the stakeholders consulted by the government on the OFR requirements. CORE issued a report in 2010 analysing the effectiveness of Section 417 on company reports, comparing Business Reviews of 105 companies.[154] Their analyses revealed a number of deficiencies of the Business Reviews when compared to the statutory requirements, and concluded that, overall, the level of disclosures were inadequate.

In respect to climate change, the report did find that CO_2 emissions were one of the best reported issues, but detailed quantitative information on CO_2 emissions was reported by fewer than 50 per cent of the companies analysed.[155] The report states that 'even where quantitative information was reported, there was rarely any description or detailed specifications of the indicators used, such as that the Greenhouse Gas Protocol was used for measuring greenhouse gases'.[156] Therefore, a lack of mandatory reporting standards under Section 417 resulted in companies not releasing detailed quantitative analyses of their CO_2 emissions. The report also concluded that, although CO_2 emissions were reported, there was almost no analysis in the companies' reports reviewed about the sensitivities of the companies to climate change itself.[157] This indicates that Section 417 has done little to improve climate risk reporting by companies, and paved the way for increased regulation around non-financial and GHG reporting.

Reporting requirements for directors are increasing in specificity, particularly in relation to climate change. In 2013, new regulations replaced the business review with a strategic reporting requirement.[158] The purpose of the strategic report was to explain how directors have discharged their duties under Section 172. The directors' report must describe principal risks and uncertainties facing the company, and quoted companies have to report on the company's performance and position regarding environmental matters, as well as new disclosure requirements on GHG emissions and methodologies not previously required under the business review.

The Department for Business, Energy and Industrial Strategy issued a green paper at the end of 2016, soliciting views on a number of corporate governance issues, including stronger reporting requirements under Section 172.[159] The report notes

---

[154] Adrian Henriques, 'The Reporting of Non-Financial Information in Annual Reports by the FTSE 100' (CORE 2010), www.henriques.info/downloads/Reporting%20of%20Non-Financial%20Information%20FINAL.pdf (accessed 29 July 2014).
[155] Ibid., 8–9.
[156] Ibid., 6.
[157] Ibid., 8–9.
[158] Companies Act 2006 (Strategic Report and Directors' Report) Regulations 2013 (SI 2013/1970).
[159] Department for Business, Energy and Industrial Strategy, *Corporate Governance Reform Green Paper*, (November 2016) para 2.30, https://assets.publishing.service.gov.uk/government/uploads/system/uploads/attachment_data/file/584013/corporate-governance-reform-green-paper.pdf (accessed 6 July 2020).

that the lack of details on how directors actually perform their duties under this section has led to a lack of clear and transparent information about corporate actions to fulfil their Section 172 duties.[160] Material financial information and non-financial information must be disclosed under the strategic report if its disclosure is necessary for an understanding of the development, performance, position or future prospects of the company.[161] For listed public companies, the strategic report must also include environmental matters (including the impact of the company's business on the environment).[162] It must also include any policies of the company relating to the environment, as well as the effectiveness of those policies.

The impacts from climate change are likely to have become a principal risk in the case of many companies and therefore should be reported in those circumstances.[163] Reporting duties under the Companies Act 2006 are enforced by the FRC. The FRC is a non-profit company which sets the UK Corporate Governance and Stewardship Codes, and standards for accounting and actuarial work. It also monitors and takes action to promote the quality of corporate reporting. The FRC has recently requested powers to investigate and prosecute breaches of directors' duties, including reporting duties.

The FRC issues guidance to directors on how to comply with their statutory duties under the Companies Act 2006. Reforms to the 2018 FRC Guidance on the Strategic Report now also expressly refer to climate risk,[164] and directors will have to include how they comply with this duty in the strategic report.[165] The full impacts, however, of Section 172 will only be fully understood as a result of subsequent cases that interpret these provisions.

3.5 POST-2006 CASE LAW

There has been very little case law on Section 172, and therefore the full effects of the new statutory provision may not be clear for some time. It is not entirely clear what the relationship is between the new codification of directors' duties and the pre-2006 Companies Act. Section 170(3) of the Act provides that the statutory provisions replace the common law rules and principles, but section 170(4) states that the old common law is still preserved as an interpretive guide, stating that duties

---

[160] Ibid.
[161] See generally Financial Reporting Council, *Guidance on the Strategic Report* (July 2018),, https://bit.ly/2n10mrX (accessed 6 July 2020).
[162] Companies Act 2006 (Strategic Report and Directors' Report) Regulations 2013, s 414C(7)(b)(i).
[163] Client Earth, 'Risky Business: Climate Change and Professional Liability Risks for Auditors' (2017) 8.
[164] Financial Reporting Council, (n 161).
[165] The Companies (Miscellaneous Reporting) Obligations 2018 require large corporations to include a separate section in their Strategic Report on how directors have complied with their duties under Sections 172(1)(a)–(f).

shall be interpreted and applied in the same way as the common law rules and equitable principles were. The few cases since the new statutory provisions have been enacted have provided very little guidance to directors. In *re Southern Counties Fresh Food Ltd*,[166] the court stated that the old statutory wording of bona fide in the interests of the company is now reflected in the wording in the new statutory language of Section 172(1) of 'in good faith' in a way most likely to promote the success of the company for the benefit of the members as a whole, thus arguing there has been little change in the law. A number of other cases intimate that Section 172 has done little but codify the previous common law.[167] In *re Phoenix Contracts (Leicester) Ltd*,[168] the court stated that what promotes the success of the company is for the director's subjective determination, referring back to the test in *re Smith and Fawcett*. In *Odyssey Entertainment Ltd. v. Ralph Kamp*,[169] Judge Barker QC noted that Section 172(1) identifies a number of matters that must take into account when directors determine what is most likely to promote the success of the company for the benefit of the members as a whole.

In *GHLM Trading Ltd v. Anil Kumar Maroo & Others*,[170] Section 172 was described as the 'touchstone' provision, requiring the directors to act in good faith in the company's interest. In this case, the change ushered in by Section 172 was described as making the duty to promote the success of the company prescriptive[171]. These cases seem to interpret Section 172 as continuing the pre-2006 common law position.

Judge Pelling QC in *Stimpson v. Southern Landlords Association*[172] provided the most comprehensive guidance on the judicial understanding of Section 172. He states that directors can act in any way they consider, in good faith, to be most likely to promote the success of the company, but where the company has mixed objectives, the interests of the members cannot be ignored. In circumstances of conflict between promoting the success of the company and benefiting the members, he states that a balancing exercise will be required.[173] His approach has been supported by Justice Popplewell in *Madoff Securities International Ltd (in liquidation) v. Stephen Raven & Others*,[174] who stated that 'the predominant interests to which the directors of a solvent company must have regard are the interests of the shareholders as a whole, present and future', which he stated was codified by

---

[166] [2008] EWHC 2810.
[167] See *Eclairs Group Ltd v. JKX Oil & Gas Plc* [2015] UKSC 71 regarding s 170–1, para 37; *Kevin Hellards & Devdutt Patel v. Horatio Luis de Brito* [2013] EWHC 2876, where Judge John Randall QC notes that s 172 'effectively codifies' the pre-existing common law position, para 88.
[168] [2010] EWHC 2375.
[169] [2012] EWHC 2316.
[170] [2012] EWHC 61.
[171] Ibid., para 193.
[172] [2010] BCC 387
[173] Ibid., 399.
[174] [2013] EWHC 3147.

Section 172.[175] These two cases elevate the interests of shareholders, and seem to be more consistent with the language in Section 172(1) when compared to the pre-2006 common law position.

One of the most interesting cases relating to Section 172 and climate change is *R (on the Application of the People and Planet)* v. *HM Treasury*.[176] HM Treasury became a majority shareholder in the Royal Bank of Scotland (RBS) through a subsidiary of HM Treasury, UK Financial Investment Ltd. (UKFI). An application for judicial review was brought by an NGO to review HM Treasury's decision not to require RBS to change its usual business practices in order to reduce its carbon emissions and be more respectful of human rights. The Government, having undergone a Green Book Assessment of its investment, determined that UKFI was to take a commercial, hands-off approach as the majority shareholder. According to HM Treasury, to take a more interventionist approach would threaten the financial health of RBS, damage investor confidence and risk the commercial freedom of the bank.[177] In addition, HM Treasury believed that regulation would be a better approach to target the entire banking industry, instead of just RBS.

HM Treasury believed that to take a more interventionist approach would cut across the fundamental legal duty of boards to manage their company in the interests of all their shareholders,[178] and violate their duties under Section 172. HM Treasury took the view that any more of an activist role by UKFI would cut across the legal obligations of Section 172, intimating that any further activity on behalf of non-shareholder constituents such as the climate would, in fact, violate Section 172. As a result, the Government, in particular through the HM Treasury, and the court in this instance, took a conservative view of the requirements of Section 172, preferring competition and profitability to climate activism on the part of a majority shareholder. The case clearly demonstrates that climate concerns are subordinated to shareholder concerns under Section 172, unless an easy and economic compatibility between the two can be found.

Alexia Staker and Alice Garton interpret the new reporting requirements in the strategic report combined with evolving FRC guidance as providing legal duties on directors to assess and take into account climate risks. They identify four key ways in which liability can arise for directors under Section 172. Where a director acts in bad faith by ignoring climate risk, where a director overlooks climate risk for honest reasons, fails to obtain expert advice or adequately consider that advice or there is a defect in the directors' decision-making process so they fail to have regard to the factors listed in Section 172(1).[179] They base this interpretation on a number of cases, including *Bhullar* v. *Bhullar*[180] where a director was still in breach of his fiduciary

---

[175] Ibid., para 187.
[176] [2009] EWHC 3020.
[177] Ibid., para 13.
[178] Ibid., para 13.
[179] Staker and Garton (n 112), 16.
[180] [2017] EWHC 407, at para 122–3, 134.

duty by giving no thought to whether certain lending activities were in the company's best interest, and ignoring cautionary advice provided by an accountant. In addition, they note the duty of competence under s174 also imposes obligations on directors to acquire and maintain a sufficient level of knowledge of the company's business, including climate risks to the business, and oversee any delegation of duties.[181] In their view, climate change for most companies has become a clearly foreseeable and material risk which directors must assess and manage.[182]

3.6 CONCLUSION

Most academics believe that Section 172 will have merely a modest, normative at best, impact on directors' duties. While the language of the statute specifically includes consideration of non-shareholder constituents, including the environment, the substantive provisions only require that directors act upon environmental interests when those interests are consistent with the long-term profitability of the company and shareholders. The case of *R (on the Application of the People and Planet)* v. *HM Treasury* specifically subordinates climate concerns to shareholder concerns. Stakeholders are excluded in Section 172 in both the goals of the company and any right to enforce the provision.[183] As such, it would appear that post-2006, company law has done little to promote a broader stakeholder view of the company, has firmly adopted a shareholder primacy approach, and therefore allowed directors to continue to focus primarily on the interests of their shareholders. Jane Dine notes that Section 172 reconfirmed shareholder primacy 'in [a] spectacular manner'.[184] However, directors' duties have always been a highly flexible concept, particularly as interpreted by the common law prior to the 2006 Act. In a speech in August 2019 given by Lord Sales of the UK Supreme Court to the Anglo-Australian Law Society, Lord Sales noted that wider regulatory reform in both England and Australia brings into question some long-held assumptions of company law, and directors are already permitted under the company law obligations to consider the impacts of climate change to their companies.[185] His speech evidences a renewed interrogation of directors' duties in the context of climate change.

Even though shareholder primacy may not have been a firm legal mandate of directors in the old common law approach, directors have often focused on shareholder interests as their primary concern. This may be due to the influence of corporate codes of conduct, which advocate a shareholder primacy position, as well

---

[181] Staker and Garton (n 112), 19.
[182] Ibid., 14–15.
[183] Bradshaw (n 122) 154.
[184] Dine (n 5), 186.
[185] Lord Sales, 'Directors' Duties and Climate Change: Keeping Pace with Environmental Challenges' (*Anglo-Australian L Society*, 27 August 2019), www.supremecourt.uk/docs/speech-190827.pdf (accessed 16 April 2020.

as market forces that have created the perception that shareholder primacy is a legal requirement for directors.[186]

Prior to 2006, the company was seen by the judiciary as a more malleable entity, subject to market forces, myths, codes, theories, and greater flexibility was afforded by company common law to directors.[187] Post-2006, the position of company law has hardened when it comes to directors' duties. Directors now have a statutory requirement to act in the best interests of the company and its shareholders. While directors should also pay heed to the interests of other stakeholders such as the environment, their duties to the shareholders stand, in priority to the interests of any other stakeholders. As a result, if acting on environmental concerns such as climate change runs counter to the profitability motive of shareholders, directors will not be obliged to reduce GHG emissions under company law. Even under the 2006 Act, though, directors will have legal duties to at least consider the impacts of climate change on their businesses, and obtain expert advice on the issue.

A helpful aspect to the new Section 172 is the focus on the long-term success of the company in Section 172(1)(a). This was specifically inserted in order to mitigate what the CLRSG determined was a myopic focus on short-term profitability by directors. This may be helpful from the climate perspective,[188] as GHGs remain in the atmosphere for long periods of time. If one adopts an entity approach to the company (as advocated in the previous chapter), and given that companies potentially have a perpetual existence, long-term profitability could potentially extend beyond the lifetimes of both shareholders and directors. However, the time periods over which climate change is usually measured and predicted extend hundreds of years into the future, and it is questionable whether directors today will either be able or willing to consider effects so far removed from the pressures of quarterly profit reporting. In addition, a number of shareholder primacists already emphasise the long-term requirements of management, and this has done little to alleviate short-termism.[189] To be clear, climate change can also pose short- and medium-term risks to a company, depending on its industry and sector.

Under the Companies Act 2006, shareholders hold a privileged place within the company. They can appoint and remove directors,[190] bring derivative actions on

---

[186] Jacob M. Rose, 'Corporate Directors and Social Responsibility: Ethics versus Shareholder Value' (2007) 73(3) *Journal of Business Ethics* 319, 320; Andrew Johnston, 'After the OFR: Can UK Shareholder Value Still be Enlightened?' (2006) 4 Eur. Business Organization L. Rev. 817, 818.

[187] Ciaran O'Kelly and Sally Wheeler, 'Internalities and the Foundations of Corporate Governance' (2012) 21 *Social & Legal Studies* 469, 470.

[188] Although, note that Keay doubts it will be effective. Andrew Keay, 'Risk, Shareholder Pressure and Short-termism in Financial Institutions: Does Enlightened Shareholder Value Offer a Panacea?' (2011) 5(6) L. Financial Markets Rev. 435, 443.

[189] Keay (n 134) 39.

[190] Companies Act 2006, s 160 and 168.

behalf of the company,[191] and have the right to attend and vote at annual general meetings.[192] They also receive the directors' and auditors' reports and have rights in takeover situations.[193] The English jurisdiction has always been fairly shareholder-centric.

Under Section 172, directors owe duties to promote not only the success of the company, but duties to benefit the members specifically. Contemporary English cases have interpreted the company as a whole to mean nothing more than its shareholders. Does this mean that directors must run the company exclusively for the benefit of shareholders? According to the CLRSG, it does. In the 'Modern company law for a competitive economy: developing the framework' report the CLRSG states that directors must run the company for the benefit of the members, as shareholders have been given the power to hold directors to account.[194] Although the shareholder primacy norm had not previously been uniformly accepted by English courts, it is now clear that under Section 172 of the Companies Act 2006, through the enlightened shareholder value theory, climate concerns cannot take priority over long-term shareholder interests where these interests are not considered compatible.

The shareholder primacy approach privileges shareholders' interests to the exclusion of all others, and assumes that wealth maximisation is the singular objective of shareholders. This provides for a simplistic explanation of a complex and powerful institution that is the company. More importantly for climate change, it provides little room within company law to deal with environmental concerns generally and externalities such as GHGs specifically, unless these interests coincide with the long-term success of the company. The shareholder primacy norm pushes externalities outside of company law, to be dealt with by voluntary codes of conduct or environmental regulation.

English corporate regulatory choices have been directed and informed by the shareholder primacy norm, and the company law reform exercise in 2006 did not consider company law the appropriate forum to deal with environmental issues. Due to the 2006 Act, company law lost much of the flexibility it historically provided to directors. Some flexibility remains, particularly if Section 172 is interpreted in light of older common law cases, and this discretion could be resurrected by the judiciary absent of any legislative amendments to Section 172 (a light green approach). A cleaner approach would be to remove, through legislation, the reference to shareholders in Section 172 entirely, to make the Act more compatible with prior common law cases and restore significant discretion to directors to act in the best interests of the company as an entity (a medium green approach). Better still, a

---

[191] Ibid., s 260.
[192] Ibid., s 306–7, s 318, s 320 (s 336–339 for public companies).
[193] Ibid., s 417, s 423 (s 437 for public companies), s 495; UK Takeover Code (n 26) Rule 21.
[194] CLRSG, *Developing the Framework* (n 103) para 2.7.

3.6 Conclusion

specific legislative provision which requires directors to balance shareholder interests with stakeholder interests equally, in the interests of the entity as a whole, would begin to negate the pervasive impact shareholder primacy corporate norms have had on company law. A clearer legal articulation of the requirement to balance shareholder interests with corporate impacts on the environment, including the climate, would provide a specific legal mandate to directors to take climate action in the interests of the company as an entity, in accordance with EMV and EMS entity theories (a dark green approach). Absence of such legislative amendments, it is still arguable that directors' duties are sufficiently flexible to require directors to pay attention to climate risks where they pose a material and foreseeable risk to the company and its shareholders, but they are not as facilitative to corporate climate action as they could, and should, be.

While company law maintains some flexibility to evolve in the face of escalating climate concerns, climate change is currently pushed by company law into the realm of environmental and energy regulation, voluntary codes of conduct, or non-regulatory mechanisms such as market mechanisms. These mechanisms are currently inadequate to force or even encourage companies to reduce their emissions, although these areas of law are changing quickly, motivated mainly by the Paris Agreement. The next chapter will examine the adequacy of international environmental law, and non-regulatory mechanisms such as market mechanisms, to temper the shareholder primacy theory and, as a result, corporate GHG emissions.

4

International and Transnational Climate Change Law and Policies

> By comparison to what it could have been, it's a miracle. By comparison to what it should have been, it's a disaster.
>
> —George Monbiot, 12 December 2015

This quote by Guardian columnist George Monbiot summed up what many negotiators and activists in the climate area felt about the Paris Agreement. With hindsight and the growing popularism amongst leaders in both developed and developing countries, the first part of this quote seems more appropriate. The Paris Agreement now looks like a miracle, even though achieving the global temperature goals agreed within it seems even further away than they did in 2015. Despite this lack of progress, the almost uniform ratification of the agreement by countries after decades of unsuccessful climate negotiations was a remarkable achievement. Companies, including some carbon-major companies, also facilitated its agreement. While the United States submitted a motion to withdraw from the agreement in 2019, and other countries have not been as ambitious as they should be to meet global temperature goals, the Paris Agreement has still served as a powerful normative catalyst to many actors, including non-state actors.

A number of international treaties and initiatives focus on climate change, and a few global initiatives focus specifically on the role of companies in climate change. While international treaties such as the UNFCCC and the Paris Agreement do not formally include companies as parties to them, the Paris Agreement negotiations, in particular, recognised the important role of non-state actors in tackling climate change. Provisions in the Paris Agreement acknowledge and reflect a growing awareness by states of the influence (both positive and negative) of companies in the area of climate change. In addition to state-made international law, transnational initiatives are also emerging. Global initiatives such as the Task Force on Climate-Related Financial Disclosures (TCFD) and the Principles on Climate Obligations of Enterprises have started to outline what existing and future corporate obligations on climate change are, and may become. Given the accelerating and intensifying impacts of climate change, it is likely that many of these obligations will crystallise into legal obligations in the near future.

This chapter assesses mitigation requirements for companies to substantially reduce or eliminate GHGs in various international and transnational agreements and initiatives, including formal and informal mechanisms. Formal international law mechanisms include state-based international law in the environmental, energy and climate change areas, such as multilateral environmental agreements (MEAs). Informal or transnational mechanisms include corporate social responsibility (CSR) initiatives, codes of practice and principles. Transnational environmental regulation can be understood as environmental regulation beyond the state.[1] Regulation has been described as a deliberate exercise of influence on a target's behaviour designed to either stabilise or modify their behaviour, performed with a certain degree of authority and persistence.[2] It is a subset of governance, which includes all processes and institutions, both formal and informal, that guide and restrain collective activities of a group.[3] Some of the initiatives in this chapter are 'quasi-regulatory' as they are fully developed and implemented by private actors and not states. Some are a combination of state and non-state actor influence, or public–private partnerships in rule-setting.[4]

This chapter will provide an overview of the role of the state in international environmental lawmaking, an analysis of key MEAs, including international agreements on climate change, such as the UNFCCC, the Kyoto Protocol (KP) and the Paris Agreement, and assess the value and efficacy of CSR initiatives and other climate-related public–private partnerships. While internationally binding agreements that deal with climate change are applicable to states only, they exert a direct pressure on states and an indirect one on companies. The chapter will analyse states' roles and obligations under international conventions, as well as corporate obligations under both formal and informal mechanisms.

Lack of binding international obligations on companies contributed to the re-emergence of transnational environmental regulation, including the CSR movement and global initiatives such as the United Nations Global Compact, and private standard-setting and disclosure efforts such as the ISO 14000 and the Carbon Disclosure Project (CDP). Newer initiatives such as the TCFD and the Principles on Climate Obligations of Enterprises highlight more specific obligations for companies at the global level and target the intersection of corporate and climate change law.

---

[1] Veerle Heyvaert, 'Transnationalization of Law: Rethinking Law Through Transnational Environmental Regulation', (2017) 6 *Transnational Environmental Law* 205, 206.
[2] Ibid.
[3] Ibid.
[4] Doris Fuchs, *Business Power in Global Governance* (Lynne Rienner 2007), 112.

4.1 INTERNATIONAL TREATIES ON CLIMATE CHANGE

Formal regulation encompasses a fairly narrow category of laws and regulations which are state-based and include international conventions and protocols, as well as domestic legislation and policy. At both the international and national level, formal regulation is the result of state-based negotiation and enforcement and is therefore compromise laden. International competitiveness concerns result in international and domestic laws and policies that are vague and often require little in the way of significant reduction of emissions from states. International agreements on climate change have led to some domestic movement on climate change with the introduction of a number of instruments to deal with climate change,[5] as well as elevating public concern and awareness both domestically in the United Kingdom and around the world, on the climate crisis.

4.1.1 *The Role of the State in Environmental Law-Making*

Climate change is a complex, transboundary and therefore global issue. Sources of GHG emissions originate at the individual, company, regional and state levels. States have traditionally been reluctant to take unilateral action to reduce their GHG emissions due to concerns about ensuring the competitiveness of their businesses, and have played a largely ambivalent role in regulating transboundary, polycentric and global environmental issues. At the international level, significant competition exists between states regarding their levels of regulation. Firms and other regulated entities may practice a type of 'regulatory arbitrage' by exploiting the differences between national regulatory environments to their advantage.[6] Regulatory arbitrage reduces the freedom and scope of regulators[7] which may affect the level of ambition and commitment states are willing to make in international treaties. As a result, in the arena of climate change, states will be constrained not only by the costs of abatement domestically, but also by international competitiveness concerns of carbon leakage.[8] These dual concerns significantly constrain states, particularly industrialised states, when enacting specific domestic regulation on

---

[5] These include the climate change levy, renewable obligations and general energy market reform in the 1990s.
[6] Amit M. Sachdera, 'Regulatory Competition in European Company Law' (2010) 30 Eu. J. L. Econ. 137, 137.
[7] Jonathan R. Macey, 'Regulatory Globalization as a Response to Regulatory Competition' (2003) 52 Emory L. J. 1353, 1362.
[8] The Department for Business, Innovation and Skills (BIS) estimates that levels carbon leakage could reach 41 per cent if non-European suppliers gain competitive advantage over EU suppliers, See 'Cumulative Impacts of Energy and Climate Change: Policies on Carbon Leakage' (*BIS* February 2012) www.gov.uk/government/uploads/system/uploads/attachment_data/file/31732/12-581-cumulative-impacts-policies-on-carbon-leakage.pdf (accessed 1 June 2015).

climate change.⁹ As a result, most progress on climate change regulation has taken place at the international level. The success of the Paris Agreement may lie not in requiring states to reduce their emissions, but in the creation of an international, normative direction of travel towards reaching the agreed long-term temperature goals in a carbon-constrained world. The agreement incentivises bottom-up, nationally determined actions by states, but also by sub-state and non-state actors, which should increase in ambition over time.

There is no international environmental parliament or lawmaking body and, as a result, international organisations, and the UN and its subsidiary bodies, in particular, have become the leading fora for international environmental lawmaking.[10] International treaties, customary international law, non-binding resolutions and state-based diplomacy constitute the main body of international environmental law.[11] States are also the central actors and subjects of international law and they play a primary role in shaping and adopting international environmental law.[12] There is a direct relationship between national goals of states and the international treaties and agreements they create. Ambitions of states, when crafting and implementing international environmental law, depend on their individual economic, political, cultural, geographical and ecological interests.[13] While the negotiation process amongst almost 200 UN member states can be a complex process in and of itself, complex environmental problems, such as climate change, pose additional challenges to the multilateral negotiation system.

Treaties are one of the main sources of international environmental law; however, they can pander to the lowest common denominator. Agreed outcomes must accommodate the interests and concerns of all states involved in the negotiations, and therefore are compromise laden. Negotiations are affected by the varying power of each state involved.[14] States are often driven by economic self-interest and the desire to secure or maintain international competitive advantages.[15] They are, to a lesser extent, concerned with environmental issues. As a result, states do commit to MEAs on particular environmental problems,[16] but often negotiate for low levels of obligations. If a number of states are reluctant to bind themselves to strict

---

[9] Jonathan Baert Wiener, 'Global Environmental Regulation: Instrument Choice in Legal Context' (1999) 108(4) Yale L. J. 677, 691–693.
[10] Patricia Birnie and Alan Boyle, *International Law & The Environment* (3rd edn, Oxford University Press 2009) 13.
[11] Ibid., 10.
[12] Philippe Sands and Jacqueline Peel, *Principles of International Environmental Law* (3rd edn, Cambridge University Press 2012) 51.
[13] Ibid., 51.
[14] Abram Chayes and Antonia Handler Chayes, *The New Sovereignty Compliance with International Regulatory Agreements* (1998) 6.
[15] Richard B. Stewart, 'Environmental Regulation and International Competitiveness' (1993) 102 (8) Yale L. J. 2039, 2041.
[16] For example, the Convention on Long-Range Transboundary Air Pollution adopted on 13 November 1979, Vienna Convention for the Protection of the Ozone Layer 22 March 1985, the London Convention on the Prevention of Marine Pollution by Dumping of

obligations, merely hortatory or weak language is often the end result.[17] This type of language can be norm-creating and lead to further and stricter obligations in the future, but this is a gradual process at best, and treaties with such weak language can be ineffectual.

While there are over 500 MEAs in existence, and compliance levels are generally high, global environmental conditions continue to deteriorate.[18] Weak MEA obligations do provide leverage and discretion to states to unilaterally decide whether to increase their national ambition in a particular environmental area. International treaties and their subsidiary bodies, such as the UNFCCC and the Conference of Parties are, at the moment, the main international negotiation forum for dealing with climate change. While the Paris Agreement is a binding legal treaty, many of its provisions are drafted in language that is not legally binding, or constitutes soft law obligations, but can provide strong normative pressures. While international treaties are binding only on states, companies do participate and play a role during the negotiations of these treaties and have been the subject of international efforts over the years to impose environmental obligations on them.

4.1.2 The First Phase of the International Environmental Movement and Corporate Environmentalism: 1972–1992

International efforts to regulate companies directly began in the 1970s, which saw the initial phase of growth by multinational companies.[19] A UN-formed group recommended that a binding Code of Conduct be developed to regulate TNC behaviour.[20] Efforts to agree to such a code continued for fifteen years under the United Nations Commission on Transnational Corporations (UNTNC) mechanism, but collapsed in 1992.[21] The OECD Guidelines for Multinational Enterprises were established in 1976 as non-binding guidelines for multinational companies to use and continue to be one of the only international guidelines directly applicable to companies. International business had a profound influence on the drafting of the Guidelines that were negotiated through the Committee on International

---

Wastes and Other Matter 29 December 1972, the United Nations Convention on the Law of the Sea 10 December 1982, the Convention on Biological Diversity 5 June 1992.

[17] Abram Chayes and Antonia Handler Chayes, 'On Compliance' (1993) 20(1) *International Organization* 175, 189.

[18] Teall Crossen, 'Multilateral Environmental Agreements and the Compliance Continuum' (2003–2004) 16 Geo. Intl. Envtl. L. Rev. 473, 474.

[19] Emily F. Carusco and Jang B. Singh, 'Towards Holding Transnational Corporations Responsible for Human Rights' (2010) 22(4) *European Business Review* 432, 434.

[20] 'Effects of TNCs on Development and International Relations' (1974) UN Doc E/5500/Rev.1/ST/ESA/6, 55.

[21] Carusco and Singh (n 20) 434; Elisa Morgera, 'The UN and Corporate Environmental Responsibility: Between International Regulation and Partnerships' (2006) 15(1) *RECEIL* 95, 96.

Investment and Multinational Enterprises (CIME), who was 'vehemently opposed'[22] to the Guidelines being anything more than voluntary guidelines. The original OECD Guidelines did not include any environmental provisions until 1991, when an environment chapter was added.

The two major international conferences held by nation states were the Stockholm Conference in 1972 and the Rio Conference in 1992. These are formally known as the 1972 United Nations Conference on the Human Environment (UNCHE) and the 1992 United Nations Conference on Environment and Development (UNCED), respectively. UNCHE resulted in the Stockholm Declaration, a non-binding set of principles that set the stage for the Rio Declaration agreed at UNCED.[23]

In 1990, in preparation for the Rio Conference, forty-eight TNCs established a lobbying group called the Business Council for Sustainable Development. Their position was that only voluntary approaches to corporate sustainable development should be agreed at the 1992 UNCED.[24] TNCs were heavily involved in the UNCED negotiations, to the point that critics claimed the entire UNCED process had been 'co-opted'[25] by business. Both the United States and the United Kingdom lobbied during the UNCED process to ensure that no binding environmental obligations fell upon companies.[26] Those efforts were successful as the outcome documents of the 1992 UNCED included Agenda 21 and the Rio Declaration, which included only voluntary, non-binding efforts on companies to act in environmentally responsible ways.[27] UNCED also produced the 1992 UNFCCC, which also included no binding emission reduction targets on either states or companies.

By the end of the 1990s, negotiations on both the Draft Code of Conduct for TNCs and the Multilateral Agreement on Investment (MAI)[28] had collapsed, and no binding international code of conduct for TNCs existed. The quasi-voluntary nature of the OECD Guidelines, together with the flexible but inconsistent and

---

[22] Sorcha Macleod and Douglas Lewis, 'Transnational Corporations Power, Influence and Responsibility' (2004) 4(1) *Global Social Policy* 77, 80.

[23] Principle 21 of the Stockholm Declaration in particular has continued to have enduring value in international environment law, setting out the customary international rule on transboundary harm. In addition to the Stockholm Declaration, the United Nations Environment Programme was established, as well as a global action plan and an environmental fund.

[24] Jennifer Clapp, 'Global Environmental Governance for Corporate Responsibility and Accountability' (2005) 5(3) *Global Environmental Politics* 23, 25.

[25] David Hallman, 'Transnational Corporations and Sustainable Development: Post-Rio Challenges' (1993) 25(4) *Peace Research* 69, 74.

[26] Ibid., 73.

[27] Successful lobbying efforts continued by the World Business Council for Sustainable Development at both the World Summit on Sustainable Development in 2002 and at the Rio+20 conference in 2012, see Clapp (n 24) 26, 29.

[28] Negotiations collapsed in 1998 in part because business did not support the OECD's concessionary efforts to include binding language on social and environmental provisions. See David Egan, 'The Limits of Internationalization: a Neo-Gramscian Analysis of the Multilateral Agreement on Investment' (2001) 27 *Critical Sociology* 74, 85.

weak nature of its enforcement through National Contact Points (NCPs),[29] meant that the Guidelines were often critiqued from an environmental standpoint. While the NCPs have been more active in recent years (as highlighted in Chapter 6), the Guidelines do not explicitly cover climate change, nor contain recommended guidelines on the reduction of GHG emissions for companies. Instead, the Guidelines recommend the use of environmental management systems by companies.

Due to political tensions and successful lobbying efforts by TNCs, at the international level, only voluntary initiatives were applicable directly to companies during this era. While the 1992 Rio Conference did produce two binding international environmental agreements, these are binding only on states, and not companies, and many of the provisions of the UNFCCC are weak and currently require little more than the status quo from states, and require no formal obligations to reduce GHGs from companies. The UNFCCC framework did, however, lead to the negotiation of a more specific protocol with binding obligations on states in the late 1990s, and then led to the Paris Agreement. Lack of an international environmental framework binding on companies in the 1990s contributed to the large volume of voluntary initiatives at the corporate level during this time, which required little climate change mitigation action from companies. Despite the proliferation of voluntary initiatives in the 1990s and lack of international regulations binding on companies, the second phase of international environmental movement galvanised more action by companies on climate change. The normative force of these newer corporate actions and initiatives can be seen as creating almost a coerced form of voluntarism around climate change amongst companies, particularly amongst more progressive companies.

4.1.3 The Second Phase of the International Environmental Movement and Corporate Environmentalism: 1992–2015

While the UNFCCC contains no binding emission reduction targets for states, it does contain a number of principles and overarching obligations which apply directly to states. It is considered to be the main umbrella framework on international climate law. Article 2 of the UNFCCC sets out the ultimate objective of the UNFCCC as the 'stabilization of greenhouse gas concentrations in the atmosphere at a level that would prevent dangerous anthropogenic interference with the climate system'.[30] While the UNFCCC itself does not contain a definition of 'dangerous

---

[29] Sarah Fink Vendzules, 'The Struggle for Legitimacy in Environmental Standards Systems: The OECD Guidelines for Multinational Enterprises' (2010) 21 Colo. J. Intl. Envtl. L. & Poly 451, 488.
[30] United Nations Framework Convention on Climate Change, 9 May 1992, Article 2.

anthropogenic interference',[31] or a specific global temperature increase or atmospheric concentration target, the parties to the UNFCCC subsequently agreed in 2010 to limit temperature rise to 2°C above pre-industrial levels.[32]

The KP is a protocol agreed under the framework of the UNFCCC. It is a binding legal agreement with specific emissions targets for developed countries listed in 'Annex I' to reduce 'net' GHG emissions[33] by certain percentages for the first commitment period of 2008–12.[34] The United States never ratified the KP, although it was heavily involved in its negotiation. The European Union participated in the UNFCCC as a regional economic integration organisation[35], and GHG targets, therefore, became applicable to the European Union and its individual member nations. The European Union initially became a leader in the climate negotiations, as climate change became a 'saviour issue for EU integration'.[36] The United Kingdom also took on a climate change leadership role under Tony Blair.[37] Negotiations and debates surrounding the KP have focused on the costs of mitigation actions.[38] As a result, the existing targets agreed and imposed on developed states are weak, although the enforcement mechanism is extensive compared with most MEAs.[39] In addition, a number of developed countries such as Canada and Japan withdrew from the protocol, and so it governs an ever-decreasing percentage of global emissions.

After the KP was agreed, the 2007 Conference of the Parties meeting in Bali produced the Bali Action Plan,[40] which called for mitigation commitments from developed country Parties only, on the basis of common but differentiated responsibilities and respective capabilities (or CBDRC), as set out in Article 3(1) of the

---

[31] P. Brian Fisher, 'Shifting Global Climate Governance: Creating Long-Term Goods through UNFCCC Article 2' (2011) 8(3) *PORTAL* 23.

[32] FCCC/CP/2010/7/Add.1, 1/CP.16, para 4.

[33] Net emissions are calculated as the gross release of GHGs minus quantities of GHGs absorbed by carbon sinks such as forests; see Richard L. Sander, Michael J. Walsh, 'Kyoto or Not: Opportunities in Carbon Trading Are Here' (2001) 10 (3) *Environmental Quality Management* 53, 54.

[34] Prior to 2008, Article 3(2) states that parties were obligated to make demonstrable progress towards meeting their commitments.

[35] Lisanne Groen and Arne Niemann, 'The European Union at the Copenhagen Climate Negotiations: A Case of Contested EU Actorness and Effectiveness' (2013) 27 *International Relations* 308, 311.

[36] Ibid., 309.

[37] Although Schreurs and Tuberglien note this was largely an effort to distance the United Kingdom from the United States after the Iraq war, Mirenda A. Schreurs and Yves Tuberglien, 'Multi-Level Reinforcement: Explaining EU Leadership in Climate Change Mitigation' (2007) 7(4) *Global Environmental Politics* 19, 38.

[38] Elliot Diringer, 'Letting Go of Kyoto' (2011) 479 *Nature* 292, 292; Alexander Golub, Anil Markanalya, and Dominic Marcellino, 'Does the Kyoto Protocol Cost Too Much and Create Unbreakable Barriers for Economic Growth?' (2006) 24(4) *Contemporary Economic Policy* 520, 520.

[39] Will Catton, 'Dynamic Carbon Caps. Splitting the Bill: A Fairer Solution Post-Kyoto?' (2009) 37 *Energy Policy* 5636, 5636; Dieter Helm, 'The Kyoto Approach' (2012) 491 *Nature* 663, 664.

[40] FCCC/CP/2007/6/Add.1.

UNFCCC. The CBDRC principle is the cornerstone of the global climate regime,[41] and was designed to ensure equity and historic responsibility for GHG emissions, imposing the burden of action on to developed countries. However, the principle has papered over major disagreements between developed and developing countries concerning who is responsible for, and will ultimately pay for, the costs of climate change. Developing country Parties' commitment to CBDRC has become deeply problematic as some of the largest global emissions have shifted since the 1990s from developed to developing countries. By 2006, China had surpassed the United States as the largest global emitter of GHGs, and by 2010 had become the largest consumer of energy. By 2014, China had exceeded the European Union for per capita emissions.[42] Two of the four largest GHG emitters are now developing countries.[43]

Developing countries have cited poverty reduction and general development goals as the reasons they have refused to commit to legally binding reduction targets in international treaties over the years. To a large extent, this position is supported by the UNFCCC, which states that developed countries are to lead the way in combating climate change[44] and that the specific needs, circumstances and vulnerabilities of developing countries are to be fully considered by the parties.[45] EU emissions have, at the same time, declined from 19 per cent of global emissions in 1990 to 10 per cent in 2019, and the admission of fossil-fuel reliant Eastern European countries into the European Union has led to fragmentation in EU climate policy.[46] Perhaps, as a result, EU leadership in global climate policy diminished.[47]

At the same time, developed countries have consistently failed to accept their historic responsibility for climate change[48] or to provide leadership or adequate

---

[41] Jutta Brunnee and Charlotte Strack, 'The UNFCCC as a Negotiation Forum: Towards Common but More Differentiated Responsibilities' (2013) 13(5) *Climate Policy* 589, 590; Jennifer Marga and David Waskow, 'A New Look at Climate Equity in the UNFCCC' (2014) 14(1) *Climate Policy* 17, 17.

[42] Sneha Shah, 'After Overtaking USA in Carbon Emissions, China Surpasses USA in Energy Consumption as Well' (*Green World Investor*, 20 Jul 2010), www.greenworldinvestor.com/2010/07/20/after-overtaking-usa-in-carbon-emissionschina-surpasses-usa-in-energy-consumption-as-well/ (accessed 4 May 2017); Douglas Main, 'China Surpasses EU in Per Capita Carbon Emissions' (22 September 2014),, www.newsweek.com/china-surpasses-eu-capita-carbon-emissions-272357 (accessed 4 May 2017).

[43] Brunee and Strack (n 41) 591.

[44] UNFCCC (n 30) Article 3(1).

[45] Ibid., Article 3(2).

[46] Carolina B. Pavese and Diarmuid Torney, 'The Contribution of the European Union to Global Climate Governance: Exploring the Conditions for EU Actorness' (2012) 55 *Revista Brasileira de Política Internacional* 125, 128.

[47] Paul Taylor, 'Snubbed in Copenhagen, EU Weighs Climate Options' (13 January 2010), http://in.reuters.com/article/2010/01/13/idINIndia-45370820100113 (accessed 4 May 2017); Gavin Hewitt, 'Europe Snubbed in Copenhagen?' (22 December 2009), www.bbc.co.uk/blogs/legacy/thereporters/gavinhewitt/2009/12/s_5.html (accessed 4 May 2017).

[48] The EU may be an exception in this regard as regionally it conditionally agreed to more emission reductions if other developed countries did the same.

funding to developing countries to assist them in the transition to a green economy. The United States refused to ratify the KP, while Canada, Australia, New Zealand and Japan have either left the KP or refused to agree to a second commitment period under it.[49] As a result, the KP only covers approximately 35 per cent of global emissions,[50] leading some to question whether any domestic action in the United Kingdom to reduce GHG emissions should be taken until developing countries committed to binding legal targets.[51]

In addition to their obligations under the UNFCCC, there are strong arguments as to why developed countries should take the lead on reducing their GHG emissions. As Henry Shue writes, to insist that no developing country emits any more carbon emissions would relegate significant parts of their populations to grinding poverty,[52] and deny them even subsistence emissions. If developed countries had taken appropriate measures as they had committed to do from 1992, they could have made room for subsistence emissions from developing countries without an increase in overall global totals of emissions.[53] These issues of increased emissions from developing countries and relative inaction historically from a number of developed countries, meant that a new international legal treaty governing climate change was required. Despite this acknowledged need, issues of equity, historic responsibility and differentiation plagued the negotiations of what was ultimately to become the Paris Agreement.

4.1.4 *The Paris Agreement*

After many years of negotiations, the Paris Agreement and its related Conference of Parties (COP) decision were concluded at the end of 2015. The Agreement itself is a historic treaty as, unlike the KP, it includes obligations for both developed and developing states, although many of the substantive provisions are collective obligations.[54] It adopted a 'bottom-up' approach to global climate regulation, and relies on quasi-voluntary nationally determined contributions (or NDCs) from states to reduce their GHG emissions. Powerful states, such as the United States, India and China, did not want result-based obligations in relation to their NDCs, and so there are no legally binding obligations imposed on individual parties to meet any

---

[49] The Doha Amendment was agreed in 2012, establishing a second commitment period of the KP, and after a considerable delay, will come into force on 31 December 2020, https://unfccc.int/process/the-kyoto-protocol/the-doha-amendment (accessed 15 November 2020).
[50] Beatriz Perez de las Heras, 'Beyond Kyoto: The EU's Contribution to a More Sustainable World Economy' (2013) 19(4) European L. J. 577, 585.
[51] David Campbell, 'After Doha: What Has Climate Change Policy Accomplished?' (2013) 25(1) J Environmental Law 125, 133.
[52] Henry Shue, 'Climate Hope: Implementing the Exit Strategy' (2012) 13 Chi J Intl L 381, 391.
[53] Ibid., 392.
[54] Daniel Bodansky, 'The Legal Character of the Paris Agreement' (2016) 25(2) *RECEIL*, 144, 150.

emission caps or targets that are included in their NDCs.[55] Instead, many of the legally binding obligations are ones of conduct or process; all parties have obligations to submit successive NDCs, which include commitments that each party intends to achieve. Parties also have obligations to pursue domestic mitigation measures, but this obligation is qualified by language that the measures are those that aim to achieve the objectives of their NDCs.[56]

The Agreement contains many positive provisions, including a collective, ambitious long-term temperature goal of holding any increase in the global average temperature to 'well below 2°C', with an aspirational goal of pursuing efforts to limit that increase to 1.5°C above pre-industrial levels.[57] There are, however, no individual obligations imposed on states to ensure that their NDCs collectively meet the agreed long-term temperature goals, or that they make emission cuts proportionate to their global or per capita emissions. The Agreement does contain some top-down provisions to help ensure ambition is collectively pursued. There is a normative or soft law expectation that successive NDCs will demonstrate progress over time.[58] The level of progressive ambition in NDCs, however, is left entirely up to each party to determine.[59] Top-down provisions include a five-yearly global stocktake to assess collective progress. The periodic global stocktakes are to consider progress towards the achievement of the goals in Article 4(1),[60] and could incentivise states to include more ambitious targets within their NDCs.

There are some collective and ambitious goals included in Article 4(1). Parties are to achieve a balance between anthropogenic emissions by sources and removals by sinks by mid-century. This balance is commonly understood as achieving net zero emissions, but the reference does not specify a particular date for achieving this goal. In order to achieve that balance, emissions of GHGs from fossil fuels should end by mid-century.[61] The date of mid-century is more ambitious than the previous language proposed for Article 4(1), which referred to 'by 2100'.[62] Article 4(1), combined

---

[55] Lavanya Rajamani, 'Ambition and Differentiation in the 2015 Paris Agreement: Interpretation Possibilities and Underlying Politics' (2016) 65(2) *Intl. and Comparative .L Q.* 1, 7.
[56] FCCC/CP/2015/L.9, Article 4(2).
[57] Ibid., Article 2(1)(a).
[58] Ibid., Articles 14(1) and 3.
[59] Rajamani (n 55) 11.
[60] Mukul Sanwal, 'The Paris Climate: A New Global Vision, Challenges of the Urban Transition Remain and Negotiations Continue' www.indiaenvironmentportal.org.in/content/424852/the-paris-climate-a-new-global-vision-challenges-of-the-urban-transition-remain-and-negotiations-continue/ (accessed 4 May 2017).
[61] Michael Gerrard, 'Legal Implications of the Paris Agreement for Fossil Fuels' (*Climate Law Blog*, 19 December 2015), http://blogs.law.columbia.edu/climatechange/2015/12/19/legal-implications-of-the-paris-agreement-for-fossil-fuels/ (accessed 4 May 2020).
[62] Kelly Levin, Jennifer Morgan and Jiawel Song, 'INSIDER: Understanding the Paris Agreement's Long-term Goal to Limit Global Warming' (*World Resources Institute*, 15 December 2015), www.wri.org/blog/2015/12/insider-understanding-paris-agreement%E2%80%99s-long-term-goal-limit-global-warming (accessed 4 May 2020).

with the long-term temperature goals, can send a strong signal to business that governments are serious about ending fossil fuel emissions,[63] and therefore can send indirect regulatory messages to companies and their directors. The language about finance flows also has the potential of sending a strong signal to the private sector for them to re-assess and redirect their investments.[64] The provision does not, however, include a date when global emissions must peak and then start decreasing, an annual rate of decline, or the date when fossil fuel use should end.[65] The agreement also does not include language about removing fossil fuel subsidies, instituting a price on carbon, or mainstreaming enabling environments.[66]

The Paris Agreement is historic as it encourages commitments from non-state actors, and over 1200 stakeholders signed the Paris Pledge of Action.[67] The Lima–Paris Action Agenda encourages non-state actors to contribute to state-based NDCs, and was established in 2014 before the Paris Agreement was agreed. Non-state actors, including many companies, were active in the negotiations and encouraged high ambition on the part of states. Many non-state actors, in fact, wanted to become a party to the agreement itself, demonstrating a very different approach to international environmental treaties than was on offer in the 1992 UNCED negotiations, but this approach was rejected by most state parties. Despite the fact that only states became parties to the Paris Agreement and are formally bound by its provisions, the process of the treaty's negotiation and the almost universal agreement to it on the part of states, established strong normative obligations and a 'direction of travel' towards collectively reaching its long-term temperature goals amongst state and non-state actors alike. As a result, non-state actors have become a core element of climate governance.[68] Even after the United States submitted a notice to withdraw from the Paris Agreement, a number of non-state actors recommitted to the obligations of the United States under the Agreement. For example, the 'We Are Still In' coalition of civil society organisations and businesses have pledged to implement the Paris Agreement targets in the United States.[69] Non-state actor contributions to the

---

[63] Daniel Bodansky, 'The Paris Climate Change Agreement: A New Hope?' (2016) 110(2) *American J. International Law* 288.
[64] Ralph Bodle, Lena Donet and Mathias Duwe, 'The Paris Agreement: Analysis, Assessment and Outlook' (Ecological Institute, January 2016), http://ecologic.eu/sites/files/event/2016/ecologic_institute_2016_paris_agreement_assessment.pdf (accessed 4 May 2020).
[65] Daniel Tanuro, 'Specter of Geoengineering Haunts Paris Climate Deal' (25 January 2016), http://climateandcapitalism.com/2016/01/25/the-specter-of-geoengineering-haunts-the-paris-climate-agreement/ (accessed 4 May 2020).
[66] Ibid., 13.
[67] Kenneth W. Abbott, 'Orchestrating Experimentation in Non-State Environmental Commitments' (2017) 26(4) *Environmental Politics* 738, 750 .
[68] See http://climateaction.unfccc.int/ (accessed 15 July 2020); Thomas Hale, '"All Hands on Deck": The Paris Agreement and Non-State Climate Action' (2016) 16(3) *Global Environmental Politics* 12, 14.
[69] See www.wearestillin.com (accessed 15 July 2020).

Paris Agreement commitments include a mix of domestic or state-level action, but also CSR and transnational private environmental governance initiatives.

4.2 CORPORATE SOCIAL RESPONSIBILITY AND PRIVATE ENVIRONMENTAL GOVERNANCE

From the 1970s to the 1990s, the international business community strongly resisted any internationally binding regulations directly governing their environmental activities. This approach was broadly consistent with the Anglo-American shareholder primacy approach, which generally denies 'any significant role for the "interventionist regulatory state"'.[70] The UK government itself has been mindful of the costs that regulation imposes upon firms, and adopted an official position in a 1985 White Paper that the costs of regulation would be taken into account when any new regulation is suggested.[71] This antagonistic approach to regulating company activities facilitated the rise of the CSR movement as a voluntary, self-regulatory approach to corporate environmentalism, and formed part of the deregulatory movement in the 1970s and 1980s.[72] While a resurgence of business responsibility took place in the 1960s and 1970s in the United States, Europe and the United Kingdom have now become the major centre of gravity for CSR since then.[73]

Many CSR initiatives relied upon by businesses over the years, particularly those used by carbon-major corporations, failed to link the CSR initiatives to significant emission reductions. But attitudes of many companies towards climate change have evolved dramatically since the 1990s. Many large and emission-intensive companies have instituted their own private environmental governance regimes, which led to significant emission reductions and committed to net zero emission targets. Some carbon-major companies are even collaborating with NGOs to commit to specific emission reductions. These initiatives are often motivated not by regulation or the fear of regulation, but by the companies themselves in fulfilment of their social licence to operate. These initiatives can no longer be seen as purely voluntary, but are in fact the result of a type of compulsion felt by the companies and their directors

---

[70] Marc Moore, *Corporate Governance in the Shadow of the State* (Hart 2013), 92, although note that some interventionist contractarians are amenable to some regulatory intervention by company law.
[71] Department of Trade and Industry, 'Lifting the Burden' (White Paper, Cm 9571, 1985).
[72] David Sadler and Stuart Lloyd, 'Neo-liberalizing Corporate Social Responsibility: A Political Economy of Corporate Citizenship' (2008) 40(4) *Geoforum* 613, 614; Rhys Jenkins, 'Corporate Codes of Conduct Self-Regulation in a Global Economy' (2001) UN Research Institute for Social Development, Progress Paper iii; Jette S Knudsen and Dana Brown, 'Why Governments Intervene: Exploring Mixed Motives for Public Policies on Corporate Social Responsibility' (2015) 30(1) *Public Policy and Administration* 51, 61.
[73] David Vogel, *The Market for Virtue The Potential and Limits of Corporate Social Responsibility* (Brookings 2006) 6–7.

to act in a socially responsible manner on climate change, often in the absence of state regulation.

4.2.1 The Early Days of Corporate Social Responsibility

The CSR is usually understood to mean non-state-based initiatives that are developed and implemented entirely by private entities. There is no universal definition of CSR,[74] although Archie Carroll has provided a pyramid approach to CSR that is often referred to by academics.[75] The economic incentive of 'be profitable' forms the base of the pyramid, followed by the legal obligation to obey the law, the ethical imperative, and lastly the philanthropic or charitable imperative.[76] The European Commission has provided another well-used definition of CSR as a 'concept whereby companies integrate social and environmental concerns into their business operations and in their interactions with their stakeholders on a voluntary basis'.[77] A number of academics have determined that CSR involves companies voluntarily going 'beyond compliance'[78] or focusing on the triple bottom line of people, profits and the planet.[79] It could also be understood as simply an

---

[74] Leonid Polishchuk, 'Corporate Social Responsibility or Government Regulation: An Analysis of Institutional Choice' (2009) 52(8) *Problem of Economic Transition* 73, 75; Abigail McWilliams, Donald S. Siegel and Patrick M. Wright, 'CSR: Strategic Implications' (2006) 43(1) *Journal of Management Studies*, 8; Dimitros Pesmatzoglou et al., 'Extractive Multinationals and Corporate Social Responsibility: A Commitment Towards Achieving the Goals of Sustainable Development or only as a Management Strategy?' (2014) 26 *Journal of Inteernational Development* 187, 188.

[75] Archie B. Carroll, 'The Pyramid of Corporate Social Responsibility: Toward the Moral Management of Organizational Stakeholders' (1991) 34(4) *Business Horizons*, 42; H Yeung, F Huang and X Liu, 'Global Influence of European Corporate Social Responsibility: China as a Case Study' (2015) University of Leicester School of Law Research Paper No. 15-17, 5; Pauline Poncy, 'Multinational Corporate Social Responsibility and Sustainable Environmental Standards across Borders: A Comparative Analysis of Five American Multinational Corporations Producing in the State of Guanajuato, Mexico', 6, www.academia.edu/7024196/Multinational_Corporate_Social_Responsibility_and_Sustainable_Environmental_Standards_across_Borders_A_Comparative_Analysis_of_Five_American_Multinational_Companies_producing_in_the_State_of_Guanajuato_Mexico (accessed 30 May 2020).

[76] Carroll (n 75) 42. Carroll subsequently developed a Venn diagram of CSR, see Mark S. Schwartz and Archie B. Carroll, 'Corporate Social Responsibility: A Three-Domain Approach' (2003) 13(4) *Business Ethics Quarterly* 503.

[77] Commission of the European Communities, 'Promoting a European Framework for Corporate Social Responsibility' Green Paper (Brussels, 18 July 2001), para 20.

[78] McWilliams, Siegel and Wright (n 74) 1; Hoje Jo and Maretmo A. Harjoto, 'The Causal Effect of Corporate Governance on Corporate Social Responsibility' (2012) 106 *Journal of Business Ethics* 53, 54.

[79] Johan Graafland, Corrie Mazereeuw and Van der Duijn Schouten, 'Motives for Corporate Social Responsibility' (2012) 160 *De Economist* 377, 379; Reinhard Steurer, 'The Role of Governments in CSR: Characterising Public Policies on Corporate Social Responsibility in Europe' (March 2010) 43(1) *Policy Sciences* 49, 50.

'umbrella' term encompassing the relationship between companies and civil society.[80] CSR can be a more cost-effective mechanism than national regulation at tackling externalities, precisely as a result of governments failing to efficiently deal with externalities which companies could be incentivised to internalise.[81] There has also been an attempt to define environmental CSR as voluntary, environmentally friendly actions, or the internalising of negative environmental externalities.[82]

Environmental debates on sustainable development in the 1990s viewed CSR as part of long-term business sustainability initiatives,[83] but these have yet to crystalise into a coherent definition.[84] Doris Fuchs notes that public–private partnerships are a means for TNCs, in particular, to exercise their structural power by enabling businesses to influence agenda-setting directly.[85] Self-regulatory arrangements such as CSR initiatives have increased in number and autonomy from the state, and provide an important channel for businesses to actively set rules and gain political influence.[86] Many environmental CSR initiatives focus on the cost-savings that could be achieved by environmental activities, such as waste reduction and reduced natural-resource consumption.[87] It could be that environmental CSR was motivated primarily only by cost savings, staving off the threat of environmental regulation and the consumer demand of green goods and services,[88] but these initiatives have evolved into something more, particularly in the context of climate change.

---

[80] Pesmatzoglou et al. (n 74) 191.
[81] Andrew Johnston, 'Facing Up to Social Cost: The Real Meaning of Corporate Social Responsibility' (2011) 20 Griffith L. Rev. 221, 226.
[82] Thomas P. Lyon and John W. Maxwell, 'Corporate Social Responsibility and the Environment: A Theoretical Perspective' (2008) 2(2) *Review of Environmental Economics and Policy*, 2; Johnston, (n 81) 221.
[83] Laura Albaredo, Josep M. Lozano and Tanyko Ysa, 'Public Policies on Corporate Social Responsibility: The Role of Governments in Europe' (2007) 74(4) *Journal of Business Ethics* 391, 403.
[84] Lyon and Maxwell (n 82) 17; Rodrigo Lozano, 'A Holistic Perspective on Corporate Sustainability Drivers' (2015) 22 *Environmental Management* 32, 33; Scott Victor Valentine, 'The Green Onion: A Corporate Environmental Strategy Framework' (2010) 17 *Corporate Social Responsibility and Envtly Management* 284, 286.
[85] Fuchs (n 4), 112.
[86] Ibid., 119.
[87] Piotr Mazurkiewicz, 'Corporate Environmental Responsibility: Is a Common CSR Framework Possible?' (World Bank, 2004), 8. https://documents.worldbank.org/en/publication/documents-reports/documentdetail/577051468339093024/corporate-environmental-responsibility-is-a-common-csr-framework-possible (accessed 30 May 2020); Commission of the European Communities, 'Promoting a European Framework for Corporate Social Responsibility' (Green Paper, Brussels, 2001) para 39.
[88] Christiane Reif and Sascha Rexhauser, 'Good Enough! Are Socially Responsible Companies the More Successful Environmental Innovators?' (2015) ZEW Centre for European Economic Research, Discussion Paper No. 15-018, 2.

4.2.2 *Corporate Social Responsibility and the Social License to Operate*

CSR attempts to align profits with socially responsible behaviour,[89] and to be more inclusive towards non-shareholder stakeholders found in wider society. It is a business-initiated response to perceived shareholder exclusivity, and an effort to reach out to other stakeholder constituents as well as to society at large. Companies tend to employ stakeholder language because they suspect that simply employing shareholder wealth maximisation rhetoric is not sufficient to satisfy public expectations of the role of companies in society.[90]

While there is no international definition of CSR, companies often see CSR as providing them with the 'social licence to operate'.[91] Some companies operate beyond the requirements of regulation as a result of the confluence of pressures of various licences.[92] These include the licence to operate (consisting of shareholder return requirements as well as social harm), the regulatory licence (consisting of regulatory compliance requirements) and the social licence (consisting of various stakeholder pressures on the company).[93] It is often only the regulatory and social licences that will demand reductions of emissions from companies,[94] and these efforts will be constrained by economic concerns if directors recommend non-incremental activities which are costly and affect shareholder returns.[95]

There are significant differences in the approach to CSR under corporate governance, connected to whether the jurisdiction is shareholder-centric or adopts a more stakeholder-inclusive approach. Therefore, even CSR initiatives are closely connected to directors' understandings of what corporate statutes require and permit. For example, the Canadian Business Corporations Act in Section 122(1)(a) expressly states that a director must act in the best interests of the company.[96] There is no mention of shareholders in this provision. This express language was included in the statute with the aim that Canadian corporate governance would move away from the English shareholder-centric approach.[97]

---

[89] Polishchuk (n 74) 76.
[90] Lisa M. Fairfax, 'The Rhetoric of Corporate Law: The Impact of Stakeholder Rhetoric on Corporate Norms' (2005) 31 J. Corp. L. 675, 699.
[91] Pesmatzoglou et al. (n 74) 189.
[92] Robert A. Kagan, Dorothy Thornton and Neil Gunningham, 'Explaining Corporate Environmental Performance: How Does Regulation Matter?' (2003) 37(1) *Law & Society Review*, 76.
[93] Ibid., 77.
[94] Ibid., 78.
[95] Ibid., 68.
[96] R.S.C. 1985 C-44.
[97] Waitzer and Jaswal note that the Dickerson Committee which recommended the language declined to give guidance on how this provision should be interpreted but with the desire that Canadian courts would escape the 'constraints' of English law, interpreted as shareholder-centric constraints, Edward J. Waitzer and Johnny Jaswal, 'Peoples, BCE and the Good Corporate Citizen' (2009) 47(3) Osgood Hall L. J. 439, 440.

Two Supreme Court of Canada decisions confirmed a more stakeholder-inclusive approach. In *Peoples Department Stores Inc. (Trustee of) v. Wise*, the Supreme Court took a broad view of the corporate purpose, stating that the best interests of the company should not be read as only the best interests of the shareholders, but it may be legitimate for directors to consider the interests of shareholders, employees, suppliers, creditors, consumers and the environment.[98] In the subsequent case of *BCE Inc. v. 1976 Debentureholders*, the Supreme Court affirmed this approach, and stated directors have broad discretion to not take a short-term, shareholder maximisation approach but instead could act in the best interests of the corporation viewed as a good corporate citizen.[99] In interviews with thirty-two Canadian corporate law practitioners, Carol Liao documents that while, theoretically, practitioners considered the best interests of the company to be different than shareholders, in practice those interests were often considered as one and the same.[100] However, after the *BCE* decisions, legal advisors have informed boards that they can and should take into account non-shareholder interests.[101]

Some developing countries have taken a more progressive approach to CSR. The first corporate governance report was published in South Africa in 1994 by the Institute of Directors in Southern Africa (IoDSA) and the King Committee on Corporate Governance. The report adopted a similar approach of comply or explain as the Cadbury Report in the United Kingdom. The King Report principles were put forward as voluntary and non-legislative principles and recommendations on corporate governance, but have gained in influence and traction within the corporate community in South Africa. The 2006 case of *Minister of Water Affairs and Forestry v. Stilfontein Gold Mining Company Limited and Others*[102] regarding breach of an environmental regulation stated that the King Report recommendations, while voluntary, were widely accepted by the corporate community. One of the foundational characteristics of the King Report has been that of social responsibility. The revised Companies Act 2008 of South Africa[103] states, in Section 7, that the Act reaffirms the concept of the company as a means of achieving both economic and social benefits, and refers to the Act as a means of promoting the Bill of Rights in the South African Constitution, which includes a right to an environment that is not detrimental to the health or well-being of the people of South Africa.[104]

The newest King IV report, issued in 2016, expressly situates itself in the global context of climate change, the UN SDGs agreed in 2015, the Africa 2063 Agenda

---

[98] [2004] 3 SCR 461, para 42.
[99] [2008] 3 SCR 560, para 81.
[100] Carol Liao, 'A Canadian Model of Corporate Governance' (2014) The Dalhousie L J 560, 572.
[101] Ibid., 576.
[102] [2006] ZAGPHC 47 (S. Afr. H. C.).
[103] Companies Act No. 71, 2008.
[104] Section 24, Constitution of South Africa, 1996.

and the South African National Development Plan 2030. It includes a foundational concept of value creation accomplished in a sustainable manner.[105] Principle 3 states that a company's governing body should ensure the organisation is and is seen to be a responsible corporate citizen.[106] This term is defined in the report as a recognition that the organisation is an integral part of the broader society in which it operates, affording the organisation standing as a juristic person in that society with rights but also responsibilities and obligations. The definition expressly connects good corporate citizenship to the recognition that broader society is the licensor of the organisation.[107]

Principle 16 advocates for the adoption of a stakeholder-inclusive approach to governance.[108] The report emphasises that stakeholder-inclusiveness is a recognition that the best interests of the company are not necessarily always equated with the shareholders, and so shareholders do not necessarily have predetermined precedence over other stakeholders.[109] Instead, directors owe duties to the company alone as a legal entity, which is represented by a variety of stakeholder interests, including shareholders, employees, consumers, the community and the environment.[110] The report emphasises that a company is dependent upon wider society to provide a conducive operating environment, a viable customer base and skills that the organisation requires.[111] Shareholder and stakeholder interests are therefore seen as interdependent.

The King IV report situates the stakeholder-inclusive approach to corporate governance in the African concept of *Ubuntu* or *Botho*, or 'I am because you are; you are because we are' – a foundational understanding of the interdependency between business organisations and society.[112] While the principles are still provided as voluntary ones, King IV adopts an 'apply and explain' approach (not an 'apply or explain' approach). It clarifies that while voluntary, courts will consider generally accepted standards of conduct which affect directors' actions, and so failure to adopt corporate governance standards may involve liability for directors.[113]

India has gone a step further by legally incorporating CSR into its Companies Act 2013. Section 135 of the Act requires companies over a certain size to spend at least 2 per cent of their average, domestic net profit over past three years on CSR initiatives.[114] This provision is applicable to certain companies based on three

---

[105] Institution of Directors of Southern Africa, Report on Corporate Governance for South Africa, 2016, 3.
[106] Ibid., 40.
[107] Ibid., 11
[108] Ibid., 41.
[109] Ibid., 26.
[110] Ibid.
[111] Ibid., 24.
[112] Ibid.
[113] Ibid., 35.
[114] Companies Act 2013, Ministry of Corporate Affairs, India.

thresholds: turnover (10 billion Indian Rupees), net profit (50 million Indian Rupees) or net worth (5 billion Indian Rupees). Companies subject to any of these thresholds also have to establish a CSR committee of the Board of Directors. Schedule VII provides an illustrative list of qualifying CSR activities which have been updated by subsequent rules. India has adopted a unique approach to CSR by including specific CSR action in a corporate statute, the first national legislation in the world to do this.

India has a long history of social consciousness in its approach to corporate law. After shedding the burden of colonialism, the first Indian Government required social consciousness and social development activities of its state-owned companies.[115] Shortly after independence, in 1951, the Supreme Court of India stated that companies have a social character where they are involved in the production of essential commodities.[116] The transition of the economy in the 1990s towards privatisation and neoliberal policies was also accompanied by significant public distrust of large multinationals. This was mainly due to the devastating chemical spill in Bhopal from the Union Carbide factory, which killed 2,500 people and left over 300,000 injured.[117] There have also been significant criticisms of Coca-Cola's CSR efforts in the country, particularly in relation to water pollution.[118] These developments led to the inclusion of the CSR spending requirement in the 2009 draft of the Act, which due to corporate resistance in 2009 was removed, but then reintroduced in the 2011 version[119] which subsequently passed. The Act has had mixed effects, with one study finding evidence of significantly increased CSR activity overall by firms and reduced advertising expenditure by firms, but that large firms which had previously spent over 2 per cent of their net profits on CSR, reduced that spending after Section 135 came into effect.[120] Another study found a 4.1 per cent drop in share price for firms affected by Section 135.[121]

While different jurisdictions take varying approaches to CSR, as public concern over climate change grows, public pressure on companies to do more to fulfil their social licence to operate will (and has) invariably increase. There is evidence of increased social pressure on corporations in the area of climate change already. As a result of increasing pressure from the social licence to operate, rather than CSR

---

[115] Alison McArdle, 'A Stick in the Global Carrot Patch: The Business of Corporate Social Responsibility' (2015) 38 Suffolk Transnat'l. L. Rev. 467, 476.
[116] *Chiranjit Lal Chowdhuri v. The Union of India, et al*, 1951 AIR 41 at 915.
[117] McArdle (n 115), 481.
[118] Ibid., 482
[119] Ibid., 484.
[120] Dhammika Dharmapala and Vikramaditya S. Khanna, 'The Impact of Mandated Corporate Social Responsibility: Evidence from India's Companies Act of 2013 (2016) University of Chicago Law School Working Papers No. 601, 1.
[121] Harion Manchirajn and Shivaram Rajgopal, 'Does Corporate Social Responsibility (CSR) Create Shareholder Value? Evidence from the Indian Companies Act 2013' (2017) 55(5) *Journal of Accounting Research* 1257.

being seen as purely voluntary initiatives which it previously was, business initiatives on climate change are now understood as more of a compelled voluntarism, or exerting a 'compliance pull' on corporate actors.[122] Companies now feel duties towards the public in various different areas,[123] although the level of commitment will vary within sectors and firms.

Most companies, even energy companies, now employ CSR or other environmental initiatives in one form or the other. Some type of CSR committee is often the mechanism to analyse environmental risks and activities within the company. It is difficult to quantify the output of CSR and compliance with voluntary codes, or their contribution to sustainable development and environmental goals.[124] Voluntary mechanisms often lack coherence as companies can pick and choose their content outside of what is required by law, and so these reports can be manipulated by companies by choosing their own baselines and methodologies for monitoring and enforcement.[125] As a result, it is often difficult to measure and verify progress towards CSR goals either within the same company, or between companies or industries. CSR mechanisms can be considered as only on ethical, non-binding responsibilities by companies, and so the overall effectiveness of CSR initiatives can be hard to assess.

Despite these deficiencies, CSR initiatives can provide real-world impacts and significant emission reductions. Many of the global companies are part of the Climate Ambition Alliance, established at the UN Secretary-General's Climate Action Forum in 2019.[126] Businesses joined regions, cities and investors in the 'Race to Zero' campaign, all pledging to achieve net zero emissions on or before 2050.[127] For example, Walmart was the first retailer to announce science-based targets which align with the Paris Agreement. This corporate giant has committed to reducing its Scope 1 and 2 emissions by 18 per cent, and to power 50 per cent of their operations by renewable power, both by 2025.[128] Walmart is also working with their extensive supplier network to avoid 1 billion metric tonnes of GHGs by 2030 under Project Gigaton.[129] In 2019, Amazon agreed to a net zero emissions target across all of its operations by 2040, and to power 100 per cent of its operations by renewable energy by 2025.[130] In January 2020, Microsoft pledged to be carbon

---

[122] Heyvaert (n 1), 216.
[123] See Barnali Choudhury and Martin Petrin, *Corporate Duties to the Public* (CUP 2019). The authors document areas such as human rights, the environment, criminal law, corruption and tax law which involve public duties for companies.
[124] Pesmatzoglou et al. (n 74) 198.
[125] Issachar Rosen-Zvi, 'You are Too Soft!: What Can Corporate Social Responsibility Do For Climate Change?' (2011) 12 *Minn. J. Sci. & Tech.* 527, 551.
[126] https://cop25.mma.gob.cl/en/climate-ambition-alliance.
[127] https://unfccc.int/climate-action/race-to-zero-campaign.
[128] https://corporate.walmart.com/esgreport/environmental#climate-change.
[129] Ibid. Although Vogel notes the long and often contentious history of WalMart in CSR, (n 73), viii.
[130] https://sustainability.aboutamazon.com.

negative (removing more carbon than it emits) by 2030, and to remove all of their historic emissions emitted from 1975, by 2050.[131] The company also pledged to support new public policies which accelerate carbon reduction and removal.[132] After extensive criticism of their funding of climate denial organisations,[133] Google also increased its climate pledges. However, not all of these emission commitments include Scope 3 emissions, and where they rely on carbon offsets to meet their targets, the environmental integrity of their efforts may be suspect.[134] What these efforts do demonstrate, however, is the strong desire of many companies to at least be seen as responsible global climate actors, which goes beyond strictly voluntary measures.

This more modern approach to CSR has yet to take hold across the board in all companies or even within all carbon-major companies. While a number of carbon-majors position GHG emission reductions at the parent level within some sort of CSR administrative grouping or approach, none of them have indicated a growth trajectory which divests them entirely away from fossil fuels and towards renewable energy. At Centrica plc, for example, it is the board-level corporate responsibility committee that analyses the group's environmental risks. BG Group's approach to climate change is incorporated through their Business Principles, which set out the group's core standard of ethical conduct, and the company's responsibility to people and the environment. Royal Dutch Shell positions their 'core values' of honesty, respect and integrity as the basis of their eight General Business Principles (which include health, safety and the environment).[135] The group's Corporate and Social Responsibility Committee was formed in 2005 and monitors the group's adherence to its Business Principles.

Despite these minimalist approaches to energy transitions, there is evidence of a splintering of approaches even within the carbon-major world. For example, ExxonMobil and Chevron have doubled down on their fossil fuel investments,[136] while Shell has indicated a willingness to transition (albeit slowly) into the general energy market and away from just being a fossil fuel company. After months of engagement with the investor initiative Climate Action 100+, Shell announced in December 2018 its aim to reduce its emissions by 30 per cent by 2035 and net

---

[131] www.microsoft.com/en-us/corporate-responsibility/sustainability/operations.
[132] Ibid.
[133] Stephanie Kirchgaessner, 'Revealed: Google Made Large Contributions to Climate Change Deniers' *The Guardian* (11 October 2019), www.theguardian.com/environment/2019/oct/11/google-contributions-climate-change-deniers (accessed 18 July 2020).
[134] Natasha Bernall, 'Google, Microsoft and the Strange World of Corporate Greenwashing' Wired (31 January 2020) available www.wired.co.uk/article/corporate-greenwashing (accessed 18 July 2020).
[135] Royal Dutch Shell Plc, 'Sustainability Report 2014' (2014), 7, https://reports.shell.com/sustainability-report/2014/servicepages/welcome.html (accessed 20 July 2020).
[136] *The Economist*, 'ExxonMobil Gambles on Growth' (9 February 2019), www.economist.com/briefing/2019/02/09/exxonmobil-gambles-on-growth (accessed 19 July 2020).

zero ambitions by 2050.[137] In 2020, BP also established net zero emissions ambitions by 2050.[138] It announced its transition from an international oil company to an integrated energy company, with an anticipated reduction in oil production and an increase in low-carbon technologies including renewables, hydrogen, bioenergy and carbon capture, use and sequestration (CCUS).[139] Despite these varying levels of commitments, all carbon-major companies have and do participate in international emissions reporting initiatives.

4.2.3 CSR and Corporate Reporting Requirements

Companies in the United Kingdom are required to report certain environmental information to shareholders under the strategic report provisions of the Companies Act, in particular Section 414.[140] Under the Companies Act 2006 (Strategic Report and Directors' Report) Regulations 2013, directors must submit a Strategic Report and a Directors' Report.[141] The Strategic Report is designed to work in conjunction with Section 172 of the Companies Act 2006 in order to enshrine the 'enlightened' part of the enlightened shareholder value principle. The 2013 Regulations also impose a requirement on quoted companies with less than 500 employees to report on their global GHG emissions, as outlined in the KP. These cover Scopes 1 and 2 emissions, which are direct emissions from the company, and indirect emissions from purchased fossil fuel based electricity and gas. These are to be included in the Directors' Report, regardless of whether the directors considered them to be material. If it was not practical to obtain the information, directors have to provide a justification for that fact.

In 2016, the Department for Business, Energy and Industrial Strategy noted that disclosure requirements were leading to unclear and unsatisfactory disclosures by

---

[137] Shell PLC, "Shell's Ambition to be a Net-Zero Emissions Energy Business" (Shell Global, The Energy Future, 2019), www.shell.com/energy-and-innovation/the-energy-future/shells-ambition-to-be-a-net-zero-emissions-energy-business.html (accessed 16 April 2020).

[138] www.bp.com/en/global/corporate/news-and-insights/press-releases/bernard-looney-announces-new-ambition-for-bp.html.

[139] www.bp.com/en/global/corporate/news-and-insights/press-releases/from-international-oil-company-to-integrated-energy-company-bp-sets-out-strategy-for-decade-of-delivery-towards-net-zero-ambition.html.

[140] In addition, The Companies, Partnerships and Groups (Accounts and Non-Financial Reporting) Regulations 2016 transposed the EU Non-Financial Reporting Directive 2014/95/EU, and amended Section 414CB of the Companies Act, which now requires a non-financial reporting statement that includes environmental matters, as well as principal risks and key performance indicators to measure activity.

[141] Prior to 2013, companies had to submit a business review which led to inadequate disclosures regarding GHG emissions, see Adrian Henriques, 'The Reporting of Non-Financial Information in Annual Reports by the FTSE 100' (CORE, 2010). Small companies and micro-entities are exempted.

directors.¹⁴² The Companies, Partnerships and Groups (Accounts and Non-Financial Reporting) Regulations 2016 were subsequently developed to impose obligations on companies with over 500 employees (defined as public interest entities) to disclose GHG emissions. These apply to traded companies, banking companies, authorised insurance companies or companies conducting insurance market activity. Quoted companies with under 500 employees continue to report under the 2013 regulations. The 2016 Regulations are designed to help companies identify sustainability risks to increase investor and consumer trust, and to manage change towards a sustainable global economy by combining long-term profitability with social justice and environmental protection.

Long-term systemic risks which may have a material effect on the entity's ability to generate and preserve value in the long-term must be disclosed by public interest entities under the 2016 Regulations. The Financial Reporting Council guidance, issued in 2019, recommends that the Strategic Report explain the potential impact on the entity's strategy and business model if those risks crystallise, using the specific example of climate change as a systemic risk.¹⁴³ The Companies (Miscellaneous Reporting) Regulations 2018, Section 414 CZA also requires large companies to include an additional report on how directors have taken into account considerations under Section 172 of the Companies Act 2006. This Section 172 statement should include matters that are of strategic importance to the company. The level of information disclosed should be consistent with the size and complexity of the business.¹⁴⁴

Just issuing a report on emissions does not always mean that emissions will be reduced or other cited sustainability goals will be achieved. When corporate GHG emissions increase, carbon-major companies often refer to some type of CSR licence as a potential tool to address this problem, but often do identify how, if at all, this CSR initiative could contribute to reductions in GHG emissions. For example, Centrica was concerned that not being seen as a low-carbon supplier of energy would affect their social licence to operate.¹⁴⁵ BP plc noted that its licence to operate is earned through real benefits delivered to the communities in which they operate.¹⁴⁶ Beyond these vague statements, it is often unclear what the connection between the social licence to operate and reduced emissions are in some companies.

---

¹⁴² UK Department of Business, Energy and Industrial Strategy, 'Corporate Governance Reform' Green Paper, (November 2016).
¹⁴³ United Kingdom Financial Reporting Council, 'Guidance on the Strategic Report' (July 2018), para 7B.31.
¹⁴⁴ Ibid., para 8.12.
¹⁴⁵ Centrica Plc, 'CDP 2009 Investor CDP Information Request' (2009), 11, www.centrica.com/media/2445/centcro9_cdp.pdf (accessed 19 July 2020).
¹⁴⁶ BP Plc, 'Sustainability Report 2014' (2014), 2, www.bp.com/content/dam/bp/business-sites/en/global/corporate/pdfs/sustainability/archive/archived-reports-and-translations/2014/sustainability-report-2014.pdf (accessed 30 June 2020).

Shell couched its ability to grasp the challenge and opportunities of climate change as integral to its 'licence to grow'.[147] When BG Group's GHG emissions rose in 2013, it put in place a 'Licence to Operate' scheme in order to satisfy its stakeholders,[148] although this scheme did not include concrete absolute GHG emission reduction pledges.

While CSR initiatives can lead to reduced emissions without regulatory prodding, at times there can be no concrete connection between CSR initiatives and GHG emission reductions, particularly in companies which are dependent on emissions and increased energy use for corporate growth and profits. Despite these criticisms, private environmental governance initiatives are still being used by companies and have the potential to incentivise real emissions reductions in some industries and sectors in the absence of regulatory requirements.

4.2.4 Private Environmental Governance

Transnational environmental regulation has appeared more prominently in private environmental governance initiatives. Michael Vandenbergh defines private environmental governance as action taken by non-government entities that are designed to achieve traditional environmental goals such as managing common pool resources or reducing environmental externalities.[149] While acknowledging that private environmental governance initiatives are neither complete nor optimal responses to existing environmental problems, Vandenbergh poses alternative ways of measuring the success of these initiatives, such as what would have occurred in their absence, and whether they can induce scholars to identify new solutions to collective action problems.[150] While technically membership is voluntary, in some industries and sectors, these initiatives can have a strong 'compliance pull'.[151] In the climate arena, private environmental governance initiatives have the potential to fill temporal or governance gaps where climate regulation at the national level is slow to emerge.[152] They can also be highly effective, with Vandenbergh and Jonathan Gilligan estimating that private environmental governance and corporate actions could reduce emissions by roughly 1,000 million tonnes of CO_2 per year between

---

[147] The Shell Group, 'People, Planet and Profits: The Shell Report 2001' (2001), 2, www.bcsd.org.tw/2010/images/doc/301/002/002_3/SHELL%20REPORT_2001.PDF (accessed 30 May 2020).
[148] BG Group, 'Sustainability Report 2012' (2012) 5, http://edg1.precisionir.com/companyspotlight/EU000395/BG12Sustain.pdf (accessed 30 May 2020).
[149] Michael P. Vandenbergh, 'Private Environmental Governance' (2013) 99 Cornell L. Rev. 129, 146.
[150] Ibid., 139.
[151] Heyvaert (n 1), 216.
[152] Vandenbergh (n 149) 163.

2016 and 2025 and so achieve major GHG emission reductions in the face of government gridlock.[153]

This turn to transnational governance initiatives has its advocates and critics. Larry Backer argues that TNCs have used this development as an opportunity to substitute themselves as the new regulators of behaviour through transnational networks of governance initiatives.[154] Groups of non-state actors are able to create autonomous regulatory communities, allowing them to mount strong functional attacks on state-based governance authority.[155] In addition to private environmental governance, codes of conduct and other transnational initiatives have also been developed.

4.3 INTERNATIONAL CODES OF CONDUCT AND PRIVATE TRANSNATIONAL INITIATIVES

While CSR and corporate governance codes are distinct concepts,[156] voluntary corporate codes were promoted as part of the CSR agenda towards the environment. For example, the OECD Guidelines included an environmental chapter in 1991, and the Ceres coalition of investors, concerned about the environmental impact of business, was formed in 1989 following the Exxon Valdez oil spill.[157] Codes can be either public (applicable to all companies or an industry) or private (developed for a specific company),[158] and are often used as a mechanism to avoid regulation.[159] Codes are flexible in that they are often voluntary and not binding, and therefore can be catered to the individual needs of a company or industry.[160] Codes can also bring predictability and stability to a particular area of corporate activity, foster public trust and align corporate activities with public expectations.[161]

---

[153] Michael P. Vandenbergh and Jonathan M. Gilligan, 'Beyond Gridlock', 40(2) *Columbia J. Env. Law* 218, (2015). See also, Michael Vandenbergh, 'The Drivers of Corporate Climate Mitigation' (2018) 29 The Environmental Forum; and Michael Vandenbergh, 'Private Actors: Part of the Problem, Part of the Solution', (2017) 48 Environmental Forum.

[154] Ibid.

[155] Larry Catá Backer, 'Private Actors and Public Governance Beyond the State: The Multinational Corporation, the Financial Stability Board, and the Global Governance Order', (2011) 18 *Indiana Journal of Global Legal Studies* 751, 755.

[156] Yeung, Huang and Liu (n 75) 5.

[157] J. Andy Smith III, 'The CERES Principles: A Voluntary Code for Corporate Environmental Responsibility' (1993) 18 Yale J. Int'l. L. 307, 308; CERES, www.ceres.org/aboutus (accessed 15 July 2020).

[158] Jenkins divides codes into five types: company codes, trade association codes, multi-stakeholder codes, model codes and inter-governmental codes, Jenkins, (n 73) iv.

[159] Gunther Teubner, 'Self-Constitutionalizing TNCs? On the Linkage of "Private" and "Public" Corporate Codes of Conduct' (2011) 18 *Indian Journal of Global Legal Studies* 617, 619.

[160] Mark B. Baker, 'Private Codes of Corporate Conduct: Should the Fox Guard the Henhouse?' (1992) 24 U. Miami Inter-Am. L. Rev. 399, 130.

[161] Ibid., 400, 405, 415.

Codes can also be used to curry favour with the public, or to respond to public outcry or concern in a particular area, without binding a company to taking specific, often costly, steps to rectify the issue, which would contravene the shareholder primacy norm of profit maximisation. Gunther Teubner states, 'They try both to overcome the primacy of shareholder value in favour of a stakeholder-orientation as well as to realise self-restraint in the areas of labour, product quality, environment and human rights'.[162] The voluntary nature of codes means that they are often not effective in ensuring compliance by companies, particularly in the environmental arena, where preventive or clean-up actions are often costly.[163] The private–public initiatives can be more effective in motivating action by companies due to their public nature.

4.3.1 The United Nations Global Compact

Given the failure of the international community to agree to international, binding obligations on companies, and the inherent challenges of regulation to effectively deal with climate change, the role of corporate environmental regulator was largely left to the UN, which relied heavily on CSR initiatives. Realising this gap in global governance,[164] the UN put forward the idea of a public–private initiative, constituting a global compact directly between the UN and global companies. However, international business organisations were resistant to the idea of the compact as a binding international code, and only agreed to engage with the United Nations on the basis that the compact remained a voluntary initiative.[165]

The UN Global Compact (or UNGC) provides for ten voluntary principles which all companies can sign on to. The principles cover broad areas of CSR such as human rights, labour rights, environmental rights and anti-corruption. Principles 7–9 cover environmental areas, and stipulate that companies should support the precautionary approach to environmental challenges (Principle 7), should undertake initiatives to promote greater environmental responsibility (Principle 8) and should encourage the development and diffusion of environmental friendly technologies (Principle 9). The principles are broad and contain guidance regarding steps that companies can take to implement them. These steps include the development of codes of conduct and strategies, and the use of environmental management, monitoring and verification programmes.

The UNGC currently has over 12,000 participants, which include companies, NGOs and other stakeholders, located in 145 countries, and is presently the largest

---

[162] Teubner (n 159) 613.
[163] Sophie Hsai, 'Foreign Direct Investment and the Environment: Are Voluntary Codes of Conduct and Self-Imposed Standards Enough?' (2002–2003) 9 Envtl. L. 673, 681.
[164] Georg Kell, 'The Global Compact Selected Experiences and Reflections' (2005) 59(1/2) Journal of Business Ethics 69, 71.
[165] Ibid.

global corporate initiative.[166] Participants include a large number of companies in the extractive industry, including energy, oil, timber and mining companies.[167] While none of the principles specifically refer to the reduction of GHGs by companies, the Caring for Climate (C4C) initiative was developed in 2007 by the UNGC, United Nations Environment Programme and the Secretariat of the UNFCCC. The goal of the C4C is to advance the role of business in addressing climate change by companies endorsing a UN 'Caring for Climate Statement', setting goals and targets, and disclosing their emissions under the UNGC Communication on Progress.[168]

Originally any company, regardless of its past environmental performance, could join the UNGC. In 2017, the UN decided that tobacco companies could no longer participate as an addition to its exclusionary criteria,[169] but fossil fuel companies remain eligible for membership, and in fact many do participate in the UNGC. Every participant can choose which four of the ten principles to cover in their communication and can choose their own methodology to measure performance. The lack of monitoring and enforcement, coherence, or minimum criteria for the corporate communications, as well as the fact that any NGO criticisms are not included in the communications themselves, has led some academics to conclude that the UNGC is ineffective, toothless,[170] and has led to a loss of public trust in the UN.[171] The UNGC has also been criticised for incorporating some assumptions of ameliorative CSR for supposing that an automatic balance can be struck between the demands of the market and socially responsible norms,[172] and for diminishing areas of conflict between the shareholder profit maximisation imperatives of business and the costs of environmentally responsible corporate behaviour.[173] However, the UNGC was designed as more of a forum for non-state actors to forge partnerships, alliances and demonstrate a commitment to principles such as human rights and sustainability.

---

[166] United Nations Global Compact, www.unglobalcompact.org/AboutTheGC/index.html (accessed 15 July 2020).
[167] Lynn Bernie, Patrick Bernhagen and Neil J. Mitchell, 'The Logic of Transnational Action: The Good Corporation and the Global Compact' (2007) 55 *Political Studies* 733, 744.
[168] See www.caringforclimate.org (accessed 15 Jul. 2020).
[169] See <www.unglobalcompact.org/participation/join/who-should-join> accessed 17 July 2020.
[170] Steve Hughes et al., 'Profile 1 – The Global Compact: Prioritizing Corporate Responsibility?' (2001) 10 *Environmental Politics* 155, 157.
[171] S. Prakesh Sethi and Donald H. Schapers, 'United Nations Global Compact: The Promise-Performance Gap' (2014) 122 *Journal of Business Ethics* 193, 206, 193; Robert W. Neson, 'Structuring the Global Marketplace: The Impact of the UN Global Compact' (2008) 28 *Journal of Macromarketing* 418, 421.
[172] Christina Garsten and Kerstin Jacobsson, 'Transparency and Legitimacy in International Institutions: The UN Global Compact and Post-political Global Ethics' (2011) 19(4) *Social Anthropology* 378, 382.
[173] Hughes (n 170) 157.

To date, there are no international codes directly binding upon companies in the environmental arena,[174] or specifically in relation to climate change and the reduction of GHGs. As a result, none of the existing global codes outside of the human rights area of law (covered in Chapter 6) ensure that companies are accountable.[175] This is particularly true where inadequate monitoring or enforcement mechanisms exist,[176] resulting in no guarantees of compliance.[177] In the absence of an international code on GHG emissions reduction, a number of private initiatives have sprung up.

4.3.2 Private, Voluntary Initiatives

Private-based initiatives have been developed to fill the international void, such as the ISO 14000, the CDP, the Global Framework for Climate Risk Disclosure and the Global Reporting Initiative (GRI), which all advocate voluntary reporting of environmental performance and GHG emissions.

The ISO standards are a hybrid of public- and private-sector standards, and are voluntary, industry-based tools[178] developed to measure environmental management procedures of companies. The ISO 14000 was developed in collaboration with the participation of the ICC and other industry representatives on the ISO technical committees.[179] The ISO 14000 family of standards provides companies with guidelines and a framework which corporations can follow to implement effective environmental management systems. The framework can be applied across any industry or sector, and provides certification systems to provide an external check on the system and its implementation. The environmental management systems focus on how companies can improve their environmental performance through more efficient use of resources and minimisation of waste.[180] It is designed to be a holistic

---

[174] The Norms on the Responsibilities of TNCs and Other Business Entities with regard to Human Rights, originally promulgated in 2003 by the Working Group under the UN Sub-Committee on the Promotion and Protection of Human Rights, had been envisaged by the Working Group to be a binding set of norms, which include environmental responsibilities. However, due to vigorous resistance by the international business community (including the ICC and Confederation of British Industry), the UN Subcommittee determined that binding norms had not been requested and so had no legal standing, and John Ruggie was appointed as a special representative of the UN to provide recommendations on whether these Norms should be binding upon business.
[175] Clapp (n 25) 26.
[176] Mark B. Baker, 'Promises and Platitudes: Towards a New Twenty-first Century Paradigm for Corporate Codes of Conduct?' (2007) 23 Comm. J. Intl. L. 123, 133.
[177] Robert J. Fowler, 'International Environmental Standards for Transnational Corporations' (1999) 12 Melb. J. Intl. L. 1, 30.
[178] Jennifer Clapp, 'The Privatization of Global Environmental Governance: ISO14000 and the Developing World' (1998) 4 *Global Governance* 295, 295.
[179] Ibid., 299; Christina C. Benson, 'The ISO 14000 International Standards: Moving Beyond Environmental Compliance' (1996–1997) 22 N.C.J. Int'l. & Com. Reg. 307, 311.
[180] ISO, 'Introduction to ISO 14001' (2015), www.iso.org/files/live/sites/isoorg/files/archive/pdf/en/introduction_to_iso_14001.pdf (15 July 2020).

management system which looks across all environmental issues affecting a business, including air and water pollution, sewage and other wastes, as well as climate change mitigation and adaptation.[181] The standards are consistently reviewed and updated, and the latest ISO 14001, issued in 2015, provides a closer focus on commitments from a company's leadership team, promotion of life cycle thinking across the organisation, pro-active activities in the areas of climate change mitigation, and a more stakeholder-focused communication strategy.[182]

The CDP was established in 2002 in the United Kingdom as a non-profit, international organisation which supports and incentivises non-state actors such as cities, investors and corporations to improve their environmental management. While it originally focused only on carbon emissions reporting, the organisation now focuses on climate, water and forestry, and helping non-state actors to measure and understand their environmental impact.[183] It requests information on corporate emissions, climate risk and low carbon opportunities from the world's largest companies. These companies publish a CDP report which publishes climate-related information in standardised categories, providing a useful tool for investors. In addition to its carbon reports, CDP publishes reports on industry leaders, as well as leading cities, in the CDP A-list for environmental performers. It also regularly reports on climate risks to a sustainable economy.

The GRI is an independent, international institution established in 1997, which focuses on sustainable reporting. It assists companies and governments in understanding and reporting on their impact on a wide range of environmental, social and governance issues, including climate change, human rights and social well-being.[184] The GRI Sustainability Reporting Standards are a uniform set of standards used by companies to disclose sustainability information but also to identify and manage sustainability-related risks and opportunities. The standards cover economic, environmental and social impacts as well as contributions to sustainable development. Companies can use the standards to issue GRI sustainability reports, which can be used as a resource by policymakers and regulators.

In addition to these more established private initiatives, many companies have either signed up to, or themselves formed, new voluntary initiatives such as the World Bank Zero Routine Flaring by 2030 initiative, or the Oil and Gas Climate Initiative launched by the UN Secretary-General in September 2014, which provides an industry-driven platform for companies to voluntarily share technical solutions to climate change.

---

[181] Ibid., 2.
[182] Ibid., 5.
[183] See www.cdp.net/en/info/about-us (accessed 15 July 2020).
[184] See www.globalreporting.org/Information/about-gri/Pages/default.aspx (accessed 15 July 2020).

4.3.3 Emerging International Initiatives

In addition to CSR, international Codes of Conduct and private initiatives, other transnational regulatory initiatives have emerged which have the potential to change the regulatory landscape and standard industry practices in relation to climate change. These more recent initiatives focus exclusively on the relationship between companies and climate change. They focus on climate-risk to corporations and the global economy, as well as the emerging legal obligations of both companies and investors on climate change. The Sustainability Accounting Standards Board (SASB) issues reporting guidance for companies in several areas, including climate change. The TCFD emerged out of the concern by the Governor of the Bank of England of the risks that climate change poses to investors and the global economy. The Principles on Climate Obligations of Enterprises is also risk-driven, but charts the emerging legal risks for investors and companies on climate change.

The SASB was established as an independent, standard-setting arm of the SASB Foundation. The Foundation's mission is to establish and improve industry-specific disclosure standards across financially material environmental, social and governance topics, in order to facilitate communication between companies and investors about decision-useful information.[185] It is the SASB that develops, issues and maintains SASB standards. They are developed using an open and transparent process, including consultation with business and industry. In 2018, the SASB launched seventy-seven industry-specific reporting standards, including environment, social and governance indicators. These reporting standards have been adopted by 120 firms, including companies and investors.[186] SASB Standards provide detailed climate-related disclosure topics and metrics which are catered for specific industries. They include areas of focus which are reasonably likely to have a material effect on the financial performance of companies in specific industries.

The TCFD developed from a recommendation made by the G20 to the Financial Stability Board (FSB) in April 2015 for the FSB to consider climate risk. In December 2015, the FSB launched the industry-led TCFD with a mandate to develop recommendations on climate-related financial disclosures. The final recommendations were published in June 2017 after several years of consultations and engagement with industry. The recommendations are designed to help companies create consistent, comparable, reliable, clear and efficient climate-related disclosures in order to provide decision-useful information to investors.[187]

---

[185] www.sasb.org/governance (accessed 16 July 2020).
[186] Ben Ashwell, 'More than 100 companies using SASB standards' IR Magazine, 12 December 2019, www.irmagazine.com/reporting/more-100-companies-using-sasb-standards (accessed 15 July 2020).
[187] See www.fsb.org/work-of-the-fsb/policy-development/additional-policy-areas/climate-related-financial-disclosures (accessed 15 July 2020).

The TCFD recommendations were crafted around a key gap in existing disclosure initiatives highlighted earlier – that managers, investors and decision makers lacked information on the financial implications of climate-related risks.[188] Existing financial disclosures on climate change, made under CSR initiatives, are often boilerplate, non-comparable and lack decision-useful content for investment, insurance and lending activities in the medium to long-term.[189] This trend was identified as problematic by the TCFD, which estimated that climate-related impacts on business may be enormous; the value of impacts on manageable assets could range from US$4.2 trillion to $43 trillion between now and the end of the century.[190] The TCFD recommendations are provided for both financial and non-financial firms, and specific guidance has also been developed and tailored for specific industries.

The recommendations are structured around four thematic areas of governance, strategy, risk management, and metrics and targets. They recommend that investors and businesses consider their long-term strategies in order to determine the most efficient allocation of capital, taking into account climate risk. Value chain assessments over reasonable timeframes can often be the first and best-starting place, and these assessments should focus on relevant transition and physical risks on and to the operations and assets of a business. These assessments should include both potential risks and an assessment of potential opportunities.[191] To overcome the fragmentation of climate-related disclosures, the TCFD recommend that businesses include disclosures on climate risk in their mainstream financial filings, which will also enable the evolution of practices and techniques more rapidly (including data analytics) to improve the quality of disclosures.[192] The process recommended by the TCFD effectively meshes value-creation timeframes with climate-related time periods.[193]

In September 2018, the TCFD published a survey of results from across a broad spectrum of industry reflecting an uneven implementation of the recommendations. While the majority of the 1,700 firms surveyed aligned with at least one of the TCFD recommendations and many reported on climate-related risks and opportunities, very few firms reported on the financial risks of climate change to their businesses.[194]

The recommendations are likely to not only become industry standard, but perhaps new global regulatory requirements. In October 2019, the Governor of the Bank of England announced that major companies have two years to agree with rules for reporting climate risks before global regulators devise and impose their own

---

[188] Ibid., 1.
[189] Ibid.; see also SASB 'SASB Climate Risk Technical Bulletin #TB001–1018 2016', October 2016.
[190] Ibid.
[191] Ibid., 7.
[192] Ibid., iv, v.
[193] Lisa Benjamin and Stelios Andreadakis, 'Corporate Governance and Climate Change – Smoothing Temporal Dissonance to a Phased Approach' (2019) 40(4) *Business Law Review* 146.
[194] Ibid.

rules on these corporations.[195] These rules are likely to be based on the TCFD recommendations, once a definitive view on what constitutes a high-quality disclosure is agreed upon.[196] The need for climate-risk reporting by companies is driven by the emerging climate emergency and the need for companies to document existing and potential effects on their businesses, and also the appetite from investors to support companies that understand the risks climate change poses to their businesses.

The Principles on Climate Obligations of Enterprises were developed in 2018, and updated in 2020, by a prominent group of legal experts, and a further description of them is provided in Chapter 6 in the context of liability for companies. The Principles follow on from the Oslo Principles on Global Climate Change Obligations, which distilled general legal obligations regarding climate change.[197] The Enterprise Principles elaborated upon the Oslo Global Principles to develop specific legal principles applicable not to states, but only to private, commercial or industrial entities, or non-private entities that carry on commercial or industrial activities. The Enterprises referred to in the Principles include both companies and investors. The Principles were developed to address the enormous contribution that businesses make to climate change, and to include businesses in the effort to achieve the required global emission reductions.[198] While the Principles are regarded as aspirational, and the authors acknowledge they are progressive, the authors also consider that as the threat of runaway climate change materialises, the law in this area will likely progress rapidly in order to meet the urgent demands of society.[199] The Principles, however, initially only adopted the global temperature goal of 2°C (updated in 2020 to 1.75°C), and do not include the aspirational goal of 1.5°C that parties included in the Paris Agreement.

The Principles are wide-ranging and include both disclosure and reduction obligations of enterprises. They state that enterprises should take all reasonable steps to reduce the emissions of their activities to the point where they are no longer excessive, in the shortest time reasonably feasible.[200] Disclosures by Enterprises should be proportionate to the size of the enterprise and its location.[201] Material

---

[195] Philip Innman, 'Corporations Told to Draw Up Climate Rules or Have Them Imposed' *The Guardian* (8 October 2019), www.theguardian.com/business/2019/oct/08/corporations-told-to-draw-up-climate-rules-or-have-them-imposed (accessed 15 July 2020).
[196] Ibid.
[197] Expert Group on Global Climate Obligations, Oslo Principles on Global Climate Change Obligations (2015), https://globaljustice.yale.edu/oslo-principles-global-climate-change-obligations (accessed 19 July 2020).
[198] Ibid., 28.
[199] The Principles also acknowledge the difficulties in temporal assessments in terms of corporate liability. Many businesses have historical emissions which the Principles do not address.
[200] Ibid., 146.
[201] The Oslo Principles differentiate between obligations of developed and developing countries, and the Enterprise Principles take a similar approach, differentiating between companies located in developed or developing countries.

disclosures are those that would influence the economic decisions of stakeholders which use the organisation's financial statements.[202] In the context of investors, short-termism and climate change, the Principles advocate that, considering the magnitude of climate risk, investors are not only allowed but may be obligated, to invest in funds that generate less profit in the near future if and to the extent that this strategy would be the only way to avoid temperature increases above 2°C. This approach marks a clear departure from the traditional approach to obligations under the fiduciary duties of investors but also directors, reflected in traditional corporate theories. Whether this investment approach will be adopted by businesses in the near future is unclear, but the authors of the Principles expect that the law will develop in this direction in the next ten to twenty years.[203]

These emerging transnational governance initiatives are more focused on companies and climate change than previous efforts were, and reflect a clear departure from corporate business as usual. They reflect the new directions that disclosure and legal obligations may lead to in the near future. They also bridge the traditional gap between voluntary transnational governance initiatives such as CSR and Codes of Conduct, and binding international law. As a result, they demonstrate the subversive effect that emerging climate risks and impacts may have on traditional and outdated approaches to company law.

4.4 CONCLUSION

International binding agreements on states such as the UNFCCC, KP and the Paris Agreement are compromise laden, and fail to provide stringent, binding targets on GHG emissions reductions. This is largely due to lack of political will and industry concerns with international competitiveness and carbon leakage. Despite the lack of ambition contained within the language of these treaties, the Paris Agreement has been a motivating factor for many non-state actors to take up the mantle of emission reductions. The Paris Agreement is a near-universal statement by countries that we are heading towards a carbon-constrained world where businesses (and emissions) as usual are no longer acceptable. Despite the progress reflected by the Paris Agreement, at present there are no internationally binding obligations on companies to reduce GHG emissions. Voluntary initiatives developed as part of transnational environmental regulation are the traditional, and for a long time were the only mechanisms, employed by the companies.

CSR relies heavily on the social licence to operate, which until recently was not taken seriously by many companies, and is an amorphous concept that is general[204]

---

[202] These are largely considered by the Principles to be investors.
[203] Ibid., 226.
[204] Polishchuk (n 74) 75.

and evolving.[205] The same can be said for strategic environmental CSR.[206] While CSR may motivate some movement, this will only be the case where the social licence requirements exceed those of licence to operate and the profit motive of companies. Although limits to these licences (even the economic licence) are as yet unclear,[207] commitments to make drastic reductions of GHG emissions by companies are evolving only because external stakeholders are exerting pressure on corporate managers. CSR should consist of internalising externalities, and may ultimately be more cost-effective than regulation, but would require changes to traditional approaches to shareholder primacy and wealth maximisation in order to be truly effective.[208]

At the moment, however, sustainability is often linked with the success of the business.[209] In many cases, future efficiency aims are linked to short pay back periods.[210] Very few carbon-major companies have long-term plans on how their business operations will change in order to dramatically reduce their GHG emissions and contributions to climate change. In fact, many of the companies, particularly ones such as ExxonMobil and Chevron, anticipate that their traditional fossil-fuel activities will continue to play a significant role in the energy future.[211] But this is not the case for all carbon-major companies. Shell and BP, for example, have recently decided to diversify generation assets and move into the energy market.[212] It remains to be seen whether and how these companies will follow through with this initiative and crucially, whether other market actors will follow.

Codes of conduct and other transnational environmental governance techniques prove to be fairly popular with companies. Initiatives such as the ISO 14000, GRI and the CDP can provide companies with much-needed guidance and tools to report their emissions and implement environmental management systems. CDP reporting in particular seems almost universally adopted by most energy companies. According to the CDP, energy companies give similar explanations for why they do not have company-wide, absolute GHG emission targets: Business is expanding and emission reduction targets will constrain their growth.[213] Expansion, profit incentives and

---

[205] Dirk Matten and Jeremy Moon, '"Implicit" and "Explicit" CSR: A Conceptual Framework for a Comparative Understanding of Corporate Social Responsibilty' (2008) 33(2) *Academy of Management Review*, 404, 408.
[206] Lyon and Maxwell (n 82) 17; Lozano (n 84) 33; Valentine (n 84) 286.
[207] Kagan, Thornton and Cunningham (n 92) 82.
[208] Johnston (n 81) 237.
[209] See John Browne, 'Addressing Global Climate Change' (19 May 1997), 6, www.bp.com/content/dam/bp/pdf/speeches/1997/Addressing_Global_Climate_Change.pdf (accessed 30 May 2015); National Grid, 'Our Contribution: A Framework for Environmental Sustainability in National Grid', 4, www2.nationalgrid.com/Responsibility/Non-financial-performance-report/ (accessed 30 May 2015); Vogel (n 73), 111.
[210] BG Group, (n 147) 1.
[211] *The Economist* (n 136).
[212] See www.shell.com/energy-and-innovation/the-energy-future.html (accessed 19 July 2020).
[213] CDP, 'Sector Insights: What Is Driving Climate Change Action in the World's Largest Companies?' (2017) Global Climate Change Report, 24.

shareholder primacy, therefore, are continuing to be the main incentives for company operations in this area, particularly carbon-major companies, and currently override any other incentives or social licences to reduce GHG emissions.

This is not the case for other industries and sectors which are adopting private environmental governance initiatives. These private-oriented initiatives are firm-specific and can contribute vast amounts of emissions reductions by individual companies. Large conglomerates such as Walmart can in fact lead value chain emissions reductions by influencing other actors along their vast supply chain to also reduce emissions. Other market leaders such as Amazon and Microsoft are making extensive commitments on emissions reductions as a result of the Paris Agreement. However, it remains to be seen how ambitious those commitments will be in practice, as actual investments linked to emission reductions and the application of climate-friendly technologies will truly demonstrate an actual commitment to climate change strategies.[214]

Newer transnational governance initiatives such as the TCFD and the Enterprise Principles are focusing exclusively on the relationship between companies and climate change. These initiatives focus both on the risks of climate change to companies and the global economy, as well as chart emerging legal obligations for companies in this area. Many investors want decision-useful information on climate-related risks and opportunities to the businesses they chose to invest in. These initiatives are bridging the gap between non-binding international law, and traditional voluntary transnational initiatives. Instead of this binary choice, certain large companies are beginning to feel compelled to reduce emissions, due to increased social pressure. In addition, transnational governance initiatives are likely to become not just industry standards, but in fact binding rules in emissions reporting as we have seen in the United Kingdom. These emerging initiatives demonstrate that law can and should evolve to respond to the urgent threat of climate change. Theoretical approaches such as shareholder primacy and wealth maximisation will have to be adjusted as well. These initiatives are being accompanied by and have in fact influenced a wave of domestic climate and energy regulation in the United Kingdom. These regulatory developments are covered in the next chapter.

---

[214] Ingvild Andressen Saeverud and Jon Birger Skjoerseth, 'Oil Companies and Climate Change: Inconsistencies between Strategy Formulation and Implementation?' (2007) 7(3) *Global Environmental Politics* 42, 45.

5

Domestic Climate and Energy Regulation

In June 2019, the then-Prime Minister of the United Kingdom, Theresa May, committed to a national net zero emissions target by 2050. The announcement took many by surprise, and in fact, preceded a subsequent EU decision to achieve the same target by 2050. Her announcement may have in fact been motivated by a perceived failure to achieve a successful Brexit outcome. Whatever the political motivations behind the announcement may have been, it was, procedurally at least, the result of legislation enacted over ten years prior. In particular, the structure of the independent UK Committee on Climate Change was a critical institutional mechanism which facilitated and incentivised her decision. Staffed by well-respected industry experts, the Committee was established under the 2008 Climate Change Act and serves to provide independent advice to successive governments. On the whole and over time, successive governments, in fact, have heeded the Committee's advice, as did Theresa May.

As part of its mandate, the Committee can review and suggest revisions to established national emissions reduction targets. In 2019, as a result of the Intergovernmental Panel on Climate Change (IPCC) 1.5°C Special Report, the Committee decided to revisit the existing national emissions reduction targets, recommending they be reduced to net zero by 2050. The Conservative government, then headed by Theresa May, accepted the Committee's advice and passed legislation to enshrine the net zero emissions target that same year. Setting a target and achieving a target are two different things, but this national target highlights how domestic climate and energy regulation, motivated by international environmental law and linked to company law, can lead to ambitious climate action by national governments.

This chapter focuses on non-corporate regulation, including climate and energy regulation as well as market mechanisms such as emissions trading schemes. The regulatory process can be flawed due to interference by lobby groups and the fast pace of climate science and technology, which cannot always be incorporated into the regulatory process at an appropriate pace. But regulation can also facilitate ambitious climate action. The focus of this chapter is on EU and UK energy and climate regulation, including developments resulting from the departure of the United Kingdom from the European Union (otherwise known as Brexit). These changes, combined with a renewed interest in Green New Deals (GNDs), have led to more ambitious regulation in the climate and energy sphere in both the European Union and the United Kingdom, despite tremendous political upheaval due to Brexit.

This chapter focuses on the types of regulations which directly intersect with companies in the context of climate change, and in particular energy companies. As a result, this chapter will assess specific climate change regulations as well as emission control measures and legislative efforts to transition energy markets away from fossil fuels and towards renewable energy. Emission reporting mandates, energy market reform and emissions trading schemes, all have direct impacts on companies. While other environmental laws (including waste, water, biodiversity and forestry management laws, environmental impact assessments, land regulation and others) also affect companies, this chapter takes a narrower approach, focusing only on climate and energy regulation. While the existing regulatory regimes focus on GHG reporting by companies, the implications of the GNDs, and recent net zero emissions targets by 2050 in the United Kingdom and the European Union, will have significant ramifications for companies, including energy companies. These targets will likely (and should) require more significant reduction requirements to be placed on companies in the future.

Climate and energy regulation can be imperfect tools, as their results are negotiated outcomes, and their enforcement can be problematic. Despite these imperfections, recent developments in the European Union and the United Kingdom have focused on achieving net zero emissions by 2050 and placed this target in the context of a GND in the European Union and a Green Brexit in the United Kingdom. This chapter will look specifically at EU approaches to energy regulation, particularly in the context of the GND. In addition, national approaches such as the enactment of the domestic Climate Change Act 2008 and the Energy Act 2013 in the United Kingdom will also be assessed, with a focus on the impacts of this regulation on energy-intensive companies. While energy legislation is directly applicable to companies, the Climate Change Act in the United Kingdom only regulates national emissions reduction efforts generally. It does overlap with the Companies Act 2006 in the area of directors' reporting regulations on GHG emissions. Gaps and opportunities of these regulatory approaches will be highlighted.

5.1 REGULATING COMPANIES

The concept of regulation is varied, and there is no universal definition of the term. Dennis Patterson provides a narrow, state-based definition as non-tax, non-criminal, legal directives issued and enforced by a governmental body, primarily through sanctions or incentives other than criminal penalties.[1] Types of regulation can vary from command-and-control types to incentive-based regulation.[2] These categories can include legal directives, performance standards, regulatory taxes, tradable permits and information (such as labelling).[3] The concept of regulation has evolved from previously narrow definitions to include less formal mechanisms, which can include market mechanisms such as emission trading schemes.[4]

Regulation is often cited as a means to correct certain market failures,[5] and in this case the negative externality of corporate GHG emissions. State intervention through regulation in corporate affairs can have efficiency justifications, and non-economic or equity justifications.[6] Corporate law contractarians, for the most part, insist that non-corporate regulatory mechanisms are preferable to mediate any negative social outcomes of corporate activities and negate the role of corporate law in dealing with externalities.[7] For example, Robert Baldwin, Martin Cave and Martin Lodge argue that while regulatory oversight is still necessary for a market economy, 'better regulation' focuses on the nature and performance of the regulation, and often includes regulatory impact assessments and cost-benefit analyses.[8] As a result, concepts of economic efficiency and shareholder primacy are folded into this neoliberal approach to regulation.

---

[1] Dennis Patterson, *A Companion To Philosophy of Law and Legal Theory* (Wiley-Blackwell 2010) 592.
[2] Jorge Riviera et al., 'Business Responses to Environmental and Social Protection Policies: Towards a Framework for Analysis' (2009) 42(1) *Policy Science* 3, 22.
[3] Patterson (n 1), 603.
[4] Robert Baldwin, Martin Cave and Martin Lodge, 'Introduction: Regulation – The Field and the Developing Agenda' in Robert Baldwin, Martin Cave and Martin Lodge (eds), *The Oxford Handbook of Regulation* (OUP 2010), 5–6.
[5] Patterson (n 1) notes that regulation is often cited to deal with a number of market failures such as externalities, public goods, monopolies and imperfect information, 596. See also Robert W Kling, 'Building an Institutionalist Theory of Regulation' (1988) 22(1) *Journal of Economic Issues* 197; Although Veljanovski cautions that viewing regulation as simply a reaction to market failure may be misleading, as both markets and governments can fail, Cento Vejanovski, 'Economic Approaches to Regulation' in Robert Baldwin, Martin Cave and Martin Lodge (eds), *The Oxford Handbook of Regulation* (Oxford University Press 2010), 19.
[6] Although Cheffins notes that non-economic justifications should be treated with caution. See Brian R. Cheffins, *Company Law Theory Structure and Operation* (2000 Oxford University Press) 126–160. Larry Reynolds, 'Foundations of an Institutionalist Theory of Regulation' (1981) XV(3) *Journal of Economic Issues* 641, 642. There is an extensive literature on judging regulation by its cost-benefit effects that is grounded in neoclassical efficiency, on the basis of either Pareto supremacy or Kaldor–Hicks efficiency. For example, see Matthew Adler, 'Regulatory Theory' in Dennis Patterson (ed) *A Companion to Philosophy of Law and Legal Theory* (2nd edn, Wiley-Blackstone 2010), 592; William J. Baumol, 'On Taxation and the Control of Externalities' (1972) 62(3) *The American Economic Review* 307; Matthew D. Adler, 'Beyond Efficiency and Procedure: A Welfarist Theory of Regulation' (2000) 28 Fla. St. U. L. Rev. 241.
[7] Marc T. Moore, *Corporate Governance in the Shadow of the State* (Hart 2013) 66.
[8] Baldwin, Cave and Lodge (n 4) 7–8.

Regulation is a political outcome, resulting from a negotiated process. Regulation can therefore be exploited either at its formative stage by powerful lobbying groups that act on behalf of companies,[9] or at its post-enactment stage, through lack of monitoring and enforcement. Explicit regulation is a product of a political mechanism that can allow narrow interests to capture the process, and overrule the interests of the majority.[10] Politicians and bureaucrats may be overly concerned with their own political ambitions, which may overcome the imperative to regulate appropriately. Politicians and policymakers also suffer from time constraints as a result of tight legislative schedules.[11] Vague or unclear legislative language may result from these time limitations.

In the United Kingdom, maintaining a relationship with industry in the regulatory environment is considered crucial.[12] Consequentially, governments tend to consult with the same interest groups, such as the Confederation of British Industry (CBI) and Institute of Chartered Accountants of England and Wales, and their views may be overly considered during the consultation process.[13] Julia Black notes that the interdependencies between social actors and governments are so intertwined that the public/private distinction of governance has collapsed, and regulation is now 'co-produced'.[14] Companies are one of the actors that may be involved in this regulatory production. The regulatory outcome may transfer wealth to specific interest groups.[15] In fact, oil and gas companies, such as Shell and BP, have been accused of heavily influencing the UK Government's climate change policies.[16] At the post-enactment stage, compliance and enforcement can depend on the character and resources of the regulator.[17] Regulators often have discretion when

---

[9] Kling (n 5) 202; Sam Peltzman, 'The Economic Theory of Regulation after a Decade of Deregulation' (Brookings Papers: Microeconomics, 1989), www.brookings.edu/bpea-articles/the-economic-theory-of-regulation-after-a-decade-of-deregulation/ (accessed 30 April 2015), 13.

[10] Kling (n 5) 202.

[11] Cheffins (n 6) 193, 184; See also J. H. Farrar, 'The United Kingdom Companies Act 1989' (1990–1991) 17 Can. Bus. L. J. 150, 159; Andre Tunc, 'A French Lawyer Looks at British Company Law' (1982) 45(1) M.L.R. 1, 8; Michael Rush, 'Making Better Law: A Review of the Hansard Society Commission on the Legislative Process' (1993) 14(2) Statute L. Rev. 75, 77.

[12] Stephen Fineman, 'Enforcing the Environment: Regulatory Realities' (2000) 9 *Business Strategy and the Environment* 62, 63.

[13] Cheffins (n 6), 182.

[14] Julia Black, 'Decentring Regulation: Understanding the Role of Regulation and Self-Regulation in a Post-Regulatory World' (2001) 54(1) *Current Legal Problems* 103, 109–110.

[15] Sam Peltzman, 'Toward a More General Theory of Regulation' (1976) 19(2) *J. L. & Econ.* 211, 212.

[16] See Felicity Lawrence and Harry Davies, 'Revealed: BP's Close Ties with the UK Government' (*The Guardian*, 20 May 2015), www.theguardian.com/environment/2015/may/20/revealed-bps-close-ties-with-the-uk-government (accessed 1 June 2015); Arthur Neslen, 'UK Accused of Hypocrisy over Plans to Limit Enforcement of EU Climate Goals' (*The Guardian*, 6 January 2015), www.theguardian.com/environment/2015/jan/06/uk-accused-hypocrisy-plans-limit-enforcement-eu-climate-goals (accessed 1 June 2015).

[17] James C. Cooper and William E. Kovacii, 'Behavioural Economics: Implications for Regulatory Behavior' (2012) 41 *Journal of Regulatory Economics* 41, 42; Stephen Fineman,

selecting compliance cases[18] and may suffer from regulatory capture by particularly powerful firms.[19] Firms themselves can often react to regulation in a number of ways, including compliance, over-compliance,[20] manipulation, avoidance and compromise.[21]

Ronald Coase made a significant contribution to the understanding of regulation through his work 'The Problem of Social Cost'.[22] In it, Coase posits that social cost, illustrated by the harm caused by environmental pollution, is a reciprocal problem,[23] and may not necessarily justify government regulation.[24] According to Coase, in order to achieve the optimal allocation of resources, both parties should take into account the harmful effects of the nuisance,[25] and bargain in order to efficiently allocate the harm. Through this reciprocal bargaining, polluters and their victims could achieve what Coase considered to be a socially optimal level of pollution.[26] In his view, the courts, through regulation and legal rights, fail to efficiently allocate the costs of regulation,[27] and government regulation can be costly and inefficient.[28] Coase's theories laid the groundwork for market-based mechanisms, and in particular cap-and-trade emissions reduction programmes, where parties bargain in the absence of transaction costs.[29] These types of schemes are also covered in this chapter, as companies often prefer market-based approaches to regulation, as market-based approaches can reduce the compliance costs of regulation or avoid the need for regulation entirely.

'Enforcing the Environment: Regulatory Realities' (2009) 9 *Business Strategy and the Environment* 62, 71.

[18] Amitai Aviram, 'Allocating Regulatory Resources' (2011) 37 J. Corp. L. 739, 741.

[19] Dale D. Murphy, 'Interjurisdictional Competition and Regulatory Advantage' (2005) 8(4) J. Int. Econ. L. 891, 891.

[20] Robert A. Kagan, Dorothy Thornton and Neil Gunningham, 'Explaining Corporate Environmental Performance: How Does Regulation Matter?' (2003) 37(1) *Journal of Law & Society Review* 51, 52.

[21] Jorge Riviera et al. (n 2) 7.

[22] R. H. Coase, 'The Problem of Social Cost' (1960) 3 J. of L. & Econ. 1, 3.

[23] Ibid., 2.

[24] Fred S. McChesney, 'Coase, Demsetz, and the Unending Externality Debate' (2006) 26 *Cato Journal* 179, 181.

[25] Ibid., 13.

[26] Robert Hahn, 'Ronald Henry Coase 1910–2013' (2013) 502 *Nature* 449, 449.

[27] Coase (n 22) 16.

[28] ibid., 18; Vejlanovski, (n 5) 22; Simpson notes that Coase's writings display a deep skepticism for government regulation. See A. W. Brian Simpson, '"Coase v. Pigou" Reexamined' (1996) 25(1). J of L. Studies, 58; and Demsetz criticizes Coase's treatment of government regulation as part of the economic system; see Harold Demsetz, 'The Problem of Social Cost: What Problem? A Critique of the Reasoning of A. C. Pigou and R. H. Coase' (2011) 7 Rev. of L. and Econ., 8, although Hahn argues that Coase did not necessarily see government regulation as less efficient; see Robert Hahn (n 26) 449.

[29] Sarah E. Light, 'The New Insider Trading: Environmental Markets within the Firm' (2015) 34 (1) Stanford Envtl. L. J., 12.

5.2 CLIMATE AND ENERGY REGULATION IN THE EUROPEAN UNION

The European Union has a long history of regulating and reducing emissions, as well as encouraging (and now mandating) increased use of renewable energy among its member states. These regulatory ambitions derive in part from the EU's leadership in international climate negotiations, including the negotiation of the Kyoto Protocol (KP) and more recently the Paris Agreement, and their associated emissions trading mechanisms. Article 94 of the Treaty on the Functioning of the EU (TFEU) states that each member state retains the right to determine conditions for exploiting its own energy resources. Member states have agreed to participate in effort-sharing agreements which mandate regional emissions reduction targets, as well as national renewable energy and energy efficiency targets. These targets have evolved and become more ambitious over time.

In 2008, the EU 2020 climate package agreed on a regional target to reduce GHG emissions by 20 per cent below 1990 levels by 2020 (with a conditional agreement to reduce by 30 per cent if other developed country parties participating in international climate negotiations made similar commitments), and by 50 per cent by 2050.[30] In 2012, the European Union signed on to a second commitment period under the KP to reduce GHG emissions by 20 per cent below 1990 levels. The United Kingdom and Germany are the two largest emitters in the European Union. The UK's share of the then EU target equated to a 16 per cent reduction of non-EU-ETS emissions relative to 2005 levels.[31]

The updated 2020 Climate and Energy Package (CARE) in the European Union contained three key, legally binding targets: a 20 per cent cut in GHG emissions (from 1990 levels), 20 per cent of EU renewable energy target and a 20 per cent improvement in energy efficiency.[32] European Union effort sharing legislation provides binding emissions targets for sectors not covered by the EU Emissions Trading System (also [EU ETS], mainly housing, waste, agriculture and transportation) which included a target of a 30 per cent reduction in emissions by 2030.[33] In preparation for the 2015 Paris Conference, the European Union agreed to increase that target, and reduce GHG emissions by 40 per cent below 1990 levels by 2030.[34] Post-2015, the 2018 RES Directive imposed binding renewable energy targets on member states of at least 32 per cent by 2030, with an upwards revision clause in

---

[30] Beatriz Perez de las Heras, 'Beyond Kyoto: The EU's Contribution to a More Sustainable World Economy' (2013) 19(4) European L. J. 577, 585.
[31] DECC, UK GHG Statistics and Inventory Team, 'UK GHG Emissions: Performance Against Emissions Reductions Targets -2012 Provisional Figures' (5 July 2013), 7.
[32] https://ec.europa.eu/clima/policies/strategies/2020_en (accessed 20 July 2020).
[33] https://ec.europa.eu/clima/policies/effort_en (accessed 20 July 20200.
[34] Arthur Neslen, 'EU Leaders Agree to Cut Greenhouse Gas Emissions by 40% by 2030' (*The Guardian*, 24 October 2014), www.theguardian.com/world/2014/oct/24/eu-leaders-agree-to-cut-greenhouse-gas-emissions-by-40-by-2030 (accessed 21 July 2020).

2023.³⁵ Most recently in 2020, as part of the European GND, the European Union established a goal and pathway to climate neutrality by 2050, meaning net zero emissions by 2050.³⁶ This pathway established binding legal obligations on member states to achieve net zero emissions by 2050.

This ambitious 2050 goal evolved as part of the recently agreed European GND. In December 2019, the European Union agreed a growth strategy that aimed to transform the European Union into a fair and prosperous society, with a modern, resource-efficient and competitive economy with no net emissions in 2050.³⁷ The concept of a GND has been around for some time as a proposed response to the 2008 financial crisis, and the 'triple threat' of economic, social and ecological crises.³⁸ It generally includes four key components: reducing carbon dependency in the world economy, reducing ecological scarcity, eliminating challenges in global capital and skills gaps, and national actions to implement the GND.³⁹ The concept has gained in popularity with the issuance of the US proposal for a GND in 2019,⁴⁰ and the European adoption of the GND, also in 2019.

The European GND focuses on energy decarbonisation, but also establishes a circular economy with sustainable product and raw materials policies. It also focuses on the renovation of buildings to ensure efficiency and affordability, as well as ensuring a sustainable food production strategy. Underpinning the entire strategy is the concept of a just and inclusive transition, ensuring regions and sectors most affected by the transition away from fossil fuels are supported. The strategy recognises the need to embed sustainability into corporate governance frameworks. In that vein, increased disclosures on climate and environmental data will need to be made, along with a review of the existing EU Non-Financial Reporting Directive.

5.3 CLIMATE AND ENERGY REGULATION IN THE UNITED KINGDOM

The United Kingdom has been an active participant in the international negotiations on climate change, and until the agreement on Brexit, contributed to the KP targets through the regional EU commitments. The UK Government has cited both moral and economic reasons for reducing domestic GHG emissions. The UK

---

³⁵ Directive 2018/2001/EU (known as the RES Directive).
³⁶ Brussels, COM (2020) 80 final 2020/0036, Proposal for a Regulation of the European Parliament and of the Council Establishing the Framework for Achieving Climate Neutrality and amending Regulation EU 2018/1999.
³⁷ COM (2019) 640 final, The European Green New Deal.
³⁸ See, for example, Heinrich Boll Stiftung, 'Green New Deal – Greening the Economy' (Article issue 2009), https://us.boell.org/en/2009/02/01/green-new-deal-greening-economy (accessed 21 July 2020); Ahment Atil Asici and Zeynap Bunul, 'Green New Deal: A Green Way Out of the Crisis?' (2012) 22 *Environment Policy and Governance* 295.
³⁹ Asici and Bunul (n 38), 299–300.
⁴⁰ House Resolution 109, 'Recognizing the duty of the Federal Government to create a Green New Deal', www.congress.gov/bill/116th-congress/house-resolution/109/text (accessed on 20 July 2020).

Government's approach is that the Paris Agreement had to be 'credible and fair', and should therefore reflect past and future climate change activities, as well as domestic capabilities.[41] In addition, climate action is motivated by the significant damages that the United Kingdom has already incurred, particularly as a result of flooding events in 2012–13,[42] and concern over future impacts that UK companies and domestic markets face as a result of climate change impacts overseas.[43] The United Kingdom historically implemented its share of the EU targets through domestic action on climate change, largely through legislative efforts such as energy market reform and the Climate Change Act 2008, as well as by participation in the EU ETS. Post-Brexit, the institutional structures of the Climate Change Act will not change, but the United Kingdom will exit the EU ETS, leading to some uncertainty regarding new domestic emissions trading mechanisms.

5.3.1 Parliamentary Supremacy in Climate and Energy Regulation

English common law has explicitly deferred the power of law-making in the environmental arena to Parliament through the landmark case of *Cambridge Water Co. v. Eastern Counties Leather Plc*.[44] In this leading judgment, Lord Goff denied the pollution claim, but also made some important statements about the role of the courts in environmental law-making. He stated that in the area of environmental protection and preservation more generally, international and national public bodies were taking steps to establish legislation on these matters, and as a result, there was less need for the courts to develop a common law principle to achieve the same environmental goal, and it may be undesirable for the courts to interfere.[45]

As a result, the common law of nuisance was nullified as an effective tool to develop standards on environmental protection and preservation, and the House of

---

[41] HM Government, 'Paris 2015 Securing Our Prosperity through a Global Climate Change Agreement' (2013), 8, 52–53, www.gov.uk/government/publications/paris-2015-securing-our-prosperity-through-a-global-climate-change-agreement#:~:text=In%20December%202015%2C%20the%20world,on%20years%20of%20hard%20work (accessed 21 July 2020).

[42] Estimated to be between £200 and 277 million, with indirect costs reaching £260–620 million, ibid., 18.

[43] Ibid., 21.

[44] [1994] 2 AC 264. Cambridge Water purchased the Sawston Mill in 1976, and constructed a facility to extract water from the existing borehole on the land. Eastern Counties Leather had been operating a tanning facility for many years on a nearby property, and had used small amounts of perchloroethylene (or PCE) to degrease leather pelts. Small amounts of PCE had seeped into the ground and infiltrated the aquifer at the Sawston Mill, leading to small amounts of PCE in the drinking water. PCE only became regulated in 1980. The House of Lords considered whether the rule of strict liability was to be enforced through the common law of nuisance to prevent environmental pollution as stated in *Rylands* v. *Fletcher* [1868] UKHL 1.

[45] Ibid., 306, paras G-H.

Lords 'abdicated' their role in developing common law principles of nuisance.[46] The courts are, as a result, reluctant to delineate explicit environmental law principles, and have relegated this role specifically to Parliament. Regulation, therefore, has become the primary mechanism to deal with environmental issues in the United Kingdom. As a result of Brexit, the Environmental Bill 2020 was introduced into Parliament on 15 October 2019 (and re-introduced due to the national election in January 2020). It is the primary legal mechanism to deliver the Government's 25 Year Environmental Plan, to establish new governance frameworks for the environment, and to deliver a 'Green Brexit'.

5.3.2 A 'Green Brexit'

The 25 Year Environment Plan was issued in 2018, and established a roadmap to tackle problems of waste and soil deprivation, improve agriculture and fisheries management and to also improve social justice.[47] These changes are designed to replace existing EU environmental monitoring mechanisms and targets, and in particular to alleviate concern regarding a lack of environmental monitoring and management domestically post-Brexit.[48] The 2020 Environment Bill requires policymakers to have due regard to environmental principles such as the preventative and precautionary principle and the polluter pays principle. It also establishes new, legally binding targets in four priority areas – air quality, waste, resource efficiency and water and nature, which will be reviewed on a five-yearly basis. The 25 Year Environment Plan, along with the Environment Bill 2020, will complement the Industrial Strategy and Clean Growth Strategy, with the latter focused on emissions reductions and increasing renewable energy. Combined with the new UK Green

---

[46] Rosalind Lee, '*Cambridge Water* v. *Eastern Counties Leather*: The Polluters' Charter?' (1994) 12(3) *Property Management* 29, 29. Although see O'Quinn, who states that this was a strategic decision by the House of Lords to avoid opening the floodgates to historic pollution claims, John C. O'Quinn, 'Not-so-strict Liability: A Foreseeability Test for *Rylands* v. *Fletcher*' (2000) 24 Harv. Env. L. Rev. 287, 296.

[47] HM Government, 'A Green Future: Our Twenty-Five Year Plan to Improve the Environment' (2018), https://assets.publishing.service.gov.uk/government/uploads/system/uploads/attachment_data/file/673492/25-year-environment-plan-annex1.pdf (accessed 20 July 2020).

[48] Alyssa Gilbert and Maria Carvalho, 'Consultation Response: Environmental Principles and Governance after EU Exit' (Grantham Institute, August 2018), www.lse.ac.uk/granthaminstitute/wp-content/uploads/2018/09/Environmental-principles-and-governance-after-EU-exit_Defra-consultation-response-2.pdf (accessed 20 July 2020). For example, as part of Brexit, the United Kingdom will lose funding from the European Investment Bank and EU research funding, as well as the share of EU budget funds that were traditionally invested in energy infrastructure projects, and the Bill's approach to environmental principles has been critiqued, Fay Farstand, Neil Carter and Charlotte Burns, 'What Does Brexit Mean for the UK's Climate Change Act?' (2018) 89(2) *The Political Q.*, 292, 293, Maria Lee and Eloise Scotford, 'Environmental Principles after Brexit: the Draft Environment (Principles and Governance) Bill' (Working Paper) (2019), https://papers.ssrn.com/sol3/papers.cfm?abstract_id=3322341 (accessed 31 August 2020).

Finance Strategy, these regulatory changes will have sweeping consequences for companies in the United Kingdom and should complement existing energy market reforms.

5.4 ENERGY MARKET REFORM IN THE UNITED KINGDOM

Action on climate change in the United Kingdom began in earnest in the 1980s, and the deregulation and reform of the energy market have been inextricably linked to domestic climate action.[49] The first UK subsidy for renewable energy was introduced in 1990 through the non-fossil fuel obligation (or NFFO).[50] During the 1990s, the 'dash for gas' in the United Kingdom meant that emissions declined nationally as the United Kingdom transitioned from coal to gas use. As a result, the reduction of GHGs was not such a challenging issue for the government in the 1990s when it signed on to the KP.[51] Further modernisation of the UK energy industry occurred in 2000 under the Utilities Act, which updated the 1989 Electricity Act that introduced the Renewables Obligation (RO) for energy suppliers.[52] However, the major piece of legislation dealing with climate change was the Climate Change Act 2008.

5.4.1 The Climate Change Act 2008

Energy reform complemented the national legislative movement on climate change, which was comprehensively set out in the Climate Change Act 2008. The United Kingdom was the first country to enact specific legislation on climate change through the Act.[53] The motivation for the Act is set out in the Explanatory Notes, which states:

---

[49] Simon Dresner, Tim Jackson and Nigel Gilbert, 'History and Social Response to Environmental Tax Reform in the UK' (2006) 34 *Energy Policy* 930, 930.

[50] Till Stengel and Alexander Frenzel, 'Regulating Technological Change – The Strategic Reactions of Utility Companies toward Subsidy Policies in the German, Spanish and UK Electricity Markets' (2008) 361 *Energy Policy* 2645, 2648; Doerte Forquest and Thomas B. Johansson, 'European Renewable Energy Policy at a Cross-roads – Focus on Electricity Support Mechanisms' (2008) 36 *Energy Policy* 4079, 4082. The Climate Change Levy (or CCL) was implemented in April 2001 as a tax on energy use by business of fuels such as gas, coal, electricity and non-transport LPG; see Adarsh Varma, 'UK's CCL: Cost Effectiveness, Competitiveness and Environmental Impacts' (2003) 31 *Energy Policy* 51, 52.

[51] Shane Fudge and Michael Peters, 'Behaviour Change in the UK Climate Debate: An Assessment of Responsibility, Agency and Political Dimensions' (2011) 3 *Sustainability* 789, 792.

[52] The 10% percentage would be increased to 15.4% by 2015; see J. J. Foxton and P. J. G. Pearson, 'Towards Improved Policy Processes for Promoting Innovation in Renewable Electricity Technologies in the UK' (2007) 35 *Energy Policy* 1539, 1539.

[53] Matthew Lockwood, 'The Political Sustainability of Climate Policy: The Case of the UK Climate Change Act' (2013) 23 *Global Environmental Change* 1339, 1339.

It is widely accepted that urgent action is required to address the causes and consequences of climate change. The 2006 Stern Review set out the economic case for action on climate change, and concluded that the cost of inaction will be far higher than tackling climate change now.[54]

The original aim of the legislation was to set a target for the reduction of GHG emissions by 2050 at least 80 per cent lower than the 1990 baseline,[55] although this target has become more ambitious over time. The main institutional mechanism of the Act is the Committee on Climate Change, which provides expert and independent advice to governments on setting and achieving appropriate reduction targets, and provides reports to Parliament on progress. Staffed by eminent scientists and technical experts, the Committee's advice has often been heeded by successive Governments.[56] This institutional structure of the Committee and the Act is unlikely to be affected by Brexit.

Despite the reputational and institutional advantage of the Committee, under the Act carbon targets can be amended by the Secretary of State, subject to certain conditions set out in section 2(1) and (2). The Secretary of State can also establish five-yearly carbon budgets, starting with the period 2008–12, and the national UK 'carbon account' cannot exceed those carbon budgets.[57] Prior to Brexit, the carbon budgets had to be in line with the European Union and international obligations.[58] Three carbon budgets were originally established, set out in the 2009 UK Low Carbon Transition Plan.[59]

The major decreases in GHG emissions in the United Kingdom from the 1990 baseline were achieved through fuel switching (the transition from coal to gas), reduced methane emissions from coal mines and upgrades and reduced leakages in national gas distribution networks.[60] The ease with which the targets were achieved meant that there was no substantive investment in low-carbon

---

[54] Climate Change Act Guidelines 2008, s 4. See also HM Government, 'Implementing the Climate Change Act 2008: The Government's Proposal for Setting the Fourth Carbon Budget' Policy Statement (May 2011), <Implementing the Climate Change Act 2008: The Government's Proposal for Setting the Fourth Carbon Budget> accessed 20 July 2020, 4.

[55] Climate Change Act 2008, Chapter 27, s 1(1).

[56] Akshat Rathi, 'The UK's trailblazing advantage against climate change' *Quartz*, 11 July 2019, https://qz.com/1662800/the-uks-committee-on-climate-change-is-a-model-for-all-countries/.

[57] Ibid., s4(1).

[58] Ibid., s8.

[59] HM Government, 'The UK Low Carbon Transition Plan' National Strategy for Climate and Energy (15 July 2009), https://assets.publishing.service.gov.uk/government/uploads/system/uploads/attachment_data/file/228752/9780108508394.pdf (accessed 20 July 2020), 39.

[60] For example, 2011 industry emissions were 41 per cent lower than 1990 (excluding power stations), HM Government, 'Government Response to the Fifth Annual Progress Report for the Committee on Climate Change: Meeting the Carbon Budgets – 2013 Progress Report to Parliament' (October 2013), www.theccc.org.uk/wp-content/uploads/2013/06/CCC-Prog-Rep-Book_singles_web_1.pdf (accessed 30 May 2020); DECC, Ricardo-AEA, 'An Introduction to the UK's Greenhouse Gas Inventory 2008–2012' (Chapter 4, 14 May 2014), 10.

capacity.[61] The increasing reliance on gas will ensure that the UK target up to 2020 can also be achieved, which may prolong and delay the necessary investment in low-carbon capacity.[62] As a result, longer-term targets of an 80 per cent reduction by 2050 were considered to be more challenging to meet, and would necessitate decarbonisation of the electricity system in the 2020s.[63] Overall, the trajectory of GHGs nationally has been decreasing in an inconsistent fashion with a 3.5 per cent increase in GHG emissions in 2012 from 2011,[64] and a 12 per cent increase in coal generation emissions in 2009.[65] As a result, UK emissions have fluctuated instead of steadily decreasing in recent years,[66] and the progress on decreasing emissions was threatened to be reversed.[67] As a result, it was 'highly uncertain' whether post-2020 targets could be achieved.[68]

In reaction to this uncertainty, the Committee on Climate Change published a report to Parliament in June 2017. In that report, the Committee advised Parliament that new domestic policies were urgently needed to cut the UK's emissions, to enable future carbon targets to be met, and to replace existing EU targets post-Brexit.[69] Partly as a reaction to the Committee's report, the UK Government published its Clean Growth Strategy in October 2017.[70] The Strategy advocated growing the national economy while cutting emissions, with a goal to end coal use for electricity by 2025. While the Committee approved of the Government's approach of placing the low-carbon economy at the heart of the UK's industrial policy, it also warned that despite the Clean Growth Strategy, more action needed to be taken in order for the Government to meet its fourth carbon budget.[71] In May

---

[61] Committee on Climate Change, 'Meeting Carbon Budgets – the Need for a Step Change' (Progress Report to Parliament, 12 October 2009), 109, www.theccc.org.uk/publication/meeting-carbon-budgets-the-need-for-a-step-change-1st-progress-report/ (accessed 4 May 2017).
[62] Ibid., 112.
[63] DECC, 'Emissions Performance Standard Impact Assessment' (July 2011), 2, www.gov.uk/government/uploads/system/uploads/attachment_data/file/204801/eps_ia.pdf (accessed 30 May 2020).
[64] HM Government (n 60) October 2013, Executive Summary, 9. The report notes that the increase resulted from greater use of coal and gas for electricity generation and a colder than average winter, but also notes this increase is not a long-term trend.
[65] Committee on Climate Change (n 61) 41.
[66] DECC and Ricardo-AEA, (n 60) 13; Committee on Climate Change (n 61) 40–41.
[67] Ibid., 109.
[68] Ibid., 112; DECC, 'Updated Energy and Emissions Projections 2015' (November 2015), 9, www.gov.uk/government/publications/updated-energy-and-emissions-projections-2015 (accessed 10 February 2020).
[69] Committee on Climate Change, 'Meeting Carbon Budgets: Closing the Policy Gap' 2017 Report to Parliament, June 2017.
[70] HM Government, 'The Clean Growth Strategy Leading the Way to a Low Carbon Future' (October 2017), https://assets.publishing.service.gov.uk/government/uploads/system/uploads/attachment_data/file/700496/clean-growth-strategy-correction-april-2018.pdf (accessed 20 July 2020).
[71] Committee on Climate Change, 'An Independent Assessment of the UK's Clean Growth Strategy – from Ambition to Action' (January 2018).

2019, in reaction to the IPCC's landmark special report on 1.5°C, the Committee recommended the Government adopt a net zero emissions reduction target by 2050, concluding that this target was necessary, feasible and cost-effective.[72] The Government agreed, and in June 2019 passed legislation to enshrine the net zero target into law, becoming the first major economy to do so.[73]

5.4.2 Intersection between the Climate Change Act and the Companies Act

In addition to establishing nationally binding emissions reductions targets, the Climate Change Act also has provisions that implicate companies directly, but currently only in relation to reporting requirements. Section 85 requires that the Secretary of State make regulations pursuant to Section 416(4) of the Companies Act to require directors to report such information as may be specified regarding GHG emissions from their corporate activities. Section 416(4) of the Companies Act 2006 allows the Financial Reporting Review Panel to monitor and amend accounts of large public and private companies. Failure to comply with reporting requirements by companies is an offence under Section 419(3) of the Companies Act. Regulations requiring mandatory reporting were made necessary as voluntary approaches to corporate GHG emissions reporting had not led to a 'sufficiently high level of reporting nor consistency of reporting'.[74]

In 2011, Department for Environment, Food and Rural Affairs (Defra) made a recommendation that only Scope 1 and Scope 2 emissions are required to be reported, and that Scope 3 emissions are encouraged to be reported.[75] Following consultation, there was clear support for mandatory reporting for all large companies, although the majority of industry and trade associations, and a 'sizeable minority of companies'[76] advocated for voluntary reporting instead of regulation. In

---

[72] Committee on Climate Change, 'Net Zero: The UK's Contribution to Stopping Global Warming' (May 2019), 8, with a net zero target for Scotland in 2045, and in Wales a 95% target by 2050.

[73] Climate Change Act 2008 (2050 Target Amendment) Order 2019, www.legislation.gov.uk/ukdsi/2019/9780111187654 (accessed 20 July 2020), see also www.gov.uk/government/news/uk-becomes-first-major-economy-to-pass-net-zero-emissions-law (accessed 20 July 2020).

[74] Defra, 'Impact Assessment of Options for Company GHG Reporting' (31 August 2011), 1, www.gov.uk/government/uploads/system/uploads/attachment_data/file/82354/20120620-ghg-consult-final-ia.pdf (accessed 30 May 2015).

[75] Ibid., 16; Scope 1 emissions are direct emissions, Scope 2 emissions are indirect from other organisations that produced steam, electricity, cooking or heat for Scope 1 emissions, and Scope 3 emissions are indirect from other organisations used as inputs into the company concerned to produce direct emissions; see Defra 'Environmental Reporting Guidelines: Including Mandatory Greenhouse Gas Emissions Reporting Guidance' (June 2013), 38, www.gov.uk/government/publications/environmental-reporting-guidelines-including-mandatory-greenhouse-gas-emissions-reporting-guidance (accessed 30 May 2020).

[76] DEFRA, 'Measuring and Reporting GHG Emissions by UK Companies. Survey of Consultation Responses' (June 2012), 5, www.gov.uk/government/uploads/system/uploads/attachment_data/file/86569/20120620-ghg-consult-sumresp.pdf (accessed 30 May 2020).

June 2012, Defra released the 'Consultation on GHG emissions reporting draft regulations for quoted companies', confirming that only UK-quoted companies would be subject to mandatory GHG reporting. The regulations do not require the use of a coherent methodology for reporting,[77] although Defra did issue guidance on GHG reporting.[78] Companies could set their own targets (on the basis of absolute reductions or intensity targets) and report on their compliance. A 2010 Defra report concluded that although reporting of GHG emissions is important, it does not automatically lead to a reduction in GHG emissions.[79] So while many Financial Times Stock Exchange (FTSE) companies reported figures on climate change or energy use, there was a lack of quantitative data in these annual reports – they tended to contain more qualitative data.[80]

As with national emissions reduction targets, there have been sweeping changes in reporting requirements as well in recent years. In 2016, the Department for Business, Energy and Industrial Strategy noted that disclosure requirements were leading to both unclear and unsatisfactory disclosures by directors.[81] The existing reporting regulations were not proving effective, and so The Companies, Partnerships and Groups (Accounts and Non-Financial Reporting) Regulations 2016 were introduced, and imposed obligations on companies with over 500 employees (defined as public interest entities) to disclose GHG emissions. These only applied to certain companies, including publicly traded companies, banking companies, authorised insurance companies or companies conducting insurance market activity. The regulations were designed to help companies identify sustainability risks, to increase investor and consumer trust, and to manage change towards a sustainable global economy by combining long-term profitability with social justice and environmental protection.

In 2019, the new Streamlined Energy and Carbon Reporting (SECR) framework became effective. This framework applies to an expanded category of companies, including all large or quoted companies and large limited liability partnership (or LLPs) in the United Kingdom.[82] Large entities are as defined in the Companies Act 2006, and include entities that have a turnover of £36 million or more, a balance sheet of £18 million or more, or 250 employees or more (unless they use under a

---

[77] DEFRA (n 76) 15, 23; Companies Act 2006 (Strategic Report and Directors' Report) Regulations 2013.
[78] DEFRA (n 76) 15, 23.
[79] DEFRA, 'The Contribution That Reporting of Greenhouse Gas Emissions Makes to the UK Meeting Its Climate Change Objectives: A Review of the Current Evidence' (November 2010), 35, www.gov.uk/government/uploads/system/uploads/attachment_data/file/69262/pb13449-corporate-reporting-101130.pdf (accessed 30 May 2020).
[80] Ibid., 7.
[81] UK Department of Business, Energy and Industrial Strategy, 'Corporate Governance Reform' Green Paper (November 2016).
[82] Companies (Directors' Report) and Limited Liability Partnerships (Energy and Carbon Report) Regulations 2018.

certain threshold of energy of 40 MWh in a reporting period). These regulations expand the number of business entities subject to reporting requirements to approximately 12,000, and are related to EU-wide environment, sustainability and governance initiatives (covered in Chapter 7), and complement ongoing domestic energy reform initiatives.

5.4.3 The Energy Act 2013

The Energy Act 2008 complemented the Climate Change Act 2008 by covering renewable energy, carbon capture and storage (or CCS) technology, and feed-in tariffs, and was quickly updated by the Energy Act 2010 and Energy Act 2013. The Energy Act 2013 led to sweeping energy market reform in the United Kingdom, with the objectives of achieving secure, reasonably priced and low-carbon sources of energy for the national market. These reforms included a contract for difference (CfD) to secure minimum purchase prices through long-term investment contracts of fifteen years for renewable energy, and the establishment of Emissions Performance Standards (or EPS) to limit annual carbon dioxide emissions from new fossil fuel power stations.[83] The EPS acts as a regulatory backstop to effectively prevent the build of new coal-fired plants without CCS technology attached to them.[84]

The regulations require that power plants over 50 MW limit their emissions to 450g CO_2/kWh.[85] Government documents have noted that the use of CCS will allow coal and gas to continue to play a role in the energy mix for the medium term.[86] As a result, existing coal-fired power plants will be grandfathered into the EPS system until 2018 at a minimum.[87] The carbon price mechanism was consequently moved from a primary to a secondary place in the legislation, possibly indicating political pressure to keep electricity affordable.[88] In addition, energy-

---

[83] The EPS effectively prevents the build of new coal-fired power plants without CCS technology, See DECC, 'Ninth Statement of New Regulation January–June 2015' (December 2014), 5, www.gov.uk/government/publications/decc-ninth-statement-of-new-regulation (accessed 30 May 2020). The Energy Act 2016 renamed the Oil and Gas Authority Limited as the Oil and Gas Authority, and transferred certain functions to it, and the 2020 OGA strategy includes reference to the United Kingdom's net zero emissions target.

[84] Clifford Chance, 'Energy Act Passed and EMR Delivery Plan Finalised' (Briefing Note, December 2013), www.cliffordchance.com/briefings/2013/12/energy_act_passedandemrdeliveryplanfinalised.html (accessed 30 May 2020); DECC (n 68) 9–10.

[85] DECC (n 68) 12.

[86] HM Government, 'Implementing the Climate Change Act 2008: The Government's Proposal for Setting the Fourth Carbon Budget' Policy Statement (May 2011), https://assets.publishing.service.gov.uk/government/uploads/system/uploads/attachment_data/file/48081/1683-4th-carbon-budget-policy-statement.pdf (accessed 20 July 2020), 15; HM Government (n 64) Executive Summary, 6

[87] DECC (n 68) 32.

[88] Ibid., 3.

intensive industries are exempted from the CfD, which means they would not be subject to any carbon price incentives to switch to renewables. This is curious, as energy-intensive industries are the very industries that must move towards renewable sources in order to transition away from fossil fuels, and market mechanisms are often touted by businesses as a more appropriate route than regulation to mediate their carbon emissions.

5.4.4 Energy Companies' Approaches to Climate Change

Many large energy companies in the United Kingdom have cited regulatory uncertainty and the costs of regulating GHG emissions as direct threats to their business operations because they result in increased operational costs. A sampling of some approaches to energy-intensive companies is set out below. While most of these companies acknowledge the risks that climate change poses to their own businesses and to society at large, they have taken disparate and sometimes contradictory approaches to Government regulation to the issue of climate change generally.

Regulation of GHG emissions is often the most influential factor in corporate internal climate change policy-formation. In the view of the BP's Head of Policy, the most effective approach to climate change for their company is to assess and then mirror government policy.[89] BP used to see regulatory approaches to GHG emissions as 'increasingly stringent regulatory constraints' on emissions.[90] Although BP has taken innovative steps on climate change very recently, it is important not to overstate its achievements as there is very little detail available on how it will achieve these targets. Miriam Cherry and Judd Sneirson noted that the Beyond Petroleum campaign was nothing more than a 'glittering public relations campaign',[91] and that the company is still focused on profit-making. BP's previous energy outlooks asserted that oil and gas will remain the dominant source of energy, contributing over three-fourths of the total energy supply in 2035.[92] However, in February 2020, BP announced one of the most progressive emissions reduction ambition of any energy-intensive company.[93] It pledged to eliminate or offset not only all of the Scope 1 and Scope 2 emissions from its operations, but also Scope 3 emissions caused by the oil and gas it produces. While the company did not provide many

---

[89] BP Plc, 'Sustainability Review 2012' (2012), 16, www.bp.com/content/dam/bp/pdf/sustainability/group-reports/BP_Sustainability_Review_2012.pdf (accessed 10 February 2020).
[90] Ibid., 7.
[91] Miriam A. Cherry and Judd F. Sneirson, 'Beyond Profit: Rethinking Corporate Social Responsibility and Greenwashing after the BP Oil Disaster' (2011) 85(4) *Tulane Law Review* 983, 1009.
[92] BP Global, 'BP Energy Outlook 2017 Edition' (2017), 15, www.bp.com/content/dam/bp/business-sites/en/global/corporate/pdfs/energy-economics/energy-outlook/bp-energy-outlook-2017.pdf (accessed 4 May 2020).
[93] www.bp.com/en/global/corporate/news-and-insights/press-releases/bernard-looney-announces-new-ambition-for-bp.html (accessed 21 July 2020).

details on how it would achieve these ambitions, the announcement illustrates the growing pressure these companies are facing from activists and investors.[94]

Royal Dutch Shell has taken a more nuanced but also progressive approach to climate change in recent years. While the company acknowledges the risks that climate change poses to its business, it continued, until September 2015, to be a member of the American Legislative Exchange Council, a political organisation that opposes policies to address climate change.[95] The expert review committee of the company's own sustainability reports has also pointed out the company's hypocrisy on this matter.[96] Following a shareholder resolution in 2015, Shell published a report specific to climate change and portfolio resilience, although the company noted that its reserves would not become stranded, and that oil and gas would remain integral to the global energy system for decades.[97] After consultations with institutional investors Climate Action 100+, in 2018 Shell agreed to set emission reduction targets and link them to executive pay.[98] In 2020, Shell agreed to a net zero emissions reduction ambition by 2050.[99]

Many of these companies used to consider GHG emissions regulations as 'stringent' even though very little formal regulation existed or still exists requiring these energy companies to comply with absolute GHG emissions reductions. The only formal regulatory mechanisms that directly regulate these companies are the emission performance specifications (EPS) and the directors' regulations to report GHG emissions. The EPS has fairly simple requirements that no new coal fuel plants can be built without CCS being attached to it. None of these companies operate many coal plants, and therefore the EPS does not have any significant impact on their operations and therefore emissions. These companies' historic approach to regulation was very much in line with the shareholder primacy and wealth maximisation

---

[94] Brad Plumber, 'BP Pledges to Cut Emissions to Zero but Offers Few Details' (*New York Times*, 12 February 2020), www.nytimes.com/2020/02/12/climate/bp-greenhouse-gas-emissions.html#:~:text=The%20British%20oil%20giant%20BP,pumps%20out%20of%20the%20ground (accessed 21 July 2020).

[95] Terry Macalister, 'The Real Story behind Shell's Climate Change Rhetoric' (*The Guardian*, 17 May 2015, www.theguardian.com/environment/2015/may/17/shell-climate-change-rhetoric-the-real-story) accessed 30 May 2020.

[96] Royal Dutch Shell, 'Sustainability Report 2014' (2014), https://reports.shell.com/sustainability-report/2014/servicepages/welcome.html 54 (accessed 20 July 2020).

[97] Royal Dutch Shell, 'Shell: Energy Transitions and Portfolio Resilience' (2016), 11, 34, www.shell.com/investors/environmental-social-and-governance/esg-news-presentations-and-annual-briefings/_jcr_content/par/tabbedcontent/tab_667142067/textimage_1262076677.stream/147932 3448964/ac5a7d526a53492af1cb2ed12357a3839349a2c3/ir-shell-and-energy-transitions-reporta4v20-124048.pdf (accessed 10 February 2020).

[98] Ivana Kottasová and Daniel Shane, 'Shell is the first energy company to link executive pay and carbon emissions' (CNN, 3 Dec 2018), www.cnn.com/2018/12/03/business/shell-climate-change-executive-pay/index.html (accessed 21 Jul 2020).

[99] 'Investors Welcome Net Zero Emissions Commitment Agreed with Shell' (IIGCC, 16 April 2020), www.iigcc.org/news/investors-welcome-net-zero-emissions-commitment-agreed-with-shell (accessed 20 July 2020).

approach to regulation. However, due to activist and investor pressure, these companies have begun to agree to more aggressive emission reduction approaches.

Existing regulations require that publicly traded companies report their GHG emissions. Many energy-intensive companies are publicly traded and therefore subject to the GHG regulations. However, the regulations only require that these companies report their GHG emissions, which they do, and therefore they are all compliant with the regulatory mechanism, and enforcement of the regulations is achievable. Failure to report GHG emissions becomes an offence under Section 419 (3) of the Companies Act 2006. The regulations, however, have very low levels of requirements. For example, they do not require a specific or coherent format of reporting, which in fact makes it difficult to compare emissions both within the same company over time, and between companies. The SECR framework does require that entities publish the methodology used, and that it must be robust, but does not mandate a specific methodology. From 2021 though, reporting is expected to be compliant with recommendations from the TCFD.

Most importantly, the current regulations do not require that companies reduce their GHG emissions, only that they report them. As a result, under the regulations, companies can voluntarily set their own targets on the basis of absolute reductions or intensity targets, and report on their own compliance. It is clear that at the moment the reporting regulations have not been effective in motivating sufficient reduction in GHG emissions in particular energy-intensive companies, although this may change as a result of increasingly ambitious national and corporate targets of net zero by 2050. While the detail on how these targets will be achieved is not entirely clear, Shell and BP's cooperation with institutional investors, and their net zero announcements by 2050, are a sign of future conduct by these types of companies. Traditionally, many companies will cite growth, expansion and profit motivators as reasons they anticipate an increase in their GHG emissions, and so shareholder wealth maximisation and the incentive to profit and grow traditionally acted as drivers of GHG emissions from energy intensive companies. Recent corporate announcements are now weighing investor and societal pressure against shareholder primacy and profit pressures, and motivating at least announcements of more progressive action.

> Formal regulatory mechanisms do not sufficiently mediate profit incentives, or, therefore, contribute to significant reductions in GHG emissions at the moment. To be clear, more ambitious regulation is required to mandate emissions reductions by companies. As noted in Chapter 2, the traditional approach to shareholder primacy and shareholder wealth maximisation may be slowly changing to reflect a broader, stakeholder-inclusive, based approach. As will be further highlighted in Chapters 6 and 7, litigation and financial incentives may also incentivise companies into making more dramatic and ambitious business decisions regarding

energy transitions and climate change. Combined with more ambitious 2050 national emissions goals in both the European Union and United Kingdom, there may be significant changes required both within these companies and their internal operations, and along with their supply chains in years to come. There is no doubt, however, that market mechanisms will complement existing or future regulatory initiatives.

5.5 MARKET MECHANISMS

Market mechanisms can be either state-based and regulated, or entirely voluntary initiatives. The KP was the main incentive for the development of the EU ETS, which is the primary carbon trading mechanism in the European Union. Market-based mechanisms are designed to lead to greater efficiency in environmental and energy policies by reducing the costs of implementing and complying with environmental measures, thereby incentivising technological change.[100] However, market mechanisms have been largely unsuccessful at ensuring adequate emission cuts in developed countries to date, particularly as a result of the reduction in carbon prices due to the 2008 financial crisis.[101] The recent COVID-19 public health and commensurate economic crisis, combined with low oil prices, might similarly affect emissions trading mechanisms, but its long-term effects remain to be seen. The short-term impact of the crisis has been a reduction in emissions and therefore a reduction in the price of carbon. If national recovery plans incorporate a just transition approach and a renewed emphasis on climate change,[102] combined with linking emissions systems internationally as well as new trading rules under the Paris Agreement (if agreed), these efforts could provide renewed impetus to carbon market mechanisms.

5.5.1 *State-Based Market Mechanisms: The Kyoto Protocol*

Market mechanisms are not ideologically neutral[103] and states often rely heavily on industry expertise to design and implement them.[104] Regulators of these

---

[100] David Pearce, 'The Political Economy of an Energy Tax: The United Kingdom's CCL' (2006) 28 *Energy Economics* 149, 149.
[101] There are also some philosophical opposition to using market mechanisms as they put a price on ecosystem services; see Erik Gomez-Baggethun and others, 'The History of Ecosystem Services in Economic Theory and Practice: From Early Notions to Markets and Payment Schemes' (2009) 69(6) *Ecological Economics* 1, 1.
[102] See letter from seventeen EU Environmental Ministers, 'European Green New Deal Must be Central to a Resilient Recovery at Covid-19' 9 April 2020, www.climatechangenews.com/2020/04/09/european-green-deal-must-central-resilient-recovery-covid-19 (accessed 20 July 2020).
[103] Gomez-Baggethun (n 101), 7.
[104] Larry Lohmann, 'Financialization, Commodification and Carbon: the Contradictions of Neoliberal Climate Policy' (2012) 48 *Socialist Register* 85, 87.

mechanisms also often become buyers and sellers within the marketplace, and therefore may not question the robustness[105] or environmental soundness of the system. As a result, long-term structural changes in developed countries needed to reduce use and reliance on fossil fuels can become divorced from the imperatives of a carbon market.[106] However, holistic approaches to greening the economy and financial systems (covered in Chapter 7) can provide a more ambitious and systemic underpinning to carbon markets.

An effective cap-and-trade system relies on robust and binding emissions targets to ensure that the permits are scarce and not oversupplied, and therefore that trading of permits will generate revenue and incentivise emissions reductions. It also requires robust reporting and strong compliance mechanisms to monitor, track and verify emission reductions, and to force state compliance with the regime.[107] The main goal of carbon trading is to make it cheaper for governments and companies to meet their GHG targets.[108] As a result, many countries have linked increased ambition of carbon targets to the availability of international market-based mechanisms to enable them to make cost-effective carbon cuts.[109]

The main mechanism used under the KP is the emissions trading mechanism, and offsets are reflected in the clean development mechanism (CDM) and the joint implementation (JI) mechanism. These are regulated through the KP and the institutions that have been established under the Protocol, and so are regulated market mechanisms; however, participation in the mechanisms is voluntary and emissions trading is designed to be supplemental to parties' domestic emissions cuts. The KP, however, made very limited demands on member states[110] to reduce emissions. While the KP is often described as a 'top-down' treaty, it was individual parties who agreed with their targets underneath it. The moral hazard at the heart of carbon trading is that the low level of commitments currently enshrined in the KP lead to delays by developed countries in making domestic reductions.[111] The use of tradable permits in the KP was introduced to overcome the rigidities of regulation, but permit allocations were often made without cost in order to 'buy the acceptance'

---

[105] Ibid., 88.
[106] Ibid., 90.
[107] Farhana Yamin and Joanna Depledge, *The International Climate Change Regime: A Guide to Rules, Institutions and Procedures* (CUP 2004) 156.
[108] Tamra Gilbertson and Oscar Reyes, 'Carbon Trading: How It Works and Why It Fails' (November 2009) Critical Currents No. 7, 9.
[109] Sampo Seppanen, 'Demand in a Fragmented Global Carbon Market: Outlook and Policy Options' (March 2013), 9, www.diva-portal.org/smash/get/diva2:702582/FULLTEXT01.pdf (accessed 30 May 2020).
[110] Bradley C. Parks and J. Timmons Roberts, 'Climate Change, Social Theory and Justice' (2010) 27(2) *Theory, Culture & Society* 134, 135.
[111] Mark Purdon, 'Neoclassical Realism and International Climate Change Politics: Moral Imperative and Political Constraint in International Climate Finance' (2014) 17 *JIRD* 301, 317.

of industry of the new cap-and-trade regime.[112] The 'grandfathering in' of existing pollution levels through the free allocation of permits effectively froze the status quo of emissions.[113] The low level of ambition in the international carbon market led to an oversupply of international carbon credits, keeping the price of carbon at very low levels.[114] New rules under the Paris Agreement for carbon trading mechanisms are therefore sorely needed in order to bolster existing international carbon trading mechanisms. The KP did lay the foundation for the development of the EU ETS, which remains the major regional emissions trading system in the world.

5.5.2 *The EU Emissions Trading System*

The EU ETS is the largest regional carbon trading mechanism, and was motivated by the establishment of the emissions trading mechanism in the KP.[115] The EU ETS is the key tool used within the European Union to reduce emissions, and covers approximately 45 per cent of all EU emissions, and the 2020 target was to reduce emissions covered by the EU ETS by 21 per cent (compared to 2005).[116] The EU ETS was originally designed as a stand-alone mechanism, but was later linked to the KP to ensure that allowances were freely bankable by the European Union at the international level. The aim of the EU ETS was to internalise the social cost of GHG emissions so that market prices would reflect the actual cost of GHG emissions. This in turn was designed to incentivise investment in low-carbon technologies and therefore lead to a low-carbon society in the EU by 2050.[117] The scheme covers approximately 11,500 power stations and other heavy-energy using installations such as industrial plants, and covers approximately half of the EU's CO_2 emissions.[118] The overall EU cap is allocated to countries on the basis of National Allocation Plans, which originally distributed the largest allocations to the worst polluters.[119]

While industry historically opposed the institution of a carbon tax at the EU level through the Union of Industrial and Employers' Confederations of Europe

---

[112] Judith Rees, 'Markets – the Panacea for Environmental Regulation?' (1992) 23(3) *Geoforum* 383, 391.
[113] Incremental reductions were to have taken place under the second commitment period of the KP.
[114] Seppanen (n 109) 44.
[115] Frank J. Convery, 'Origins and Development of the EU ETS' (2009) 43 *Environmental Resource and Economics* 391, 392.
[116] Ibid. Emissions outside of the EU ETS are covered by national emission reduction targets which differ according to a country's national wealth, and are covered by the EU effort-sharing decision, https://ec.europa.eu/clima/policies/effort_en (accessed 20 July 2020).
[117] PBL Netherlands Environment Assessment Agency, 'Evaluation of Policy Options to Reform the EU Emissions Trading Scheme: Effects on Carbon Price, Environment and the Economy' (2013) 1, 8.
[118] Gilbertson and Reyes (n 108) 32.
[119] Ibid., 32.

(UNICE), industry supported the introduction of a market-based trading system. This was largely based on the experience of BP, which had instituted its own internal carbon trading scheme. There was, however, significant opposition to the EU ETS from German industry. To overcome this opposition, it was agreed that free initial allowances would be provided to industry under the scheme.[120] During the first trading period of the EU ETS from 2005 to 2007, free allocations of permits were provided to installations covered by the scheme, which meant that industry was not forced to make substantial GHG reductions.[121] In 2013, 80 per cent of allowances were allocated for free for the third trading period. This will decline to 30 per cent by 2020 for the fourth trading period, and 0 per cent by 2027 for the fifth trading period.[122] Although the percentage of free allowances are expected to decline, granting free allowances divorced from historic emission amounts provides subsidies to polluters.[123] While subsequent trading periods have implemented more stringent measures for emissions reductions, the oversupply of permits on the market has meant that the EU ETS has not successfully ensured large-scale reductions of GHG emissions, as industry is able to cheaply acquire pollution permits instead of making required GHG cuts.

When the EU ETS was designed, it assumed an upward trajectory of emissions, which was reflected in the initial supply of permits on the market. The recession from 2008 to 2009 led to a reduced demand for allowances.[124] In addition, at the end of the second trading period from 2008 to 2012, there were leftover permits available to be banked in the third trading period (2013–20).[125] This meant that there was an oversupply of permits available in the market, and as a result the price of carbon permits crashed. In January 2013, the price remained low at €5/tCO$_2$. Because of the oversupply of carbon permits in the marketplace and fluctuations in fossil fuel prices, technology costs and electricity prices,[126] it was anticipated that the price of carbon would remain below €10/tCO$_2$ to the end of the third trading period in 2020.[127] In addition, in the United Kingdom, the proposed carbon price mechanism in the Energy Act 2013, which would have provided a minimum price for carbon, was moved from a primary to secondary place in the legislation, possibly indicating political pressure to keep electricity affordable,[128] and further weakening the legislative signal to support a high carbon price. The low price of carbon did not send an

---

[120] Frank J. Convery, 'Origins and Development of the EU ETS' (2009) 43 *Environmental and Resource Economics* 391, 402.
[121] Javier de Centra de Larragan, 'Case Note: *Republic of Poland v. Commission*' (2010) 1 Climate L. 199, 201.
[122] PBL (n 117) 19.
[123] Ibid., 24.
[124] Committee on Climate Change (n 61) 59.
[125] PBL (n 117) 14.
[126] Committee on Climate Change (n 61) 70.
[127] PBL (n 117) 10.
[128] Ibid., 3.

adequate price signal to industry to decarbonise,[129] and led to changes within the trading system.

To counter price volatility, the European Union added a market stability mechanism to the EU ETS, called a market stability reserve. Market stability mechanisms provide flexibility to emissions trading schemes, allow them to react to new knowledge, costs, or unexpected exogenous shocks by moderating the number of allowances available.[130] In 2019, the market stability reserve began operating in the European Union. It established an upper and lower band of available emissions based on the total number of allowances in circulation, which would be announced on a yearly basis. The introduction of this mechanism, combined with new EU policies on climate and energy which began to be announced in 2018 and 2019, led to a rebound in the price of carbon. Increased carbon prices negatively impacted coal facilities, helping to phase them out of operation, and incentivised investments in renewable energy.[131] The price of carbon was expected to increase for a third consecutive year in 2020, almost reaching €30/tCO_2, when the COVID-19 crisis hit. One of the outcomes of the crisis is the shrinking of emissions both globally and within the European Union, which led to an immediate decrease in the price of carbon permit prices.[132] It is unclear whether and how long the crisis may last, and therefore what its medium- and long-term impacts on the economy and emissions trading schemes may be. The dual health and economic crisis may also affect the establishment of a UK emissions trading scheme.

5.5.3 Brexit-ing the EU Emissions Trading System

As a result of Article 96 of the Withdrawal Agreement between the United Kingdom and the European Union, the United Kingdom will remain in the EU ETS during the implementation period and comply with the 2019 and 2020 scheme years, but will leave the European Union in 2021. From 1 January 2021, the United Kingdom will have the ability to enforce the EU ETS 2020 allowance surrender obligation. This means that any UK facilities with access to the Union Registry under the EU ETA will retain access to the registry and the United Kingdom will remain a full

---

[129] OECD, 'Economic Survey United Kingdom', (OECD Publishing March 2011), 146.
[130] International Carbon Action Partnership, 'Market Stability Mechanisms in Emissions Trading Systems' (February 2020), https://icapcarbonaction.com/en/?option=com_attach&task=download&id=669 (accessed 21 July 2020).
[131] Matthew Carr, 'Carbon Pollution Costs Are Likely to Rise Again in Europe' (6 February 2020), www.bloomberg.com/news/articles/2020-02-07/carbon-prices-headed-higher-in-2020-tightening-eu-climate-policy (accessed 20 July 2020).
[132] Nina Chestney and Susanna Twidale, 'Coronavirus pushes EU Carbon Permits to 16-Month Low' (18 March 2020) Reuters, www.reuters.com/article/us-eu-carbon-prices/coronavirus-pushes-eu-carbon-permits-to-16-month-lows-idUSKBN2151DP (accessed 20 July 2020).

participant in the EU ETA through 30 April 2021.¹³³ After this date, there will be a new UK emissions trading system (UK ETS), although all of the details of the system are yet to be finalised.

In June 2020, the UK Government issued its response to consultations on the UK ETS. The first phase of the system will run from 2021 to 2030 with reviews scheduled for 2023 and 2028.¹³⁴ It will largely mirror the EU ETS, but it may operate as either a stand-alone system or be linked to the EU ETS (as Switzerland is) if it is beneficial to parties for it to be linked. The UK ETS will apply to energy-intensive industries with a total rated thermal input over 20MW (with exceptions for small, ultra-small facilities and hospitals), which includes power generators, refining, heavy industry, manufacturing and aviation.¹³⁵

As a result of the national net zero emissions goal, the level of ambition in the UK ETS may increase, depending on the Committee on Climate Change's Sixth Carbon Budget, due in September 2020. Any increased ambition would be effective from January 2024. Like the EU ETS, allowances will be auctioned, with some free allowances allocated to new entrants as well as to existing industries that have to significantly adjust their activity levels. These allowances would mirror those allowed under Phase IV of the EU ETS, with a calculation based upon historic activity level and carbon leakage exposure factors as well as existing industry caps.¹³⁶ At the moment, the UK ETS will not accept international offsets, for example, from Article 6 of the Paris Agreement or CORSIA,¹³⁷ until these are more formally settled.

It is still unclear whether the United Kingdom will maintain its own national trading system fully independent of the EU ETS as currently proposed, or will link to the EU ETS. Maintaining a fully independent UK ETS may be difficult and complicated to achieve.¹³⁸ Alternatively, a UK system could be linked with the EU ETS after the transition period. The EU ETS is able to link to other compatible emissions trading systems. This linking ability enables participants in one system to use units from another system for compliance purposes. Linking provides several benefits, which include reducing the cost of cutting emissions, increasing market liquidity and stabilising the market price of carbon as well as increasing global cooperation in

---

[133] www.gov.uk/government/publications/meeting-climate-change-requirements-if-theres-no-brexit-deal/meeting-climate-change-requirements-if-theres-no-brexit-deal#actions-euets (accessed 20 July 2020).

[134] UK Government, 'The Future of UK Carbon Pricing – UK Government and Devolved Administration's Response' (June 2020).

[135] Ibid., 5.

[136] These caps based on Phase IV of the EU ETS amount of 58 million allowances in 2021, due to decline by 1.6 million allowances annually, Ibid., 17.

[137] CORSIA is the Carbon Offsetting and Reduction Scheme for International Aviation, agreed at the International Civil Aviation Organization (ICAO), see www.icao.int/environmental-protection/CORSIA/Pages/default.aspx (accessed 21 July 2020).

[138] Fay Farstand, Neil Carter and Charlotte Burns, 'What Does Brexit Mean for UK's Climate Change Act' (2018) 89(2) 291, 294, pointing to problematic issues such as scale, stability and longevity of a completely independent emissions trading system.

carbon markets.[139] For example, in 2017, the EU and Switzerland agreed to link their systems. Having an international trading mechanism agreed under Article 6 of the Paris Agreement to replace the KP system would be advantageous for both the United Kingdom and other countries.

5.5.4 The Paris Agreement: Article 6 Trading Mechanism

Carbon trading systems can direct large-scale financing towards the most effective and efficient mitigation activities.[140] Market harmonisation across economies provides a broader base for a given carbon price, making its operation more cost efficient.[141] International linkages between carbon markets can therefore achieve deeper emissions cuts and raise more climate finance, which would be used by parties around the world to help fund the emission cuts established in their nationally determined contributions under the Paris Agreement.[142] The parties to the Paris Agreement acknowledged the need to replace the emissions trading system under the KP with a new system which could include all the parties to the Paris Agreement. It was anticipated that the international carbon market would play a key role in increasing the ambition of all parties in their NDCs in 2020. Unfortunately, that may not be the case.

Article 6 of the Paris Agreement establishes two primary market-based approaches to a new carbon trading mechanism. The first are the cooperative approaches laid out in Article 6.2. The cooperative approaches are based on the concept of internationally transferred mitigation outcomes (or ITMOs). ITMOs are carbon units which can be exchanged by the parties and used to achieve reductions in parties' NDCs, promote sustainable development and ensure environmental integrity. While these cooperative approaches would be voluntary and the system would be largely decentralised, parties did anticipate they would involve linking of national emissions trading systems, direct government-to-government transfers, as well as international crediting mechanisms.[143]

The second approach is the emissions mitigation mechanism, otherwise known as the sustainable development mechanism, established in Article 6.3. This mechanism was anticipated to replace the CDM under the KP, and so be subject to a more coordinated and centralised governance approach. Both approaches required more detailed rules, modalities and procedures than articulated under Article 6. The rules, modalities and procedures were agreed for all other elements of the Paris Agreement at COP 24 held in 2018 in Katowice, Poland. (These operational rules

---

[139] https://ec.europa.eu/clima/policies/ets/markets_en (accessed 20 July 2020).
[140] IETA, 'A Vision for the Market Provisions of the Paris Agreement' (May 2016), 3.
[141] Ibid.
[142] Ibid.
[143] Gao Shuai et al., 'International Carbon Markets under the Paris Agreement: Basic Form and Development Prospects' (2019) 10 *Advances in Climate Change Research* 21, 22.

are otherwise known as the Paris Rulebook). Unfortunately, parties could not agree on the rules for the trading mechanisms under Article 6, and so its status remains unclear. In particular, issues remain regarding the scope of the ITMOs and whether they can only cover activities and units outlined in NDCs. It is also unclear what the shelf life of ITMOs will be, and how many ITMOs can be used towards an NDC.[144]

While Article 6 clearly establishes a requirement for environmental integrity, and a prohibition on double-counting (use by two parties of the same emissions reduction towards an NDC), there is currently vigorous opposition from countries such as the United States, Brazil and Australia regarding re-use of existing emissions reductions credits.[145] Including weak language regarding the eligibility of carbon units could undermine the integrity of the system, and its ability to achieve emissions reductions.[146] The Conference of Parties meeting due to be held in Glasgow in December 2020 has been postponed due to the COVID-19 crisis, and so it is unclear when or whether new rules to implement Article 6 will be agreed. Despite these uncertainties, companies have traditionally advocated for the use of market-based mechanisms.

5.6 COMPANIES' APPROACHES TO TRADING MECHANISMS

BP Plc was originally a leader in emissions trading, establishing its own internal trading system in 1997, which was a key element in meeting its internal GHG emission reduction targets.[147] BP calculated emissions and allocated targets for each individual business unit, and grandfathered in historic emissions.[148] The company's scheme did not actually involve the exchange of money for the purchase of permits, and there was no real penalty if targets were missed.[149] While the scheme was innovative for its time, it was not renewed after 2002, possibly due to cost.[150] The Shell group launched an internal pilot emissions trading scheme for three years, ending in 2002,[151] but not many details of the results of the scheme were included in

---

[144] Ibid., 22–23.
[145] Umair Irfan, 'The US, Japan and Australia Let the Whole World Down at the UN Climate Talks' (18 Dec. 2019) VOX available at www.vox.com/energy-and-environment/2019/12/18/21024283/climate-change-cop25-us-brazil-australia-japan (accessed 20 July 2020).
[146] Carbon Brief, 'How 'Article 6' Carbon Markets Could 'Make or Break' the Paris Agreement' (29 November 2019), www.carbonbrief.org/in-depth-q-and-a-how-article-6-carbon-markets-could-make-or-break-the-paris-agreement (accessed 20 July 2020).
[147] Mark Akhurst, Jeff Morheim and Rachel Lewis, 'Greenhouse Gas Emission Trading in BP' (2003) 31 *Energy Policy* 657, 657.
[148] David G. Victor and Joshua C. House, 'BP's Emission Trading System' (2006) 34 *Energy Policy* 2100, 2103.
[149] Ibid., 2108.
[150] Ibid., 2112.
[151] The Shell Group, 'Meeting the Energy Challenge: The Shell Report 2002' (2002), 26, http://reports.shell.com/sustainability-report/2012/servicepages/previous/files/shell_report_2002.pdf (accessed 30 May 2020).

its reports. It started to apply a shadow price to major investments of $40 per tonne.[152] BP and Royal Dutch Shell participate in the EU ETS and are members of the UK Emissions Trading Group, an industry-led association that informs and represents companies that are subject to the EU ETS,[153] but there is a general lack of transparency in this mechanism. It is difficult to determine how many permits each company has acquired, and how many tonnes of GHG emissions this has allowed them to continue to emit.

Six of the major oil and gas companies issued an open letter to the Executive Secretary of the UNFCCC and the President of COP 21 on 29 May 2015. The Chairmen of BP Plc, Royal Dutch Shell Plc and BG Group were three of the six signatories. The companies stated that they required clear, stable, long-term, ambitious policy frameworks, preferably global in nature, in order for their companies to do more on climate change. In particular, they called for a price on carbon, and to eventually connect national trading systems into an international system.[154] These companies have expressed a clear preference for market mechanisms, through a pricing and trading scheme, in order for them to be incentivised to reduce their GHG emissions. Progress on establishing rules for both an international trading scheme under Article 6 of the Paris Agreement, as well as on the UK emissions trading scheme, would be very helpful for companies.

5.7 CONCLUSION

In recent years both the European Union and United Kingdom have increased their climate ambitions and imposed net zero emissions targets for 2050. This is partly due to the impact the climate crisis is having, and is projected to have, around the world but also in their economies. Energy market reform has accompanied climate legislation, and the Climate Change Act 2008 has been a significant force driving ambition in the United Kingdom. There are clear linkages between the Climate Change Act 2008 and the Companies Act 2006, with increasing requirements on reporting imposed on companies. Generational shifts in attitudes towards climate change and the recent public health and economic crisis may help entrench the GND proposal recently enacted in the European Union, which may have a knock-on effect in the United Kingdom and plans for a Green Brexit.

While there is certainly increasing ambition on climate regulation, the carbon markets' picture looks less certain. Historically, the EU ETS failed to ensure GHG

---

[152] Royal Dutch Shell Plc (n 97) 2.
[153] See ETG, www.etg.uk.com/ (accessed 20 July 2020).
[154] UN Climate Change Newsroom, 'Six Oil Majors Say: We Will Act Faster with Stronger Carbon Pricing'. Open Letter to UN and Governments' (1 June 2015), https://unfccc.int/news/major-oil-companies-letter-to-un (accessed 1 January 2020).

emissions were significantly reduced.[155] This position was slowly changing as a result of the market stability mechanism introduced in the EU ETS, combined with more ambitious climate targets. The shift in approach by Shell and BP to agree emission reduction targets reflects growing pressure on these types of companies to take climate change seriously. However climate targets in both the European Union and the United Kingdom will most likely rely on some type of market mechanism, and so an agreement on operational rules for Article 6 of the Paris Agreement is important both for EU and UK climate goals, but also for companies which want to use these trading mechanisms. Net zero emissions targets are not the same as a zero emissions target. Countries are very likely to rely on some type of offsetting or trading mechanism to achieve a net zero target. If these systems are not environmentally sound, net zero targets will be ineffective to mitigate the climate crisis.

Many energy companies still view formal regulatory action to reduce emissions as a risk to their business, and many seem to prefer the market mechanism of carbon trading, as well as pricing carbon to regulatory action. While many of these companies have experimented with voluntary targets, and in the case of BP even a trading scheme, cost and growth constraints still take precedent. Instead of emissions reductions, many companies appear to prefer reporting initiatives. But even these initiatives are becoming more stringent, with most European countries tending towards encouraging or requiring reporting in line with TCFD recommendations. Companies are also starting to react to increased societal and investor pressure on climate change. Recent events such as climate litigation initiatives against energy companies, as well as shifts in approach to climate risks by institutional investors (covered in Chapters 6 and 7, respectively), may provide the final push needed to complement these regulatory and market-based initiatives and move towards more progressive corporate climate action.

---

[155] Seppanen (n 109) 44.

6

Companies, Human Rights and Climate Litigation

In 2019 at the 25th UNFCCC Conference of Parties, the Philippines Human Rights Commission announced their finding that carbon-majors could be liable for human rights violations resulting from climate change.[1] This announcement was the culmination of a multi-jurisdictional investigation that lasted for several years. The investigation was launched on the basis of a petition submitted by Greenpeace South-East Asia as well as other local groups and citizens of the Philippines. Motivated by the significant loss of life and damage caused by Super Typhoon Haiyan, the groups sought to establish the legal liability of forty-seven carbon-major companies for the violations of human rights caused by the typhoon, and other climate-related impacts. While the Philippines Human Rights Commission has no powers to enforce its findings, it can make recommendations to the Government. This type of investigation could also be replicated by Human Rights Commissions in other countries.

The process of the investigation as well as its outcome highlights the important and evolving relationship between companies, human rights and climate litigation.[2] This evolving relationship questions long-held assumptions about the role of companies in climate change, and their liability for climate-induced harms. Climate litigation often falls outside of the traditional remit of state-centred regulation. Litigation can expose gaps in the existing transnational governance structures, particularly in relation to human rights and climate change.[3] It can also highlight

---

[1] Isabella Kaminski, 'Carbon Majors Can Be Held Liable for Human Rights Violations, Philippines Commission Rules' (*The Climate Docket* 9 December 2019), www.climateliabilitynews.org/2019/12/09/philippines-human-rights-climate-change-2/ (accessed 11 July 2020).

[2] For an overview of the broader relationship of business and human rights, see Barnali Choudhury and Martin Petrin, *Corporate Duties to the Public* (Cambridge University Press 2018) ch 8.

[3] Lisa Benjamin, 'The Responsibilities of Corporations: New Directions in Environmental Litigation' in Veerle Heyvaert and Leslie-Anne Duvic-Paoli (eds), *Research Handbook on Transnational Environmental Law* (Edward Elgar 2020) 229-247.

the role of companies in climate-induced human rights violations, and pose questions as to whether more regulation and liability should be imposed on these entities in the area of both climate change and human rights.

This chapter will begin with an analysis of the connection between businesses and human rights, then between climate change and human rights, and finally cover the increase of global climate change litigation against states and companies. Combined with Chapter 7 which focuses on fiscal initiatives, this chapter draws on a more holistic and pluralistic approach to regulation than the state-centred approaches covered in Chapters 4 and 5. The previous chapters focused more intently on black letter law, international conventions where states have direct obligations, and market mechanisms in which states and companies participate directly. Instead, Chapters 6 and 7 expand the theoretical analysis of regulation initiated in Chapter 4 and expanded upon in Chapter 5, through the exploration of broader, more contextual approaches to regulation by relying more heavily on the 'decentred' concept of regulation employed by Black.[4] According to Julia Black, decentred regulation can be defined as follows:

> Regulation is the sustained and focused attempt to alter the behaviour of others according to defined standards or purposes with the intention of producing a broadly identified outcome or outcomes, which may involve mechanisms of standard-setting, information-gathering and behaviour-modifications.[5]

According to her approach, a wider concept of regulation disperses power between social actors, and between non-state actors and the state.[6] Although she notes that once untethered from the state, it is not clear where the boundaries of decentred regulation lie,[7] the concept would include the courts, and as such, litigation, as well as soft law approaches.[8]

Litigation involves mediated rights of litigants against regulated bodies such as states, which indirectly affects companies through associated national regulation. Decentred regulation could also include actions by private groups and associations, including private environmental governance regimes.[9] Chapters 6 and 7 also draw on Heyvaert's concept of transnational environmental law, which includes a 'richer, more diversified notion' than state-centred regulation.[10]

The initiatives covered in the next two chapters are new or emerging ones, and often transnational. They are also generally excluded from traditional

---

[4] Julia Black, 'Critical Reflections on Regulation' (2002) 27 *Australian Journal of Legal Philosophy* 1.
[5] Ibid., 26.
[6] Ibid., 5–6.
[7] Ibid., 2.
[8] Ibid., 17.
[9] Ibid., 35.
[10] Veerle Heyvaert, 'Regulating Competition – Accounting For the Transnational Dimension of Environmental Regulation' (2013) 25(1) J. Environmental L. 1, 1.

understandings of state-based regulation or market mechanisms. Some of these initiatives also fall beyond the direct control of companies but can exert a tremendous influence over climate-related policies, and therefore are likely to impact corporate policies and practices on climate change in the near future. For example, the Guiding Principles on Business and Human Rights impose responsibilities on companies, although these constitute soft law obligations at the moment. The outcomes of climate litigation, even if unsuccessful, can have an enormous influence on public opinion and potentially motivate regulatory changes on climate liability.

The emerging relationship between human rights and climate change, and climate litigation, are both relatively new phenomena, and their long-term impacts are yet unknown. However, combined with innovations in investor approaches to climate change covered in Chapter 7, these emerging issues can accelerate a new way of thinking about companies and corporate liability in the context of climate change.

6.1 COMPANIES AND HUMAN RIGHTS

International law has traditionally considered human rights violations to be cabined within a vertical relationship between the state and its citizens. As companies are not considered to be formal actors under international law, they have not been fixed with enforceable legal obligations for human rights violations. Similar to international environmental law, while the power of companies has grown over the years, human rights law has not made similar progress by imposing legal liability on these entities under international law for human rights violations they may be involved in either directly or indirectly. While attempts have been made in the past to impose liability on to companies for human rights violations under transnational governance initiatives, these were unsuccessful largely due to resistance by companies as well as developed states. This resistance was based on an understanding that companies should not and could not be fixed with legal liability for human rights violations.

At the moment, companies are subject to soft law obligations under the United Nations Guiding Principles for Business and Human Rights. Just a few years after they were adopted in 2011, developing states submitted a proposal to the Human Rights Council for a binding treaty on business and human rights. This demonstrates lingering dissatisfaction regarding the current approach of international law, and most national law, at the interface of companies and human rights. This situation is exacerbated by climate change, which can be the driver for significant human rights violations, and companies lie squarely within the nexus of climate change and human rights due to their significant corporate emissions.

6.2 HUMAN RIGHTS AS AN ENVIRONMENTAL CONCERN TO COMPANIES: THE DEVELOPMENT OF THE UN NORMS

Concerns regarding the negative impact of corporate activities on human rights grew in the 1970s, particularly with the rise of TNC operations in developing countries which often focused on natural resource extraction.[11] The OECD Guidelines for Multinational Corporations were agreed to in 1976,[12] followed by the International Labour Organization's Tripartite Declaration of Principles Concerning Multinational Enterprises and Social Policy in 1977.[13] Concerns continued to grow in the 1990s about corporate activities, which affected labour issues such as the employment and exploitation of children and intimidation of union leaders. These concerns were exacerbated by environmental pollution by companies, and indirect participation by companies in human rights abuses.[14] These concerns were fuelled by the execution of Ken Saro-Wiwa in Nigeria, implicating Shell's operations there, the activities of the Occidental Petroleum Corporation in Colombia, and ExxonMobil's activities in Indonesia.[15]

Global initiatives were promulgated as a partial response to these concerns, such as the United Nations Global Compact and the Voluntary Principles on Security and Human Rights in 2000, the Kimberley Process Certification Scheme and the Extractive Industries Transparency Initiative in 2002. These initiatives reflected the traditional understanding that companies could not be fixed with legal liability for international human rights violations. However, there was also a push to go 'beyond voluntarism'[16] globally, a push that resulted in the United Nations Norms on the Responsibilities of Transnational Corporations and Other Business Enterprises with regard to Human Rights ('UN Norms').[17]

The UN Norms were controversial as they sought to impose legal obligations on transnational corporations to 'promote, secure the fulfilment of, respect, ensure respect of and protect human rights'.[18] They sparked a divisive debate between

---

[11] Giovannia Mantilla, 'Emerging International Human Rights Norms for Transnational Corporations' (2009) 15(2) *Global Governance* 279, 279.
[12] See The Organization for Economic Co-operation and Development, 'Guidelines for Multinational Enterprises' (*OECD.org*), www.oecd.org/corporate/mne/ (accessed 16 July 2020).
[13] See International Labor Organization, 'Tripartite Declaration of Principles Concerning Multinational Enterprises and Social Policy' (*ILO.org*, March 2017), www.ilo.org/empent/Publications/WCMS_094386/lang--en/index.htm (accessed 16 July 2020).
[14] Mantilla (n 11) 282; Matthew Murphy and Jordi Vives, 'Perceptions of Justice and the Human Rights to Protect, Respect, and Remedy Framework' (2013) 116 *Journal of Business Ethics* 781, 781–2.
[15] Murphy and Vives (n 14).
[16] Mantilla (n 11) 285–6.
[17] U.N. Doc. E/CN.4/Sub.2/2003/12/Rev.2 (2003).
[18] Ibid Article A.1.

human rights advocacy groups, which supported binding obligations, the business community, such as the International Chamber of Commerce, and countries, such as the United States and United Kingdom, which strongly resisted the imposition of legal obligations on companies.[19]

Imposing human rights obligations on companies is difficult and complex, mainly due to the fact that companies are not formal legal actors under international law and therefore are not directly bound by international human rights law.[20] The traditional understanding is that human rights emanate from the state, which has the authority to ratify international human rights treaties and therefore carries the obligation to protect human rights. These obligations are traditionally considered to be positive vertical obligations of the state to protect its citizens' human rights. Some academics have claimed that imposing legal obligations on non-state actors would undermine the very nature of human rights.[21]

The relative decline in state power and the significant increase in the influence of non-state actors have not been met with a corresponding increase in transnational obligations of companies in the realm of human rights. Amid this global governance gap, companies are exercising power without restraint, leading to the rights of individuals becoming vulnerable to corporate power abuse.[22] States remain the traditional addressees of international human rights obligations, and the dominant method to address business and human rights therefore currently comprises soft-law initiatives.[23]

The UN Norms were eventually abandoned, but the issue of the legal liability of companies for human rights violations remained alive and contentious. In order to resolve this deep divide, John Ruggie was appointed in 2005 as special representative of the Commission of Human Rights on the issue of business and human rights, with the mandate to 'identify and clarify' international standards and policies.[24] The UN Human Rights Council unanimously welcomed the 2008 Framework.

---

[19] Mantilla (n 11) 288; Human Rights Council, 'Report of the Special Representative of the Secretary-General on the Issue of Human Rights and Transnational Corporations and Other Business Enterprises, John Ruggie' (March 2011) A/HRC/17/31, para 3; Pni Pavel Miretski and Sascha-Dominik Bachman, 'The UN "Norms on the Responsibility of Transnational Corporations and Other Business Enterprises with Regard to Human Rights" – A Requiem' (2012) 17 Deakin L. Rev. 5, 8.

[20] Janet Dine, *Companies, International Trade and Human Rights* (Cambridge University Press 2010) 167–168.

[21] Nien-Hê Hsieh, 'Should Business Have Human Rights Obligations?' *Journal of Human Rights* 14 (2015) 218, 219.

[22] Barnali Choudhury and Martin Petrin, *Corporate Duties to the Public* (Cambridge University Press 2019) 207; Janet Dine, 'Corporate Regulation, Climate Change and Corporate Law: Challenges and Balance in an International and Global World' (2015) 25 Eur. Bus. L. Rev. 173, 180.

[23] Lee McConnell, 'Assessing the Feasibility of a Business and Human Rights Treaty' (2017) 66 I.C.L.Q. 143, 144.

[24] Mantilla (n 11) 289; Janice R. Bellace, 'Hoisted on Their Own Petard? Business and Human Rights' (2014) 56(3) *Journal of Industrial Relations* 442, 453.

6.3 THE UNITED NATIONS GUIDING PRINCIPLES

Perhaps having learned the lesson of the UN Norms,[25] Ruggie's 2008 Framework established a three-pronged approach of 'protect, respect and remedy', but only included a responsibility, not a legal duty, of companies to 'respect' human rights. While this responsibility includes a duty to avoid causing or contributing to adverse human rights impacts (negative duties to do no harm), as well as positive duties to establish policies and processes to meet the responsibility to respect,[26] it has no enforcement mechanism for companies. This corporate responsibility to respect is interpreted as mandatory but not enforceable (as opposed to the state obligation to protect human rights which is both binding and enforceable).[27]

Ruggie also produced a set of 'Guiding Principles' in 2011 to operationalise the framework.[28] The UNGPs state that companies should institute a formal policy to respect human rights, a human rights due diligence process to identify impacts, and a remediation process.[29] The responsibility to respect human rights requires companies to avoid causing or contributing to adverse human rights impacts, and to address any impacts where they occur. The responsibilities extend beyond the company and include human rights impacts linked to a company's products or services, or through its business relationships.[30] The 2015 UN Guiding Principles Reporting Framework provides further procedural details for companies.[31]

Just three years after the UNGPs were adopted, Ecuador and South Africa submitted a proposal in 2013 at the 24th session of the Human Rights Council for a binding treaty on multinational corporations and human rights. While it is unclear what progress (if any) this proposal will make, it reflects the ongoing frustration with the inability of the law, including company law, to impose liability for violations on companies.

---

[25] Miretski and Bachman (n 19), 35; Bjorn Fasterling and Geert Demuijnck, 'Human Rights in the Void? Due Diligence in the UN Guiding Principles on Business and Human Rights' (2013) 116 *Journal of Businsess Ethics* 799, 800.
[26] Human Rights Council (n 19) Annex, Article II.
[27] Barnali Choudhury and Martin Petrin, 'Corporate Governance That "Works for Everyone": Promoting Public Policies Through Corporate Governance Mechanisms' (2018) 18 J. Corp. L. Studies 381, 414.
[28] See UN Human Rights Council, 'The Guiding Principles on Business and Human Rights: Implementing the United Nations 'Protect, Respect and Remedy' Framework', HR/PUB/11/04 (2011), www.ohchr.org/Documents/Publications/GuidingPrinciplesBusinessHR_EN.pdf (accessed 16 July 2020).
[29] Ibid., 13–25.
[30] Ibid., principle 13.
[31] See UN Guiding Principles, 'Reporting Framework' (UNGPReporting.org, 2018), www.ungpreporting.org/ (accessed 16 July 2020).

6.4 THE OECD GUIDELINES AND NATIONAL CONTACT POINTS

The OECD Guidelines, originally agreed in 1976, were updated in 2011 to take into account the UNGPs. Unlike the UNGPs, the OECD Guidelines do have a type of non-judicial enforcement mechanism where states establish National Contact Points (or NCPs). While the Guidelines are voluntary, adhering states make a binding commitment to implement them, and establish NCPs.[32] There was originally very little activity on human rights within the NCP system. After the Guidelines were updated to reflect the UNGPs, the number of human rights-related complaints submitted through the NCPs escalated.[33]

In relation to climate change, a 2019 statement by the Dutch NCP responded to a complaint brought by four NGOs against the financial institution ING. The complaint concerned the lending practices of ING, as well as the lack of disclosure of indirect GHG emissions resulting from ING's lending practices. The NGOs claimed these practices were not in line with the OECD Guidelines in the context of climate change.[34]

Partly as a result of the binding nature of the Paris Agreement on the Dutch Government, the Dutch NCP accepted the complaint, and facilitated good offices between the parties. The parties eventually agreed on a methodology which would enable ING to monitor and disclose its indirect GHG emissions, as well as a target date to end ING's exposure to thermal coal to zero by 2025, and a commitment from ING to refrain from financing new coal fire projects. The parties also agreed to jointly call upon the Dutch Government to reduce its national emissions in line with the 1.5°C target articulated by the Intergovernmental Panel on Climate Change (IPCC) Special Report (see the *Urgenda* litigation covered below). While there are no formal, binding outcomes as a result of the NCP process, as illustrated by the ING dispute, the NCP process can lead to dialogue and agreed outcomes between the parties, including more progressive climate action by companies. As a result, it may become a more popular venue in the future for climate-related complaints based on the OECD Guidelines.

6.5 BROADER EFFECT OF THE UNITED NATIONS GUIDING PRINCIPLES ON COMPANIES

Academics are divided as to the actual impact the Ruggie Framework and Guiding Principles have and will have. It is clear that they have led to an update of the

---

[32] Sara Seck, 'Indigenous Rights, Environmental Rights or Stakeholder Engagement: Comparing IFC and OECD Approaches to Implementation of the Business Responsibility to Respect Human Rights' (2016) 12 McGill J, Sustainable Development L. & Policy 51, 53.
[33] Lottie Lane, 'The Horizontal Effect of International Human Rights Law I Practice' (2018) Eur. J. Comparative L. & Governance 5, 19.
[34] Netherlands Ministry of Foreign Affairs, 'Final Statement Dutch NCP Specific Instance, 4 NGOs versus ING Bank' (19 April 2020), www.oecdguidelines.nl/latest/news/2019/04/19/final-statement-dutch-ncp-specific-instance-4-ngos-versus-ing-bank (accessed 16 July 2020).

OECD Guidelines and the potential use of the NCP dispute resolution forum going forward. Janice Bellace notes that the Guiding Principles have 'changed the landscape'[35] of human rights. Other commentaries have taken a less enthusiastic approach, noting that the UNGPs constitute the least common denominator of recommendations,[36] are too expensive and time-consuming for companies to institute, and are unlikely to be effective unless policymakers put pressure on companies to incorporate them.[37]

The UNGPs constitute soft law instruments, and do not impose enforceable obligations on companies to abide by international human rights standards. Businesses have no direct positive legal obligations under the UNGPs besides largely procedural ones, which include obligations to institute policies and remediation procedures. They do, however, have duties and responsibilities under the UNGPs. Sara Seck and Michael Slattery argue that the normative value and nature of these responsibilities should not be underestimated or overlooked, as they are explicitly framed to extend beyond the boundaries of states' territorial jurisdictions.[38] In this regard, they attempt to fill the gap of transnational human rights regulation. Larry Backer argues that the social licence to operate, out of which the UNGPs were developed, may, in fact, be just as important as legal norms.[39] Barnali Choudhury and Martin Petrin focus on the obligation of companies to respect human rights as a fundamental condition of society, and failure to do so risks their social licence to operate.[40]

The UNGPs have led to some domestic action in the realm of business and human rights, and therefore may have an indirect effect on state initiatives. For example, the 2017 French 'Duty of Vigilance' imposed an obligation on companies to establish a vigilance plan. Section 172(1)(d) of the UK Companies Act 2006 imposes a set of circumstances that directors must have regard to, including the impacts of the business on the community and the environment.

Motivated by the UNGPs, the Office of the UN High Commissioner for Human Rights has confirmed that both states and companies are 'duty bearers' in the context of human rights and climate change. This means that companies must be accountable for their climate impacts, participate responsibly in both climate change

---

[35] Bellace (n 24) 454.
[36] Robert C. Blitt, 'Beyond Ruggie's Guiding Principles on Business and Human Rights: Charting an Embracive Approach to Corporate Human Rights Compliance' (2012) 48 Texas Intl. L. J. 33, 35.
[37] Susan Ariel Aaronson and Ian Highham, 'Re-righting Business: John Ruggie and the Struggle to Develop International Human Rights Standards for Transnational Firms' (2013) 35(2) Human Rights Q. 333, 333–334.
[38] Sara Seck and Michael Slattery, 'Business, Human Rights and the IBA Climate Justice Report' (2016) 34(1) J. Energy & Natural Resources L. 75, 78.
[39] Larry Catá Backer, 'On the Evolution of the United Nations "Protect-Respect-Remedy Project": The State, the Corporation and Human Rights in a Global Governance Context' (2011) 9 Santa Clara J. Intl. L. 37, 61.
[40] Choudhury and Petrin (n 27), 411.

mitigation and adaptation efforts, with full respect for human rights.[41] Even within the context of the UNGP, clearer linkages are being forged between companies, climate change and human rights.

6.6 CLIMATE CHANGE AND HUMAN RIGHTS

While there is no clear, hard law yet in the area of businesses and human rights at the transnational level,[42] there is emerging jurisprudence and activity on human rights and climate change. The United Nations has determined that climate change can potentially violate a number of existing human rights, such as the rights to life, adequate food, attainment of the highest standards of physical and mental health, adequate housing, self-determination, safe drinking water and sanitation, and the right to development.[43] Many state constitutions also specifically protect the right to a healthy environment as a collective, third-generation human right.[44] There have also been arguments that there is a human right not to be exposed to dangerous climate change,[45] otherwise deemed as 'climate rights'. It is not clear whether climate rights would be recognised as traditional, enforceable human rights, or, as Eric Brandstedt and Anna-Karin Bergman have argued, simply as criteria by which certain political, social and economic developments and institutions could be judged.[46]

The 2007 Male' Declaration on the Human Dimension of Global Climate Change was the first intergovernmental statement on the relationship between climate change and human rights.[47] In the lead-up to the 21st UNFCCC Conference of Parties in Paris, a number of countries made voluntary pledges to facilitate the sharing of knowledge and experience between human rights and

---

[41] Office of the UN High Commissioner for Human Rights, 'Understanding Human Rights and Climate Change' (UNFCCC COP21, 2015) message 8.

[42] Lise Smit, 'Human Rights Litigation Against Companies in South African Courts: A Response to *Mankayi v. Anglogold Ashanti*' (2011) 27 *S. African J. Human Rights* 354, 367.

[43] UNGA Human Rights Council A/HRC/RES/41/21 (23 July 2019); Office of the UN High Commissioner for Human Rights, 'The Effects of Climate Change on the Full Enjoyment of Human Rights' (Climate Vulnerable Forum, 30 April 2015).

[44] These include countries such as Republic of Azerbaijan, Kingdom of Belgium, Republic of Chile, Costa Rica, Colombia, Cape Verde, Federal Republic of Ethiopia, Finland, Greece, Kenya, South Korea, Republic of Turkey, Ukraine and Republic of Yugoslavia; see Binod Prasad Sharma, 'Constitutional Provisions Related to Environment Conservation: A Study' (2010), 3–5, www.iucn.org/backup_iucn/cmsdata.iucn.org/downloads/constitutional_provisions_related_to_environment_conservation___a_study.pdf (accessed 4 May 2020).

[45] Eric Brandstedt and Anna-Karin Bergman, 'Climate Rights: Feasible or Not?' (2013) 22 *Environmental Politics* 394, 395.

[46] Ibid.

[47] Republic of Maldives, 'Male' Declaration on the Human Dimension of Global Climate Change' (Conference of the Alliance of Small Island States, 2007), www.ciel.org/Publications/Male_Declaration_Nov07.pdf (accessed 16 July 2020).

climate change.[48] The Paris Agreement is the first international environmental agreement to explicitly recognise the relationship between climate change and human rights.[49] It contains a preambular reference acknowledging that states, when taking climate action, should respect, promote and consider their obligations on human rights.[50] John Knox notes that, 'In an important sense, the Paris Agreement signifies the recognition by the international community that climate change poses unacceptable threats to the full enjoyment of human rights'.[51] However, he also states that the causal links on attribution for specific effects of climate change are still uncertain,[52] and further work needs to be done in order to fully implement and strengthen the rights set out in the Paris Agreement.[53] While the Paris Agreement made great strides in the context of climate change and human rights, company law has been left out of the discussion of how to improve the impact business has on society, and how to address linkages between corporate activity and human rights violations.[54]

In his 2015 report to the Human Rights Council, Knox outlines specific obligations that states have in respect of climate change. These include largely procedural obligations to assess environmental impacts, facilitate public participation and provide access to remedies for harm.[55] They also include obligations on states to adopt legal and institutional frameworks to protect against and respond to environmental harm.[56] These obligations on states also apply to harm caused by companies, as companies have an obligation to respect human rights.[57]

In a July 2019 Safe Climate Report, the new United Nations Special Rapporteur for the Environment, David Boyd, affirmed the responsibility of businesses for human rights violations, especially in the context of climate change. The Report notes that businesses 'must adopt human rights policies, conduct human rights due diligence, remedy human rights violations for which they are responsible, and work to influence other actors to respect human rights where relationships of leverage exist'.[58] These responsibilities include the reduction of GHG emissions from

---

[48] See Republic of Costa Rica, 'Geneva Pledge for Human Rights in Climate Action' (UNFCCC COP21, 2015), https://carbonmarketwatch.org/wp-content/uploads/2015/02/The-Geneva-Pledge-13FEB2015.pdf (accessed 16 July 2020).
[49] See UN FCCC/CP/2015/L.9/Rev.1 Preamble; UN GA Human Rights Council, 'Report of the Special Rapporteur on the Issue of Human Rights Obligations Relating to the Enjoyment of a Safe, Clean, Healthy and Sustainable Environment' (1 February 2016) A/HRC/31/52, para 20.
[50] Ibid.
[51] Ibid., para 22.
[52] Ibid., para 34.
[53] Ibid., 22.
[54] Beate Sjafjell, 'How Company Law Has Failed Human Rights – and What to Do About It' (2020) Business and Human Rights Journal 5(2), 179–199. doi:10.1017/bhj.2020.9.
[55] Human Rights Council (n 49), para 50.
[56] Ibid., para 66.
[57] Ibid.
[58] UNGA, 'Human Rights Obligations Relating to the Enjoyment of a Safe, Clean, Healthy and Sustainable Environment' (15 July 2019) A/HRC/31/52, para 20.

activities, products and services, minimising emissions from suppliers, and ensuring those impacted can access remedies.[59]

Whether or not specific climate obligations have emerged for companies, there is a clear international consensus that the impacts of climate change will affect a number of existing human rights, and that businesses have existing responsibilities for human rights violations. States may become liable for violations of human rights not only within their own state, but also potentially extraterritorially.[60] While actions for human rights violations are traditionally made against the state (vertically), there is an argument that companies should also be held directly or indirectly liable (horizontally). The extractive industry, in particular, has been criticised for their close proximity to, if not liability for, human rights violations in general.[61] These types of suits would involve significant operational, regulatory and reputational risks for businesses.[62] Globally, there have been a number of pieces of litigation that have employed a human rights discourse against both states and private entities, particularly energy companies, in the context of climate change.

6.7 CLIMATE CHANGE LITIGATION

Climate litigation has been a self-help tool used for several years to motivate regulatory action on climate change. While it is difficult to define the parameters of what constitutes 'climate litigation', it is generally thought that the first climate action was initiated in the United States in 1990.[63] This type of litigation has taken a variety of forms, including using public law tools such as human rights, constitutional law and judicial review,[64] but also private law mechanisms, such as tort, nuisance or negligence.[65] Hari Osofsky has noted that most traditional climate change litigation was targeted towards incentivising stricter carbon regulation as well as generating greater public attention, and therefore greater social pressure on

---

[59] Lisa Benjamin, Meinhard Doelle and Sara Seck, 'Climate Change, Poverty and Human Rights: An Emergency without Precedent' (*The Conversation*, 4 September 2019), https://theconversation.com/climate-change-poverty-and-human-rights-an-emergency-without-precedent-120396 (accessed 17 July 2020).

[60] John Knox, 'Linking Human Rights to Climate Change at the United Nations' (2009) 33 *Harvard Environmental L. Rev.* 477, 491; See International Law Association 'Legal Principles Relating to Climate Change' Draft Articles, Article 7A(1) (2014), www.ila-hq.org/en/committees/index.cfm/cid/1029 (accessed 4 May 2020).

[61] Rory Sullivan, 'NGO Expectations of Companies and Human Rights' (2003) 3 Non-State Actors & Intl. L. 303, 316.

[62] UN PRI, 'Human Rights and the Extractive Industry: Why Engage, Who to Engage, How to Engage' (UNEP Finance Initiative, 2015), 5–6, www.unpri.org/download_report/8530 (accessed 17 July 2020); Josephine Balzac, 'Corporate Responsibility: Promoting Climate Justice Through the Divestment of Fossil Fuels and Socially Responsible Investment' in Randall S. Abate (ed), *Climate Justice* (Environmental L Institute 2016), 125–148.

[63] Brian J. Preston, 'Climate Change Litigation (Part 1)' (2011) 5 Carbon & Climate L. Rev. 3, 4.

[64] Brian J. Preston, 'Climate Change Litigation (Part 2)' (2011) 5 Carbon & Climate L. Rev. 244, 258.

[65] Preston (n 63) 4.

states to take action.[66] More recently, there has been a turn to human rights-motivated climate litigation, with varying levels of success in jurisdictions.[67] James Flynn notes that, even if litigation suits are unsuccessful, they can persuade companies to shift assets to more sustainable sources, put pressure on them to lobby legislatures to develop comprehensive climate change legislation, and also keep the issue of climate change alive in the public consciousness.[68]

There has been a small but growing spate of climate litigation in Europe,[69] but even less in the United Kingdom. Jurisdictions such as New Zealand, the United States and Australia have been more active in terms of suits filed against the government and private entities. Citizen action has taken place in jurisdictions such as Pakistan, and more recently, the Philippines and South Africa.[70] As part of the common law tradition, these cases can throw light on potential suits in other common law jurisdictions. The recent *Urgenda* case in the Netherlands has direct relevance for EU climate and energy policy, and has been cited in other human rights-related cases. In the United Kingdom, the case of *R v. Secretary of State for the Environment, Food and Rural Affairs*[71] deals with government policy on an air pollutant, and may also have regulatory implications for climate change, although the air pollutant involved was not a GHG. The United States, however, has been the most active jurisdiction by far for climate litigation.

6.7.1 US Climate Litigation

The United States has seen the bulk of climate change litigation, and several countries have looked to this jurisdiction for 'normative and legal developments'[72] to support other climate change litigation suits. United States claims can be broadly

---

[66] Hari M. Osofsky, 'Climate Change Litigation as Pluralist Legal Dialogue?' (2007) 43 Stanford J. Intl. L. 181, 190; see also Jacqueline Peel and Hari M. Osofsky, *Climate Change Litigation: Regulatory Pathways to Cleaner Energy* (Cambridge University Press 2015).

[67] Jacqueline Peel and Hari Osofsky, 'A Rights Turn in Climate Litigation?' (2018) 7(1) Transnational Environmental L. 37.

[68] James Flynn, 'Climate of Consensus: Climate Change Litigation in the Wake of *American Electric Power v. Connecticut*' (2013) 29 Georgia State U.L. Rev. 823, 862.

[69] International Bar Association, 'Achieving Justice and Human Rights in an Era of Climate Disruption' (Climate Change Justice and Human Rights Task Force, 2014), 82, www.ibanet .org/Document/Default.aspx?DocumentUid=C6462899-63E7-4A22-B869-3419E38DFF56 (accessed 17 July 2020).

[70] See *Ashgar Leghari v. Federation of Pakistan*, Lahore High Court P. No. 25501/2015, as well as a citizen petition filed in The Philippines against 47 carbon major companies in May 2016, www.greenpeace.org/philippines/press/1237/the-climate-change-and-human-rights-petition/ (accessed 17 July 2020), and a case brought by an NGO against the Government for failing to take into account climate change considerations when approving a new coal-fired power plant, *Earthlife Africa Johannesburg v. Minister of Environmental Affairs (and others)*, High Court of South Africa, Pretoria Case number 65662/16 decided 8 March 2017, www.saflii. org/za/cases/ZAGPPHC/2017/58.html (accessed 17 July 2020).

[71] [2015] UKSC 28.

[72] Phillip Dirisek, 'Climate Change Torts: *American Electric Power v. Connecticut*' (2011) 7 Macquarie J. Intl. & Comparative Environmental L. 108, 110.

divided into nuisance-based claims directed against private entities, and regulatory challenges, directed mainly against the Environmental Protection Agency (EPA).[73] Private entities, particularly carbon-major entities, have also been subject to climate change litigation.[74] The cases in the United States can be divided into two main waves, which involve both government and private entities as defendants.

In the first wave, the *American Electric Power Co. v. Connecticut*[75] case was an example of a public nuisance suit brought by eight states and New York City against six electric and utility companies. The states and New York City essentially argued that the emissions of these companies were interfering with public rights, and asked the court to impose emission caps on them, with a scale of decreasing caps to force them to reduce their emissions.[76] The Supreme Court rejected the claim of the plaintiffs on the basis of that the Clean Air Act 'displaced' any federal nuisance action dealing with climate change.[77] Justice Ginsberg provided the unanimous decision of the court which stated that there was no 'parallel track' for federal nuisance claims on climate change in addition to federal regulatory action already taken under the Clean Air Act.[78] This definitive statement by the Supreme Court has effectively closed the door to future federal nuisance common law claims on climate change,[79] even though Flynn notes that the EPA had not taken comprehensive action on climate change at the time.[80]

Also part of the first wave, the case of *Native Village of Kivalina v. ExxonMobil Corporation*[81] involved the self-governing village of Kivalina in the Arctic bringing a suit for public nuisance against twenty-two fossil-fuel producers. The Tribe of Iñupiat Eskimos claimed that these companies had contributed to climate change, which had led to the dramatic erosion of the Arctic sea ice that had sheltered their village from winter storms.[82] In September 2012, the Ninth Circuit Court of Appeals dismissed their claim on the basis that common law claims had been 'displaced' by legislation. In May 2013, the Supreme Court dismissed their appeal without giving

---

[73] Flynn (n 68) 832.
[74] See *Connecticut v. American Electric Power* 406 F.Supp.2d 265 (SDNY 2005); *Genesis Power Ltd v. Greenpeace New Zealand* [2008] 1 NZLR 803 (NZ App Ct 2008); *Kivalina v. ExxonMobil* 663 F Supp. 2d 863 (ND Cal 2009).
[75] 564 US 410 (2011); Anita Foerster, 'Climate Justice and Corporations' (2019) 30(2) King's L. J. 305.
[76] Ibid., 419.
[77] Flynn (n 68) 846; Fredric Eisenstat, '*American Electric Power Company v. Connecticut*: How One Less Legal Theory Available in the Effort to Curb Emissions Is Actually One Step Forward for the Cause' (2012) 25 Tulane Environmental L. J. 221, 222; Dirisek (n 71) 108.
[78] *American Electric Power* (n 74).
[79] Flynn (n 68) 856; Dirisek (n 72) 109.
[80] Flynn (n 68) 847–8. Flynn argues that the Clean Air Act only addresses domestic air resources whereas the impacts of climate change are more complex, exceeding impacts on air, and are also transboundary.
[81] *Kivalina* (n 74).
[82] Flynn (n 68) 836; Peter Manus, '*Kivalina* at the Supreme Court: A Lost Opportunity for Federal Common Law' 8(2) (2014) J. Environmental & Public Health L. 223, 225.

reasons, leaving the Ninth Circuit ratio intact.[83] Quin Sorenson has argued that the Kivalina decision relied heavily on the 'displacement' argument in the American Electric Power case, confirming that American Electric Power applies to all federal climate change litigation cases, regardless of whether it is mitigation action or damages being sought.[84] Both the American Electric Power case and the Kivalina case made clear that US courts are employing the displacement doctrine to ensure that climate change is decided by the legislature. While regulatory litigation has seen more success in the United States,[85] it is clear that federal common law nuisance claims on climate change will be very difficult if not impossible to win for plaintiffs.

In the second wave of litigation,[86] companies have faced an escalating number of claims based on a variety of legal arguments. Cities and municipalities from around the United States, including New York City,[87] Oakland and San Francisco,[88] San Mateo,[89] Marin County,[90] the City of Imperial Beach,[91] County of Santa Cruz,[92] City of Santa Cruz[93] and the City of Richmond in California,[94] King County in Washington,[95] the State of Rhode Island,[96] the City and Mayor of Baltimore,[97] the City and County of Honolulu,[98] as well as crab fishermen in California and

---

[83] Karine Péloffy, '*Kivalina* v. *Exxonmobil*: A Comparative Case Commentary' (2013) 9 McGill J. Sustainable Development L. & Policy 119, 122.
[84] Quin M. Sorenson, '*Native Village of Kivalina* v. *Exxonmobil Corporation*: The End of "Climate Change" Tort Litigation?' (2013) 44 *Trends* 1, 6.
[85] For example see *Massachusetts* v. *EPA* 549 US 497 (2007), where several states and NGOs successfully sued the EPA for not regulating greenhouse gases.
[86] Martin Olszynski, Sharon Mascher and Meinhard Doelle, 'From Smokes to Smokestacks: Lessons from Tobacco for the Future of Climate Change Liability' (2017) 30 Georgetown Environmental L. Rev. 1, 14–15; Geetanjali Ganguly, Joana Setzer and Veerle Heyvaert 'If At First You Don't Succeed: Suing Corporations for Climate Change' (2018) 38 Oxford J. L. Studies 841, 842; Foerster (n 74).
[87] David Hasemyer, 'Fossil Fuels on Trial: Where the Major Climate Change Lawsuits Stand Today' (*Inside Climate News* 8 November 2019), https://insideclimatenews.org/news/04042018/climate-change-fossil-fuel-company-lawsuits-timeline-exxon-children-california-cities-attorney-general (accessed 17 July 2020). (detailing the 'wave of legal challenges ... washing over the oil and gas industry, demanding accountability for climate change, [which] started as a ripple after revelations that ExxonMobil had long recognized the threat fossil fuels pose to the world').
[88] *California* v. *BP PLC*, No. C 17-06011 WHA (ND California 27 February 2018) and *City of Oakland* v. *BP PLC*, 325 F.Supp.3d 1017 (ND Cal. 2018), *vacated and remanded sub nom. City of Oakland* v. *BP PLC*, 960 F.3d 570 (9th Cir 2020).
[89] *County of San Mateo* v. *Chevron Corp*, 294 F.Supp.3d 934, 938 (ND California 2018).
[90] *City of Marin* v. *Chevron Corp. et al.*, Case No. 17-cv-4935 (ND California 2017).
[91] *City of Imperial Beach* v. *Chevron Corp. et al.*, Case No. 3:17-cv-4394 (ND California 2017).
[92] *County of Santa Cruz* v. *Chevron Corp. et al.*, Case No. 5:18-cv-00450 (ND California 2017).
[93] *City of Santa Cruz* v. *Chevron Corp. et al.*, Case No. 3:18-cv-00458 (ND California 2018).
[94] *City of Richmond* v. *Chevron Corp. et al.*, Case No. 3:18-cv-00732 (ND California 2018).
[95] *King County* v. *BP PLC, et al.*, Case No. 2:18-cv-00758 (WD Washington 2018).
[96] *Rhode Island* v. *Chevron Corp et al.*, Case No. PC-2018-4716 (Rhode Island Super Ct 2018).
[97] *Mayor and City Council of Baltimore* v. *BP PLC*, 388 F.Supp.3d 538 (D Maryland 2019).
[98] *City and County of Honolulu* v. *Sunoco LP*, Case No. 1CCV-20-0000380 (Hawaii Cir Ct 2020).

Oregon,[99] have all initiated claims against carbon-major companies. These types of companies have been popular targets of litigation for a number of reasons, including their organisational structure of large, transnational groups, combined with their long history in the industry. They have continued to operate around the globe, largely unregulated in terms of their GHG emissions.[100] Lack of regulatory oversight may be another reason for the recent emergence of this second wave of litigation against these entities.[101] In almost all of these cases in the second wave, plaintiffs have cited Heede's 2014 paper which established the historic contribution of fossil fuel and cement producers to climate change.[102]

On 25 June 2018, one of the first cases brought by the cities of Oakland and San Francisco against the five largest private carbon-major companies was dismissed on numerous grounds, including the federal displacement doctrine, foreign affairs powers to regulate a transnational issue and that the issue was largely a political one. The cities had requested abatement, not damages, for costs of adapting to sea-level rise on the basis of public nuisance. Judge Alsop famously conducted a climate tutorial, and his understanding of climate science is reflected in the judgment which clearly states that the case is not about climate science but about the law, 'whether these producers of fossil fuels should pay for anticipated harm that will eventually flow from a rise in sea level'.[103] Ultimately, his answer was no, based on a number of factors, including the public utility of these industries' contributions to global development.

New York's claim was similar to the Oakland and San Francisco claims, based upon both public and private nuisance law, as well as illegal trespass due to sea-level rise. In July 2018, the US District Court for the Southern District of New York granted a motion to dismiss filed by the defendant companies on the basis that federal common law governed the City's claims, as they were based on transnational emissions, and their claims were displaced by the Clean Air Act and presented non-justiciable political questions.[104]

---

[99] *Pacific Coast Federation of Fishermen's Associations, Inc v. Chevron Corp.*, Case No. CGC-18-571285 (California Super Ct 2018). See also Dana Drugmand, *Commercial Fishermen Sue Fossil Fuel Industry for Climate Impacts*, (*The Climate Docket*, November 15, 2018), www.climate-docket.com/2018/11/15/fisheries-crab-climate-change-liability/ (accessed 19 July 2020) ("Crabbers in California and Oregon have suffered significant economic losses and are seeking to hold fossil fuel companies accountable . . . .").

[100] Peter C. Frumhoff, Richard Heede and Naomi Oreskes, 'The Climate Responsibilities of Industrial Carbon Producers' (2015) 132 *Climatic Change* 157, 158–62.

[101] Hari M. Osofsky and Jacqueline Peel, 'Energy Partisanship' (2016) 65 *Emory L. J.* 695, 717–18.

[102] Richard Heede, 'Tracing Anthropogenic Carbon Dioxide and Methane Emissions to Fossil Fuel and Cement Producers, 1854–2010' (2014) 122 *Climatic Change*, 229. See the Introduction for a breakdown of this report.

[103] *City of Oakland*, 325 F.Supp.3d (n 88) 1022.

[104] An appeal is currently pending in the U.S. Court of Appeals for the Second Circuit, and oral arguments were held in November 2019. *City of New York v. BP PLC*, No. 18-2188 (2d Cir. argued November 22, 2019).

These cases were both heard in federal courts (even though the claimants in the Oakland case brought the case under California-based nuisance laws), but other cases in the second wave have successfully been remanded back to state court, where they may avoid the federal displacement doctrine. These latter cases have deliberately attempted to avoid the federal displacement doctrine by claiming violations based on state common law or statutes, including public and private nuisance, strict liability for failure to warn customers of the dangers of climate change, design defect, negligence and trespass. For example, King County in Washington State filed a suit against the five largest fossil fuel corporations for coastal harms, flooding, storm surge and decreased mountain snowpack.[105] In July 2018, the State of Rhode Island and the Mayor and City of Baltimore filed similar suits against fossil fuel companies citing public and private nuisance, strict liability for failure to warn and design defect, negligence design defect and breaches of the Rhode Island State Environmental Rights Act[106] and Maryland Consumer Protection Act.[107] These strategies have been successful in some of these cases to keep them in state court. The US District Court for the Northern District of California agreed to remand *County of San Mateo* v. *Chevron Corp.*, to the state level.[108] In March 2020, an appeal by carbon-majors to remove the Baltimore suit to federal court was denied by the US Court of Appeals for the Fourth Circuit. The Fourth Circuit affirmed the district court's remand order that the suit remains in state court, and the case has been appealed to the Supreme Court.[109] Despite these jurisdictional wins, claims in state court may not be entirely successful due to the inter-state nature of GHG emissions.[110]

Even if these cases are not successful, they serve a useful role in highlighting the inadequacies of the law in fixing liability on to entities which have contributed extensively to climate impacts. These cases attempt to stretch legal concepts such as tort, causation and proximity, and serve an expository role – laying bare the role of these companies in the evolving climate crisis. This elevates the issue in the public consciousness as well as in the minds of directors and other fiduciaries.[111] These

---

[105] *King County* (n 95) First Amended Complaint at 1,
[106] *Rhode Island* (n 96) Complaint at 115–39.
[107] *Mayor and City Council of Baltimore* (n 96). In addition, in November 2018 a group of crab fishermen in California sued 30 oil and gas companies for damage to their livelihoods due to global warming induced algae blooms which have shortened the crab season. See *Pacific Coast Federation* (n 99) complaint at 1.
[108] *County of San Mateo* (n 89); *City of Marin* (n 90).
[109] *Mayor of Baltimore v. BP P.L.C.*, No. 19-1644 (4th Cir. March 6, 2020), *aff'g* 388 F.Supp.3d 538 (D. Md. 2019). For a more detailed breakdown of these cases, see Lisa Benjamin, 'The Road to Paris Runs Through Delaware: Climate Litigation and Directors' Duties' (2020) 2(1) Utah L. Rev. 313.
[110] See Benjamin (n 109).
[111] Lisa Benjamin, 'How to Eat an Elephant: a New "Corporate" Climate Litigation Trend' (*Global Policy* 2019) www.globalpolicyjournal.com/blog/05/07/2018/how-eat-elephant-new-corporate-climate-litigation-trend (accessed 17 July 2020).

cases serve, at the very least, an indirect function in elevating the nature of climate risks and implicating directors' duties along the way. These duties include the obligation to at least consider, assess and communicate to investors both the risks and opportunities that climate change poses to their businesses.

While these claims in the second wave involve mainly tort and public nuisance actions and not human rights, they still have implications for companies. These cases highlight the bidirectional nature of climate risk for companies. Companies contribute directly to climate impacts, but are also on the receiving end of these climate impacts.[112] These risks in turn put pressure on directors to comply with their fiduciary duties in assessing the risks of climate change, communicating these risks to their investors, and in some cases taking action.[113] In addition to the business risks of climate change, these cases generate public interest as well, with the majority of Americans now 'alarmed' or 'concerned' about the issue of climate change.[114] These cases feed into the evolving normative pressures involved in the social licence to operate for companies, as well as highlight companies' public role and impact on society.

Apart from the corporate cases, the US jurisdiction has also seen human rights-based claims, including one based on a class action suit launched in the District Court of Oregon. In *Juliana, et al. v. United States of America, et al.*, American youth claimed that failure by the US government to take action on climate change violated their Fifth Amendment rights by denying them the same protections provided to previous generations, by favouring economic short-term interests and depriving future generations of essential natural resources.[115] Their case also relied on the public trust doctrine, which would be exempt from any federal displacement principles which proved to be a tremendous obstacle to many of the previous cases in the first wave.

The case has taken convoluted procedural turns, with the US government making several applications to the Supreme Court.[116] In January 2020, the Ninth Circuit

---

[112] Benjamin (n 109), 314.
[113] Ibid.
[114] Abel Gustafson, Anthony Leiserowitz and Edward Maibach, 'Americans Are Increasingly "Alarmed" About Global Warming' (Yale Program on Climate Change Communication, 12 February 2019), https://climatecommunication.yale.edu/publications/americans-are-increasingly-alarmed-about-global-warming/ (accessed 17 July 2020). (noting that 6 in ten Americans are either alarmed or concerned about climate change, with the proportion of Americans alarmed about climate change doubling from 2013 to 2018); although almost half of Americans are unwilling to pay for climate policies. *See* Adam Aton, 'Most Americans Want Climate Change Policies' (*Scientific American*, E&E News 3 October 2017), www.scientificamerican.com/article/most-americans-want-climate-change-policies/ (accessed 17 July 2020) (noting that in a 2017 poll seven out of ten Americans believed climate change was happening but half would be unwilling to pay even $1.00 more on their electricity bills to lower emissions).
[115] 217 F.Supp.3d 1224 (D Oregon 2016).
[116] For example, Chief Justice Roberts in the Supreme Court granted a temporary halt in response to a request by the federal government to stay the case although the stay was ultimately lifted. *In*

Court in Oregon dismissed the claim in a 2-1 decision.[117] While the court accepted climate science and that urgent action was needed, it dismissed the suit on the basis of lack of standing due to the perceived inability of the court to provide redress. However, Judge Josephine Staton's dissent provides a strong condemnation of the Court's unwillingness to intervene in the climate crisis. She accused her judicial colleagues of throwing up their hands by choosing to not deal substantially with the issue of climate change.[118] Pointing to the existential threat that climate change poses to the integrity of the nation, she based her dissent on the perpetuity principle which undergirds the US Constitution, and which prohibits the wilful dissolution of the nation.[119] In her view, the plaintiffs had a right to be free from irreversible and catastrophic climate change.[120]

While the *Juliana* case has attracted the most media attention, class action suits by young people have been launched in other states and countries in North America as well.[121] The violation of human rights of current and future generations provides a powerful narrative in these cases. While governments are the main target of the cases, the *Juliana* case originally included industry actors too. These intervenors ultimately removed themselves from the case, although Michael Blumm and Mary Wood note that the exposure of the relationship between these companies and the US government would be one of the more devastating outcomes of the case.[122] As illustrated in the following section, human rights-based claims against governments for climate change can have implications for companies. Where successful, such as in the Dutch *Urgenda* case, national governments will be forced to reduce their national emissions targets, which will have direct consequences for companies based in those jurisdictions.

6.7.2 *Non-US Climate Litigation*

Despite difficulties encountered in the US corporate climate litigation trend, two new cases have emerged that reveal some interesting liability issues for states. The

---

re United States, 139 S. Ct. 16, *vacated*, 139 S. Ct. 452 (2018); *see also* Michael Blumm and Mary Wood, 'These Kids and Young Adults Want Their Day in Court on Climate Change' (*The Conversation*, 26 October, 2018), http://theconversation.com/these-kids-and-young-adults-want-their-day-in-court-on-climate-change-105277 (accessed 17 July 2020).

[117] 947 F.3d 1159, 1175 (9th Circuit 2020). At the time of writing the plaintiffs had submitted a request for an *en banc* review of the Ninth Circuit decision.
[118] Ibid., at 1175.
[119] Ibid., at 1178.
[120] Ibid., at 1182.
[121] *Canada, ENvironnement JEUnesse v. Procureur Général du Canada*, [2018] No. 500-06; *R J Reynolds Tobacco v. Schleider*, 273 So.3d 63 (D Florida 2018); *Aji P. v. Washington*, Case No. 96316-9 (Washington Super Ct 2018); and *Sinnok v. Alaska*, Case No. 3AN-17-09910 (Alaska Super Ct 2018).
[122] Michael C. Blumm & Mary Cristina Wood, *'No Ordinary Lawsuit': Climate Change, Due Process and The Public Trust Doctrine*, 67 (2017) Am. U. L. Rev. 1.

first case of *Urgenda Foundation* v. *State of the Netherlands*[123] in June 2015 allocated vicarious liability to the Dutch state for emissions from all national sectors, including private entities.[124] Urgenda, a Dutch NGO, claimed the Dutch state had a legal obligation to impose stricter climate regulation.[125] Urgenda, along with 900 Dutch citizens, brought a suit against the Dutch state, claiming that the national target of a reduction of 17 per cent against 1990 levels by 2020 was not sufficient to avoid the dangerous impacts of climate change. The Dutch District Court agreed, stating that climate science would require a reduction of at least 25–40 per cent below 1990 levels by 2020. It is interesting to note that the 17 per cent target that the Netherlands originally adopted was in line with existing EU national targets. The Court found that, on the basis of scientific reports, the risks of later-action were much greater than earlier, lower-cost action. As a result, the court was concerned that locked-in carbon-intensive infrastructure, economic disruption and failure to meet the 2°C global goal, as a result of higher rates of emissions and greater dependence on certain technologies in the medium term would be irreversible.[126] The court relied directly on IPCC reports and evolving scientific understandings of the climate crisis.

The state argued, in its defence, that requiring more ambitious targets than had been agreed regionally or internationally would lead to the risk of carbon leakage and competitiveness concerns.[127] The Court disagreed with these arguments and took a 'pioneering'[128] approach to tort law by deciding that the state had a requirement to reduce GHG emissions by 25 per cent against 1990 levels by 2020, and failure to do so would trigger liability for endangerment under Dutch tort law.[129] The Court found a sufficiently close nexus between Dutch emissions, global climate change and a changing Dutch climate, to establish a duty of care upon the state.[130]

The Court also found that the state did not have unlimited discretion to establish its own climate policy, due to the risk of dangerous climate change.[131] As a result, while Urgenda was not permitted to rely exclusively on human rights under the European Convention on Human Rights, the Court held that one of the fetters to state discretion in establishing a national climate policy was the jurisprudence of the

---

[123] C/09/00456689/HA ZA 13-1396, (24 June 2015) (aff'd 9 October 2018) (D Hague, and Hague App Ct).
[124] Christopher Y. Nyinevi and Kwame Nkrumah, 'Universal Civil Jurisdiction: An Option for Global Justice in Climate Change Litigation' (2015) 3 J. Politics & L. 136, 143.
[125] Josephine van Zeben, 'Establishing a Governmental Duty of Care for Climate Change Mitigation: Will Urgenda Turn the Tide?' (2015) 4(2) Transnational Environmental L. 339, 342.
[126] *Urgenda* (n 123) 13.
[127] van Zeben (n 125) 343.
[128] Ibid., 344.
[129] Ibid., 352.
[130] *Urgenda* (n 123) para 4.90.
[131] Ibid., para 4.74.

European Court of Human Rights.[132] While the decision is unusual in its treatment of attribution, Patrícia Ferreira argues the case offers persuasive normative arguments that can and have been used in other national courts.[133] The Dutch Court of Appeal upheld the lower court's decision in 2018 with reference to the European Convention on Human Rights, and in 2019 the decision was appealed to the Dutch Supreme Court.

On 20 December 2019, the Dutch Supreme Court's upheld the lower courts' decisions, but based their reasoning firmly on Articles 2 (which protects right to life) and 8 (which protect the right to a private and family life) of the European Convention on Human Rights. The Court cited recent IPCC reports and in particular the urgent necessity to keep mean average global temperature increases to 1.5°C, and the reference to global temperature goals in the Paris Agreement. Based on the positive obligations of the Dutch state to protect the lives of its citizens and their right to a private and home life, and the real threat that climate change created to the right to life or family life of current generations, the Court found the Dutch state had a positive obligation to act to prevent these impacts.

The Netherlands is a monist state under international law, and so international treaties are directly incorporated into domestic law. As a result, the UNFCCC and Paris Agreement have a direct effect. In addition, it is a civil law jurisdiction, and so this decision may have a limited impact on other non-EU common law jurisdictions. However, the case has been cited in other litigation, and will have impacts on EU countries which are subject to the European Convention on Human Rights, as well as jurisdictions where the Convention's jurisprudence is persuasive. As a result, it remains an important decision connecting human rights and climate change.

A recent decision in Pakistan is also important in the evolving climate litigation and human rights nexus, as it held that inaction by the state in the face of climate change is a breach of human rights.[134] Mr Ashgar Leghari brought a suit against the state of Pakistan for its failure to implement its National Climate Change Policy and Framework for Implementation of Climate Change Policy, on the basis that such inaction violated his rights. The court decided that the lethargy exhibited by the state on this issue did violate the fundamental rights of the citizens of Pakistan, and in particular the rights of the weak and vulnerable segments of the population. The court ordered that a climate change focal point be appointed and a Climate Change Commission, responsible for appointing key personnel to the institution.[135] This case illustrates the active role of the judiciary in addressing the human rights

---

[132] Ibid., paras 4.45 and 4.74.
[133] Patrícia Galvão Ferreira, 'Common but Differentiated Responsibilities in the National Courts: Lessons from *Urgenda* v. *The Netherlands*' (2016) 5(2) Transnational Environmental L. 329, 351.
[134] *Ashgar Leghari* (n 70).
[135] Ibid., 5–7 and 11–13.

dimensions of climate change by forcing the Government to address some of the capacity constraints which face many governments in the global South.[136]

In relation to climate litigation suits against companies, there have been mixed results outside of the United States, and some cases are still pending. Many hurdles arise because of the difficulty of establishing a direct causal link between corporate emissions and impacts on the ground. A case in the Commonwealth region is the New Zealand case of *Greenpeace New Zealand Inc. v. Genesis Power Ltd*,[137] where an NGO, Greenpeace New Zealand, launched a suit against the Auckland District Council for failing to consider climate change when issuing a resource permit to Genesis Power to build an electricity generating plant.[138] The majority opinion relied heavily on a textual interpretation of Section 104E of the Resource Management Act 1991, deciding that the legislative text only required a consideration of climate change when issuing resource consents for renewable energy projects.[139] A powerful dissenting judgment by Chief Justice Elias focused instead on the purpose of the legislation, and the importance of mitigation of GHG emissions.[140]

The more recent case of *R v. Secretary of State for the Environment, Food and Rural Affairs*[141] provides some insight into what a climate change suit could look like in the United Kingdom. In this case, an NGO, ClientEarth, brought a claim against UK Department for Environment, Food and Rural Affairs (Defra) for not complying with an EU Air Quality Directive[142] on nitrogen dioxide. Nitrogen dioxide can cause respiratory problems and can lead to premature death. Despite the fact that the levels of nitrogen dioxide had failed to reach mandatory levels by 2010 due to issues beyond the Government's control,[143] the Supreme Court held that Defra had to prepare new air quality plans to remedy the 'real and continuing danger to public health'.[144] While the mandatory nature of the Directive differs from the national carbon budgets under the Climate Change Act 2008, parallels could be drawn between the public health hazard of nitrous oxide and domestic impacts due to

---

[136] Joana Setzer and Lisa Benjamin, 'Climate Litigation in the Global South: Constraints and Opportunities' (2020) 9(1) Transnational Environmental L. 77.
[137] [2008] NZSC 112 (NZ Sup Ct 2008).
[138] Ibid.
[139] Ibid., para 65.
[140] Ed Steane and Teresa Weeks, 'Climate Change and the Resource Management Act: Implications of *Greenpeace New Zealand Inc v. Genesis Power Ltd*' (2009) Resource Management Journal 1, 3.
[141] [2015] UKSC 28.
[142] 2008/50/EC
[143] Defra claimed that the high levels of nitrous oxide were largely due to diesel vehicles whose emission levels in real-world scenarios were different than emission levels in regulatory test cycle scenarios.
[144] Ibid., para 27, Maria Lee, 'Brexit and Environmental Protection in the United Kingdom: Governance, Accountability and Lawmaking' (2018) 36(3) J. Energy Nat. Resour. Law, 351

climate change on public health, including heatstroke, increased vector diseases and effects of flooding.

In 2020, NGOs won a case challenging the expansion of Heathrow Airport runway in the United Kingdom, partly on the grounds of climate change and the UK Government's obligations under the Paris Agreement.[145] The Court of Appeal carefully analysed the amended Government target of net zero emissions by 2050 under the Climate Change Act,[146] as well as communications between the Secretary of State and the Climate Change Committee. The Court of Appeal decided that Section 5(8) of the Planning Act required the Secretary of State to take into account 'Government policy', which included not just legal obligations under the Climate Change Act, but also commitments the Government had made under the Paris Agreement. The Court found the Government had failed to take its commitments under the Paris Agreement into account when approving the runway. The Government chose not to appeal the decision but Heathrow Airport Ltd. and Aurora Holdings Ltd. have been granted permission to appeal the case to the Supreme Court. In response, Dale Vince, George Monbiot and the Good Law Project launched a judicial review to challenge the Government's decision not to review its National Policy Statements on energy infrastructure in the context of climate change.[147]

Not all climate cases in the United Kingdom have been successful. A case brought by the NGO Plan B and ten UK citizens was refused by both the High Court and the Court of Appeal. The claim described the UK Government's then 2050 climate target as misaligned with the Paris Agreement.[148] The High Court refused a full hearing of the case, and the Court of Appeal refused to hear the case on the basis that it had no prospects of success. As described in Chapter 5, in 2019 the UK Government revised its 2050 targets to net zero, without being forced to do so by a court.

While much of this litigation has been between domestic actors, there is an argument that carbon-major entities could also be sued for harm caused to other international actors, especially low-lying states.[149] There are a number of hurdles for tort-based actions, in particular, the issues of causation due to the diffuse nature of GHG emissions, how to identify an appropriate class of defendants, as well as the difficulty in linking any harm caused to specific emissions either from one state or

---

[145] The other issues in the case revolved around the *EU Habitats and SEA Directives*, R v. *Secretary of State for Transport* [2020] EWCA Civ 214.

[146] Climate Change Act 2008 (2050 Target Amendment) Order 2019 (SI 2019/1056).

[147] The statement of claim is available here: https://drive.google.com/file/d/1eiE_Nn40-cjzGY_C4 OF2Tv_op1-W5X-M/view?ths=true.

[148] For more information, see https://planb.earth/plan-b-v-uk/ (accessed 20 July 2020).

[149] Nyinevi and Nkrumah (n 124) 136; Tim Stephens, 'Low-Lying Pacific Islands Sue Over Climate Change' The Maritime Executive (*The Maritime Executive*, 30 October 2019), www .maritime-executive.com/editorials/low-lying-pacific-islands-sue-over-climate-change (accessed 17 July 2020).

one company.¹⁵⁰ However, as the scientific knowledge on attribution evolves, these causation hurdles may become easier to navigate.¹⁵¹

6.7.3 An Assessment of Global Climate Litigation Trends

The US cases demonstrate a clear difficulty in overcoming the displacement doctrine applied in these cases. The judiciary is generally reluctant to step into the shoes of the legislature, even though domestic climate legislation in that jurisdiction is currently not progressive or ambitious. In addition, US cases also demonstrate that federal common law nuisance claims are very difficult to launch successfully. Tort-based actions struggle to overcome the hurdles of causation, as GHG emissions are diffuse and difficult to attribute to one particular class of defendants, such as companies. It is also challenging for courts to link harm caused to specific emissions from a company or state, and the *Kivalina* case illustrates these difficulties well.

In contrast, the *Urgenda* case has wide-ranging implications both internationally and regionally within the European Union. This case managed to overcome the hurdles mentioned above, and to clearly attribute liability and responsibility to the state as a global actor to reduce emissions. It is not clear what the implications are for the Netherland's compliance with EU targets, particularly in relation to the EU ETS.¹⁵² However, it is clear that the Court's decision is progressive compared to other jurisdictions, particularly the US human rights cases, and therefore may motivate new climate change litigation suits within the European Union. For example, there are claims by the NGO Klimaatzaak in Belgium to challenge government inaction on climate change,¹⁵³ and a suit in France by four NGOs that the Government is not taking sufficient action on climate change,¹⁵⁴ and a case in Ireland regarding the country's domestic climate targets,¹⁵⁵ so climate change is likely to continue to be an ongoing issue for state liability. Both the Netherlands and Pakistan are highly vulnerable to the impacts of climate change, and so the decisions

---

¹⁵⁰ Preston (n 63) 7; van Zeben (n 125) 348.
¹⁵¹ Péloffy (n 83) 143; Human Rights Council (n 43); see also a recent report on attribution and climate change, Committee on Extreme Weather Events and Climate Change Attribution, Board on Atmospheric Sciences and Climate, Division on Earth and Life Studies, National Academies of Sciences, Engineering, and Medicine, *Attribution of Extreme Weather Events in the Context of Climate Change* (National Academies Press, 2016).
¹⁵² van Zeben (n 123) 352.
¹⁵³ See Klimaatzaak, www.klimaatzaak.eu/en (accessed 17 July 2020).
¹⁵⁴ Karen Savage, 'French Government Sued for Inadequate Climate Action' (*The Climate Docket*, 14 March 2019), www.climatedocket.com/2019/03/14/france-government-sued-climate-greenpeace-oxfam/ (accessed 17 July 2020).
¹⁵⁵ *Friends of the Irish Environment v. Ireland* [2017]. While initially unsuccessful in the High Court, in November 2019 the NGO had their request to appeal directly to the Supreme Court accepted on the basis of the urgency of the issue.

regarding state liability make sense in that context. There are a growing number of cases in the global South as well.[156] Climate litigation in these countries, particularly where based on human rights violations, reflects the traditional vertical relationship between state obligations to protect human rights for its citizens but does not necessarily reflect issues of climate justice internationally.

Litigation in the United Kingdom has mainly involved renewable energy companies suing the state for changes in policies regarding renewable energy subsidies and have relied little on human rights jurisprudence.[157] Recent action on the Heathrow runway case evidence that judicial attitudes towards climate change may be changing, although the case is the subject of an appeal. The successful *ClientEarth* case provides a useful model demonstrating what a claim against the state for inadequate GHG targets could look like. Analogies can be drawn between the *Urgenda* case and the *ClientEarth* case in the United Kingdom. In the latter case, Defra was clearly found to be in violation of regulations dealing with environmental pollution. Parallels between the health impacts of nitrogen dioxide and climate change are obvious, and this case provides an interesting example that could motivate more national litigation on health impacts from climate change in the United Kingdom.

6.8 THE CONVERGENCE OF HUMAN RIGHTS-BASED CLIMATE LITIGATION AGAINST COMPANIES

There are only one case and one investigation to date which are situated directly in the nexus between companies, human rights and climate change. The *Lliuya v. RWE* case in Germany and the Philippines Human Rights investigation both illustrate the convergence of these evolving areas of law – climate litigation against companies based on violations of human rights resulting from climate-induced impacts. While these two disputes take very different approaches and therefore may have very different impacts, they mark important and novel legal developments in this space.

In 2017, Saúl Luciano Lliuya, a Peruvian farmer and mountain guide, sued a German utility company for their proportionate contribution to adaptation costs needed to protect his village from glacial outbursts and flooding. Mr Lliuya argued that Rhenish–Westphalian Power Plant's (RWE) historic GHG emissions contributed to increased global temperatures, which have in turn caused the glaciers around Lake Palcacocha to melt. The lake sits North of Huaraz, where more than 50,000 residents, including Mr Lliuya, face an increased risk of severe flooding

---

[156] Jacqueline Peel and Jolene Lin, 'Transnational Climate Litigation: The Contribution of the Global South' (2019) 113(4) American J. Intl. L. 679; Joana Setzer and Lisa Benjamin, 'Climate Litigation in the Global South: Filling in Gaps' (2020) 114 American J. Intl. L. Unbound 56.
[157] *Solar Century Holdings Ltd v. Secretary of State for Energy and Climate Change* [2016] BLR 341 and R *(Drax Power Limited and another) v. HM Treasury and others* [2016] EWHC 228.

which could lead to loss of life, property and other damage. Mr Lliuya based his claim on paragraph 1004 of the Germany Civil Code, which deals with interference with property. However, the potential impacts of any flooding would have extensive implications for human rights. Interestingly, this case is the first to look at corporate liability for the impacts of climate change experienced transnationally, including incidents of loss and damage where the impacts of climate change go beyond the capacity of states or communities to adapt to them. Most other litigation, except for the US cases, focuses on mitigation obligations of governments or companies, and not corporate liability for adaptation and loss and damage.

The remedy Mr Lliuya seeks is related to the costs of adapting to the impacts of climate change. Mr Lliuya is asking for contributions by RWE to these adaptation costs, which consist of building protective barriers around the lake to protect the village from flooding. Basing his case on Heede's attribution study which traces the contributions of carbon-major companies to climate change (see the Introduction), Mr Lliuya asked for damages commensurate to Heede's estimate of RWE's historical contribution to global emissions of 0.47 per cent, Mr Lliuya consequentially requested 0.47 per cent of the total costs of adaptation for his village from RWE.[158]

The Higher Regional Court of Hamm, in Germany, agreed with Lliuya's approach, accepting his arguments of contributory or partial causation by one company to global climate change, and let the case proceed to the evidentiary stage. No matter what the outcome, the court's statements that climate harms can, in principle, give rise to corporate liability, is historic; no other court has made this decision before.[159] RWE appealed the decision in December 2017, and that appeal was denied in February 2018. The evidentiary phase of the case is to follow, and parties are currently wrangling over the appointment of experts. While the decision that RWE could, in principle, be responsible for climate-related harms is historic, it is not a substantive decision yet. To date, no court has held a company liable for climate-related harms, but the case is evidence of the growing nature of climate claims connected with climate harms, and the human rights nature of those harms.

The Philippines Commission on Human Rights' investigation of forty-seven carbon-major companies' contributions to climate impacts also focuses on the liability for companies for adaptation and loss and damage. The Commission's investigation focused on damages experienced by Filipino citizens, specifically as a result of the impacts of Typhoon Haiyan The process of the investigation was

---

[158] Benjamin (n 109). The Voltum was read out in court as a preparatory opinion but it is an internal court document and is not publicly available, although it will be the basis for the final court order.
[159] Lisa Benjamin, 'Directors Are in the Crosshairs of Corporate Climate Litigation' (*The Conversation*, 8 July 2019), https://theconversation.com/directors-are-in-the-crosshairs-of-corporate-climate-litigation-117737 (accessed 17 July 2020).

novel, being the first National Human Rights Commission to hold hearings in a number of jurisdictions around the world. It held several hearings, with three sittings in the Philippines, one in New York from 27 to 28 September 2018, and another in London from 6 to 9 October 2018. The Commission's outcomes are also unlike most litigation outcomes. Unlike litigation, the Commission does not attempt to pin legal liability for damage on corporate entities but instead to explore potential avenues of legal liability. It also served as an expository exercise to highlight the damaging role these entities continue to play in the context of climate change.[160]

While the Commission's investigation cannot pin legal liability on companies, its process and outcomes can play an important role in highlighting the devastating impact of carbon-majors on the environment in a specific context; amplifying the often overlooked voices and experiences of the climate-vulnerable, while linking the activities of these powerful transnational entities to the global impacts of climate change.[161] The Petition and the Commission's approach raises novel questions about prevention, responsibility and accountability for climate change harms framed as human rights violations.[162] In December 2019, the Commission announced its findings – that carbon-majors can be held liable for human rights violations.[163] Commissioner Roberto Eugenio T Cadiz said the commission found these companies played a clear role in anthropogenic climate change, and could be held legally liable for its impacts.[164] He urged countries to establish national climate liability legislation to hold entities such as these accountable under the law.

These two cases illustrate the emerging issue of state and company liability in the face of growing threats from climate change. Annalisa Savaresi and Jacques Hartmann note the Commission's process illustrates how human rights can be used as a gap filler, while other areas of law linking climate harms to legal obligations of companies take time to develop.[165] The initiatives that have been developed to try to fill the gap, are the Oslo Global Principles and the Enterprise Principles. The Oslo Global Principles and Enterprise Principles attempt to summarise the existing and near-future obligations of both states and business enterprises in relation to climate change.

---

[160] Benjamin (n 3).
[161] Ibid.
[162] Sara Seck, 'Revisiting Transnational Corporations and Extractive Industries: Climate Justice, Feminism, and State Sovereignty' (2017) 26(2) TLCP 383, 398.
[163] Isabella Kaminski, 'Carbon Majors Can Be Held Liable for Human Rights Violations, Philippines Commission Rules' (*The Climate Docket*, 9 December 2019), www.climatedocket.com/2019/12/09/philippines-human-rights-climate-change-2/ (accessed 17 July 2020). The formal outcome of the investigation is still awaiting publication.
[164] Ibid.
[165] Annalisa Savaresi and Jacques Hartmann, 'The Impacts of Climate Change and Human Rights: Early Reflections on the Carbon Majors Inquiry' in Jolene Lin and Doug Kysar (eds) *Climate Change Litigation in Asia* (Cambridge University Press 2018), 15.

6.9 THE OSLO GLOBAL PRINCIPLES AND ENTERPRISE PRINCIPLES

In addition to ongoing climate litigation, two new sets of principles have been promulgated with important implications for states and business enterprises in the context of climate change. While they remain soft law, these global principles develop an outline of potential (and increasingly likely) state and enterprise obligations in relation to climate change. They do differ in nature from the multilateral environmental agreements covered in Chapter 4, which bind states only. Unlike, for example, the UNFCCC or the Paris Agreement, the Principles have not been signed or ratified by any states, and have been formed not by state parties or companies, but by a group of legal experts and academics.

In March 2015, a group of experts in international law, human rights, tort and environmental law published the Oslo Principles on Global Climate Change Obligations to reduce climate change.[166] The Principles distil existing legal obligations relevant to both states and companies to constrain the dangerous impacts of climate change and to avert 'critical levels of global warming'.[167] The Principles are designed to set out the basic obligations of states and companies. Principle 1 is based on the precautionary principle, and requires GHG emissions to be reduced, and reduced at a pace that would protect against the threats of climate change that can still be avoided. States and companies have a requirement to take measures to achieve this without regard to cost (unless that cost is completely disproportionate to the reduction in emissions).[168]

On the basis of Principle 1, states and enterprises should take measures to ensure that global average surface temperatures never exceed pre-industrial temperatures by more than 2°C.[169] In addition, states and enterprises should refrain from starting any new activities that would cause excessive GHG emissions unless they take countervailing measures (with exceptions for least developed countries or GHG-emitting activities that are indispensable).[170]

The Oslo Global Principles are new and therefore their implications are uncertain. While the Principles are not directly legally binding on states, they are designed to crystalise existing international obligations. They are innovative for a number of reasons. They have been promulgated by international legal experts, and therefore could be deemed to be part of customary international law.[171] They avoid the contentious issue of foreseeability and liability for future emissions by attempting

---

[166] See 'Oslo Principles on Global Climate Change Obligations' (Dickson Poon School of Law 2015), https://globaljustice.yale.edu/sites/default/files/files/OsloPrinciples.pdf (accessed 17 July 2020). ('Oslo Global Principles').
[167] Ibid., 1.
[168] Ibid., para 1.b.
[169] Ibid., para 6.
[170] Ibid., para 8.
[171] Statute of the UN International Court of Justice (1945) ch 2, art 38(1)(d)

to establish current international obligations, and they apply to both developed and developing countries, with some exceptions for least developed countries. Interestingly, these obligations are specifically identified as persisting even if national or international law set lower standards.[172] The Principles, therefore, flesh out legal obligations that would avoid the risk that any commitments under the Paris Agreement are not sufficient to reach the new 'well below 2°C' global goal.

The Oslo Global Principles may provide further guidance and support for future climate litigation efforts against both states and companies. The Principles are innovative in that they specifically attempt to impose obligations on companies, an achievement that general international human rights law has so far failed to achieve. However, it is important to note that the Principles have not been adopted by the UN or any nation state, and therefore constitute soft law, at best. While the Principles are an innovation in international law on climate change, fiscal incentives, including fossil-fuel subsidies, continue to persist and present barriers to the transition to a low-carbon economy.

In 2018, a prominent group of legal experts developed the Principles of Climate Obligations of Enterprises ('The Enterprise Principles'), which follow on from the Oslo Global Principles. The Enterprise Principles apply only to private, commercial or industrial entities, or non-private entities that carry out commercial or industrial activities. The Principles recognise the enormous contribution that businesses make to climate change, and that it is impossible to achieve significant global emission reductions without major contributions from enterprises.[173] The Enterprise Principles are wide-ranging and include reduction obligations of enterprises, as well as disclosure obligations. They note that enterprises should take all reasonable steps to reduce the emissions of their activities to the point where they are no longer excessive, in the shortest time reasonably feasible.[174] The Enterprise Principles clearly state that carbon-majors deserve special consideration in the climate context, and therefore may attract liability first. The Enterprise Principles are the first global governance tool that specifically attempts to articulate, and therefore to impose, reduction obligations on corporations in the context of climate change.[175] Although they do not deal with liability directly, the Enterprise Obligations also provide a window into where existing normative frameworks could crystalise into legal obligations as the impacts of climate change increase and worsen over time.

While these initiatives are exciting legal developments, they do not deal specifically with liability or the human rights implications of climate change. Instead, they

---

[172] Oslo Global Principles (n 166), para 12.
[173] Expert Group on Climate Obligations of Enterprises, 'Five Principles on Climate Obligations of Enterprises: Legal Perspectives for Global Challenges' (Eleven Intl Publishing 2018) 28. These were updated in 2020 https://climateprinciplesforenterprises.org (accessed 17 November 2020).
[174] Ibid., 146.
[175] Lisa Benjamin, 'Corporations, CSR and Climate Change' in Sara Seck and Meinhard Doelle (eds), *Research Handbook on Loss and Damage* (Edward Elgar, forthcoming).

focus mainly on obligations of mitigation. In the context of companies, some further hurdles or stumbling blocks remain for fixing liability on companies for climate-induced impacts.

6.10 SOME STUMBLING BLOCKS TO CLIMATE LITIGATION EFFORTS AGAINST COMPANIES

In addition to some of the difficulties under tort law highlighted above, another potential stumbling block in relation to both human rights as well as climate litigation against companies is the structure of corporate groups. In the human rights realm, in particular, this has posed a significant obstacle for plaintiffs located in other jurisdictions making claims against the parent company located in a different jurisdiction. Janet Dine notes that the power of MNCs has left the human rights structure in disarray, particularly because MNCs hide their irresponsibility in opaque and complex structures located across multiple jurisdictions.[176]

This has been a long-standing problem, particularly in the area of human rights. In 2017, the UN Economic and Social Council's General Comment No. 24 highlighted that corporate groups routinely escape liability by hiding behind the so-called corporate veil.[177] In particular, victims of activities of transnational corporations face specific obstacles in establishing a causal link between the conduct of the defendant company in one jurisdiction resulting in a violation in another jurisdiction, due to, among other things, the *forum non conveniens* doctrine which allows courts to decline jurisdiction if another forum is available.[178]

The Council emphasised that states do have a duty to address challenges which prevent a denial of justice, and ensure effective remedies and reparations, by removing substantive, procedural and practice barriers to remedies, including by establishing parent company liability or group liability regimes.[179] In the United States, the main route of the Alien Tort Statute route has been all but stymied by a series of cases.[180] Progress may be occurring, slowly, in jurisdictions such as the United Kingdom as well as in Canada and the Netherlands in relation to common law claims. For example, in 2015 the Dutch Court of Appeals decided that Shell could be sued, in principle, for its subsidiary's negligence, although proof of liability

---

[176] Janet Dine, 'Stopping Jurisdictional Arbitrage by Multinational Companies: A National Solution?' (2014) 11(2) Eur. Company Law 77, 77.

[177] UN Committee on Economic, Social and Cultural Rights, 'General Comment No. 24 (2017) on State Obligations under the International Covenant on Economic, Social and Cultural Rights in the Context of Business Activities' (2017) E/C.12/GC/24, para 42.

[178] Ibid., para 43. The extraterritoriality issue is also a potential stumbling block, but this chapter will not cover that doctrine.

[179] Ibid., para 44.

[180] *Kiobel v. Royal Dutch Petroleum Co*, 569 US 108 (2013) and *Joseph Jesner et al. v. Arab Bank plc* 138 S.Ct. 1386, No. 16-499 (US Sup Ct 2019).

had to be established.[181] In the United Kingdom, the tort-based approach has made some headway. For example, in *Chandler v. Cape Industries*,[182] it was established that a parent company could have a duty of care for its subsidiary where it created expectations or responsibility through actions of the parent company. In the Canadian context, there have been similar developments. Direct actions by a parent company were held to include knowledge by the parent that there was a risk of violence that was so reasonably foreseeable by the parent that authorising the use of force could lead to human rights violations as a result of past behaviour of security forces.[183]

In a more recent set of cases,[184] claimants sought damages as a result of serious and ongoing pollution from leaks of oil from a pipeline in the Niger Delta from the parent company of the Royal Dutch Shell group located in the United Kingdom.[185] The local subsidiary, Shell Petroleum Development Company of Nigeria Ltd (SPDC) was also a respondent. The claimants brought a negligence claim under the common law of Nigeria, which is the same as the common law test in the United Kingdom, and brought a suit in the English courts, which was appealed to the Court of Appeal.[186] The Court of Appeal considered the three-part test of the duty of care as foreseeability, proximity and reasonableness, and considered that a parent company could owe a duty of care to an employee of a subsidiary or a party directly affected by its operations in certain circumstances: where the parent has taken direct responsibility for devising a material health and safety policy and its adequacy is the subject of the claim, or the parent controls the operations which give rise to the claim.[187] However, issuing mandatory policies was not sufficient, in the majority's opinion, to demonstrate the sufficient nexus of control by the parent over the operations of the subsidiary.[188] The policies in question were at a high level, and none came close to establishing the sort of proximity necessary to establish a duty of care.[189]

Despite this decision, in 2019 the UK Supreme accepted jurisdiction to hear the appeal of another case regarding a claim brought by 1,800 Zambian rural farming community members against UK-based Vedanta and its Zambian subsidiary

---

[181] A. F. Akpan v. Royal Dutch Shell plc. Court of Appeal of the Hague (18 December 2015).
[182] [2012] EWCA (Civ) 525 [80].
[183] *Choc v. Hudbay Minerals Inc.*, 2013 ONSC 1414 (Ontario Sup Ct 2013).
[184] *HRH Emere Godwin Bebe Okpabi v. Royal Dutch Shell* [2018] EWCA (Civ) 191.
[185] Ibid., [1].
[186] Ibid., [3].
[187] *Lungowe v. Vendanta Res.* [2017] EWCA (Civ) 1528; [83] In *HRH Emere*, the issue of proximity was problematic for the court. The court was concerned about whether RDS was in control of the SPDC operations. Five elements of the relationship of proximity were examined: mandatory policies, standards and manuals on engineering design and practice, systems of supervision and oversight, financial control over SPDC, and a high level of direction and oversight of SPDC's operations were exercised by RDS. [86].
[188] *HRH Emere* at [89].
[189] Although there was a strident dissent by LJ Sale, based on the *Chandler v. Cape* test.

regarding waste discharges from a copper mine, specifically on the basis that group policies can, in fact, establish a sufficient nexus of control between parent and subsidiary.[190] The outcome of this case, if it establishes a theory of group enterprise liability, would be historic. However, absent such a ruling, the cases illustrate how difficult establishing liability by a parent company for the actions of its subsidiaries in the context of climate change might be. Dine proposes an alternative solution, of making one jurisdiction responsible for the actions of all companies within a group, including the parent company and its subsidiaries.[191] Choudhury and Petrin argue for imposing a form of enterprise liability for traditional corporate groups combined with a modified vicarious liability.[192]

6.11 CONCLUSION

Company law, human rights law and climate change regulation have all developed independently. As a result, there has been little jurisprudence, litigation, or academic investigation of the overlaps among these three regimes, until recently. In recent years there have been significant developments in relation to business and human rights, climate change and human rights, and climate litigation. In fact, these three areas began to overlap just in 2019 with the investigation of forty-seven carbon-majors by the Philippines' Human Rights Commission, as well as the case brought by Mr Lliuya against RWE.

The inclusion of references to human rights in the Paris Agreement was a historic achievement, even though it is a preambular reference only. It is clear that states have obligations to protect human rights and these extend to the arena of climate change at the national level. In terms of international obligations, these are primarily characterised as international cooperation obligations between states, and soft law obligations characterised as responsibilities of companies under the UNGPs.[193] National obligations to mitigate climate change under human rights jurisprudence is emerging, but is not yet widespread, as few states have a singular responsibility for global climate change.[194] In addition, imposing human rights obligations on companies is challenging, and public nuisance suits against companies have been particularly difficult in the US jurisdiction.

Tort actions all over the world have been difficult due to the federal displacement doctrine and issues of causation. Most tort actions against states and companies have been defeated by difficulties in attributing climate impacts to specific emissions or specific emitters. In addition, the judicial reluctance in the United States to

---

[190] *Vendanta Res. v. Lungowe* [2019] UKSC 20. Subsequent actions by the Government of Zambia mean the case is unlikely to be heard in the Supreme Court.
[191] Dine (n 176), 78–9.
[192] Choudhury and Petrin (n 22), 120.
[193] Human Rights Council (n 43).
[194] Ibid.

circumvent the legislature might be instructive for other litigation claims worldwide. Despite these setbacks, litigation in other countries is continuing apace. Recent European jurisprudence under the *Urgenda* case has highlighted that states are vulnerable to climate change litigation suits targeting a lack of state regulatory action. In this case, courts were willing to overcome the complex issues of attribution and rely directly on human rights arguments. With the increases in certainty regarding climate change attribution science, it is likely that litigation across the globe will increase. In addition, the recent case against Defra and the Government in relation to the expansion of Heathrow Airport in the United Kingdom illustrates that, where public health issues arise, the judiciary may become more active in holding states responsible for regulatory inaction.

As the impacts of climate change escalate and continue to negatively affect human rights, more litigation will be pursued both against states as well as against companies. A convergence between human rights, climate change and company law, particularly in the contested site of climate litigation, is clearly emerging. Regulatory approaches which impose transnational liability on companies would prove a more comprehensive solution, but may be difficult to achieve as the UN Norms exercise illustrates. But courts can, and are, forcing states to take more proactive approaches to reduce carbon emissions, and litigants are forging a connection between corporate activities and the cost (in human lives as well as monetary values) of climate-induced harms, adaptation, and the impacts of loss and damage. Even if this litigation is unsuccessful, it implicates the fiduciary duties of directors. The Enterprise Principles foreshadow where these developments may crystallise into hard law obligations in the future, and corporate directors would do well to pay attention to, and prepare for these future legal developments now. Markets and investors are certainly paying attention, as illustrated in the next chapter.

7

Fiscal Barriers and Incentives to Corporate Climate Action

On 29 September 2015, Mark Carney, the then Governor of the Bank of England and Chairman of the Financial Stability Board, gave a speech entitled 'Breaking the Tragedy of the Horizon – Climate Change and Financial Stability'. The timing and location of his speech were as important as its contents. The speech preceded the 2015 UNFCCC Paris Agreement Conference of Parties by several months, and was held at the Lloyd's of London headquarters in Lime Street. Lloyd's is located in the heart of London's central business district, and is an incorporated marketplace of insurers and reinsurers which collectively manage billions of dollars of risk premiums from all over the world. Founded in 1686 by Edward Lloyd who sold marine insurance from his coffee shop in London (including to mariners involved in the slave trade), Lloyd's has grown to be one of the largest marketplace of syndicates, insurance buyers and brokers, managing agents and cover holders who buy, sell, manage and hedge insurable risks.

Called an 'unlikely climate champion',[1] as a former Goldman Sach's banker, Carney's approach to climate change is couched in language that investors and other financial intermediaries such as insurers understand – risk. In his 2015 speech, Carney pointed to the enormous risks to UK investors of climate change, including stranded assets, as 19 per cent of FTSE 100 companies operated in natural resources and extraction, and another 11 per cent in utilities, chemicals, construction and industrial goods.[2] Carney emphasised the temporal dissonance between business risk cycles and climate risk cycles. He noted that business cycles vary from monetary policy cycles of 2–3 years, to financial stability credit cycles of 10 years, so by the time

---

[1] Ed King, 'Mark Carney, the Unlikely Climate Champion' (*Climate Home News*, 15 December 2016), www.climatechangenews.com/2016/12/15/mark-carney-the-unlikely-climate-champion (accessed 20 July 2020).

[2] Mark Carney, 'Breaking the Tragedy of the Horizon – Climate Change and Financial Stability' (Lloyd's of London, 29 September 2015) 11, www.bankofengland.co.uk/speech/2015/breaking-the-tragedy-of-the-horizon-climate-change-and-financial-stability (accessed 20 July 2020).

climate change becomes a defining issue for financial stability, it may already be too late to address it.[3] He also emphasised the necessity of a smooth and phased transition towards a low-carbon economy. An abrupt devaluation of assets as a result of non-linear climate impacts could lead to pro-cyclical crystallisation of losses and a tightening of financial conditions – a Minsky Moment – which in itself could jeopardise fiscal stability.[4]

Carney's speech set out the broad and systemic risks that climate change poses to financial systems and financial stability, and the important role financial policy-makers have in the context of climate change. The extensive nature of this risk is partly due to historical financial incentives, such as fossil-fuel subsidies, that have, and continue to embed carbon into economies. His speech also provides an initial roadmap of financial opportunities available to firms for transitioning away from fossil fuel-intensive economies by internalising carbon risks, using tools such as carbon taxes and clean energy investments. This chapter looks at three financial elements of climate change in turn – fossil-fuel subsidies, carbon taxes and the emerging role of institutional investors in climate action. These financial elements involve government regulation and non-governmental approaches in terms of investor action.

These initiatives are related to company theories and law analysed in Chapters 2 and 3, but focus less on corporate theories and corporate law. Instead, this chapter focuses on initiatives taken by investors on climate change, including some evolving interpretations of investor-related duties. The chapter concludes by highlighting some parallels between fiduciary duties of directors and the fiduciary duties of investors in the context of environmental, social and governance (ESG) indicators. Some fiscal mechanisms can fall under the concept of decentred and transnational regulation concepts covered in Chapter 6. Investors are starting to take action by engaging with directors, divesting, or even initiating climate litigation against companies. While divorced from more traditional concepts of state regulation, these less formal initiatives can exert a tremendous influence over firms as well as climate and energy regulation and policies. For example, decisions made by institutional investors may fall outside the control of companies, but may have a significant effect on corporate decisions, investments and operations.

7.1 FOSSIL-FUEL SUBSIDIES

Fossil fuel subsidies remain a controversial subject. Part of the controversy surrounding subsidies is in the inability or unwillingness of states to adopt a universal definition. As a result, subsidies are difficult to quantify and estimate. Some

---

[3] Ibid., 4.
[4] Ibid., 11. A Minsky Moment refers to the onset of market collapse due to a sudden shift or decline in market sentiment, named after the economist, Hyman Minsky's, credit cycle.

definitions focus on the benefit conferred on a specific group through a price-gap between the actual price and a benchmark price (based on fuel unit prices).[5] Others focus on producer or consumer subsidies (the latter being more popular in developing countries). Beyond direct transfers to producers or allowing fossil fuel purchases below domestic market prices, there remains significant political disagreement on their definition,[6] and therefore their existence. The OECD recently estimated the level of fossil fuels subsidies amongst forty-four states to equal approximately US$150–200 billion per year between 2010 and 2016, increasing slightly to US$178 billion in 2019.[7] The International Energy Agency estimated consumption subsidies to be approximately US$400 billion in 2018, declining to US$120 billion in 2019.[8] The International Monetary Fund broke with tradition by adopting an expansive definition of fossil-fuel subsidies including any non-pricing of environmental externalities, which led to a staggering number of US$4.7 trillion in subsidies in 2015, rising to US$5.2 trillion in 2017.[9]

Subsidies can affect both the price and quantity of available goods and services.[10] Fossil-fuel subsidies encourage the consumption of fossil fuels and consequently GHG emissions, and are therefore inconsistent with policies to combat climate change.[11] They can also disincentivise investments in energy efficiency and renewable energy.[12] Externalities, such as GHG emissions, can also be a subsidy given that pollution is often not internalised by the emitters.[13] William Blyth argues that the lack of a carbon price also constitutes a subsidy to GHG emitters as they do not pay for the full cost of their production.[14] Removing subsidies would therefore provide significant climate and other environmental benefits, as well as cost savings for governments, but political will to reform or remove them remains low.[15] On the other hand, arguments in support of the use of subsidies include the protection of

---

[5] Jakob Skovgaard, 'The Devil Lies in the Definition: Competing Approaches to Fossil Fuel Subsidies at the IMF and OECD' (2017) 17 *International Environmental Agreements* 341, 343.
[6] Jakob Skovgaard and Harro van Asselt, 'An Introduction' in Jakob Skovgaard and Harro van Asselt (eds), *The Politics of Fossil Fuel Subsidies and Their Reform* (Cambridge University Press 2018), 4, 41.
[7] 'OECD-IEA Fossil Fuel Support and Other Analysis' (*OECD.org*, 5 June 2020), www.oecd.org/fossilfuel/data (accessed 20 July 2020).
[8] 'Energy Subsidies: Tracking the Impact of Fossil-fuel Subsidies' (*International Energy Agency*), www.iea.org/topics/energy-subsidies (accessed 20 July 2020).
[9] David Coady et al., 'Global Fossil Fuel Subsidies Remain Large: An Update Based on Country-Level Estimates' (2019) International Monetary Fund Working Paper 19/89.
[10] William Blyth, 'Energy Subsidies in the UK' (Environmental Audit Committee, 2013), 8.
[11] Environmental Audit Committee, *Energy Subsidies* (HC 2013-14, 61) 3; Shelagh Whitley, 'Time to Change the Game. Fossil Fuel Subsidies and Climate' (*Overseas Development Institute*, 2013), 1.
[12] Shelagh Whitley and Laurie Van Der Burg, 'Reforming Fossil Fuel Subsidies The Art of the Possible' in Jakob Skovgaard and Harro van Asselt (eds), *The Politics of Fossil Fuel Subsidies and Their Reform* (Cambridge University Press 2018) 48, 48.
[13] Blyth (n 10) 10.
[14] Ibid., 10.
[15] Skovgaard and van Asselt (n 6) 4.

infant industries, protection from foreign competition, and to support pro-poor policies,[16] specifically affordable energy. Subsidies' benefits extend beyond the oil and gas industry beneficiaries to any other business or industry that relies heavily on fossil fuel-based electricity or transportation.

In September 2009, G20 leaders committed to rationalise and phase out inefficient fossil-fuel subsidies that lead to wasteful consumption.[17] More recently, G7 states agreed to phase out fossil-fuel subsidies by 2025.[18] However, there is no systematic reporting of fossil-fuel subsidies at the international level,[19] and the definition and phasing out of harmful subsidies remain a national decision.[20] Since the 2009 commitment, there has been little action or political appetite for the phasing out of fossil-fuel subsidies. As a result, the only definition of subsidies at the international level remains one developed by the World Trade Organization (WTO).[21]

7.1.1 *Subsidies under the WTO Rules*

For a long time, energy and energy subsidies were considered to fall outside of the General Agreement on Tariffs and Trade (GATT) 1947, primarily because between the period of 1940s and 1970s, energy remained concentrated within a cartel of a few international companies.[22] As a result, it was felt that there was no need for special rules on energy at the WTO.[23] There is still no 'energy agreement' within the WTO agreements, however, energy is covered by the WTO agreements as discussed during various rounds of the GATT.[24] Further, energy is covered in the Agreement

---

[16] Ibid., 5.
[17] 'G20 Leaders' Declaration', (G20 Saint Petersburg Summit, 2009), para 94, www.oecd.org/g20/summits/saint-petersburg/Saint-Petersburg-Declaration.pdf (accessed 20 July 2020).
[18] Karl Mathieson, 'G7 Nations Pledge to End Fossil Fuel Subsidies by 2025' (*The Guardian*, 27 May 2016), www.theguardian.com/environment/2016/may/27/g7-nations-pledge-to-end-fossil-fuel-subsidies-by-2025 (accessed 20 July 2020).
[19] G20, IEA, OPEC, OECD, and World Bank, 'Analysis of the Scope of Energy Subsidies and Suggestions for the G-20 Initiative' (G20 Toronto Summit, 2010), 4, www.oecd.org/env/45575666.pdf (accessed 20 July 2020).
[20] Ibid., 9.
[21] Henok Birhanu Asmelash, 'Energy Subsidies and WTO Dispute Settlement: Why Only Renewable Energy Subsidies are Challenged' (2015) 18 J. Intl. Economic L. 261, 267.
[22] Anna-Alexandra Marhold, 'The World Trade Organization and Energy: Fuel for Debate' (2013) 2(8) Eur. Society Intl. L. Reflections, 2.
[23] Cottier, T., Malumfashi, G., Matteotti-Berkutova, S., Nartova, O., De Sépibus, J., & Bigdeli, S. (2011). Energy in WTO law and policy. In T. Cottier & P. Delimatsis (Eds.), The Prospects of International Trade Regulation: From Fragmentation to Coherence (pp. 211–244). Cambridge: Cambridge University Press. doi:10.1017/CBO9780511792496.007.
[24] Rafael Leal-Arcas and Ehab S. Abu Gosh, 'Energy Trade as a Special Sector in the WTO: Unique Features, Unprecedented Challenges and Unresolved Issues' (2014) Queen Mary University London School of Law Legal Research Paper No. 176/2014, 28.

on Subsidies and Countervailing Measures (SCM Agreement), and in rules on government procurement and competition.[25]

The SCM Agreement has the clearest definition of subsidies within the suite of the WTO-covered agreements. It divides subsidies into two types: prohibited and actionable. The third category of subsidies, non-actionable subsidies, expired on 1 January 2000.[26] Article 3 governs prohibited subsidies, which include export subsidies (where a subsidy is tied to export performance) or import substitution subsidies.[27] Actionable subsidies are those that must be withdrawn only if they cause adverse impacts to the interests of member states. Actionable subsidies are further defined in Article 5 and include injury to domestic industries, nullification or impairment of benefits, and serious prejudice to the interests of another member state.[28]

Thousands of subsidies have been notified by WTO member states, indicating their widespread use by national governments.[29] Governments use fossil-fuel subsidies and subsidies to support renewable energy deployment. While fossil-fuel subsidies can distort markets, discourage the production and use of clean energy and hamper the transition to low-carbon energy,[30] they are hard to dispense with because they have helped to 'lock in' fossil-fuel technologies and infrastructure with large sunk costs.[31] Removing fossil-fuel subsidies could expedite the development and deployment of renewable energy technology through reallocating this monetary resource to renewable energy sellers and by levelling the playing field for renewables.[32] Governments have also used subsidies as an 'essential tool' to introduce emissions reduction schemes.[33] These so-called 'green subsidies' can be used to enhance public goods, redistribute income and compensate for market failure or

---

[25] Cottier et al. (n 23), 8; Steve Charnovitz, 'Green Subsidies at the WTO' (2014) World Bank, Policy Research White Paper 7060, 16.

[26] Aaron Cosbey and Petros C. Mavroidis, 'A Turquoise Mess: Green Subsidies, Blue Industrial Policy and Renewable Energy: The Case for Redrafting the Subsidies Agreement of the WTO' (2014) 17 J. Intl. Economic L. 11, 37–38.

[27] Peter van den Bossche and Werner Zdouc, *The Law and Policy of the World Trade Organization* (3rd edn, Cambridge University Press 2013) 770.

[28] Agreement on Subsidies and Countervailing Measures, (WTO Uruguay Round Agreements, 1994) Article 5(a)-(c), www.wto.org/english/docs_e/legal_e/24-scm.pdf (accessed 20 July2020).

[29] Bossche and Zdouc (n 27) 748.

[30] Valeria Jana Schwanitz and others, 'Long-term Climate Policy Implications of Phasing Out Fossil-Fuel Subsidies' (2014) 67 *Energy Policy* 882, 882.

[31] Cees van Beers and Jeroen C. J. M. van den Bergh, 'Perseverance of Perverse Subsidies and Their Impact on Trade and Environment' (2001) 36 *Ecological Economics* 475, 485.

[32] Asmelash (n 21) 267; Liesbeth Casier and others, 'Shining a Light on Fossil Fuel Subsidies at the WTO: How NGOs Can Contribute to WTO Notification and Surveillance' (October 2014) 13(4) *World Trade Review* 603, 604.

[33] Lauren Henschke, 'Going It Alone on Climate Change – A New Challenge to WTO Subsidies Disciplines: Are Subsidies in Support of Emission Reduction Schemes Permissible under the WTO?' (2012) 11(1) *World Trade Review* 27, 28. It is questionable whether cap-and-trade permits would be covered by the SCM, but renewable energy measures can span services areas such as metering, scoping, engineering, maintenance as well as intellectual property rights; see

government failure to remove fossil-fuel subsidies.[34] The SCM Agreement has no environmental exception,[35] so fossil-fuel subsidies are theoretically treated in a fashion similar to subsidies to support renewable energy within member states, but to date, there have only been disputes at the WTO regarding renewable energy subsidies, and none involving fossil-fuel subsidies.[36]

The first WTO renewable energy disputes involved a Canadian Renewable Energy Feed-in Tariff. In 2009, Ontario introduced a feed-in tariff with a fixed price over the next 20–40 years to support renewable energy deployment. Included in the scheme was a local content requirement that a certain percentage of wind turbine or solar panels used had to be produced in Ontario in order to make the higher prices of energy more palatable to the public.[37] The Appellate Body found that there was no benefit to the industry based on a market analysis of the renewable energy market (not the electricity market as a whole). While the case was a victory for renewable energy subsidies, it has been criticised for 'legal acrobatics'[38] in order to exempt renewable energy subsidies from the SCM disciplines.[39] In subsequent cases, wind and solar subsidies which involve local content requirements have all been held to violate WTO agreements.[40]

Given the number of disputes regarding renewable energy subsidies, it is curious that there have been no disputes at the WTO regarding fossil-fuel subsidies. Commentators have argued that, while the SCM Agreement attempts to balance the legitimate use of public funds for public purposes through subsidies against

Thomas Cottier, 'Renewable Energy and WTO Law: More Policy Space or Enhanced Disciplines?' (2014) 1 Renewable Energy L. Policy Rev. 42.

[34] Charnovitz (n 25) 11.
[35] Mark Wu and James Salzman, 'The Next Generation of Trade and Environment Conflicts: The Rise of Green Industrial Policy' (2014) 108 Northwestern U. L. Rev. 401, 453.
[36] These disputes include India – Certain Measures Relating to Solar Cells and Solar Modules (WT/DS456/1/Add.1); Canada – Certain Measures Affecting the Renewable Energy Sector (WT/DS412/AB/R); China – Measures Concerning Wind Power Equipment (WT/DS419/1), Canada – Measures relating to the Feed-in Tariff Program (WT/DS426/AB/R), European Union and Certain Member States – Certain Measures Affecting the Renewable Energy Sector (WT/DS452/1), European Union and Certain Member States – Certain Measures on the Importation and Marketing of Biodiesel and Measures Supporting the Biodiesel Industry (WT/DS459/1), United States – Certain Measures Relating to the Renewable Energy Sector (WT/DS510/R).
[37] Alexandre Genest, 'The Canada-FIT Case and the WTO Subsidies Agreement: Failed Fact-Finding, Needless Complexity and Missed Judicial Economy' (2014) 10 *McGill J. Sustainable Development L. & Policy* 237, 240; Samuel Griffin, 'The World Trade Organization: A Barrier to Green Energy' (2013) 22 Transnational L. & Contemporary Problems 205, 209.
[38] Cosbey and Mavroidis (n 26) 28.
[39] Rajib Pal, 'Has the Appellate Body's Decision in Canada-Renewable Energy/Canada- Feed-in-Tariff Programme Opened the Door for Production Subsidies?' (2014) 17 J. Intl. Economic L., 123, 136.
[40] See Wu and Salzman (n 35); Lisa Benjamin, 'Renewable Energy and Trade: Meeting the Paris Agreement's Goals Through a Two-Step Jurisprudential Advance' 22 Minnesota Journal of Law, Science and Technology (2021) 1.

unfairly promoting domestic industries,[41] it still requires that the adverse impact from a subsidy be tied to a specific industry.[42] Fossil-fuel subsidies, which often take the form of dual-pricing subsidies, lack the requisite specificity as they are tied to all industries and enterprises, and therefore are very difficult to challenge at the WTO.[43] Fossil-fuel subsidies also rarely rely on local content requirements, and strong domestic lobby groups for the fossil-fuel industry can also dissuade a country from initiating a dispute at the WTO.[44] This leaves the unfortunate circumstance that subsidies tailored towards supporting the renewable energy industry will continue to be challenged under the WTO system, particularly where they involve local content requirements, but fossil-fuel subsidies will remain difficult to challenge at the WTO. This reality has led a number of commentators to advocate for the revitalisation of the non-actionable subsidy list, particularly for subsidies that promote public goods.[45] To date, the WTO has failed to create such a list.[46] In December 2017, a number of member states adopted the 'Fossil Fuel Subsidies Reform Ministerial Statement',[47] seeking the rationalisation and phase-out of fossil-fuel subsidies and the central role of the WTO in facilitating this action, but very little action has followed. In 2019, five small, trade-dependent WTO member states, Fiji, New Zealand, Iceland, Costa Rica and Norway, announced negotiations towards an Agreement on Climate Change, Trade and Sustainability (ACCTS).[48] ACCTS includes the reduction of tariffs and other trade barriers on environmental goods and services, elimination of fossil-fuel subsidies and voluntary guidelines on eco-labelling.[49] Once ACCTS is agreed, other WTO member states will be able to join it. This recent initiative attempts to overcome the obstacles experienced in previous stalled negotiations at the WTO to establish an Agreement on Environmental Goods and Services.

---

[41] Henschke (n 33) 29.
[42] Timothy L. Meyer, 'Energy Subsidies and the World Trade Organization' (2013) 17(22) American Society Intl. L. Insights, 4; Genest (n 37) 248.
[43] Meyer (n 42) 4; Asmelash (n 21) 281.
[44] Asmelash (n 21) 281–282.
[45] For example, in 2014, thirteen countries pledged to proceed to negotiate a 'Green Goods Agreement' to liberalise trade in goods that had environmental, trade and development benefits, Henschke (n 33) 51; Cosbey and Mavroidis (n 26) 46; Luca Rubini, 'Ain't Wastin' Time No More: Subsidies for Renewable Energy, The SCM Agreement, Policy Space and Law Reform' (2012) 15(2) J. Intl. Economic L. 525, 571.
[46] Meyer (n 42) 3; See the WTO website on plurilateral negotiations to develop a list of environmental goods and services www.wto.org/english/tratop_e/envir_e/envir_neg_serv_e.htm (accessed 22 July 2020).
[47] 'Fossil Fuels Subsidies Reform Ministerial Statement' (WTO Ministerial Conference, 2017) WT/MIN(17)/54.
[48] See www.mfat.govt.nz/en/trade/free-trade-agreements/climate/agreement-on-climate-change-trade-and-sustainability-accts-negotiations/ (accessed 22 July 2020).
[49] Ibid.

7.1.2 Industry-Based Subsidies

The fossil-fuel industry has received subsidies in many forms over the decades. The Overseas Development Institute (ODI) characterised these subsidies as 'tantamount to G20 governments allowing fossil fuel producers to undermine national climate commitments, while paying them for the privilege'.[50]

The main type of subsidy provided in the United Kingdom has been tax allowances to the oil and gas sectors, which partially offset the petroleum revenue tax, but the level of subsidies to the fossil-fuel industry has gradually decreased over time.[51] The Environmental Audit Committee estimated that in the United Kingdom, energy subsidies amounted to approximately £12 billion per year, much of which benefits the fossil-fuel industry.[52] The ODI reported that the United Kingdom was listed as one of the top OECD-subsidising countries, with approximately £280 million tax subsidies provided to oil and gas production alone in 2011.[53] The majority of these subsidies include field allowances to oil and gas development, which are most damaging to the environment because they create incentives for companies to find and develop new fossil-fuel resources.[54]

In 2013, the Environmental Audit Committee recommended that the new budget reduce the proportion of energy subsidies that support the fossil-fuel industry.[55] In response, the Government denied that it provides harmful energy policies, rejected that subsidies amounted to £12 billion per year, and denied that it provides subsidies to the fossil-fuel industry.[56] This denial may be related to a failure of the 2009 G20 to agree on a definition of fossil-fuel subsidies, leading eleven of the G20 members to claim that they had no inefficient fossil-fuel subsidies to report.[57] Fossil fuel subsidies can also include the transfer of health or environmental reclamation risks to the public, as well as subsidised borrowing for government-owned energy infrastructure.[58] None of these types of subsidies is properly captured by US data on fossil-fuel subsidies, and so both the United Kingdom and the United States provide large subsidies to industry and yet fail to properly record the level of subsidies provided.[59] The United States also denies that key interventions supporting the fossil fuel

---

[50] Elizabeth Bast and others, 'Empty Promises G20 Subsidies to Oil, Gas and Coal Production' (ODI and OCI, 2015), 11, www.odi.org/sites/odi.org.uk/files/odi-assets/publications-opinion-files/9957.pdf (accessed 20 July 2020).
[51] Blythe (n 10) 20.
[52] Environmental Audit Committee (n 11), para 67.
[53] Whitley (n 11) 1.
[54] Ibid 17.
[55] Environmental Audit Committee (n 11) para 71.
[56] Ibid., para 9–12.
[57] Casier and others (n 32) 609.
[58] Skovgaard and van Asselt (n 6), 40.
[59] Ibid.

industry amount to subsidies at all.[60] By introducing uncertainty at the political level, governments deflect attention away from subsidy reform or removal.[61]

In the face of government opposition regarding the very existence of fossil-fuel subsidies, it is difficult to imagine that any change in policy on fossil-fuel subsidies will take place in the near future. In fact, subsidies for renewable energy are facing uncertain futures by governments around the world. From 2015 to 2017, the UK government cut tax incentives for both wind[62] and solar farms.[63] In 2020, the UK government reinstated the incentives for both wind and solar,[64] a ban on the onshore wind was removed[65] and subsidies extended in the United States for wind but not solar facilities.[66] While both fossil fuel and renewable subsidies remain contentious and uncertain, fiscal mechanisms like carbon taxes, have gained in popularity with firms seeking regulatory certainty.

7.2 CARBON TAXES

A carbon tax is a fee added to the price of a good or service to reflect its carbon context.[67] While carbon taxes cannot guarantee a certain emissions pathway, they can establish a price pathway on goods and services to dissuade consumers from purchasing carbon-intensive goods or services.[68] One of the main problems with climate change is that it produces externalities that are not factored into the price of goods and services, or internalised by the producers of carbon-intensive products.

---

[60] Skovgaard and van Asselt (n 6), 40.
[61] Ibid.
[62] See 'Onshore Wind Farms Cancelled as Subsidies Cut' (*BBC News*, 22 June 2015), www.bbc.com/news/uk-politics-33227489 (accessed 21 July 2020).
[63] Rosie Marray-West and Ruth Lumley, 'Solar Firms to Sue Government for Ending Support' (*The Ecologist*, 9 August 2014), www.theecologist.org/News/news_round_up/2509245/solar_firms_to_sue_government_for_ending_support.html (accessed 21 July 2020); 'Senseless and Damaging: UK's Solar Cuts' (*The Ecologist*, 22 July 2015), www.theecologist.org/News/news_round_up/2958550/senseless_and_damaging_uks_solar_cuts.html (accessed 21 July 2020); Adam Vaughan and Terry Macalister, 'The Nine Green Policies Killed Off by the Tory Government' (*The Guardian*, 24 July 2015), www.theguardian.com/environment/2015/jul/24/the-9-green-policies-killed-off-by-tory-government (accessed 20 July 2020).
[64] 'UK Government Reinstates Subsidies for Wind, Solar from 2021' (*Smart Energy International*, 17 April 2020), www.smart-energy.com/industry-sectors/policy-regulation/uk-govt-reinstates-subsidies-for-wind-solar-from-2021/ (accessed 21 July 2020).
[65] Jim Pickard, 'Johnson Revives Onshore Wind Farms After 4-Year Ban' (*Financial Times*, 2 March 2020), www.ft.com/content/b8ddb2f4-5c83-11ea-8033-fa40a0d65a98 (accessed 21 July 2020).
[66] Emma F. Merchant, 'US Lawmakers Stiff Solar, Wind Gets Modest Victory in Tax Deal' (*Green Tech Media*, 17 December 2019), www.greentechmedia.com/articles/read/u-s-lawmakers-hand-clean-energy-tax-credits-a-loss-though-wind-gets-a-win (accessed 21 July 2020).
[67] Kevin Kennedy, Michael Obeiter and Noah Kaufman, 'Putting A Price on Carbon: A Handbook for US Policy Makers' (2015) World Resources Institute Working Paper, 2, www.wri.org/sites/default/files/carbonpricing_april_2015.pdf (accessed 21 July 2020).
[68] Ibid.

A carbon tax internalises these externalities, and encourages individuals to consider the carbon content of the goods and services they consume.[69] Carbon taxes were first applied in the 1990s in Scandinavian countries, and have since spread to countries such as the United Kingdom and France.[70]

7.2.1 The Benefits of a Carbon Tax

Imposition of a carbon tax sends an economic signal to industry motivating the reduction of their emissions.[71] It is often touted as the most cost-effective method to achieve a low-carbon global trajectory.[72] Given that the estimated emissions gap after the Paris Agreement contributions remains at 12–18 $GtCO_{2e}$ by 2030[73], a mechanism is required to stimulate cost-effective decarbonisation globally.[74] Carbon pricing can align private and social costs of carbon, and factor the adverse impacts of climate change into everyday decision-making by consumers.[75]

Carbon taxes are often simpler to administrate than a cap-and-trade system. A carbon tax does not require a reduction in emissions but instead establishes a 'stable price trajectory',[76] providing a signal and certainty to industry.[77] Environmental taxes generally work to shift consumer behaviour away from polluting activities, and they can also encourage the development of newer and cleaner technologies.[78] Carbon taxes shift the burden of externalities from society to the emitters.[79] With respect to energy, a carbon tax can make alternative and cleaner sources of energy more cost-competitive with fossil fuels.[80] Carbon taxes can also

---

[69] Mai Farrid et al., 'After Paris: Fiscal, Macroeconomic and Financial Implications of Climate Change' (International Monetary Fund, January 2016), 5, www.imf.org/external/pubs/cat/longres.aspx?sk=43484 (accessed 21 July 2020); Gilbert E. Metcalf and David Weisbach, 'The Design of a Carbon Tax' (2009) 33 Harvard Environmental L. Rev. 499, 500.

[70] Kennedy, Obeiter and Kaufman (n 67) 3.

[71] Lara Dahan et al., 'The Paris Agreement: A New International Framework to Facilitate the Uptake of Carbon Pricing' (Institute for Climate Economics, April 2016) Climate Brief No. 39, 2, www.i4ce.org/download/the-paris-agreement-a-new-international-framework-to-facilitate-the-uptake-of-carbon-pricing/ (accessed 21 July 2020).

[72] Ibid., 1.

[73] UN Environment, 'Emissions Gap Report 2019' (UN Environment: 2020), xix.

[74] Dahan et al. (n 71) 3.

[75] Farid et al. (n 69) 6.

[76] Kennedy, Obeiter and Kaufman (n 67) 10.

[77] Ted Gayer, 'On the Merits of a Carbon Tax' (U. S. Senate Energy and Natural Resources Committee, 2 December 2009) 2, www.urban.org/sites/default/files/publication/31041/901308-On-the-Merits-of-a-Carbon-Tax.PDF (accessed 21 July 20200.

[78] Reyer Gerlagh and Wietze Lise, 'Carbon Taxes: A Drop in the Ocean, or a Drop That Erodes the Stone? The Effect of Carbon Taxes on Technological Change.' (2004) 54 Ecological Economics, 241, 241.

[79] Kennedy, Obeiter and Kaufman (n 67) 2.

[80] Fan-Ping Chiu et al., 'The Energy Price Equivalent of Carbon Taxes and Emissions Trading – Theory and Evidence' (2015) 160 Applied Energy 164, 165.

provide a stable price for carbon, which can in turn make emissions trading mechanisms more effective.[81]

Carbon taxes can also generate state revenue for use in a variety of ways. Tax revenues can offset decreases in real incomes, particularly in relation to household energy bills.[82] Revenues can be invested in public infrastructure such as energy grids, research and development towards more clean energy technologies, or as tax credits given directly to households to offset increased taxes.[83] Revenues can reduce public deficits, provide transitional assistance to displaced workers and combat climate change, such as funding climate-change adaptation activities.[84] Revenues could also be used to assist and support industries that have been adversely and disproportionately affected by the tax.[85] Additional benefits include the generation of co-benefits for the state, such as reduced pollution, enhanced energy security, increased deployment of renewable energy and increased energy efficiency.[86]

7.2.2 Development and Application of a Carbon Tax

Carbon taxes can be based on several environmental principles, such as the polluter pays, precautionary principle and least-cost abatement principle.[87] The main design considerations of a carbon tax are its scope, point of regulation, reporting and verification mechanisms and establishment of a carbon price.[88] In terms of its scope, a tax could be imposed on all GHGs, or just a select few, such as carbon.[89] A tax could also be applied to specific fossil fuels, or to sectors of the economy.[90] Ideally, a carbon tax would cover all activities that produce climate externalities.[91]

Establishing a price on carbon is difficult. In theory, the rate of the tax should equal the marginal harm from emissions.[92] The tax should be able to compensate for the social marginal damages from the production of an additional unit of emissions.[93] While there is no disagreement between economists that the costs to

---

[81] Ibid., 165.
[82] Kennedy, Obeiter and Kaufman (n 67) 3.
[83] Ibid 24; In British Columbia the proceeds of the carbon tax has been used entirely as tax credits, see also Clean Energy Canada, 'How to Adopt a Winning Carbon Price' (2008), cleanenergycanada.org/wp-content/uploads/2015/02/Clean-Energy-Canada-How-to-Adopt-a-Winning-Carbon-Price-2015.pdf (accessed 21 July 2020).
[84] Kennedy, Obeiter and Kaufman (n 67) 2.
[85] Dahan et al. (n 71) 2.
[86] Ibid., 2.
[87] Carl von Essen, 'Carbon Taxation – a Forgotten Climate Policy Tool?' (Global Utmaning, 2009), 9, www.globalutmaning.se/wp-content/uploads/sites/8/2010/09/Carbon_taxation_GU.pdf (accessed 21 July 2020).
[88] Kennedy, Obeiter and Kaufman (n 67) 4.
[89] Ibid., 4.
[90] Ibid., 4; von Essen (n 87) 22.
[91] Metcalf and Weisbach (n 69) 521.
[92] Ibid., 501.
[93] Ibid., 511.

society of burning carbon exceed its private costs, there is no agreement on the exact social costs of carbon.[94] Information on climate change and its impacts are continuously evolving, and tremendous uncertainties remain regarding the scale and scope of the damage.[95]

Predicting and modelling impacts of climate change, and then monetising those impacts, remains challenging.[96] The World Bank estimates that carbon taxes are rarely set high enough to trigger substantial reductions.[97] They range from £1/tCO$_2$ in the Ukraine to £100/tCO$_2$ in Sweden. Some initiatives are subnational, such as the imposition of a carbon tax in 2008 by British Columbia at $10/tCO$_{2e}$, which has recently been increased to $40/tCO$_{2e}$ in 2019.[98] In 2009, the Obama Administration developed a social cost of carbon which was updated in 2016 by an Interagency Working Group and used in Federal regulatory analyses to value emissions changes over several GHGs over several years. For carbon, the cost ranged from $105 per tonne in 2015 to $212 in 2050.[99] In 2017, the Trump Administration disbanded the Interagency Working Group and reduced the social cost of carbon to $1 per tonne.[100] In the United Kingdom, the price of carbon is proposed at £16/tCO$_{2e}$ rising to £78/tCO$_{2e}$ in 2030 and £220/tCO$_{2e}$ in 2050. Much of the detail around a carbon tax will depend on the establishment of the UK ETS (see Chapter 5), however, industries like agriculture, forestry and other land-use sectors may be difficult to incorporate into an ETS, and therefore may only be subject to a carbon tax.[101]

Bob Litterman points to two major difficulties with pricing carbon: first, the long time between emissions and impacts leads to difficult questions about the appropriate discount rate to apply; and second, the potential for low-probability but catastrophic scenarios are often not included in calculating the social costs of carbon.[102] Not only will establishing an initial price be difficult, but the price will have to be

---

[94] Robert S. Pindyck, 'Pricing Carbon When We Don't Know the Right Price' (2013) 36(2) *Regulation Magazine* 43, 43.
[95] Ibid., 44; Metcalf and Weisback (n 69) 519.
[96] Adele C Morris, 'Proposal 11: The Many Benefits of a Carbon Tax' (New Sources of Revenue and Efficiency, The Hamiltonne Project, 2013), 3, www.brookings.edu/~/media/research/files/papers/2013/02/thp-budget-papers/thp_15waysfedbudget_prop11.pdf (accessed 21 July 2020).
[97] The World Bank, 'State and Trends of Carbon Pricing 2019' (2019), documents.worldbank.org/curated/en/191801559846379845/State-and-Trends-of-Carbon-Pricing-2019 (accessed 21 July 2020).
[98] 'British Columbia's Carbon Tax' (British Columbia, 2020), www2.gov.bc.ca/gov/content?id=DB88EFE64EE84E9AAFF7628EC8EFEEA3 (accessed 21 July 2020).
[99] See 'The Social Cost of Carbon' (US Environmental Protection Agency 2017), https://19january2017snapshot.epa.gov/climatechange/social-cost-carbon_.html (accessed 21 July 2020).
[100] 'Promoting Energy Independence and Economic Growth' EO No. 13,783 § 5(b), 82 Fed. Reg. 16,093 (Executive Office of the President 31 March, 2017).
[101] 'The Future of Carbon Pricing in the UK' (Committee on Climate Change 2019) 18.
[102] Bob Litterman, 'What is the Right Price for Carbon Emissions?' (2013) 36(2) *Regulation Magazine* 38, 38.

monitored and modelled over time, taking into account evolving climate science.[103] Ultimately, the application of a carbon tax will require the balancing of objectives, including meeting emissions targets against the near-term economic effects of a tax.[104]

In addition to the difficulties of establishing and maintaining a price on carbon, the application of a tax at the industry level has raised concerns about competitiveness and carbon leakage. This is particularly acute where the application of a carbon tax is made at the national and not global level. The benefits of a carbon tax would be felt globally, but the costs would be applied nationally.[105] The application of a tax at the consumption level has raised issues of equity and welfare, particularly for low-income homes that spend more of their income on energy-intensive goods and services.[106] While this latter concern can be mediated through the application of revenues to households, the former issue of carbon leakage is more difficult to address.

The idea of a carbon tax historically encountered resistance from the business community particularly due to concerns about loss of competitiveness.[107] Businesses were concerned that goods and services produced in jurisdictions that do not have carbon taxes would be sold at lower prices, forcing firms to move overseas. But, the extent of the carbon leakage problem may be overblown, given that energy costs are often only a small fraction of the costs of goods or services, and affected industries such as energy companies are primarily domestic industries and do not often trade their services internationally.[108] These competitiveness concerns can be mediated. Options for mediation include providing free allocations on the taxes to exposed industries, or applying border tax adjustments (BTAs).[109] BTAs apply a tax on imported goods or services to compensate for the domestically imposed carbon tax. BTAs are not without their own difficulties, as it can be a complex task to determine the carbon content embedded in imported products.[110] It is also not clear whether BTAs would survive a challenge at the WTO, although the WTO has stated that it is possible to design a BTA that does not violate WTO agreements.[111] A way to circumvent carbon leakage arguments would be to impose a uniform carbon tax globally.

---

[103] Kennedy, Obeiter and Kaufman (n 67) 20.
[104] Ibid., 22.
[105] Kennedy, Obeiter and Kaufman (n 67) 5.
[106] Yazid Dissou and Muhammad Shahid Siddiqui, 'Can Carbon Taxes Be Progressive?' (2014) 42 *Energy Economics* 88, 88.
[107] Dahan et al. (n 71) 2.
[108] Henry Clarke, 'Some Basic Economics of Carbon Taxes' 44(2) (2011) *Australian Economic Review* 123, 128, although the steel and cement industries do trade internationally.
[109] Dahan et al. (n 69) 2; von Essen (n 87) 20.
[110] Kennedy, Obeiter and Kaufman (n 67) 20; Metcalf and Weisbach (n 69) 540.
[111] Kennedy, Obeiter and Kaufman (n 67) 40; Fiona Harvey, 'WTO Signals Backing for Border Taxes' (*Financial Times*, 26 June 2009), www.ft.com/cms/s/0/d9d8ad2e-61e9-11de-9e03-00144feabdc0.html?ft_site=falcon&desktop=true (accessed 21 July 2020).

7.2.3 Towards a Global Carbon Tax?

A global carbon tax would promote a uniform rationalisation of the costs of carbon and promote alternative energy.[112] A globally coordinated carbon tax would eliminate carbon leakage concerns, as well as the free-rider problems and disparate levels of nationally based taxes.[113] A uniform, globally imposed but nationally collected carbon price, would also disincentivise countries from wanting to impose a low tax.[114]

Recent initiatives, such as the G7 Carbon Market Platform established in 2015, aim to link G7 carbon markets and to explore avenues for cooperation between developed carbon markets. In addition, global initiatives like the World Bank Carbon Pricing Leadership Coalition are designed to coordinate both private and public sector actors to share their experiences and recommendations regarding the imposition of carbon taxes. Such high-level, multilateral initiatives have played a leading role in sending a strong signal to businesses regarding the likely expansion of projects on which a carbon tax will be placed.[115] They also note that the 2015 Paris Agreement establishes a global framework that could be suitable for the establishment of transnational carbon pricing policies.[116] While the establishment of a globally determined carbon price may not be imminent, and calculations of a minimum carbon price are challenging, carbon pricing has been determined to have a key role in the transition to a low-carbon economy.

Many companies, including BP and Royal Dutch Shell, have already begun to place a shadow price on carbon in their projects, although the levels of those prices have been contested.[117] While energy companies may apply a shadow price on carbon, doing so has not detracted from initiatives by these same companies to access hard-to-reach and therefore more expensive oil and gas reserves (such as shale oil and seams). Clearly, an informal carbon price is not effectively disincentivising these companies from expanding their production to high-emitting resources, although the recent tumble in oil prices may do just that. The COVID-19 crisis combined with political conflicts within Organization of the Petroleum Exporting Countries has significantly reduced the price of oil. Instituting a carbon tax while the price of oil remains low may provide significant public benefits. A strong carbon

---

[112] von Essen (n 87) 27.
[113] Martin L. Weitzman, 'Can a Uniform Price Commitment Help?' in Peter Cramtonne and others (eds.), *Global Carbon Pricing: We Will if You Will* (2015) 38, http://carbon-price.com/wp-content/uploads/Global-Carbon-Pricing-cramton-mackay-okenfels-stoft.pdf (accessed 21 July 2020).
[114] Ibid., 43.
[115] Dahan et al. (n 71) 3.
[116] Ibid 1.
[117] Glenn Fleishman, 'Exxon Mobil Sued by New York State for Deceiving Stockholders on Future Costs of Greenhouse Gas and Carbon Rules' (*Fortune*, 24 Oct 2018), https://fortune.com/2018/10/24/ny-ag-sues-exxon-alleging-deceit-on-carbon-costs/ (accessed 21 July 2020).

price could provide much-needed revenue to Governments to aid in the COVID-19 recovery while preventing a robust recovery in oil and incentivising a shift to clean energy.[118] Implementing a carbon price while reducing fossil-fuel subsidies should be central to any COVID-19 stimulus package to prevent a distorted, high carbon recovery, reduce fiscal deficits and increase consumer spending.[119]

Other forward-looking businesses have both imposed an internal carbon tax and advocated for a uniform global tax. Microsoft, Novartis, Coca-Cola, BT Group and BNP Paribas have all become signatories to the UN Global Compact Leadership Criteria on Carbon Pricing.[120] Investors are taking action on climate change despite the imminence of a global carbon tax being unclear and fossil-fuel subsidy reform being politically contentious. Institutional investors, in particular, are becoming increasingly concerned about the risks climate change poses across their portfolios, and in many cases are taking action without the benefit of regulatory action.

7.3 INSTITUTIONAL INVESTORS AND CLIMATE CHANGE

Institutional investors include banks, insurance companies, pension funds and pooled investment vehicles, such as hedge funds, mutual funds, endowments, unit trusts, sovereign wealth funds and private equity.[121] The types, activities and behaviours of institutional investors vary across jurisdictions.[122] Dispersed ownership in the United States means that American institutional investors hold less power and influence over the corporate boardroom than those in Germany and Japan.[123] However, in the United States, the 'big three' index mutual funds of BlackRock, Vanguard and Fidelity control approximately 20 per cent of all shares on the Standard & Poor's 500 companies, and constitute some of the largest shareholders

---

[118] Grantham Research Institute and Centre for Climate Change Economics and Policy, 'Policy Brief – Pricing Carbon During the Economic Recovery from the COVID-19 Pandemic' (May 2020), 1.

[119] Ibid., 2.

[120] 'Carbon Pricing' (We Mean Business Coalition, 2020), www.wemeanbusinesscoalition.org/commitment/put-a-price-on-carbon/ (accessed 21 July 2020).

[121] Jean Jinghan Chen and Petra Nix, *The Role of Institutional Investors in Corporate Governance An Empirical Study* (Palgrave MacMillan 2013), 44; Paul Myners, 'Institutional Investment in the United Kingdom: A Review' (HM Treasury 2001), para 1.2, http://webarchive.nationalarchives.gov.uk/20130129110402/www.hm-treasury.gov.uk/media/2F9/02/31.pdf (accessed 21 July 2020) ("Myners Review").

[122] Richard M. Buxbaum, 'Comparative Aspects of Institutional Investment and Corporate Governance' in Theodor Baums, Richard M. Buxbaum and Klaus J. Hopt (eds), *Institutional Investors and Corporate Governance* (Walter de Gruyter 2010), 10; Mark J. Roe, 'Some Differences in Corporate Governance in Germany, Japan and America' in Theodor Baums, Richard M. Buxbaum and Klaus J. Hopt (eds), *Institutional Investors and Corporate Governance* (Walter de Gruyter 2010), 28.

[123] Roe (n 122) 24.

in many publicly traded companies.[124] In the United Kingdom, institutional investors 'dominate' the domestic equity markets, and include mainly pension funds and insurance companies.[125]

Institutional investors cover a number of actors, including the asset owner (the institution having direct rights over the asset), and asset managers or investment/fund managers who are responsible for the day-to-day management of the schemes the assets are invested in.[126] Authority is delegated to these managers by the asset owners, and instructions are often included in the investment mandate, though trustees remain the ultimate decision maker.[127] Many financial intermediaries will owe fiduciary duties and so should be concerned about the extensive and systemic risks climate change poses to financial systems. In this vein, some asset owners have recently taken progressive action on climate change by forming the Asset Owners Disclosure Project[128] and Net-Zero Asset Owners Alliance.[129] However, in 2018 the Asset Owners Disclosure Project discovered that most pension funds published little to no information on climate responses, putting them at risk of violating their legal duties to their beneficiaries.[130]

The risks of transition to a low-carbon economy are so great that the Financial Stability Board determined that, if the re-pricing of assets occurs at an abrupt rate, it could negatively impact financial stability.[131] Institutional investors, in particular, should be concerned about these risks as they are 'universal owners' in that they invest in highly diversified and long-term portfolios.[132] Financial regulators are just

---

[124] Michael Barzuza, Quinn Curtis and David Webber, 'Shareholder Value(s): Index Fund Activism and the New Millennial Corporate Governance' (forthcoming) 93 Southern California L. Rev., 3.

[125] Paul L. Davies, 'Institutional Investors in the United Kingdom' in Theodor Baums, Richard M. Buxbaum and Klaus J. Hopt (eds), *Institutional Investors and Corporate Governance* (Walter de Gruyter 2010), 258.

[126] Tony Hoskins and Martin Batt, 'Corporate Responsibility and Environmental Investing' in Angelo Calvello (ed), *Environmental Alpha: Institutional Investors and Climate Change* (John Wiley & Sons 2010), 347; The Law Commission, 'Fiduciary Duties of Investment Intermediaries' (HC 2014-15, 368) Law Com No. 350, xiii, www.gov.uk/government/uploads/system/uploads/attachment_data/file/325509/41342_HC_368_LC350_Print_Ready.pdf (accessed 21 July 2020); *Myners Review* (n 121) para 2.1.

[127] Law Commission (n 126) xxiii; *Myners Review* (n 121) para 2.1.

[128] Asset Owners Disclosure Project, https://aodproject.net (accessed 21 July 2020).

[129] Net Zero Asset Owner Alliance Members (UNEP Finance Initiative 2020), www.unepfi.org/net-zero-alliance/alliance-members (accessed 21 July 2020).

[130] Asset Owners Disclosure Project, 'Pensions in a Changing Climate' (AOD Project 2018), 2. https://aodproject.net/changing-climate/ (accessed 21 July 2020).

[131] Financial Stability Board, 'Proposal for a Disclosure Task Force on Climate-related Risks' (2015), 1, www.fsb.org/wp-content/uploads/Disclosure-task-force-on-climate-related-risks.pdf (accessed 21 July 2020).

[132] PRI and UNEP, 'Universal Ownership: Why Environmental Externalities Matter to Institutional Investors' (2010), 3, www.trucost.com/published-research/43/universal-ownership-why-environmental-externalities-matter-to-institutional-investors-full-report (accessed 21 July 2020); Mindy S. Lubber, 'Risks and Their Impacts on Institutional Investors' in Angelo Calvello (ed), *Environmental Alpha: Institutional Investors and Climate Change* (John Wiley & Sons 2010), 87.

recently starting to react to the clear, systemic risks that climate change poses to financial institutions and markets, although action varies amongst jurisdictions, and the issue of stranded assets is particularly controversial.

7.3.1 Stranded Assets and Systemic Risks

Carbon-major entities are vulnerable to transition risks which can include the risk of stranded assets. Fossil-fuel assets can become stranded due to regulation, carbon pricing, energy innovation, reduced costs of renewable energy,[133] social and economic pressures, the growing risk of litigation against fossil fuel companies, as well as physical environmental challenges.[134] Prior to the Paris Agreement, Carney estimated that if the world were to meet the 2°C global temperature goal, it would render the vast majority of fossil-fuel reserves as stranded assets, 'literally unburnable without expensive carbon capture technology'.[135] He also emphasised that the exposure of UK investors to such shifts was 'potentially huge'.[136]

The new lower global temperature goals in the Paris Agreement increase the likelihood that fossil-fuel reserves may become stranded assets if states decide to limit domestic emissions to reach the global temperature goal. LINGOs, an organisation dedicated to confronting the climate crisis, estimates that achieving a 33 per cent chance of meeting the 1.5°C global temperature goal would mean that only 16 per cent of global fossil-fuel reserves could be used, and 84 per cent or 2,427 Gigatonnes of reserves must be kept in the ground.[137] These assets would become stranded, losing value before the end of their estimated life cycle, leading to asset devaluations which can occur abruptly and have consequential effects throughout the economy.

The investment community is and will be faced with significant opportunities as well as risks as a result of climate change. Opportunities include investing in cleaner technology, jobs creation and increased returns.[138] Risks include physical risks to assets and infrastructure, liability risks to compensate those who have suffered from the negative impacts of climate change, transition risks of the transition to a low-carbon economy – which could include changes in policy and technology, as well

---

[133] Ashim Paun, Zoe Knight and Wai-Shin Chan, 'Stranded Assets: What Next?' (HSBC Global Research, 2015), https://pdfslide.net/news-politics/hsbc-report-stranded-assets-whats-next.html.
[134] Nancy Schneider, 'Revisiting Divestment' (2015) 66 Hastings L. J. 589, 608.
[135] Carney (n 2) 11.
[136] Ibid., 11.
[137] Kjell Kühne, 'The Global Carbon Budget after the Paris Agreement' (LINGO 2016), http://leave-it-in-the-ground.org/wp-content/uploads/2016/02/Post-Paris-Carbon-Budget-LINGO.pdf (accessed 21 July 2020).
[138] Ceres Investor Action Network on Climate Risk and Sustainability, '2012 Investor Action Plan on Climate Change Risks and Opportunities', 1, www.ceres.org/investor-network/investor-summit/summit-files/2012-investor-action-plan (accessed 4 May 2020).

as the re-assessment of the value of assets.[139] Risks to investors also include transition risks which include increased costs due to technology changes, regulation and potential non-compliance, including litigation.[140] Transition risks are mostly a concern to investors as changes to regulation could have a short-term impact on them.[141]

Climate exposure at financial institutions in particular, such as banks and other lending agencies, can have knock-on effects for other actors in the financial system. Physical impacts at large, complex and interconnected financial institutions could transmit financial stress throughout the financial system,[142] having impacts on firms that may not be traditionally considered vulnerable to climate risks. As pointed out by Carney, the risks of climate change are systemic and have the potential to destabilise the normal functioning of the financial system, and could lead to serious negative consequences for the real economy.[143]

Climate change can create 'systemic risks' to the whole economy, and therefore directly impact long-term investors like pension funds.[144] These types of investors have a direct interest in ensuring the long-term overall health of the economy.[145] Despite these extensive risks, investors have generally been slow to realise the impact of climate change, and have not actively encouraged the mitigation of GHG emissions. Although the CDP estimated in 2010 that 78 per cent of companies reported at least one significant risk from climate change to their business,[146] another analysis noted that the majority of respondents took a very narrow view of climate risk, and 44 per cent said they did not consider climate change a material issue to their portfolio investments.[147] According to this study, 82 per cent of asset managers relied on Securities Exchange Commission (SEC) filings, and 72 per cent relied on sustainability reports of companies.[148] Even the insurance industry has been slow to realise the damages caused by climate change. Leurig notes that the

---

[139] Financial Stability Board (n 131); Carney (n 2).
[140] Carbon Disclosure Project, 'Global 500 Report' (2010), 33, http://pwc.blogs.com/files/cdp-g500-9.17_online.pdf (accessed 21 July 2020).
[141] Lubber (n 132), 81.
[142] Gregg Gelzinis and Graham Steel, 'Climate Change Threatens the Stability of the Financial System' (Center for American Progress, 21 Nov 2019) 2.
[143] Ibid., 1–2.
[144] Craig Mackenzie and Francisco Ascui, 'Investor Leadership on Climate Change: An Analysis of the Investment Country's Role on Climate Change, and Snapshot of Recent Investor Activity' (PRI, UNGC, UNEPFI 2009) 11, www.unglobalcompact.org/library/127 (accessed 21 July 2020).
[145] PRI and UNEP (n 132) 9; Lubber (n 132) 79.
[146] Carbon Disclosure Project (n 140) 29.
[147] Kirsten Snow Spalding, 'Investors Analyze Climate Risks and Opportunities: A Survey of Asset Managers' Practices' Investor Network on Climate Risk (CERES 2010) 1–2
[148] Ibid., 16.

industry focuses mainly on coastal threats, and does not pay sufficient attention to other threats such as floods, droughts, snowstorms or climate change litigation.[149] This lack of attention may be due to the misunderstanding by financial actors that climate change is only a long-term risk.

7.3.2 Short-Termism and the Emergence of Climate Risk

In the late 1980s to mid-1990s, institutional investors were not very interested in climate change in the United Kingdom.[150] However, the Amendments to the Pensions Act,[151] the Myners and Kay Reviews and the socially responsible investment movement began to create momentum.[152] The 2001 Myners Review highlighted the problem of quarterly reporting reviews of asset managers leading to short-termism,[153] and encouraged institutional investors to be more active and mindful of social, environmental and governance issues.[154]

The 2012 Stewardship Code also led to increased attention by institutional investors in corporate governance generally. The motivation behind the Code is to promote the long-term success of the company by having institutional investors play a role in keeping the directors accountable.[155] The Code sets out principles that are to be employed by institutional investors to achieve effective stewardship of the companies they invest in.[156] These include monitoring the activities of companies, and being willing to act collectively with other investors.[157] The Guidance, which accompanies the Code, suggests that institutional investors should identify issues that may result in significant losses to their investment values, and make the company's board aware of their concerns, where appropriate. These risks could include impacts from climate change.

The 2012 Kay Review concluded that short-termism was a problem in UK equity markets, stemming from a decline of trust as well as a misalignment of investment

---

[149] Sharlene Leurig, 'Climate Risk Disclosure by Insurers: Evaluating Insurer Response to the NAIC Climate Disclosure Survey' (CERES 2011) 5.
[150] Stephanie Pfeifer and Rory Sullivan, 'Public Policy, Institutional Investors and Climate Change in a UK Case Study' (2008) 89 *Climate Change* 245, 252.
[151] Amendments made in 2000 to the 1995 Pensions Act required trustees to disclose the extent to which they had taken into account social, environmental or ethical considerations in their investment process.
[152] Pfeifer and Sullivan (n 150) 255.
[153] *Myners Review* (n 121) para 51.
[154] Pfeifer and Sullivan (n 150) 255.
[155] Financial Reporting Council, 'The UK Stewardship Code' (2012), para 2, www.frc.org.uk/Our-Work/Codes-Standards/Corporate-governance/UK-Stewardship-Code.aspx (accessed 21 July 2020).
[156] Ibid., para 3.
[157] Ibid., Principles 2 and 3 respectively.

horizons and incentives throughout the investment chain.[158] The Kay Review also found that hyperactivity in equity trading was also contributing to short-termism.[159] The churning of stocks was in part due to divergences in investment time horizons, an issue raised by Carney.[160] The Kay Review found that performance horizons, by which asset managers are judged, was much shorter than value discovery horizons where the fundamental value of an asset is revealed.[161] Shortening of the performance horizon to quarterly performance reports led to an emphasis on short-term profits and away from longer-term values of assets.[162]

In the United States, the SEC has provided mixed policy responses to the issue of climate change for investors. The SEC is responsible for regulating capital markets, and for implementing statutory requirements related to corporate disclosure. The Securities Act of 1933 requires that a company disclose important financial information through the registration of securities. Regulations S-K form the foundation of SEC disclosure requirements. The key issue threshold which triggers a disclosure is that of materiality of information. According to the leading case of *Basic Inc. v. Levinson*, information has been defined as material if there is a substantial likelihood that a reasonable investor would consider it important in deciding how to vote or make an investment decision.[163]

The SEC considered climate risk to be so significant that it issued risk guidance to investors in 2010.[164] The 2010 interpretive guidance clarified that climate-related disclosures could appear under several obligations of disclosure under the SEC regime.[165] Item 101 of Regulation S-K requires a firm registered with the SEC to describe its business and that of its subsidiaries. In relation to any GHG control mechanisms, Item 101 may require disclosure of any material estimated capital expenditures for environmental control facilities for the remainder of a registrant's current fiscal year and its succeeding fiscal year, and for any further periods. Climate risks could also be disclosed under the Management's Discussion and Analysis of Financial Condition and Results of Operations (most commonly referred to as MD&A) which must disclose known trends, events, demands, commitments and uncertainties that are reasonably likely to have a material effect on the financial

---

[158] 'The Kay Review of UK Equity Markets and Long-Term Decision Making: Final Report' (UK Department for Business, Innovation & Skills 2012), 9, www.gov.uk/government/uploads/system/uploads/attachment_data/file/253454/bis-12-917-kay-review-of-equity-markets-final-report.pdf (accessed 21 July 2020) ("Kay Review").
[159] Ibid., 14.
[160] Carney (n 2) 4.
[161] Kay Review (n 158) 39.
[162] Ibid., 40; see also Law Commission Report (n 126) 24.
[163] 485 US 224 (1988).
[164] US Securities & Exchange Commission, 'Commission Guidance Regarding Disclosure Related to Climate Change' (2010) 17 CFR §§ 211, 231 and 241, www.sec.gov/rules/interp/2010/33-9106.pdf (accessed 21 July 2020).
[165] Ibid., 12–16.

7.3 Institutional Investors and Climate Change

condition or operating performance of the registrant.[166] The MD&A analysis will turn upon the registrant's interpretation of materiality, and the *Basic v. Levinson* definitions of contingent or speculative events are cited in the 2010 guidance in regard to materiality.

In October 2019, a petition was submitted to the SEC calling on the Commission to require ESG disclosure by issuers under Regulation S-K. In January 2020, the SEC issued guidance on the modernisation of Regulation S-K, but this guidance was silent on the issue of ESG indicators as well as climate change, prompting a dissenting critique from one SEC Commissioner that the current definitions of materiality are not providing sufficient disclosures around climate risk for investors.[167] The 2010 guidance has been poorly implemented and enforced by both firms and the SEC. Based on this mixed policy environment, some institutional investors have asked for more guidance around fiduciary duties to beneficiaries in the context of climate change and climate risk.

7.3.3 Fiduciary Duties and Short-Termism

While institutional investors are shareholders without fiduciary duties owed to companies in which they are shareholders, asset owners, in contrast, are often trustees who have fiduciary duties to their beneficiaries. Similar to directors' fiduciary duties covered in Chapter 3, asset managers will have fiduciary duties to invest prudently in order to facilitate profitability, diversification, liquidity and ultimately the safety of investments as well as the preservation of investment capital.[168] While fiduciary duties are an 'intractable problem'[169] in law, the Law Commission recently characterised the duty as an 'undertaking to act to advance the interests of another'.[170] Trustees of pension funds are also governed by Section 34 of the Pensions Act 2004 in the United Kingdom, which provides pension trustees with wide investment powers, with fiduciary duties being defined in case law,[171] particularly the problematic case of *Cowan v. Scargill* (see later in this chapter).[172]

---

[166] The SEC confirmed that reasonably likely is a lower disclosure standard than 'more likely than not'. US Securities and Exchange Commission, 'Commission Statement About Management's Discussion and Analysis of Financial Condition and Result of Operations' (2000) Release No. 33-8056 [67 FR 3746].

[167] See Commissioner Allison Herren Lee, '"Modernizing" Regulation S-K: Ignoring the Elephant in the Room' (US Securities and Exchange Commission 2020), www.sec.gov/news/public-statement/lee-mda-2020-01-30 (accessed 21 July 2020).

[168] Mirjam Staub-Bisang, *Sustainable Investing for Institutional Investors Risks, Regulations and Strategies* (John Wiley & Sons, 2012) 82.

[169] Law Commission (n 126) para 3.14.

[170] This includes elements of trust, vulnerability and expectation, ibid., para 3.17.

[171] Ibid., para 4.12–4.35.

[172] [1985] Ch 270; see also Regulation 4(2) of the Occupational Pensions Schemes (Investment) Regulations 2005 SI 2005 no. 3378.

It is, in fact, the effort to maximise profits in the short-term and the misunderstanding of fiduciary duties that may be undermining action by institutional investors on climate change. A report by Freshfields Bruckhaus Deringer reported that fiduciary duties are a key limitation on the exercise of discretion by investment decision makers.[173] However, they note that the profit maximisation incentive exercised by trustees managing investments on behalf of institutional investors stems from a misunderstanding of the *Cowan v. Scargill* case,[174] and a perceived requirement of profit maximisation has become a barrier to the better integration of ESG issues into institutional investment activities.[175] According to this case, there is a duty on trustees to act in the best interests of their beneficiaries, interpreted 'exclusively in financial terms as the optimisation of investment returns'.[176] This interpretation, combined with a focus on short-term profits, has led to environmental issues such as climate change being 'ignored'[177] by institutional investors.

But these interpretations of legal obligations are also subject to re-evaluation as the risks of climate change escalate, and the regulatory environment around requirements to consider ESG change rapidly. As noted in Chapter 3, legal obligations around fiduciary duties are often open-textured, and can change and adapt in response to external factors such as climate regulation and climate risk. In a recent speech to the Anglo-Australian Law Society in 2019, Lord Sales of the UK Supreme Court stipulated that wider regulatory reform around ESG creates a question mark around the priority given to financial returns under the *Cowan v. Scargill* approach.[178]

Others have echoed his approach. The Freshfields report was groundbreaking in that it determined that asset managers and institutional investment consultants have a proactive duty to raise ESG considerations with their clients.[179] This finding has been commented on by a recent Law Commission report that stated that trustees are not required to maximise returns but instead must strive to secure realistic returns over long-term.[180] The report noted that, while there is no duty on trustees to take ESG factors into account, they should take into account risks to the long-term sustainability of a company's performance.[181]

The policy environment, as Lord Sales noted, is changing rapidly on ESG. In 2018, the UNEP Finance Initiative and PRI issued a new report on fiduciary duties

---

[173] Freshfields Bruckhaus Deringer, 'A Legal Framework for the Integration of Environmental, Social and Governance Issues into Institutional Investment' (UNEP FI 2005) 8.
[174] Ibid., 9.
[175] Ibid., 82.
[176] Pfeifer and Sullivan (n 150) 247; See also Paul Q Watchman, 'The Case for Climate Change as the Paramount Fiduciary Issue Facing Institutional Investors' in Angelo Calvello (ed), *Environmental Alpha: Institutional Investors and Climate Change* (John Wiley & Sons 2010), 101.
[177] Ibid., 248.
[178] Lord Sales, 'Directors' Duties and Climate Change: Keeping Pace with Environmental Challenges' (Anglo-Australian L Society, Sydney 2019), 13.
[179] Staub-Bisang (n 168) 81 and 121.
[180] Law Commission Report (n 126) para 5.52.
[181] Ibid., 5.76.

7.3 Institutional Investors and Climate Change

which stated that fiduciary duties of loyalty and prudence require the incorporation of ESG issues for three reasons.[182] The first is that ESG consideration is now an investment norm, second that ESG issues are financially material and third that policy and regulatory frameworks are changing to require ESG incorporation.[183] That same year the UK Department for Work and Pensions issued guidance on trustees' investment duties, noting that changes in the Occupational Pension Schemes (Investment) Regulations 2005 will now require trustees to prepare a Statement of Investment Principles which must include how trustees have taken into account ESG considerations, including climate change.[184] In February 2020, the Department for Work and Pensions submitted proposed amendments to the Pensions Act 1995 which would confer powers to require occupational pension schemes to report in line with recommendations from the TCFD, with powers of enforcement for non-compliance being conferred on the Pensions Regulator.[185] Part of the rationale behind the proposals is the acknowledgement that the fiduciary duty of pension fund trustees means that all pension schemes should be taking account of climate risks appropriately and proportionately.[186] KPMG recently stated that consideration of ESG factors sits squarely within an investing institution's fiduciary duty, even when there is no regulatory imperative to do so.[187]

Despite these new interpretations, asset owners and advisors often point to fiduciary duties as one of the barriers to responsible investing.[188] In addition, traditional valuation tools relied on by institutional investors emphasise short-termism and can directly contravene the longer time frames that need to be considered for many ESG impacts.[189] Concerns about climate change are often considered too long-term for the short-termism employed by many investment managers.[190] This is based on a misunderstanding of the short, medium and long-term impacts of climate change. Emphasis by institutional investors on short-term profits, particularly in carbon-intensive industries, will create a barrier to the

---

[182] PRI and UNEP FI, 'Fiduciary Duty in the Twenty-first Century: Final Report' (2018), 8.
[183] Ibid.
[184] Department for Work and Pensions, 'Clarifying and Strengthening Trustees' Investment Duties' (2018).
[185] Department for Work and Pensions, 'Pension Schemes Bill introduced into House of Lords' (11 Feb 2020).
[186] Ibid., para 5.
[187] KPMG, 'Impact of ESG Disclosures' (2019), 4.
[188] Rory Sullivan et al., 'Fiduciary Duty in the Twenty-first Century' (UNEP Finance Initiative, PRI, and UN Global Compact 2015), 16, www.unepfi.org/fileadmin/documents/fiduciary_duty_21st_century.pdf (accessed 21 July 2020).
[189] ESG Integration Working Group, 'Integrated Analysis: How Investors are Addressing Environmental Social and Governance Factors in Fundamental Equity Valuation' (PRI 2013), 6; Rob Lake, 'Financial Reform, Institutional Investors and Sustainable Development: A Review of Current Policy Initiatives and Proposals for Further Progress'(2015) UNEP Inquiry Working Paper No. 15/07, 19, http://unepinquiry.org/wp-content/uploads/2015/04/Financial_Reform_Institutional_Investors_and_Sustainable_Development.pdf (accessed 21 July 2020).
[190] Pfiefer and Sullivan (n 150) 259.

transition to low-carbon economies,[191] but will also put these fiduciaries out of step with their legal obligations.

Tony Dhar and Sarah Barker have noticed a recent spate of activity with more investors engaging with companies on climate change at an 'unprecedented rate'.[192] This is partly due to the recognition that climate change involves short, medium and long-term risk implications, and therefore is attracting the interest of more mainstream investors whose focus is firmly centred on risk and return.[193] It also partly reflects the rapidly changing regulatory environment on ESG. Virginia Harper Ho points to recent literature that links better governance on ESG metrics with better financial health of firms.[194] A recent study of FTSE 100 firms found that while higher profit margins are associated with an increased share of revenue from green goods and services, overall profitability based on the rate of return was not.[195] This could be due to higher capital investment costs for the production of green goods and services.[196] An exception to this finding was the energy sector where firms with higher green profit margins also experienced higher overall profitability as well as better stock market performance.[197]

The rise of material risk due to climate change and other ESG factors may now be so great that fiduciaries may be exposed to liability for breach of duties of care and diligence by failing to take them into account.[198] Where there is liability, litigation is soon to follow.

7.3.4 Investor-Initiated Climate Litigation

While climate litigation against companies has taken root, with a second wave of cases targeting carbon-major companies, in particular, litigation initiated by

---

[191] McKenzie and Ascui (n 144) 36.
[192] Tony Dhar and Sarah Barker, 'From "Ethical Crusade" to Financial Mainstream – Institutional Investors Raise the Accountability Bar on ESG Risk Management' (MinterEllison 2015) 2, http://documents.lexology.com/9f724c12-1b64-4a88-ab24-a9094f312563.pdf, accessed 21 July 2020.
[193] Ibid.; Sarah Barker and Maged Girgis, 'A New COP on the Beat – Heightened Expectations for Corporate Sustainability Governance and Disclosure' (MinterEllison 2016), 1.
[194] Virginia Harper Ho, 'Risk-related Activism: The Business Case for Monitoring Non-financial Risk' (2016) 41(3) J. Corp L. 647, 665. A recent report on US Fortune 500 companies notes that significant financial benefits have been yielded by these companies' pursuit of clean energy goals, particularly energy efficiency, although energy companies are still 'laggards' in this area, WWF and others, 'Power Forward 3.0. How the Largest US Companies Are Capturing Business Value While Addressing Climate Change' (2017), 3, https://c402277.ssl.cf1.rackcdn.com/publications/1049/files/original/Power_Forward_3.0_-_April_2017_-_Digital_Second_Final.pdf?1493325339 (accessed 21 July 2020).
[195] Misato Sato and others, 'Does It Pay For Firms to Go Green?' (GRI, LSE and CCCEP 2020), 7.
[196] Ibid.
[197] Ibid., 1.
[198] Laura E. Deeks, 'Discourse and Duty: University Endowments, Fiduciary Law, and the Cultural Politics of Fossil Fuel Divestment' (2017) 47(1) Environmental L. 1, 9.

7.3 Institutional Investors and Climate Change

investors has been less popular. A few cases have emerged, and as climate risks escalate, more investors may use climate litigation as a way to negotiate with the directors of companies they invest in. At the moment, investor litigation has yielded uneven results.

Pension funds, with their long investment horizons, would seem to be a prime target for litigation. Pension fund trustees have varying ages within their beneficiary class and therefore should act objectively to balance the risk between these different groups. Climate-related pension litigation could focus on three areas: a failure to act in the best interest of beneficiaries by knowingly investing in carbon-intensive businesses which reduce the value of the fund's assets, a failure to treat beneficiaries fairly by investing in climate-unfriendly businesses which provide short-term returns but long-term risks and a failure to disclose material financial risks that climate change poses to beneficiaries.[199]

In *Fentress v. ExxonMobil Corp.* in Texas,[200] a class action suit was brought by employees of the ExxonMobil Savings Plan on the basis that senior corporate officers of the company, who were fiduciaries of the employee stock pension plan, knew or should have known that the stock was artificially inflated due to the risks of climate change. The plaintiffs claimed that the pension managers purchased $800 million worth of ExxonMobil stocks despite the climate change risks, instead of marking its assets as stranded. Plaintiffs claimed this was a breach of the duty of prudence, which requires fiduciaries to manage the assets with care, skill, prudence and diligence pursuant to 29 USC. §§ 1104(a)(1)(B). A motion to dismiss by Exxon on 30 March 2018 was granted by the US District Court for the Southern District of Texas on the basis that the plaintiffs failed to show the risks of climate change had not already been included in the stock price. Relying on the efficient market hypothesis, the judge decided that the markets could take into account public information on climate change, and the plaintiffs had not plausibly linked the realities of climate change to the future health of an oil and gas company.

In another case out of Texas, *Ramirez v. ExxonMobil*,[201] the Northern District of Texas court held that the plaintiffs, the Greater Pennsylvania Carpenters Pension Fund, successfully pleaded alleged material misrepresentations or omissions constituting securities fraud by ExxonMobil regarding losses incurred to publicly traded stock acquired between 2014 and 2017. These losses were attributed by the plaintiff to the failure by the directors of ExxonMobil to recognise and inform investors of the business risks of climate change, and the value impairment of unconventional fossil fuel operations in the Canadian tar sands. This led, in 2016, to the company disclosing that 20 per cent of its once 'proved reserves' were no longer economically

---

[199] Alastair Marke, 'Establishing the Legal Obligations of Pension Fund Trustees to Divest from Climate-Unfriendly Portfolios' (2018) 4 Climate & Carbon L. Rev. 297, 303.
[200] 304 F. Supp. 3d 569, 572 (SD Texas 2018).
[201] 334 F.Supp.3d 832 (ND Texas 2018).

feasible, and therefore fell outside of the SEC definition of 'proved reserves', constituting a $2 billion impairment, as announced in 2017. As the plaintiffs in *Ramirez* were successful at the pleadings stage, the suit is continuing.

In Australia, litigation was initiated by a pension fund holder, Mark McVeigh, against the Retail Employees Superannuation Trust (REST).[202] The claims allege violations of the Corporations Act 2001 and Superannuation Industry (Supervision) Act 1993 (SIS Act), both of which require disclosure of information as well as fiduciary obligations. In this case, plaintiff McVeigh specifically requested information from REST regarding its knowledge of – and action plan for – business risks related to climate change, as well as its compliance with the Australian Corporations Act.[203] Under Section 180 of the Australian Corporations Act, directors of REST are to exercise their powers and discharge their duties with care and diligence. The SIS Act imposes fiduciary duties on trustees to act honestly with care, skill and diligence, and to perform their duties and exercise their powers in the best interests of their beneficiaries. The plaintiff alleges that a prudent trustee and director would have known about the risks to the fund from climate change, and that those risks would have a major impact on the financial conditions of the fund. The issue brought forward by the plaintiff is whether, and how, retirement fund managers like REST are taking steps to ensure that workers' savings are secure and guaranteed in the face of rising global temperatures.[204] The parties settled at the end of 2020, with REST agreeing to align its portfolio against a net zero target by 2050, and disclose climate risks according to the TCFD framework. In July 2020 a law student at University of Melbourne sued the Government of Australia over failure to disclose climate risks to investors in sovereign bonds.[205]

While climate litigation in financial markets is a relatively recent phenomenon, the number of cases is increasing rapidly.[206] In response to this issue and the rising

---

[202] *McVeigh v. Retail Employees Superannuation Pty Ltd*, [2019] FCA 14 (AUS Fed Ct. 17 January 2019) 2019 WL 246608.

[203] Ibid., at 7.

[204] Bloomberg, "A 24-year-old is Suing Rest Super for Not Being Green Enough" (*Pensions & Investments, Courts*, 15 November 2019), www.pionline.com/courts/24-year-old-suing-rest-super-not-being-green-enough (accessed 21 July 2020).

[205] Jacqueline Peel and Rebekkah Markey-Towler, 'A Wake-up Call: Why This Student Is Suing the Government Over the Financial Risks of Climate Change' *The Conversation* 27 July 2020 available https://theconversation.com/a-wake-up-call-why-this-student-is-suing-the-government-over-the-financial-risks-of-climate-change-143359#:~:text=Katta%20O'Donnell%20%E2%80%93%20a%2023,investors%20in%20Australia's%20sovereign%20bonds.&text=Sovereign%20bonds%20involve%20loans%20of,at%20a%20fixed%20interest%20rate. (accessed 15 August 2020).

[206] Javier Solano, 'Climate Litigation in Financial Markets: A Typology' (2020) 9(1) TEL. 103, 105. See also the new suit launched against the Australian government for failing to disclose climate risks to investors when it issued sovereign bonds, see Jacqueline Peel and Rebekkah Markey-Towler, 'A Wake-up Call': Why This Student Is Suing the Government Over Financial Risks of Climate Change' *The Conversation* (27 July 2020) available: https://theconversation.com/a-wake-up-call-why-this-student-is-suing-the-government-over-the-financial-risks-of-climate-change-143359 (accessed 27 July 2020).

profile of climate risks, in 2017 eight central banks established the Network for Greening the Financial System.[207] The network is designed to bring together central banks and supervisors to better understand and manage the financial risks and opportunities of climate change, as well as to mainstream green finance. While the US Federal Reserve is notably absent from its membership, this network signals that climate risks are of increasing concern to financial regulators and financiers.

Stock exchanges are also taking action. The Australian Securities Exchange issued guidance in 2019 requiring that directors of listed companies follow the TCFD guidelines. New Zealand is also consulting on regulations requiring financial firms and listed companies to report on climate impacts on their businesses and investments. In March 2020, the UK Financial Conduct Authority issued a proposal to enhance climate-related disclosures by listed issuers on the London Stock Exchange.[208] The consultation document proposes a new rule for commercial companies with a UK premium listing, requiring them to state whether they comply with TCFD-aligned disclosures, and if not, why not.[209] Premium listed firms account for approximately 480 issuers with an approximate market capitalisation of £2.3 trillion, constituting about 60 per cent of the main London Stock Exchange's total market capitalisation.[210] The rule would come into effect on or after 1 January 2021. While disclosures are not yet required under this proposal, this is mainly due to a recognition that firms need to build their disclosure capacity, and this proposal contemplates further requirements, and an expansion beyond premium listed issuers.

While there has been some litigation by investors and action by central banks, there remains resistance by many businesses to disclosing climate risk to investors. This may be due to the complexity of climate change, but also the concern that disclosure may make investment options in a particular firm less attractive. However, lack of consideration of ESG factors may also stem from a problem matching supply and demand of low-carbon capital, as investors need a level of market and policy expertise for low-carbon investing that is currently missing, and acquiring this expertise involves high transaction costs that are unattractive to investors.[211] A recent OECD paper confirms that the financial sector faces information and knowledge barriers, but attributes this to a lack of standardised corporate information

---

[207] 'Central Banks and Supervisors Network for Greening the Financial System' (Climate Action in Financial Institutions 2019), www.mainstreamingclimate.org/ngfs (accessed 21 July 2020).
[208] FCA, 'Proposals to Enhance Climate-Related Disclosures by Listed Issuers and Clarification of Existing Disclosure Obligations' Consultation Paper, March 2020.
[209] Ibid., para 1.7.
[210] Ibid., para 4.5
[211] Sani Zou and others, 'Mainstreaming Climate Change into Financial Governance Rationale and Entry Points' (2015) CIGI Policy Brief No. 5, 4, www.i4ce.org/download/policy-brief-no-5-%E2%80%A2-june-2015-fixing-climate-governance-series (accessed 4 May 2017).

on GHG emissions and climate risks.[212] In response to this inertia, the concept of sustainable investing has emerged.

7.4 SUSTAINABLE INVESTMENT AND ENVIRONMENT, SOCIAL AND GOVERNANCE FACTORS

There have been several definitions of sustainable investing, and there is no one stable international definition.[213] The European Sustainable Investment Forum defines it as 'any type of investment process that combines investors' financial objectives with their concerns about ESG issues'.[214] Institutional investors can adopt a variety of sustainable investment strategies that include active and passive approaches such as including ESG factors into the investment process, and shareholder activism through the use of shareholder resolutions and engagement with management.[215]

The three broad courses of action investors are taking on ESG issues which include shareholder resolutions, mandated disclosures through public listing agencies and voluntary disclosure initiatives.[216] A number of groups of institutional investors are taking the lead rolling out voluntary initiatives, such as the CDP, Ceres, the Investor Network on Climate Risk, Climate Action 100+ and the Institutional Investor Group on Climate Change. Ceres has been particularly active in providing support to institutional investors who are putting in place shareholder resolutions against fossil-fuel companies. These voluntary, transnational networks are forming a type of private environmental governance that aims to re-orient the behaviour of investors regarding climate change.[217]

The United Nations Environment Programme and PRI have a central premise that responsible investing must acknowledge and consider the relevance to investors of ESG factors, as well as the long-term health and stability of the entire economy.[218] PRI defines responsible investing as recognising that 'the generation of long-term

---

[212] Yoko Nobouka, Jane Ellis and Sarah Pymalt Anderson, 'Encouraging Increased Climate Action by Non-Party Stakeholders' (OECD Publishing 2015) OECD/IEA Climate Change Expert Group Paper, No. 2015/05, 11.

[213] Meg Voorhes and Joshua Humphries, 'Recent Trends in Sustainable and Responsible Investing in the United States' (2011) 20(3) *Journal of Investing* 90, 91. Kierman also notes that sustainable investing differs from socially responsible investing, which is only values-based, whereas sustainable investing focuses on investment risk and return; see Matthew J. Kierman, 'SRI or Not SRI?' in Angelo Calvello (ed), *Environmental Alpha: Institutional Investors and Climate Change* (John Wiley & Sons 2010), 131–132.

[214] Eurosif, 'European SRI Study' (2014), 8, www.eurosif.org/sri-study-2014 (accessed 21 July 2020).

[215] Staub-Bisang (n 168) 15; Sullivan et al. (n 188) 61.

[216] Lubber (n 132) 88.

[217] Michael McLeod and Jacob Park, 'Financial Activism and Global Climate Change: The Rise of Investor-Driven Governance Networks' (2011) 11(2) *Global Environmental Politics* 54, 55.

[218] PRI and UNEP (n 132) 6; Sullivan et al. (n 188) 3.

7.4 Sustainable Investment & Environment

sustainable returns is dependent on stable, well-functioning and well-governed social, environmental and economic systems'.[219]

As with fiduciary duties in the director context, fiduciary duties in the investment context are a relatively flexible concept in many jurisdictions. In the United States, the case of *Board of v. City of Baltimore*[220] established that if social investments yield economically competitive returns at comparable levels of risk investments, they should not be deemed imprudent. Therefore, significant discretion has been provided to trustees to make ESG-related investments, provided they yield competitive returns. Despite this flexibility, there have been some mixed policy messages in terms of pension funds. In the United States, the Department of Labor (DOL) oversees fiduciaries for private-sector retirement plans under the Employee Retirement Income Security Act (ERISA). The DOL periodically issues policy pronouncements in the form of Field Assistance Bulletins (FABs). In 2018, DOL released a FAB which, instead of providing clarity regarding ESG reporting, only created further confusion for fiduciaries of private-sector pension plans.

The FAB reiterated DOL's long-standing position that fiduciaries are obliged to consider ESG factors as part of investment decisions, '[t]o the extent ESG factors, in fact, involve business risks or opportunities that are properly treated as economic considerations themselves'.[221] Simultaneously, the DOL stated that fiduciaries 'must avoid too readily treating ESG issues as being economically relevant to any particular investment choice'.[222] While this development did not constitute a substantive change to the DOL's position that material economic factors, including ESG factors, are to be considered by investment fiduciaries, United Nations Environment Programme Finance Initiative (UNEP FI) considered that the explanatory language provided in the FAB created uncertainty for fiduciaries of private pension plans.[223] In June 2020, the DOL announced a proposed rule to 'clarify' its previous investment duties regulations.[224] The proposal restricts the ability of fiduciaries to invest in ESG vehicles when there is an underlying investment strategy to subordinate return for non-financial objectives.[225] Other countries have adopted more uniform approaches to ESG factors.

China has made great strides in greening its financial sector. China's Ecological Civilisation mandate now guides its 13th Five-Year economic planning cycle.[226] Reforms include establishing green development funds for direct investment, green

---

[219] PRI and UNEP (n 132) 7.
[220] 317 Md. 72, (Maryland App Ct 1989).
[221] Department of Labor, *Field Assistance Bulletin* No. 2018-01 (23 April 2018).
[222] Ibid.
[223] Sullivan et al. (n 188), 22.
[224] See www.dol.gov/newsroom/releases/ebsa/ebsa20200623.
[225] Ibid.
[226] Caroline Goran, 'Ecological Civilization and the Political Limits of a Chinese Concept of Sustainability' (2018) China Perspectives Online 39; Alex Wang, 'The Symbolic Aspects of Environmental Reform in China' (New York U L & Development Colloquium 2017).

credit plans for the banking sector and stimulating a green bond market for capital markets which was worth approximately US$21.9 billion in the first half of 2019.[227] The 13th Five-Year Plan also requires mandatory disclosure of environmental information for listed companies and ratings and assessment tools to help financial institutions in their due diligence efforts.[228] While it is unclear how integrated this approach will be in overseas investment through the Belt and Road Initiative, a recent update to China's Green Taxonomy to remove 'clean coal' puts the taxonomy on par with that of the European Union.[229]

The European Union has been a leader in regulatory reform on ESG, including climate change disclosures. In 2017, the High-Level Expert Group on Sustainable Finance issued their key recommendations to clarify investor duties and extend associated time horizons of investments, and to bring greater focus on ESG factors. The 2018 EU Directive on Disclosure of Non-Financial information requires large public interest entities to disclose material information on key ESG aspects. Guidance was issued to investors to help them make disclosures in line with TCFD recommendations. In March 2019, Regulation on Sustainability-Related Disclosure in the Financial Services Sector was adopted, which establishes transparency rules on integration of sustainability risks.

The EU Ten-Point Action Plan for sustainable finance was followed by three key pieces of legislation to promote private sector investment in sustainable development. These include a Unified EU Green Classification System or 'Taxonomy', legislation requiring that corporations and investors disclose to their clients the impact of sustainability (ESG factors) on financial returns and the impact of their investment decision on sustainability (applicable from March 2021), and finally Climate Benchmarks and Benchmarks' ESG disclosures. This creates a new category of low-carbon benchmarks which provide investors with better information on the carbon footprint of their investments.

Following the lead of the European Union, the United Kingdom made climate-related disclosures mandatory for certain types of companies (see Chapters 4 and 5). The UK Financial Reporting Council provides persuasive (not mandatory) guidance to directors on what should be included in the Directors' Strategic Report. In particular, it provides guidance on what directors should consider to be material information. The Guidance specifically notes that when considering whether information on the impact of an entity's activities on the environment is

---

[227] Luiza Mello, 'China Green Bond Market Mid-Year Report 2019: Latest on Green Bond Issuers, Market Trends and Developments in the World's Second Largest Green Bond Market' (*Climate Bonds Initiative* 2019)

[228] Sean Gilbert and Lihuan Zhou, 'The Knowns and Unknowns of China's Green Finance' (2017) New Climate Economy, 7.

[229] Leena Fatin, 'China's Top Regulators Announce They Will Exclude Fossil Fuels From Their Green Bonds Taxonomy' (*Climate Bonds Initiative* 2020), www.climatebonds.net/2020/06/chinas-top-regulators-announce-they-will-exclude-fossil-fuels-their-green-bonds-taxonomy-it (accessed 21 July 2020).

material, directors should consider the implications for the company's long-term value generation arising from stakeholder, legal or regulatory responses.[230] The Regulations require the disclosure of GHG emissions by quoted companies unless directors explain why these are not material. The Financial Reporting Council guidance recommends that the Strategic Report explain the potential impact on the entity's strategy and business model if those risks crystallise, using the specific example of climate change as a systemic risk.[231]

In terms of pension funds specifically, the Occupational and Personal Pensions Scheme (Disclosure of Information) Regulations 2013 requires trustees to include in their Statement of Investment Principles (SIPs) how they take into account ESG considerations, including climate change. By 1 October 2020, trustees will be required to include in the SIPs an implementation statement on how they acted on those principles in the selection, retention and realisation of investments.

Other countries have taken progressive approaches to ESG indicators in the context of pension legislation. For example, in Ontario, Canada, the Pension Benefits Act 2016 requires that the statement of investment policies and principles includes information on whether ESG factors have been incorporated, and if so, how.[232] The South Korean National Pension Service, the third-largest pension fund in the world, amended its National Pension Services Act in 2015 to require consideration of ESG issues.[233] The Pension Fund Act 2013 in South Africa requires trustees to consider all factors, including ESG factors, that may be related to the fund's long-term success.[234] In Brazil, Resolution 4.661 of 2018 requires that pension funds consider ESG and corporate governance aspects whenever possible.[235]

These recent regulatory developments show the global direction is moving towards increased incorporation of ESG factors, including climate change, into investment decisions. Investors can use their influence as shareholders to incentivise companies to be more proactive on climate change, and also to explicitly factor in climate change to core business plans and processes.[236] Responses to climate change by institutional investors can be tailored to their investment approach and asset class mix. The PRI and UNEP provide a detailed list of suggested actions by investors on environmental costs, which in the context of climate change, include evaluating impacts on companies, incorporating climate change costs and risk into shareholder

---

[230] Ibid., para 5.5.
[231] UK Financial Reporting Council, 'Guidance on the Strategic Report' (2018), para 7B.31.
[232] Financial Services Commission of Ontario, 'Environmental, Social and Governance Factors' (Investment Guidance Notes 2016) IGN-004, reg 909, s78(3).
[233] PRI, UNEP FI and The Generation Foundation "Investor Obligations and Duties in Six Asian Markets" (2016), www.unpri.org/fiduciary-duty/investor-obligations-and-duties-in-six-asian-markets/266.article (accessed 21 July 2020).
[234] Financial Services Laws General Amendment Act, No. 45 (S. Africa 2013), *Amending Pension Funds Act*, No. 24 (S. Africa 1956).
[235] Res. CMN n° 4.661 (Brazil 2018).
[236] Pfiefer and Sullivan (n 150) 245.

voting initiatives, engaging with policymakers and regulators, and regular monitoring and reporting by investment managers.[237]

Measuring a portfolio's carbon footprint and improving investor engagement with companies and policymakers are important parts of the transition to a low-carbon economy.[238] Institutional investors are a critical piece of the transition to a low-carbon economy, and the private sector will have to participate in the trillion-dollar investment price tag needed through 2050 to meet increased energy needs through clean technology.[239] Pension funds are one of the most important drivers of the sustainable investment movement, which is being led by European countries such as Norway, Sweden and the United Kingdom.[240]

While awareness of climate change has increased amongst institutional investors in the past few years, there has been limited action on the ground to mainstream climate change into investment strategies.[241] There is an assumption that more and better disclosure on climate change risks will by itself create market incentives that will motivate investors to promote and encourage climate change mitigation.[242] However, the profitability barrier persists in the mind of some investors. Many investors still believe it is difficult to prove a causal relationship between sustainability and financial returns.[243] Many institutional investors continue to only be concerned with climate change when it has short-term or immediate impacts on assets and performance.[244] As a result, the majority of the discourse on climate change by institutional investors remains economics-centred and risk-driven.[245] This attitude is slowly changing as ESG investing gains prominence in some jurisdictions. The Global Sustainable Investment Alliance data shows that US$22.9 trillion of assets were professionally managed under responsible investment strategies in 2016, up

---

[237] PRI and UNEP (n 132) 5.
[238] PRI Climate Change Strategy Project, 'Discussion Paper: Reducing Emissions Across the Portfolio' (2015), 4, www.unpri.org/page/reducing-emissions-across-the-portfolio-launched-a (accessed 21 July 2020).
[239] Mark Fultonne and Bruce M. Kahn, 'Investing in Climate Change' in Angelo Calvello (ed), *Environmental Alpha: Institutional Investors and Climate Change* (John Wiley & Sons 2010), 190.
[240] Staub-Bisang (n 168) 43–47.
[241] Kierman (n 213) 129; Fultonne and Kahn (n 239) 177.
[242] Adam Harnes, 'The Limits of Carbon Disclosure: Theorizing the Business Case for Investor Environmentalism' (2011) 11(2) *Global Environmental Politics* 98, 101; Carney (n 2) 12; Financial Stability Board (n 128) 1.
[243] Ingeborg Schumacher Hummel, 'Equities' in Staub-Bisang (n 218), 148; Eun-Hee Kim and Thomas Lyon, 'When Does Institutional Investor Activism Increase Shareholder Value?: The Carbon Disclosure Project' (2011) 11(1) *Journal of Economic Analysis & Policy* 1, 23, although note Harper Ho (n 194) who cites literature connecting ESG and better financial health of firms.
[244] Harnes (n 242) 104–105; Ole Beier Sorensen and Stephanie Pfeifer, 'Climate Change Issues in Fund Investment Practices' (2011) 64(4) *International Social Security Review*, 67.
[245] Jill F. Solomon and others, 'Private Climate Change Reporting: An Emerging Discourse of Risk and Opportunity?' (2011) 24(8) *Accounting, Auditing & Accountability Journal* 1119, 1139–1140.

from US$13.3 trillion in 2012.[246] In the United States, sustainable and responsible investing assets reached US$12 trillion in early 2018.[247]

Despite this movement, substantial obstacles still remain for institutional investors interested in incorporating climate change into their investment strategies. These include the perception that greater involvement in governance will not increase performance and may be incompatible with fiduciary duties, concerns about insider trading allegations from pro-active engagement with management, as well as a lack of research linking environmental performance with financial performance.[248] According to Matthew Kierman, investors still need an investment case in order to take climate change more seriously, as well as better, company-specific analytics to enable them to assess climate risks.[249] While sustainable investing initiatives are just one of the ways through which investors try to motivate the transition to a low-carbon economy, the divestment movement is a more dramatic tact taken by some investors.

7.5 THE DIVESTMENT MOVEMENT

In the face of increasing risks confronting carbon-major entities due to climate change, investors can either hold on to their investments and minimise the downside of these risks, or divest from these companies.[250] The divestment movement began in US colleges in 2011[251] by students asking their institutions to freeze new investments in the fossil-fuel industry and divest existing stocks.[252] These student movements were assisted by NGOs such as '350.org', and popularised by Bill McKibben and his cross-country road trip in the United States in 2012 advocating for divestment.[253]

Since 2011, the divestment movement has grown, with the Rockefeller Brothers Fund announcing in September 2014 that it will decrease its investments in fossil

---

[246] Ibid.
[247] Hazel Bradford. 'Public Funds Taking the Lead in Spectacular Boom of ESG'. (*Pensions & Investments, Special Report*, 19 August 2019), www.pionline.com/special-report/public-funds-taking-lead-spectacular-boom-esg (accessed 23 March 2020).
[248] Tom Hadden, 'Corporate Governance by Institutional Investors? Some Problems from an International Perspective' in Theodor Baums, Richard M. Buxbaum and Klaus J. Hopt (eds), *Institutional Investors and Corporate Governance* (Walter de Gruyter 2010), 100; Kierman (n 213), 131; Sorensen and Pfeifer (n 244) 67.
[249] Ibid., 133; See also Ans Kolk, David Levy and Jonathan Pinske, 'Corporate Response in an Emerging Climate Regime: the Institutionalization and Commensuration of Carbon Disclosure' (2008) 17(4) *Eur. Accounting Rev.* 719, 727.
[250] Paun, Knight and Chan, (n 133) 13.
[251] The movement began in Swarthmore College in 2011 and quickly spread to other academic institutions such as the University of North Carolina and the University of Illinois.
[252] Martina K Linnenluecke et al., 'Divestment from Fossil Fuel Companies: Confluence between Policy and Strategic View Points' (2015) 40(3) *Australia J. Management* 478, 479.
[253] Jessica Grady-Benson and Brinda Serathy, 'Fossil Fuel Divestment in US Higher Education: Student-led Organizing for Climate Justice' (2016) 21(6) *Local Environment* 1, 4–5.

fuel. It has also reached the United Kingdom, with the Church of England announcing its divestments in thermal coal and tar sands in May 2015,[254] and a long-standing campaign by *The Guardian* newspaper called 'Keep it in the Ground', advocating for divestment in fossil-fuel industries.[255] In May 2016, the Gates Foundation divested its entire holdings in BP, an investment of approximately US$187 million.[256] In 2015, Oslo became the first capital city in the world to completely ban investments in fossil fuels, and had agreed to divest its pension fund from coal, oil and gas companies.[257] A number of other cities around the world have made divestment commitments, including Belfast, Oxford, Berkeley, Palo Alto, San Francisco, Seattle, Victoria and Melbourne, and in January 2017 the Irish Parliament decided to divest its national strategic investment fund from fossil fuels.[258]

Divestment can take a number of forms, including 100 per cent divestment from all fossil-fuel-producing companies, partial divestment, value-chain analysis of companies involved in fossil fuels and divestment from the 'worst-in-class', based on the carbon intensity of companies.[259] The divestment initiatives mentioned above are diverse in their approaches, and have involved some or all of these approaches. The divestment movement has grown significantly in the past few years, and is motivating stakeholder-driven support for taking action on climate change.[260]

Nancy Schneider has noted that there are three phases of divestment: action taken by public organisations, followed by action taken by investors, cities and public institutions, and finally, market recognition of risks in continued investment.[261] She notes that in 2015, the divestment movement was in its second phase,[262] which

---

[254] Leon Kaye, 'Church of England Announces Divestment from Coal and Tar Sands' (*Triple Pundit*, 4 May 2015), www.triplepundit.com/2015/05/church-of-england-announces-divestment-from-coal-and-tar-sands/ (accessed 21 July 2020).

[255] See 'Keep It in the Ground' (*The Guardian*, 2020), www.theguardian.com/environment/series/keep-it-in-the-ground (accessed 21 July 2020).

[256] Damian Carringtonne, 'Bill and Melinda Gates Foundation Divests Entire Holding in BP' (*The Guardian*, 12 May 2016), www.theguardian.com/environment/2016/may/12/bill-and-melinda-gates-foundation-divests-entire-holding-in-bp (accessed 21 July 2020).

[257] See Damian Carringtonne, 'Oslo Divests From Coal Companies' (*The Guardian*, 2 March 2015), www.theguardian.com/environment/2015/mar/02/oslo-divests-from-coal-companies (accessed 21 July 2020).

[258] For a list of investors, including cities, that have divested, see '1000+ Divestment Commitments' (Fossil Free: Divestment 2020), http://gofossilfree.org/commitments (accessed 21 July 2020); Samuel Osborne, 'Ireland Votes in Favour of Law to Become World's First Country to Fully Divest from Fossil Fuels' (*Independent*, 27 January 2017), www.independent.co.uk/news/world/europe/ireland-votes-divest-fossil-fuels-climate-change-world-first-country-parliament-renewable-energy-a7549121.html (accessed 21 July 2020).

[259] Paun, Knight and Chan (n 133) 15.

[260] Linnleuecke et al. (n 252) 486.

[261] Schneider (n 134) 592.

[262] Ibid., 592.

means that market investors had not systematically started to divest from the fossil-fuel industry.

Critics of the divestment movement in South Africa have noted that divestment movement had no effect on the targeted companies, and there is no evidence that the current divestment movement is affecting the stock prices or business decisions of targeted firms.[263] Critics also note that the divestment movement will potentially replace environmentally sensitive investors with neutral investors, thereby removing one mechanism to pressure companies to make changes.[264] Divestment can also involve high transaction costs for firms because there is no uniform set of standards by which to judge firms that are either fossil-fuel intensive or environmental friendly.[265] Critics have also pointed out that divestment may be a breach of fiduciary duties, as it may be difficult to replace these types of industrial investments in portfolios, and neutral investors will simply replace divesting investors.[266] It is unlikely that the divestment campaign will have a significant impact on firms until it enters the third phase: when the markets systematically begin to divest from the fossil-fuel industry. In addition, it is important for a re-investment in renewables strategy to accompany any flight of capital from fossil-fuel intensive firms.[267] Another tact taken by investors is to submit shareholder resolutions requiring more action on climate change by companies.

7.6 SHAREHOLDER CLIMATE ACTION VIA RESOLUTIONS

In most jurisdictions around the world, shareholders are entitled to submit resolutions to be discussed and voted on at the annual general meeting of the company. There are some minimum requirements and restrictions placed on these resolutions, and not all of them will be included in company proxy statements, and therefore not all will reach a shareholder vote.[268] Shareholders have been using this avenue to put forward demands that the companies they invest in take action on climate change, or at the very least disclose climate risks to them. Many of these resolutions have been couched in the context of the Paris Agreement. Shareholder resolutions put forward by concerned investors in conventional energy companies often cite the temperature goals in the Paris Agreement.

In April and May 2015, at the AGMs of both BP and Royal Dutch Shell, shareholder resolutions were passed, supported by a majority of shareholders and

---

[263] Daniel R. Fischel, 'Fossil Fuel Divestment: A Costly and Ineffective Investment Strategy', 20, 26, http://divestmentfacts.com/pdf/Fischel_Report.pdf (accessed 21 July 2020).
[264] Linnenluecke et al. (n 252) 480.
[265] Fischel (n 262) 13–14.
[266] Schneider (n 134) 591.
[267] Hari Osofsky et al., 'Energy Re-Investment' (2019) 94 Indiana L. J. 595.
[268] See SEC proposals to impose further restrictions on shareholder resolutions, 'SEC Proposes Amendments to Modernize Shareholder Proposal Rule' (US Securities and Exchange Commission 2019), www.sec.gov/news/press-release/2019-232 (accessed 21 July 2020).

the management. The shareholder resolutions requested enhanced reporting by these companies on their exposure to climate change, including portfolio resistance to the International Energy Agency's 2030 energy scenarios. They also requested further information on operational environmental management and public policy positions on climate change. The resolutions were submitted specifically in light of the upcoming Paris negotiations. The reasoning behind the shareholder resolution, as shared by 'Aiming for A', was to understand how these companies were preparing for the low-carbon transition, reveal systemic risks that may impact investors, and to engage in more collective fiduciary duties and enhance shareholder voice on climate change.[269]

At the end of May 2016, a similar resolution requesting more action on climate change, including increased disclosure, was put forward at the AGM of ExxonMobil and Chevron with the support of British insurer Aviva, as well as the Church of England. However, this resolution was not accepted by the majority of shareholders. Shareholders did, however, pass a resolution that could enable them to appoint board members who are more concerned about climate change.[270] The CEO for 'As You Sow', an American non-profit promoting corporate accountability, stated that investors are asking companies to take a broad, systemic analysis of their climate policies, and how they affect the broader economy. In 2017, shareholders of Occidental Petroleum approved a shareholder proposal requiring that the company disclose the business impacts of climate change.[271] This vote marks the first time that a climate-related shareholder resolution was passed over the objections of the board.[272]

On 9 March 2017, Shell announced that, due to investor pressure to mitigate climate change, it was selling most of its Canadian oil sands assets, and that 10 per cent of directors' bonuses would be tied to how well it manages GHG emissions.[273]

---

[269] BP: April 2015 AGM 'Special Resolution – Strategic Resilience for 2035 and Beyond' "Aiming for A' Coalition", https://b.3cdn.net/sactionlive/07bab6677cf0b8579f_b8m6bhff7.pdf (accessed 21 July 2020).

[270] Rupert Neate, 'ExxonMobil CEO: Ending Oil Production "Not Acceptable for Humanity"' (The Guardian, 25 May 2016), www.theguardian.com/business/2016/may/25/exxonmobil-ceo-oil-climate-change-oil-production (accessed 21 July 2020).

[271] Emily Chasan, 'Occidental Holders Override Board in Approving Climate Proposal', (Bloomberg News, 12 May 2017), bloomberg.com/news/articles/2017-05-12/blackrock-to-back-climate-shareholder-proposal-at-occidental (accessed 21 July 2020).

[272] It is important to note that shareholder proposals on their own are not binding on the corporation. In November 2019, the SEC proposed amendments to, amongst other things, increase the thresholds of shareholder eligibility to submit proposals under Rule 14a-8(b). See SEC Procedural Requirements and Resubmission Thresholds under Exchange Act Rule 14a-8, US Securities and Exchange Commission, 'Procedural Requirement and Resubmission Thresholds Under Exchange Act Rule 14a-8 (2019) 17 CFR § 240, www.sec.gov/rules/proposed/2019/34-87458.pdf (accessed 21 July 2020).

[273] Karolin Schaps, 'Shell Sells Canadian Oil Sands, Ties Bonuses to Emissions Cuts' (Reuters, 9 March 2017), www.reuters.com/article/us-shell-divestiture-cdn-natural-rsc-idUSKBN16G0PH (accessed 21 July 2020).

The Climate Action 100+ group of investors pledged to use their shareholder power to pressure companies to adopt long-term, emission reduction targets.[274] After months of engagement with the group, Shell announced in December 2018 that it aims to reduce its emissions by 30 per cent by 2035, and 65 per cent by 2050, subsequently updating that to a net zero emissions ambition by 2050.[275] BP has made similar commitments. There has certainly been increased investor activity since the Paris Agreement on climate change, but it is unclear what impact, if any, this is having on companies.

7.7 IMPACT OF INITIATIVES ON COMPANIES

These different initiatives, from fossil-fuel subsidies, carbon taxes and investor action, all have varying levels of impacts on companies. While renewable energy subsidies have been subjected to numerous disputes at the WTO, fossil-fuel subsidies have faced very little scrutiny at the international level beyond platitudes made by G7 and G20 leaders. The absence of a category of non-actionable subsidies at the WTO, combined with very slow progress during the Doha Development Round in agreeing to a list of environmental goods and services, means this forum is unlikely to lead to swift progress on trade and energy in the near future. Despite recent assertions by G7 states to phase out fossil-fuel subsidies by 2025, the lack of definition and concrete regulatory plans at the national level amongst most of these nations also cast doubt on their ability to achieve their stated target. The circumstances surrounding fossil-fuel subsidies in the United Kingdom and the United States are non-transparent, and it is unlikely that fossil-fuel subsidies will be eliminated any time soon.

Carbon taxes appear to be a more viable approach. Their implementation is simple, and some companies have been advocating for them for some time, although this may be simply a calculated attempt to avoid regulation of carbon. While a global carbon tax would overcome the issues of competitiveness and carbon leakage, the difficulties of orchestrating a global price on carbon may be challenging. The Paris Agreement provides a framework for the implementation of such a tax, and there is no barrier to states imposing it themselves. Several states and subnational states and provinces have already done so. However, establishing the price of the tax is complex and may be unpopular with the public.

The trend of sustainable investing is, by contrast, hopeful. Investors are 'unseen polluters', because the emphasis for the low-carbon transition is often focused on

---

[274] 'Global Investors Driving Business Transition' (Climate Action 100+, 2020), www.climateaction100.org (accessed 21 July 2020).

[275] Shell PLC, "Shell's Ambition to be a Net-Zero Emissions Energy Business" (Shell Global, The Energy Future, 2019), www.shell.com/energy-and-innovation/the-energy-future/shells-ambition-to-be-a-net-zero-emissions-energy-business.html (accessed 21 July 2020).

energy companies or other direct polluters.[276] But investors provide the capital required for these industries to function, and therefore will provide a significant part of the trillions of dollars of capital that is required to fund the clean energy transition.[277] A number of large institutional investors, with the assistance of transnational governance networks, are taking climate change seriously. They are particularly concerned with the issue of stranded assets, and some shareholder resolutions and other management engagement have been successful in forcing companies to at least consider the risks of climate change to their operations.

In his 2020 letter to global CEOs, Larry Fink, the CEO of BlackRock, stated that climate risk was compelling investors to reassess core assumptions about modern finance.[278] He stated that due to this risk, he believed that the world would soon see a fundamental reshaping of finance and a significant reallocation of capital.[279] In 2020, BlackRock would be asking the companies they invest in to publish a disclosure in line with industry-specific SASB guidelines by year-end and disclose climate-related risks in line with the TCFD's recommendations. While BlackRock's history of climate-friendly investment is patchy, this statement is groundbreaking. As one of the largest indexed funds in the United States, BlackRock is publicly putting its target investor companies on notice regarding its expectations around climate action.

The divestment movement has also attracted a lot of publicity, although it is clear that it is not an ideal tool to convince companies to transition away from fossil-fuel resources. While this movement has reached its second phase with public institutions and even cities divesting from fossil-fuel companies, it is unlikely that the divestment campaign will have a significant impact until it enters the third phase: when the markets systematically begin to divest from the fossil-fuel industry.

There are also some practical and methodological barriers for investors. The variety of information sources and lack of company-specific impacts of climate change on assets poses information barriers for many institutional investors. The first report by the TCFD identified some of the barriers facing investors on climate change, which include fragmented and incomplete reporting by companies, as well

---

[276] Benjamin J. Richardson, *Financial Markets and Socially Responsible Investing*, in *Company Law and Sustainability* (Beate Sjåfjell & Benjamin J. Richardson eds, 2015), 227–28.

[277] IEA, 'World Needs $45 Trillion in Investment to Meet Its Energy Needs by 2035' (3 June 2014), www.iea.org/news/world-needs-48-trillion-in-investment-to-meet-its-energy-needs-to-2035; Ceres, 'Clean Trillion' (identifying a trillion dollars of investment required annually to limit global temperature rise to 1.5°C), www.ceres.org/initiatives/clean-trillion; European Commission, 'Factsheet: Financing Sustainable Growth'. (*Commission's action plan on sustainable finance – visual materials*, January 2020), https://ec.europa.eu/info/sites/info/files/business_economy_euro/banking_and_finance/documents/200108-financing-sustainable-growth-factsheet_en.pdf (accessed 18 March 2020).

[278] Larry Fink, 'A Fundamental Reshaping of Finance' (2020), www.blackrock.com/corporate/investor-relations/larry-fink-ceo-letter (accessed 16 April 2020).

[279] Ibid.

as weak corporate governance mechanisms.[280] The Task Force Initiative identified seven principles for effective reporting of climate-related financial disclosures.[281] Adherence to the principles would be voluntary and would help to establish the needs of investors regarding disclosures and to develop common disclosure principles or recommendations.[282] While this is a welcome and timely initiative, investors need a uniform and mandatory disclosure framework, as well as jurisdictional clarifications of investor fiduciary duties in the context of climate change.

7.8 CONCLUSION

Fossil-fuel subsidies have yet to be phased out, and a global carbon tax is not yet on the immediate international agenda. Despite uneven progress in these areas, investors are taking action on climate change due to rising concern regarding its risk to fiscal stability. Investors usually take a variety of approaches to investment-related activity on climate change. These are integrating climate change into their investments, reducing the carbon intensity of their portfolios, investing in climate solutions, divesting from fossil fuel-intensive investments and engaging with corporations and policymakers (either publicly or privately).[283] Investor action on climate change can be understood as a desire to mitigate climate change risks and damage to their economy-mirroring portfolios,[284] as well as an effort to attract millennial capital.[285]

While awareness of climate change has increased amongst institutional investors in the past few years, there has been limited action on the ground to mainstream climate change into investment strategies.[286] There is an assumption that more and better disclosure on climate change risks will by itself create market incentives that will motivate investors to promote and encourage climate change mitigation.[287] However, the profitability barrier persists. It is still difficult to prove a causal relationship between sustainability and financial returns across all market actors,[288]

---

[280] Task Force on Climate-Related Financial Disclosures, 'Phase I Report of the Task Force on Climate-Related Financial Disclosures' (31 March 2016), 7–12, www.fsb-tcfd.org/wp-content/uploads/2016/03/Phase_I_Report_v15.pdf (accessed 4 May 2020).
[281] Task Force on Climate-Related Financial Disclosures, 'Recommendations of the Task Force on Climate-Related Disclosures' (14 December 2016), www.fsb-tcfd.org/wp-content/uploads/2016/12/TCFD-Recommendations-Report-A4-14-Dec-2016.pdf (accessed 4 May 2020).
[282] Financial Stability Board (n 131) 4.
[283] Rob Lake, 'Action on Climate: A Practical Guide for Fiduciaries' (*Action on Climate*, September 2015), 19.
[284] Madison Condon, 'Externalities and the Common Owner' (2019) New York U School L & Economics Research Paper Series, 5.
[285] Barzuza, Curtis and Webber (n 124).
[286] Kierman (n 213) 129; Fultonne and Kahn (n 239) 177.
[287] Harnes (n 242) 101; Carney (n 2) 12; Financial Stability Board (n 131) 1.
[288] Hummel (n 243) 148; Kim and Lyon (n 243) 23.

although this is slowly changing. Institutional investors continue to be concerned with climate change only when it has short-term or immediate impacts on assets and performance.[289] As the risks of climate change increase, the issue of mitigation of climate change risk is likely to figure more prominently on the agenda of mainstream investors.

Asset owners and advisors often point to fiduciary duties as one of the barriers to responsible investing.[290] In addition, traditional valuation tools used by institutional investors emphasise short-termism and can directly contravene the longer time frames that must be considered for many ESG impacts.[291] Concerns about climate change are often considered too long-term for the short-termism employed by many investment managers.[292] The pressures of short-termism and confusion around the extent of fiduciary duties on trustees of institutional investments, still pose a barrier to the mainstreaming of climate change into investment strategies.

Benjamin Richardson poses an alternative approach in financial markets, advocating for investing in nature's trust.[293] This concept focuses on reorienting fiduciary responsibility to accommodate and support society's dependence on long-term environmental well-being by imposing public-like responsibilities on investors to manage assets for environmental integrity.[294] While a holistic approach involving environmental regulation as well as company reform is needed, these tools alone will not reorient existing market incentives which favour the short-term. Therefore, legal measures targeted at economic institutions requiring them to take action on climate change is still required.[295] In Richardson's view, while disclosure obligations in statutes may help address investment policies, they will not address investment practices, which often focus on the short-term.[296] Instead, fiduciary laws and practices must also be updated to include sector-wide decision-making procedures, a new prudential investment duty and a public-trust duty imposed on the state in its supervisory role over financial markets.[297] Market incentives must be changed through reform or clarification of fiduciary duties, as well as changing the investment practices of market actors.[298]

---

[289] Harnes (n 242) 104–5; Sorensen and Pfeifer (n 244) 67.
[290] Sullivan et al. (n 183) 16.
[291] PRI and UNEP (n 131) 6; Lake (n 189) 19.
[292] Pfiefer and Sullivan (n 150) 259.
[293] Benjamin J. Richardson, *Fiduciary Law and Responsible Investing in Nature's Trust* (Routledge 2015) 2.
[294] Ibid., 2.
[295] Ibid., 7.
[296] Ibid., 172.
[297] Ibid., 269.
[298] For the relationship between the financial industry and climate change generally, see Megan Bowman, *Banking on Climate Change How Finance Actors and Transnational Regulatory Regimes Are Reacting* (Wolters Kluwer 2014).

7.8 Conclusion

While progress has been uneven, changes are occurring in the context of investors and climate change. These shifts, combined with other developments identified in this and previous chapters, all have the potential to garner significant action by companies to make the transition to clean energy, reduce climate risks and manage the climate crisis.

8

Conclusion

The United Kingdom has made progress on the issue of climate change, although critics argue these changes are both insufficient and long overdue.[1] A net zero emissions target is ambitious but not sufficient, and as climate impacts escalate over time, this target will have to be revisited and improved. However, over the course of approximately a decade, from the establishment of the Committee on Climate Change under the Climate Change Act 2008, to the historic net zero emissions target announced in 2019, the country has made policy progress on climate change. The Paris Agreement in 2015 provided momentum to the United Kingdom and other countries and non-state actors to move towards a low or zero-emissions economy. Progress has been made in all of the areas assessed in previous chapters (although not evenly so) from the codification of the enlightened shareholder value theory, progress under international initiatives such as the Paris Agreement, the TCFD and the Enterprise Principles, human rights approaches and climate litigation, as well as on investor and market-based incentives to assess and manage climate risk. Despite these changes, the fundamental approach of this book is that the shareholder primacy and shareholder wealth maximisation norms that have undergirded company law for so many decades are increasingly outdated and inappropriate in the context of the climate crisis, and must be adapted.

This chapter will review and assess key findings from previous chapters, and then pull together the cumulative impacts of company law, environmental law, as well as human rights, climate litigation and financial initiatives on company law and theory in the context of climate change. The first part of this chapter will revisit some of the key findings from previous chapters. The second part of this chapter will assess the

---

[1] Caroline Lucas, 'Theresa May's Net-Zero Target Is a Lot Less Impressive Than It Looks' *The Guardian* (12 June 2019), www.theguardian.com/commentisfree/2019/jun/12/theresa-may-net-zero-emissions-target-climate-change (accessed 22 July 2020).

impacts of these developments on the theoretical underpinnings of company law, what the future might hold for companies in the context of climate change, and some practical tools and guidance that directors might need to prepare for a climate-constrained world.

8.1 KEY FINDINGS

The climate crisis shifts the focus on to the public functions of companies – these entities are responsible for significant historic emissions and yet have almost no international regulatory responsibilities on climate change. This is because most corporate theory focuses on and privileges the private wealth generating functions of companies. These private functions have benefited companies and their shareholders for many decades, but have also led to dramatic negative effects for the climate. As society better understands the significant risks that climate change holds, and the contributions companies have made to these risks, attitudes have changed towards climate change in general, and corporate responsibilities for the climate in particular.

8.1.1 *Corporate Norms and Their Entrenchment in Company Law*

From the initial establishment of companies as separate legal entities, they were understood as entities with distinctly public functions.[2] During the industrial revolution, they undertook vital public projects, creating infrastructures such as roads, railways and bridges. Modern society as we know it has been shaped and built by these entities. Dispersed ownership of shareholders along with the rise of a new managerial class of directors led to significant shifts and changes in how companies understood themselves. Berle and Means' debate in the 1920s illustrated shifting approaches to the corporate vehicle, with shareholders emerging as the most important constituent of the companies.

The predominance of neoliberal economic theories and a negative approach to government regulation cemented this shift towards privatisation and private law as the most important regulatory device for companies. Shareholders became reified in this normative approach, and the maximisation of their wealth became the most important objective of the company. These private law approaches are not always reflective of actual corporate activities or even the wants or needs of shareholders. Despite competing theories which emphasised the importance of a variety of stakeholders in the corporate project, in the early 2000s ideological convergence around shareholder primacy and shareholder wealth maximisation was assumed by

---

[2] Barnali Choudhury and Martin Petrin, *Corporate Duties to the Public* (Cambriidge University Press 2019), 357.

many corporate academics and the business community, and that these norms would be the enduring approach of company law in the future.[3]

Chapter 3 assessed how these corporate norms were deeply embedded in the revised UK Companies Act 2006. Prior to this codification, English common law provided a significant amount of deference to directors, leaving them free to make profit-sacrificing actions provided they were ultimately for the benefit of the company. Prior to 2006, company law adopted a more entity-based theoretical approach to the company, and did not require that directors unquestioningly focus on maximising the wealth of shareholders. Despite the Company Law Review Steering Group's desire to 'clarify' that directors did not have to emphasise short-term profit making, the new section 172 of the Companies Act actually included shareholders in the legal directive that directors must work in the best interests of the company. This statutory shift equated shareholders with the company, and moved away from an entity approach to the company. While Section 172 also includes a requirement for directors to have regard to the long-term interests of the company, and corporate impacts on the environment and communities, this statutory shift arguably re-entrenched existing corporate norms which privilege shareholders and profit making. These shifts in corporate norms and company law set the tone for the remainder of the book, which highlights how detrimental these legal approaches have been for the climate.

These private-based norms certainly do not reflect the significant public impacts of corporate activities. These norms have justified and incentivised the externalisation of corporate GHG emissions. This externalisation has created tremendous wealth for shareholders and the companies they are a part of, but shifted the risks and impacts of climate change directly on to the public. Climate impacts are escalating quickly, and have caused a loss of life, been a driver of mass migration, and may even endanger the sovereignty of vulnerable countries and social stability. These risks are becoming bidirectional for companies. Millions of people in the United States and around the world will relocate away from hazards and this migration will have significant impacts for the private sector.[4] Businesses that operate, have infrastructure in, and serve populations in vulnerable areas, including developers, real estate agents, banks, insurers and financiers will be affected.[5] Companies are used to operating in a stable climate, and this stability can no longer be taken for granted. These dramatic shifts and consequences are systemic across financial systems, countries and societies. While there may be climate winners and losers, as certain thresholds are breached, all countries and societies become vulnerable to some extent.

---

[3] Henry Hansmann and Reinier Kraakman, 'The End of History for Corporate Law' (2000) 89 Geo. L. J. 439.
[4] A. R. Siders and Carni Hulet, 'Climigration and the Private Sector' (2019) *Community Development Innovation Review*, 79.
[5] Ibid.

The remainder of the book assessed other regulatory approaches in the climate context. These regulatory approaches highlight how outdated traditional normative approaches to the company are, and why they should be adjusted.

8.1.2 *International Consensus-Shifting on Climate Change*

The impacts of climate change will vary across geographic regions and even within countries. To be clear, some countries in the global North may benefit from increased temperatures, but it is debatable how long these benefits will last.[6] Varying incentives, capacities and historic contributions to climate change among countries have been the major stumbling blocks in climate negotiations over the decades. A pathway through these stumbling blocks was reached in 2015 through the sophisticated architecture of the Paris Agreement. All countries that ratified the Agreement have procedural obligations to submit nationally determined contributions. These contributions are supposed to demonstrate progressive climate action over time. Despite the lack of binding obligations of result within the treaty, and the withdrawal of the United States from the Agreement, non-state actors and even sub-national actors in the United States took on the message of the Paris Agreement, and regarded its global temperature goals seriously. The Agreement was a catalyst for increased regulatory action in many countries, as well as increased climate litigation around the world.

The Paris Agreement was the first international climate agreement to include human rights in its text, even though it was only a preambular reference. This reference reflected the increasing awareness that the impacts of climate change have on human rights. The international regulatory picture on companies and human rights has a checkered history. Business and industry historically resisted the imposition of hard, binding duties on human rights. Instead, they are subject to responsibilities on human rights under the UN Guiding Principles. These soft law obligations do impose procedural and remedial responsibilities on these actors, and this is often not sufficient to mediate corporate abuses. As climate impacts escalate, these avenues may become more used in the context of climate change, but more obligations and duties must be imposed on companies in the context of human rights and climate change under international governance initiatives. This movement has begun (again) with the proposals and negotiations for a binding instrument on Transnational Corporations and Other Business Enterprises with respect to human rights. While political will on this initiative may be weak, it is important that companies are subject to more detailed duties on human rights, particularly in the climate context.

---

[6] Oxford Economics, 'Global Modelling the Economic Cost of Global Warming' (6 July 2020), 6.

Regulating companies is a complex task due to the transnational impacts of climate change, and the lack of global governance of transnational corporations. Divorced from national oversight and with considerable power and flexibility to move operations (and profits) to varying jurisdictions and even within the corporate group, transnational legal regimes on the whole, and particularly in the realm of climate change, have failed to appropriately regulate these companies. This is also problematic in the area of climate litigation, where parent companies are often insulated from suits due to the doctrine of separate legal personality. While some inroads have been made into this principle in the United Kingdom, it still poses a barrier to successful climate litigation.

Companies are facing liability attempts through the dramatic increase in climate litigation all over the world. While the bulk of the litigation is taking place in the United States and is unlikely to be successful due to hurdles around causation and inter-state emissions, other more creative suits internationally may eventually create some type of liability for companies for climate harms. Litigation against RWE in Peru, as well as the Philippines' Commission on Human Rights' investigation, all pose difficult questions about corporate collusion in the climate crisis, and elevate the public conscience around corporate liability.

Regulatory frameworks are also evolving in some jurisdictions, including in the United Kingdom. The Paris Agreement combined with Brexit, incentivised ambitious climate policy making in the United Kingdom. The net zero emissions target, announced in 2019, further accelerated policy making at the national level. Existing climate and energy regulations are likely to be ramped up in this context, and targets in a new UK emissions trading scheme increased over time. While the United Kingdom has been moving away from coal for some time, some factors made the announcement of a net zero national target feasible. The commitment to establishing flexible regulations which can appropriately adapt to scientific developments, adhering to the advice of independent, qualified advisors, and having the political will to implement appropriate policy responses with the support of financial regulators, are all actions that many developed countries and large developing countries can and should take.

Despite progress and developments in these areas, significant legal and market-based challenges, remain. The pressures of short-termism underpinned by the theory of shareholder wealth maximisation, combine to leave companies free to continue to extract, accumulate, exploit, invest in and fundamentally to rely on fossil fuels, thereby exacerbating the climate crisis. These norms impact corporate action in all of the areas covered in this book, and so these norms must be adapted and updated to better facilitate global transitions. Updating company law with a light, medium or preferably dark green approach as advocated in Chapter 3, would update these norms accordingly. Shifts in market approaches to climate change are also important, and can facilitate an appropriate adaptation of company law.

8.1.3 Systemic Financial Risks of Climate Change as a Market Driver

The recent rise of ESG awareness among corporate managers and the investors who finance them is undeniable.[7] The 'E' in ESG has become particularly prominent in ESG disclosures.[8] A new approach to ESG investing emphasises that because investors value the reduction of environmental costs, a trade-off between prioritising risk-adjusted returns and minimising environmental impacts may no longer be necessary.[9] This may not be true in all circumstances across all industries. Profits are still important, and will remain important. However, investors, financial regulators and financiers in many jurisdictions are concerned about the systemic scale of climate risks. The situation is acute in particularly vulnerable industries such as coal, oil and gas, utilities, forestry and agriculture, but most companies are now concerned or at least considering climate change in a bidirectional manner.

Climate risk has evolved from an 'ethical externality' to a material financial issue, and a material risk for many industries, sectors and markets.[10] A report by SASB in 2016 stated that climate-related risks are now present in seventy-two of seventy-nine industries, comprising approximately US$27.5 trillion or 93 per cent of US equities by market capitalisation.[11] In the United Kingdom, climate change is anticipated to have a significant and complex impact on most if not all listed companies.[12] Even beyond listed firms, the Financial Conduct Authority in the United Kingdom considers that climate-related risks and opportunities are relevant to all companies, and likely to be material for most.[13]

Due to the ubiquity of climate risks, investors cannot diversify away from this risk, but instead must focus on managing climate risks.[14] The level and scale of these risks vary. Specific risks are attached to certain industries or even companies due to their locations, business models, technology or corporate preparedness.[15] Climate risks can also be systematic, as they are inherent to entire markets and are un-diversifiable.[16] Finally, climate risks can be systemic, and so can trigger the collapse of an entire market or financial system.[17] Corporate norms must be adjusted to permit or

---

[7] S & P Global Market Intelligence, 'Environmental Impact and Outperformance: A Data Driven Approach to Integrating Carbon Footprinting into the Investment Process' (May 2020), 1.
[8] Ibid.
[9] Ibid.
[10] Sarah Barker, 'An Introduction to Directors' Duties in Relation to Stranded Asset Risks' in Ben Caldecott (ed.) *Stranded Assets and the Environment Risk, Resilience and Opportunity* (Routledge 2018), 199–200.
[11] SASB, 'Climate Risk Technical Bulletin' (October 2016), 1-2.
[12] Financial Conduct Authority, 'Proposals to Enhance Climate-Related Disclosures by Listed Issuers and Clarification of Existing Disclosure Obligations' Consultation Paper (March 2020), para 1.1.
[13] Ibid., para 1.3.
[14] SASB (n 11), 2.
[15] Ibid., 8.
[16] Ibid.
[17] Ibid., 9.

even require governments to limit corporate governance decisions that cause systemic externalities to the public,[18] such as climate change.

Anglo-American corporate theory and company law have failed to keep pace with these developments. This book has illustrated most of these failings within certain contexts. But it is also important to stress that significant opportunities exist for companies in the realm of climate change as well. ESG initiatives in the EU facilitate energy transitions and the rethinking of capital allocation into more sustainable avenues. In South Africa, the recent King IV report on corporate governance advocates for a more diverse and holistic understanding of capital. It focuses on the six capitals articulated by the Integrated Reporting Council, of financial, manufactured, human, intellectual but also natural and social and relationship capital.[19] The report recommends that directors shift away from an exclusive focus on financial capitalism to a more inclusive approach to capitalism as the engine of shared prosperity and value creation in a long-term and sustainable manner.[20]

Directors' duties, at least as interpreted in Anglo-American jurisdictions, provide directors with significant flexibility to act on climate change if there are benefits to be had for shareholders and their companies. Sarah Barker notes that even within Anglo-American jurisdictions, there may be different potential to manage climate change.[21] While the United Kingdom still has a fairly flexible approach to directors' duties, US jurisprudence provides less leeway for directors to cater for business risks but some flexibility remains.[22] The Australian jurisdiction, with its unique investigatory and enforcement mechanism by the Australian Securities and Investment Council, could provide the most progressive corporate landscape.[23] The recent speech by Lord Sales in the Anglo-Australian law society on the impact of environmental litigation on corporate law in these jurisdictions cements the ongoing jurisprudential dialogue among Anglo-American jurisdictions, even on the topic of climate change. Anglo-American corporate theory has always emphasised the importance of long-term value creation for shareholders, which accords well with short, medium and long-term time scales of climate change. Therefore, when short term incentives are removed, company law in most Anglo-American jurisdictions does not in fact act as a barrier to climate action by companies, but company law could be improved to better facilitate and incentivise corporate climate action.

---

[18] Steven L. Schwarcz, 'Misalignment: Corporate Risk-Taking and Public Duty' (2016) 92 Notre Dame L. Rev. 1, 27.
[19] Institute of Directors of Southern Africa, 'King IV Report on Corporate Governance for South Africa' (2016), 3.
[20] Ibid., 4.
[21] Barker (n 10), 207.
[22] Ibid., 210–211.
[23] Ibid., 207.

While capital markets have turned their attention to the financial issues associated to climate change,[24] it is important, however, not to overstress these recent shifts and potential changes in market incentives. Market-based incentives as well as short-term investment cycles still currently provide strong countervailing pressures to corporate action. These pressures are often successful in persuading directors to act in the short-term. But these fiscal incentives may slowly be changing as investors and financial institutions see the benefits of climate action, and the significant costs of climate change.

At the moment, for example, most energy companies see their oil and gas resources as a necessary and significant part of the energy future for several decades to come, even though they acknowledge that they are tapping mature fields, accessing hard-to-reach hydrocarbons and are involved in the shale gas boom. Many of these companies did not agree with the position that their reserves may become 'stranded assets' if society meets the global temperature goal of keeping temperature increases to well below 2°C.[25] However, even among the most fossil-fuel intensive sector, positions on climate change and approaches to climate action are splintering and differentiated among actors. This is primarily due to the pressure imposed on these companies by institutional investors. Carbon-majors in the United Kingdom have been the most progressive, illustrating that regulatory changes combined with shifting investor and market-based approaches to climate risks can have an impact even on carbon-major companies.

Whether and how these companies meet their emissions targets is still unclear. It is also unclear whether other energy companies around the world will follow. For example, ExxonMobil and Chevron, both based in the United States, have yet to make much movement on climate change. While a number of companies across a variety of sectors have invested in GHG emission reductions and renewable energy technologies, their commitments to these endeavours usually ebb and flow, and profits appear to continue to be the primary motivator. Making commitments on Scope 3 emissions is usually the most difficult to achieve. Regardless, as outlined previously, US investors such as BlackRock are publicly engaging on the issue of climate change. While this action is novel and exciting, it should also raise concern about the role of such concentrated investors acting as de facto regulators in a democratic society.[26]

---

[24] Ibid., 200.
[25] BP Plc, 'Sustainability Review 2014' (2014), 16, www.bp.com/content/dam/bp/pdf/sustainability/group-reports/Sustainability_Report_2014.pdf; Royal Dutch Shell Plc, 'Response to Shareholder Resolution on Climate Change' (19 May 2015), 12, http://s01.static-shell.com/content/dam/shell-new/local/corporate/corporate/downloads/pdf/investor/agm/response-to-shareholder-resolution-on-climate-change.pdf (accessed 30 May 2020).
[26] Madison Condon, 'Externalities and the Common Owner' (2019) New York U School L & Economics Research Paper Series, 6.

Financial regulators in some jurisdictions are also taking action. The stark warnings from the Governor of the Bank of England at the end of 2015 about the risks climate change poses to general fiscal stability sparked the attention of institutional investors. Central Banks around the world, through the Network for Greening the Financial System, issued a call for action in 2019. In their report, they emphasised the structural and systemic nature of climate risks. The distinctive features of climate risks include far-reaching impacts in breadth and magnitude across all sectors and geographies, non-linear impacts, the foreseeability of the risks, the irreversibility of the impacts, and the dependency on short-term actions for climate stability.[27]

Despite these warnings, the markets are not yet systemically pricing the emerging risk of stranded assets in fossil-fuel companies. A shift in market attitudes towards climate change is vital for corporate norms and company law to adopt a more climate-friendly approach. Climate-related financial risks are not fully reflected in asset valuations, and there is a need for globally coordinated action.[28] Asset valuation tools need to be recalibrated, as the markets should not reward the replacement of fossil fuel reserves, and should take into account increasing global temperatures and re-price assets accordingly.[29] The recent drop in oil prices may change the profitability equation regarding certain hard to reach reserves, but it is unclear whether this will herald a swifter transition away from these resources.

These challenges mirror the challenges of shareholder wealth maximisation and short-termism identified in Chapters 2 and 3. As highlighted previously, the shareholder wealth maximisation privileges shareholders as the primary constituent of the company to the detriment of the interests and values of other shareholders. It focuses on shareholder wealth maximisation as the most important function of the company, and therefore can lead to a myopic focus on short-term profitability, and an economic commodification of the environment and negative externalities which have fuelled the climate crisis. These norms must be updated and adapted to focus not just on shareholders and the maximisation of their wealth, but on the company as an entity, capable of serving a number of stakeholders, including the climate. In particular, under company law directors should be required to consider climate change and climate risks as an element of their strategic governance and their duties within the company, and as part of serving the best interests of the company as an entity. Looking forward, companies must take more progressive action on climate change and some rationales and tools for action are suggested below.

---

[27] Network for Greening the Financial System, Executive Summary, 'A Call for Action: Climate Change as a Source of Financial Risk' (April 2019), 1 available, www.ngfs.net/sites/default/files/medias/documents/synthese_ngfs-2019_-_17042019_0.pdf (accessed 25 July 2020).
[28] Ibid.
[29] Carbon Tracker Initiatives and GRI, 'Unburnable Carbon 2013: Wasted Capital and Stranded Assets', 36, http://carbontracker.live.kiln.digital/Unburnable-Carbon-2-Web-Version.pdf (accessed 21 July 2020).

8.2 WHAT THE FUTURE HOLDS FOR COMPANIES IN THE CONTEXT OF CLIMATE CHANGE

Despite significant challenges in market approaches to climate change and a short-term bias, financial regulators and financial systems are waking up to the systemic and irreversible nature of climate risks. Company law must be a part of the transition to a net zero economy. Part of this justification is an economic one. Companies must avoid and manage the financial risks of climate change for their own survival. But part of this justification is also a reaction to societal expectations of companies. Companies have public functions and responsibilities, and so are sensitive to the changing demands of their social licence to operate. Businesses must face up to their moral responsibility as well as their expanding social and political roles in order to retain their perceived legitimacy.[30]

As Doris Fuchs notes, an important element of corporate power is discursive power which is diffuse, pervasive and socially comprehensive.[31] This corporate power rests on perceived legitimacy.[32] While it is a strong source of corporate influence, discursive power is also fragile and the most dangerous power if undermined by changes in dominant societal norms and ideas.[33] As social and market attitudes begin to shift on climate change, corporate attitudes and approaches must also shift. These shifts are beginning to happen, at least in the language and commitments some companies and countries are making on climate change. Whether and how these commitments are met remains to be seen, but changing social expectations due to escalating impacts of climate change will continue to be an indirect monitor of corporate climate action.

Beyond that social licence, companies are also likely to have increased legal obligations in relation to climate change. Disclosure obligations are already crystallising, but emission reduction obligations are likely to follow and are necessary. CSR alone will not be sufficient to ensure ambitious corporate climate action. Global governance and nationally binding emission reductions imposed on companies will be necessary. While it is important not to 'festishise' business regulation, as most state-based regulation has been for (not on) business,[34] domestic regulation will be a necessary part of the global transition towards a net zero world. Business responses to regulation will vary depending on the size, sector and industry,[35] but climate regulation must accompany and motivate corporate action on climate change.

Corporate action is incentivised by climate risk. The focus on climate risk, while important, does cabin this issue into one of business risk.[36] This type of framing has the

---

[30] Doris Fuchs, *Business Power in Global Governance* (Lynne Reinner 2007), 144.
[31] Ibid, 147.
[32] Ibid.
[33] Ibid, 148–9.
[34] Peter Newell, 'CSR and the Limits of Capital' (2008) 39(6) 1063, 1074.
[35] Ibid.
[36] Christopher Wright and David Nyberg, *Climate Change, Capitalism and Corporations: Processes of Creative Self-Destruction* (CUP 2015) 25.

danger of legitimising and justifying particular corporate responses which are market-based and can be solely profit-serving.[37] Public-facing regulation, which ensures that corporate responses also benefit society, will be an important part of the global climate transition. In addition, changes to prevailing corporate norms must accompany any regulatory action. Companies must equally consider both shareholders and climate impacts, and where these climate impacts have systemic and significant implications beyond the company, companies must act to reduce these impacts. These interests can be balanced if directors owe duties to the company as an entity, not just the shareholders. Entity theories such as EMV and EMS covered in Chapter 2, which require the balancing of sustainability and the duty to respect, protect and fulfil the interests of those involved in or affected by the activities of the company with the viability of the company as an entity, would require directors to balance climate concerns, particularly where they are material to the company and society. The levels and scale of their actions should be proportionate to the size, capacity and climate contributions of their companies. But they should have legal obligations to act on climate change, and it is very likely that the law will move in this direction in the near future, at least for some industries and sectors. Climate change highlights the significant and largely negative impacts companies have on the public at large, all over the world. These climate impacts must be reduced and managed, and company law must facilitate climate action.

In many jurisdictions, including the United Kingdom, company law is able, although not perfectly primed, to do this. As markets and financiers shift capital away from fossil fuel intensive sectors, and towards low-carbon choices, directors will be forced to make similar capital allocation choices within their companies and sectors. Most Anglo-American jurisdictions are concerned with the process, if not the content, of directorial decision making. Failure to become aware of, and remain adequately informed of, climate risks may already implicate the legal duties of directors. Company law frameworks and theories should be updated to focus the attention of directors on the company as an entity and to specifically require both consideration and action on climate change. Where risks of climate change are material to a company, directors should act appropriately and proportionately to mitigate and manage these risks. Directors need tools and guidance to do this.

8.2.1 *Disclosure Obligations on Climate Risks*

The systemic nature of climate risks requires a holistic approach to understanding and identifying the full range of possible direct and indirect impacts.[38] Companies should rethink models they currently use to quantify risks,[39] as historic baseline

---

[37] Ibid.
[38] *McKinsey Quarterly*, 'Confronting Climate Risk' (15 May 2020) available, www.mckinsey.com/business-functions/sustainability/our-insights/confronting-climate-risk# (accessed 27 July 2020).
[39] Ibid.

8.2 What Future Holds for Companies in Climate Change 225

assumptions may no longer be relevant. A more systemic analysis of climate risks should lead to more comprehensive and high-quality climate-related disclosures.[40] Improved disclosures should lead to better market analysis, better informed metrics and ratings, in turn, reducing market harms and enhancing market integrity.[41] With better information, financial firms and providers should be able to develop products and services that better meet consumers' climate-related preferences, capital should be reallocated accordingly and financial flows should become more supportive of the transition to net zero emissions.[42] With more accurate and tailored information on climate change, directors should be better able to meet their new legal obligations to consider climate change and act appropriately to reduce and mitigate climate risks. Climate-related disclosures, therefore, provide an important function.

There are, however, a myriad of disclosure templates. Directors are faced with a complex disclosure ecosystem, and in this environment should cater their disclosures based on the needs of the users of their disclosures.[43] Firms can start with simple disclosures, and add complexity over time.[44] Disclosures should be dynamic, not static, and the metrics, targets and outcomes should be comparable over time.[45] Mandatory and standardised guidelines and requirements for companies should be implemented by governments, based on international guidance. Clear methodological approaches included in regulatory requirements will support high-quality disclosures, reduce the cost of meeting ad-hoc investor requests and promote structural dialogues and broader governance on climate change within firms.[46]

The TCFD has created tools and recommendations on appropriate and proportionate climate disclosures. It has also created a TCFD Knowledge Hub in collaboration with the Climate Disclosure Standards Board, which provides a large body of resources to help organisations implement the TCFD recommendations. These recommendations are quickly becoming industry standard, and mandatory in jurisdictions. This trend is only likely to continue in the future, as investors demand more decision-useful information on climate change. The Network for Greening the Financial System is issuing a Handbook on climate and environment-related risks management for supervising financial authorities.

In 2021, the Bank of England will conduct a biennial exploratory scenario on the financial risks of climate change. This will give participating firms practical experience of how their strategies on identifying and managing climate-related risks hold up. Where climate risks are material to businesses, company and securities laws in

---

[40] FCA (n 12), para 1.24.
[41] Ibid.
[42] Ibid.
[43] Climate Financial Risks Forum Guide (June 2020), 'Disclosures Chapter', available www .bankofengland.co.uk/news/2020/june/the-cfrf-publishes-guide-to-help-financial-industry-address-climate-related-financial-risks (accessed 25 July 2020).
[44] Ibid., 10.
[45] Ibid.
[46] FCA (n 12), para 1.27.

many jurisdictions already require these are measured, managed and disclosed to investors. The ultimate societal benefit of better climate-related disclosures is that markets are better able to manage risk and allocate capital to support a transition to a net zero economy.[47]

Disclosure obligations are unlikely to be the only legal obligations imposed on companies. Emission reductions and contributions to climate adaptation and perhaps even liability for corporate-induced climate harms, are also likely to be emerge as legal obligations. Companies should play a part in climate action early in order to avoid or minimise legal obligations, by developing strategic and holistic governance based approaches to climate change and climate action.

8.2.2 Strategic and Governance Approaches to Climate Change

Addressing the physical and transitional risks of climate change requires a more systemic approach to risk management, accelerating corporate decarbonisation and adaptation efforts.[48] Understanding, oversight and accountability for the financial and societal risks of climate change should be instituted at all levels of the firm, with effective management and oversight from the board of directors.[49] Corporate strategies and governance approaches will have to be adjusted in order to this. Climate change, its risks and opportunities, must be mainstreamed into corporate decision making, based on the firm, sector and industry levels of risks, risk appetites and opportunities. Climate change must be incorporated into capital allocation decisions, product and service development, as well as supply chain management.[50] Broader and indirect market impacts of climate change should also be considered as these may affect consumer spending, employee health and the financial resilience of economies. Implicit market assumptions which held in the past, should be interrogated in the context of climate risks. Companies should develop short, medium and long-term perspectives on how risks, costs and opportunities will develop and evolve, and should integrate the voices of affected communities into decision making.[51] A more stakeholder-inclusive approach would be consistent with changing corporate norms, which should balance shareholder interests with climate risks and impacts.

Innovation is also critical to bring new financial products, services, policies and approaches to meet climate goals.[52] Financial regulators are important actors that can help align market incentives in the private sector with net zero emission targets.

---

[47] Ibid., para 1.27.
[48] McKinsey Global Institute, 'Climate Risk and Responses: Physical Hazards and Socioeconomic Impacts' (January 2020), 22.
[49] Climate Financial Risk Forum Guide (n 43), 'Risk Management Chapter', 5.
[50] McKinsey Quarterly (n 38), 9.
[51] Ibid., 9.
[52] Climate Financial Risk Forum Guide (n 43), 'Innovation Chapter', 2.

Re-orientating incentives in capital markets, including in lending institutions, project finance markets, retail and bank lending, as well as pension investments will provide capital incentives to corporate action and innovation in climate change. Directors should be aware of emerging climate opportunities, and the market-incentives and financial flows that can help their businesses take advantage of these opportunities.

In order to implement these tools and react to changing market incentives, boards will need climate expertise. Board-level understanding of the firm's approach to climate change is critical to embedding climate change effectively in firm governance.[53] This can either be established through a subcommittee of the board, or hired through ad hoc expertise. For more climate exposed companies, adding a climate expert on to the Board itself may be the more coherent and holistic approach. Strategic and governance approaches are intended to promote a structural dialogue within companies on the nature of climate risk and opportunities to their firm.[54] Finally, companies should support progressive climate policies at the domestic and international level. A more holistic understanding of the systemic risks of climate change should incentivise companies to do this. Adapting corporate norms to balance climate risk and actions against profit-making is a necessary and fundamental component to corporate climate action.

8.3 FINAL THOUGHTS

Policy changes in the United Kingdom over the past decade illustrate that a combination of flexible legislative structures which establish an independent and scientifically sound advisory Committee with the political will to adhere to the scientific advice of the Committee, can lead to progressive policy decisions. Supported by informed and proactive financial regulators, a national re-assessment of financial strategies and market regulation, as well as instituting mandatory disclosure obligations on companies and institutional actors such as pension funds, creates a coherent policy pathway towards achieving a net zero economy. Not all countries have the same level of capacity, economic flexibility or political will as the United Kingdom. Even in the United Kingdom, progress has been uneven over the past decade. However, all of this activity has taken place during a politically tumultuous period for the country. Perhaps these dramatic policy and regulatory shifts have taken place precisely because the United Kingdom had to reconsider its national priorities in the context of Brexit, but the country could just have easily moved away from climate change in order to obtain perceived competitive advantages. Flexible and appropriate regulatory mechanisms that can evolve according to climate science, independent and qualified experts whose advice is heeded by

---

[53] Climate Financial Risk Forum Guide (n 43), 'Risk Management Chapter', 5.
[54] FCA (n 12), para 1.24.

successive governments, combined with appropriate support from financial regulators have been the key ingredients to progressive climate action.

This jurisdiction, which is the birthplace of modern corporate law and is heavily shareholder-centric, has managed to bypass powerful corporate norms and usher in at least a policy pathway to a net zero emissions economy. While much work remains to be done to achieve this target and ensure it is environmentally sound, regulatory changes in the past ten years have not been stymied by company law. In fact, the United Kingdom has been the birthplace for the TCFD, mandatory disclosure of climate risks by companies, Central Bank market assessments of climate change, along with other sweeping market-based shifts in the understanding of climate risk. Company law has not blocked progressive policy making on climate change, but it has not facilitated it either. Companies have the power to facilitate and accelerate the climate transition. While corporate power is generally accepted, it is not well understood.[55] This book has hopefully contributed to a fuller understanding of the power and vulnerabilities of companies in the context of climate change, and how updating existing corporate norms and company law can usher in the sweeping legal, market and societal changes needed to ensure a stable climate.

Global responses are also needed across companies, industries and international financial markets. These shifts are beginning to take place as institutional investors, and political and business leaders take climate change seriously. The ultimate test of these commitments will be the level of emission increases or decreases experienced in the next ten, twenty and thirty years.

Climate change is the great disruptor. Climate change is striking harder and more rapidly than many expected.[56] No business or society will be spared of negative climate impacts. Cumulative physical impacts will compound slowly over time, with the most draconian effects felt after 2030.[57] Significant climate action in the 2020s is therefore extremely important. Without ambitious climate action in the next decade, it is possible that as climate impacts escalate, global consensus could fray, leading to significant economic and societal disruption.[58] The implications of climate change are catastrophic, wide-ranging and intersectional, and some impacts are unknown.[59]

For centuries, companies, financial markets, governments and individuals have made decisions against the backdrop of a stable climate, but the looming risks of climate change means atmospheric conditions could be non-stationary and climate

---

[55] Global Justice Now, 'Ending Corporate Impunity the Struggle to Bring About a Binding UN Treaty on Transnational Cooperation and Human Rights' (July 2018), 2.
[56] McKinsey Quarterly (n 38), 6.
[57] Moody's Analytics, 'The Economic Implications of Climate Change' (2019), available, www.moodysanalytics.com/-/media/article/2019/economic-implications-of-climate-change.pdf (accessed 25 July 2020).
[58] World Economic Forum, 'The Global Risks Report 2020' (15th ed), 33.
[59] Ibid., 30.

8.3 Final Thoughts

impacts could be non-linear.[60] Natural systems and societal systems may falter, break down or stop working altogether.[61] Replacing a stable environment with one that is ever-changing means that decision making based on past experience may be unreliable.[62] In the context of these dramatic risks to business and society, it is imperative that companies, and company law, respond appropriately. Existing corporate norms which privilege profit above everything else are no longer relevant or appropriate. Neither companies nor society can operate fully and effectively without a stable and safe climate. Corporate action, aided by company law should ensure climate stability for this, and for future generations.

---

[60] *McKinsey Quarterly* (n 38), 3.
[61] Ibid.
[62] Ibid.

Index

3M, 20

Accenture, 20
Action Aid, 70
Agency costs, 8, 13, 21, 24–6, 28
Allen v. Gold Reefs of West Africa, 56
Amazon, 20, 97, 112
American Electric Power v. Connecticut, 152–4
American Legislative Council Exchange, 129
Amnesty International, 70
Anglo-American, 1, 5, 7–9, 17–18, 22, 31, 46, 59, 68, 90, 220, 224
Anglo American Plc, 5
Anthropocene, 1–2, 40
Anthropogenic, 2–3, 5, 36, 84–5, 88, 155, 166
Apple, 20
As You Sow, 208
Asset Owners Disclosure Project, 188
Australia, 17, 58, 74, 87, 138, 152, 198, 205
Australian Corporations Act 2001, 58–9, 198
Australian Securities and Investment Council, 58, 220
Australian Securities Exchange, 199

Bali Action Plan, 85
Bank of England, 16, 107–8, 173, 222, 225
Basic Inc. v. Levinson, 192–3
BCE Inc. v. 1976 Debentureholders, 94
Benefit companies, 9–10
Berle and Means, 23–4, 26
Berle, Adolf, 23–6, 37, 52, 60, 215
BG Group Plc, 98, 101, 111, 139
Bhullar v. Bhullar, 73
Biological diversity, 14
BlackRock, 187, 210, 221
Blair, Tony, 85

BNP Paribas, 187
Board of Trustees v. City of Baltimore, 201
Border Tax Adjustments, 185
BP Plc, 5, 20, 99–100, 111, 116, 128–30, 134, 138–40, 154–6, 186, 206–9, 221
Brexit, 17–18, 113–14, 119, 121, 123–4, 135–6, 139, 218, 227
Business Council for Sustainable Development, 83
Business Roundtable, 20, 44

Cadbury Review, 47–9, 94
Cambridge Water Co. Ltd. v. Eastern Counties Leather Plc, 120–1
Canada, 17, 85, 87, 94, 158, 169, 178, 183, 203
Canadian Business Companies Act, 93
Capital, 1–2, 7, 9–10, 13, 15–16, 19, 34–5, 37, 56, 59, 108, 119, 192–3, 196, 199, 202, 206–7, 210–11, 220–1, 224–7
Carbon Market Platform, 186
Carbon Pricing Leadership Coalition, 186
Caring for Climate, 6, 104
Carney, Mark, 173, 189–90, 192, 204, 211
CDP, 6, 100, 105–6, 111, 190, 200
Centrica Plc, 98, 100
Ceres, 102, 190, 200
Chandler v. Cape Industries, 170
Chevron Plc, 5, 20, 98, 111, 154, 156, 208, 221
China, 12, 86–7, 91, 178, 201
Church of England, 206, 208
ClientEarth, 161, 164
Climate Action 100+, 98, 129, 200, 209
Climate Ambition Alliance, 97
Climate Change Act 2008, 17, 57, 113–14, 120–3, 125, 127, 136, 139, 161–2, 214
Coase, Ronald, 26, 36, 117
Coca-Cola, 20, 96, 187

231

Common but Differentiated Responsibilities and Respective Capabilities, 85–6
Community interest companies, 10
Companies (Miscellaneous Reporting) Regulations 2018, 68, 100
Companies Act 1862, 52
Companies Act 1985, 56–7, 61
Companies Act 2006, 8, 17–18, 41–2, 46, 49, 51, 53, 57, 60–1, 63–71, 75–6, 94–5, 99–100, 114, 116, 125–6, 130, 139, 148, 216
Companies Act 2006 (Strategic Report and Directors' Report) Regulations 2013, 61, 70–1, 99, 126
Companies, Partnerships and Groups (Accounts and Non-Financial Reporting) Regulations 2016, 100, 126
Company Law Review Steering Group, 31, 41–2, 47, 49, 61–6, 75–6
ConocoPhillips Plc, 5
CONSOL Energy Plc, 5
Corporate Responsibility Coalition, 70
Corporate Social Responsibility, 13–15, 18, 36, 66, 79, 90–100, 102–4, 107–8, 110–11, 168, 223
Cowan v. Scargill, 193–4

Defra, 125–6, 161, 164, 172
Delaware, 10–11, 34, 42–3, 58, 156
Denmark, 204
Department for Business, Energy and Industrial Strategy, 70, 99, 126
Department for Works and Pensions, 195
Department of Trade and Industry, 31, 41, 61, 65, 90
Directors' duties, 1, 8, 17–18, 22, 29. 44, 46–7, 49, 53, 55, 58–9, 62–3, 67, 71, 74–5, 77, 157, 219–20
Dodd, Merrick, 24, 37–8, 60
Dodge v. Ford Motor Co, 58

eBay v. Newmark, 42, 58
Ecuador, 146
Employee Retirement Income Security Act, 201
Energy Act 2013, 114, 127, 134
Enlightened Shareholder Value, 17, 41–2, 46, 51, 60–3, 65–7, 69, 76, 99, 214
Entity theories, 38–9, 41
Environment, social and governance indicators, 174, 193–6, 199–204, 219–20
EU, 17–18, 80, 85–6, 99, 113–14, 116, 118–19, 121, 123–4, 127, 131, 133–6, 139, 152, 159–61, 163, 202, 220
EU Climate and Energy Package, 118
EU Emissions Trading System, 118, 120, 133–6, 139–40, 163

European Commission, 91, 210
European Convention on Human Rights, 159–60
European Sustainable Investment Forum, 200
Externalities, 2–3, 7–8, 22, 29–32, 35–6, 45, 66, 76, 92, 101, 111, 115, 175, 181–3, 188, 211, 220–2
Extractive Industries Transparency Initiative, 144
ExxonMobil Plc, 5, 98, 102, 111, 144, 153–4, 186, 197, 208, 221

Fidelity, 187
Fiduciary duty, 63, 74, 195
Fiji, 179
Financial Conduct Authority, 199, 219
Financial Reporting Council, 48–50, 71, 73, 100, 191, 202–3
Financial Stability Board, 15, 102, 107, 173, 188, 190, 204, 211
French Duty of Vigilance, 148
Friends of the Earth International, 69–70
FTSE 100, 70, 99, 173, 196

G20, 17, 107, 176, 180, 209
G7, 176, 186, 209
GE, 20
General Motors, 20
Germany, 118, 164–5, 187
GHLM Trading Ltd v. Anil Kumar Maroo & Others, 72
Global Framework for Climate Risk Disclosure, 105
Global Reporting Initiative, 105–6, 111, 196, 222
Globalisation, 2, 38, 80
Goldman Sachs, 20
Good Law Project, 162
Google, 98
Green New Deal, 114, 119, 139
Greenbury Review, 49
Greenhalgh v. Arderne Cinemas, 39, 55–6, 59
Greenhouse gas, 1–3, 5–6, 8, 22, 28–32, 35–6, 45, 55, 65, 68–70, 75–7, 79–80, 84–8, 97–100, 102, 104–5, 110–11, 114, 118–19, 122–3, 125–6, 128–30, 132–4, 138–9, 147, 150, 152, 154–6, 159, 161–4, 167, 175, 183–4, 190, 192, 200, 203, 208, 216, 221
Greenpeace New Zealand v. Genesis Power Ltd, 161
Guterres, António, 4

Hampel Review, 49
Heede, Richard, 5–6, 12, 36, 155, 165
Higgs Review, 48, 50
High-Level Expert Group on Sustainable Finance, 202
Hutton v. West Cork Railway Company, 54

IBM, 20
ILO Tripartite Declaration of Principles Concerning Multinational Enterprises, 144
IMF, 175
In re Walt Disney Company Derivative Litigation, 43
India, 17, 87, 95–6, 178
Indian Companies Act, 95
ING Plc, 147
Institute of Directors in Southern Africa, 94
Institutional investors, 2, 13, 19, 34, 129–30, 140, 174, 187, 191, 193–5, 200, 203–4, 210–12, 221–2, 228
Intergovernmental Panel on Climate Change, 3, 113, 125, 147, 159–60
International Chamber of Commerce, 145
International Energy Agency, 4, 175, 208
Internationally Transferred Mitigation Outcomes, 137–8
Investor Network on Climate Risk, 190, 200
Iran, 12
ISO 14000, 79, 105, 111

Japan, 12, 85, 87, 138, 187
Joint Stock Companies Act 1844, 7
Joint Stock Companies Act 1856, 7, 52
Juliana et al. v. United States of America et al., 157–8

Kay Review, 191
Kimberley Process Certification Scheme, 144
King Report on Corporate Governance South Africa, 94–5, 220
Kivalina v. ExxonMobil Corporation, 153–4, 163
KPMG, 195
Kyoto Protocol to the United Nations Framework Convention on Climate Change, 79, 85, 87, 99, 110, 118–19, 122, 131–3, 137

Licence to operate, 93, 100, 111
Lima–Paris Action Agenda, 89
Limited Liability Act of 1855, 7
Limited Liability Corporations, 11
Limited Liability Partnerships, 11, 126
LINGO, 189
Lliuya v. RWE, 164
Lloyd's of London, 173
London Stock Exchange, 9, 48, 199
Low-profit company, 11

Madoff Securities International Ltd (in liquidation) v. Stephen Raven & Others, 72
Male' Declaration on the Human Dimension of Global Climate Change, 149
May, Theresa, 113, 214

Microsoft, 97, 112, 187
Minister of Water Affairs and Forestry v. Stilfontein Gold Mining, 94
Multilateral Agreement on Investment, 83
Multilateral Environmental Agreements, 79, 81–2, 85, 167
Myners Review, 188, 191

National Contact Points, 84, 147–8
Nationally Determined Contributions, 4, 87–9, 137–8, 217
Network for Greening the Financial System, 199, 222, 225
Net zero, 17–18, 88, 90, 97, 99, 113–14, 119, 125, 129–30, 136, 139–40, 162, 188, 209, 214, 218, 223, 225–8
Net Zero Asset Owners Alliance, 188
New York Stock Exchange, 9
New Zealand, 87, 152–3, 161, 179, 199
New Zealand Resource Management Act 1991, 161
Nexus of contracts theory, 28, 31–2, 39
Nigeria, 144, 170
Norway, 179, 204

Occidental Petroleum, 144, 208
Occupational and Personal Pensions Scheme (Disclosure of Information) Regulations 2013, 203
Occupational Pension Schemes (Investment) Regulations 2005, 195
Odyssey Entertainment Ltd. v. Ralph Kamp, 72
OECD, 4, 13, 17, 48, 82–3, 102, 135, 144, 147–8, 175–6, 180, 199
OECD Guidelines for Multinational Enterprises, 82–3, 102, 144, 147–8
OECD Principles of Corporate Governance, 17, 48
Oil and Gas Climate Initiative, 106
OPEC, 176, 186
Oslo Principles on Global Climate Change Obligations, 109, 166–8
Overseas Development Institute, 175, 180

Pakistan, 17, 19, 152, 160, 163
Paramount Communications Inc. v. Time Inc., 58
Paris Agreement, 4, 12, 18, 77–9, 81–4, 87–9, 97, 109–10, 112, 118, 120, 131, 133, 136–40, 147, 150, 160, 162, 167–8, 171, 173, 178, 182, 186, 189, 207, 209, 214, 217–18
Parke v. The Daily News, 57
Peabody Energy Plc, 5
Peoples Department Stores Inc. v. Wise, 94
Percival v. Wright, 54
Peru, 19, 218

Philippines Human Rights Commission, 141, 165, 171, 218
Poland, 134, 137
Principles of Responsible Investing, 151, 188, 190, 194–5, 200, 203–4, 212
Principles on Climate Obligations of Enterprises, 78–9, 107, 109, 112, 166, 168, 172, 214

R v. Secretary of State for Environment, Food and Rural Affairs, 152, 161
R (on the Application of the People and Planet) v. HM Treasury, 73–4
Re Caremark International Inc. Derivative Litigation, 43
Re Citigroup Inc. Shareholder Derivative Litigation, 43
Re Lee Behrens, 55
Re Phoenix Contracts (Leicester), 72
Re Smith and Fawcett Limited, 55, 72
Re Southern Counties Fresh Food Ltd, 72
Re Waste Recycling Group Plc, 56
Revlon Inc v. MacAndrews & Forbes Holdings Inc, 58
Rio Declaration, 83
Rockefeller Brothers Fund, 205
Ruggie, John, 105, 145–7
RWE AG, 164–5, 171, 218

Salomon v. Salomon, 9
Saudi Arabia, 12
Securities and Exchange Commission, 190, 192–3, 198, 207–8
Shareholder primacy, 1, 7–8, 11–13, 17–18, 20–6, 28–9, 31–3, 36–7, 39–42, 44–8, 50–1, 55, 57–60, 63, 66, 74–7, 90, 103, 111–12, 115, 129–30, 214–15
Shareholder wealth maximisation, 1, 7–8, 11–12, 21–2, 27–8, 31, 33–5, 37–8, 40–2, 44–5, 50–1, 57–8, 62, 65–6, 68, 93, 111–12, 129–30, 214–15, 218, 222
Shell Plc, 98, 101, 111, 116, 129–30, 138–40, 144, 169–70, 186, 207–8, 221
Shlensky v. Wrigley, 58
Short-termism, 12–13, 20–2, 31, 33–6. 45, 62, 75, 94, 110, 131, 157, 190–1, 194–5, 197, 204, 212, 216, 218, 221–3
Shuttleworth v. Cox Bros and Co., 56
Sidebottom v. Kershaw, Leese and Company Ltd, 56
Social licence, 15, 90, 93, 96, 100, 110, 112, 148, 157, 223
South Africa, 17, 94–5, 146, 152, 203, 207, 220
South African Companies Act, 94
South African National Development Plan 2030, 95
Stakeholder theories, 25, 37–9, 60
Standard & Poor 500, 187
State-owned companies, 12–13, 96
Stimpson v. Southern Landlords Association, 72
Stone v. Ritter, 42
Subsidies and Countervailing Measures Agreement, 177–8
Supreme Court
    Canada, 94
    Delaware, 42
    India, 96
    The Netherlands, 160
    UK, 74, 153, 161–3, 194
    US, 153, 157
Sustainability Accounting Standards Board, 107–8, 210, 219
Sweden, 184, 204

Takeover Code, 47, 51, 76
Task Force on Climate-Related Financial Disclosures, 78–9, 107–8, 112, 130, 140, 195, 199, 202, 210–11, 214, 225, 228
Team production theory, 38–40
The Gap, 20
The Netherlands, 152, 159–60, 163, 169
The Philippines, 17, 19, 141, 152, 164–5, 171, 218
Traidcraft, 70
Transnational corporations, 2, 7, 13, 15, 19, 82–3, 92, 102, 105, 169
Treaty of the Functioning of the EU, 118
Turnbull Review, 50

UK Clean Growth Strategy, 121, 124
UK Committee on Climate Change, 113, 123–4, 134, 136, 184, 214
UK Corporate Governance Code, 46–50
UK Electricity Act 1989, 122
UK Emissions Performance Standards, 127
UK Emissions Trading System, 136, 184
UK Energy Act 2008, 127
UK Energy Act 2010, 127
UK Environment Bill 2020, 121
UK Green Finance Strategy, 122
UK Low Carbon Transition Plan, 123
UK non-fossil fuel obligation, 122
UK Pensions Act 2004, 193
UK Stewardship Code, 191
UK Streamlined Energy and Carbon Reporting, 126, 130
UN Economic and Social Council, 169
UN Environment, 3, 83, 104, 200

UN Global Compact Leadership Criteria on Carbon Pricing, 187
UN Guiding Principles on Business and Human Rights, 143, 146–8, 171, 217
UN High Commissioner for Human Rights, 148–9
UN Human Rights Council, 143, 145–6, 149–50, 163, 171
UN Norms, 144–5, 172
UN Special Rapporteur for the Environment, 150
UN Sustainable Development Goals, 14, 94
UNEP Finance Initiative, 3, 30, 151, 188, 194–5
Union of Industrial and Employers' Confederation of Europe, 133
United Kingdom, 2, 6–7, 9–10, 16–18, 34, 44, 47–8, 51, 57, 59–60, 63, 68, 71, 74, 80, 83, 90, 99–100, 106, 112, 114, 116, 118–19, 121–4, 126–8, 131, 134–7, 139, 145, 152, 161–2, 164, 169–70, 172–3, 180, 182, 184, 188–9, 191, 194–5, 199, 202, 206, 209, 214, 218–21, 224, 227
United Nations Conference on Environment and Development, 83, 89
United Nations Conference on the Human Environment, 83
United Nations Framework Convention on Climate Change, 2–4, 14, 78–9, 82–7, 104, 110, 139, 141, 149, 160, 167, 173
United Nations Global Compact, 79, 103–4, 144, 190
United Nations Secretary-General, 4, 106

United States, 5, 7, 9–14, 17–20, 30, 42–4, 51, 57–8, 78, 83, 85–7, 89–90, 119, 138, 145, 151–8, 161, 163, 165, 169, 171, 178, 180–1, 187, 192, 197, 199–201, 205, 209–10, 216–21
Urgenda Foundation v. *State of the Netherlands*, 147, 152, 158–9, 163–4, 172
US Alien Tort Statute, 169
US Clean Air Act, 20, 153, 155
US Environmental Protection Agency, 153–4, 184

Vanguard, 187
Vedanta Resources, 170
Voluntary Principles on Security and Human Rights, 144

Walmart, 97, 112
War on Want, 70
We Are Still In coalition, 89
World Bank, 28, 92, 106, 176–7, 184, 186
World Bank Zero Routine Flaring by 2030, 106
World Trade Organization, 19, 176–9, 185, 209
World Wildlife Fund, 70
WTO Agreement on Climate Change, Trade and Sustainability, 179
WTO Appellate Body, 178

Zambia, 170

CPSIA information can be obtained
at www.ICGtesting.com
Printed in the USA
LVHW080920030821
694401LV00004B/291